# Successful Freelance Court Reporting

AF784726

# The West Legal Studies Series

## Your options keep growing with West Legal Studies

Each year our list continues to offer you more options for every area of the law to meet your course or on-the-job reference requirements. We now have over 140 titles from which to choose in the following areas:

- Administrative Law
- Alternative Dispute Resolution
- Bankruptcy
- Business Organizations/Corporations
- Civil Litigation and Procedure
- CLA Exam Preparation
- Client Accounting
- Computer in the Law Office
- Constitutional Law
- Contract Law
- Criminal Law and Procedure
- Document Preparation
- Environmental Law
- Ethics
- Family Law
- Federal Taxation
- Intellectual Property
- Introduction to Law
- Introduction to Paralegalism
- Law Office Management
- Law Office Procedures
- Legal Research, Writing, and Analysis
- Legal Terminology
- Paralegal Employment
- Real Estate Law
- Reference Materials
- Torts and Personal Injury Law
- Will, Trusts, and Estate Administration

## You will find unparalleled, practical support

Each book is augmented by instructor and student supplements to ensure the best learning experience possible. We also offer custom publishing and other benefits such as West's Student Achievement Award. In addition, our sales representatives are ready to provide you with dependable service.

## We want to hear from you

Our best contributions for improving the quality of our books and instructional materials is feedback from the people who use them. If you have a question, concern, or observation about any of our materials, or you have a product proposal or manuscript, we want to hear from you. Please contact your local representative or write us at the following address:

West Legal Studies, 3 Columbia Circle, P.O. Box 15015, Albany, NY 12212-5015

For additional information point your browser at

**www.westlegalstudies.com**

WEST

THOMSON LEARNING™

# Successful Freelance Court Reporting

Dana Chipkin

WEST
THOMSON LEARNING™

Australia Canada Mexico Singapore Spain United Kingdom United States

WEST
THOMSON LEARNING™

WEST LEGAL STUDIES

**Successful Freelance Court Reporting**
by Dana Chipkin

**Business Unit Director:**
Susan L. Simpfenderfer

**Executive Editor:**
Marlene McHugh Pratt

**Acquisitions Editor:**
Joan M. Gill

**Editorial Assistant:**
Lisa Flatley

**Executive Marketing Manager:**
Donna J. Lewis

**Channel Manager:**
Nigar Hale

**Executive Production Manager:**
Wendy A. Troeger

**Production Editor:**
Betty L. Dickson

**Cover Design:**
Connie McKinley

COPYRIGHT © 2001 by Delmar
West Legal Studies is an imprint of Delmar, a division of Thomson Learning, Inc. Thomson Learning™ is a trademark used herein under license

Printed in the United States
1 2 3 4 5 XXX 05 04 03 02 01 00

For more information, contact Delmar, 3 Columbia Circle, PO Box 15015, Albany, NY 12212-5015.

Or find us on the World Wide Web at http://www.westlegalstudies.com

ALL RIGHTS RESERVED. No part of this work covered by the copyright hereon may be reproduced or used in any form or by any means—graphic, electronic, or mechanical, including photocopying, recording, taping, Web distribution or information storage and retrieval systems—without written permission of the publisher.

For permission to use material from this text or product, contact us by
Tel (800) 730-2214
Fax (800) 730-2215
www.thomsonrights.com

Library of Congress Cataloging-in-Publication Data

Chipkin, Dana.
Successful Freelance Court Reporting / Dana Chipkin
p. cm.
"West Legal Studies series"
Includes index.
ISBN 0-7668-1746-6
1. Law reporters—United States. 2. Law reporting—United States. I. Title

KF8805 .C48 2001
347.73'16—dc21 00-063327

## NOTICE TO THE READER

Publisher does not warrant or guarantee any of the products described herein or perform any independent analysis in connection with any of the product information contained herein. Publisher does not assume, and expressly disclaims, any obligation to obtain and include information other than that provided to it by the manufacturer.

The reader is notified that this text is an education tool, not a practice book. Since the law is in constant change, no rule or statement of law in this book should be relied upon for any service to any client. The reader should always refer to standard legal sources for the current rule or law. If legal advice or other expert assistance is required, the services of the appropriate professional should be sought.

The Publisher makes no representation or warranties of any kind, including but not limited to, the warranties of fitness for particular purpose or merchantability, nor are any such representations implied with respect to the material set forth herein, and the publisher takes no responsibility with respect to such material. The publisher shall not be liable for any special, consequential, or exemplary damages resulting, in whole or part, from the readers' use of, or reliance upon, this material.

# TABLE OF CONTENTS

# PREFACE

The average person's knowledge of court reporting is greatly influenced by the film and television industry's portrayal of it. Inaccurate perceptions are often created by actors pretending to be writing stenographically in courtroom dramas. The actor may be physically located in a setting in which no court reporter would dare report. The actor may be writing when no one is speaking or, conversely, resting his or her hands while so-called valuable testimony should in fact be on the record. On occasion, you may even spot actors whose stenography machines are backward!

A majority of these scenes occur in courtroom settings rather than lawyers' offices, which are also a venue for legal proceedings. Therefore, when told someone is a court reporter, the response that usually follows is, "Oh. What court do you work in?" Granted, the title *court reporter* connotes that one is employed within the court system; however, roughly 72 percent of court reporters are actually freelancers.

Although some may freelance in order to gain work experience as a stepping-stone toward a career in the court system (official reporting) or in the United States House of Representatives or Senate (legislative official reporting), others enjoy their entire reporting career as a freelancer. Why, then, has there been such limited material available on freelance court reporting to date?

## AN EVER-CHANGING INDUSTRY

Court reporting is an industry that experiences continual changes due to legislation, equipment technology, supply-and-demand fluctuations, and so on. This requires court reporters and court reporting educators to keep an ear to the ground, so to speak. Information put into print today may very well be outdated in a month.

*Successful Freelance Court Reporting* offers reporters of the Millennium an up-to-date accounting of the freelancing profession. It speaks to some of the changes evidenced by tape-recording technology, the use of computerized machines, and the obsolescence of inked writers, Dictaphones, and the like.

## DIFFERENCES BY LOCALITY

The differences in freelance court reporting practices and protocols from locality to locality are vast. Not only does each state have its requirements of freelance court reporters, but from county to county and town to town, reporters will observe variations. Therefore, it is up to the educators and state court reporting associations to teach court reporting students and reporters what transpires within their state.

*Successful Freelance Court Reporting* informs the reader about locality differences pertaining to such things as exhibit maintenance, the use and placement of stipulation pages, and reporter certification requirements in each state in order to apprise readers that what applies in one state may be unheard of in another.

## AGENCY DIFFERENCES

In addition to variations by locality, freelance court reporting agencies have individual preferences regarding such things as style of work sheet on which reporters list job information, transcript formats, and on-the-job protocols. Therefore, books on freelance court reporting may offer general freelancing principles and scenarios but cannot state with 100 percent accuracy each freelance court reporting agency's personal requirements of its reporters.

*Successful Freelance Court Reporting,* written by a working senior reporter, stresses the importance of being amenable to agency and client preferences, despite what the reporter may view as the "correct" punctuation or protocol. It also instructs the reader on matters such as how to obtain the necessary tools to understand and emulate a freelance court reporting agency's transcript format, how to learn about an agency's clientele, and how to successfully interview with freelance court reporting agencies.

## SEGREGATION OF OFFICIAL AND FREELANCE PRINCIPLES

Many books to date have integrated freelance and official principles in an attempt to help reporters pass state or national certification examinations and/or obtain official positions. As such, the freelancing material provided is often limited to basic tenets and lacks the kind of detail about the freelance industry that aspiring freelancers desire.

Information pertaining to official and freelance reporting is frequently relayed to court reporting students within the same academic class, Court Procedures. As students generally have limited knowledge of either subject at this stage, they oftentimes will be confused by which principles apply to freelancing and which apply to official reporting.

*Successful Freelance Court Reporting,* while addressing certain aspects of official reporting, shares with the reader details about the freelance profession that only a working freelance reporter would think to impart. It is a soup-to-nuts, how-to-succeed-at-freelance-court-reporting book. This book apprises the reader pondering freelancing as a career on a variety of subjects, such as options regarding the specific tools that are required of freelance reporters, interviewing with freelance court reporting agencies, and professional protocol.

This book concentrates on training the reader to appear experienced even though it may be the reader's first assignment. It contains a beginner's checklist and recommendations for those first few freelance jobs. It offers practical tips in communication areas, such as requesting breaks, getting spellings/clarifications, and obtaining documents necessary for accurate transcript preparation.

## SUBJECTIVITY

Authors attempting to characterize freelance court reporting across the board run the risk of subjectivity, incorporating material from one's personal experience and opinion and being limited to knowledge of one's local practice. *Successful Freelance Court Reporting* attempts to introduce its readers to rudimentary freelance court reporting principles so that those considering a career as a freelance court reporter can have a glimpse into what the job really entails. It covers the details that are best learned prior to accepting assignments as opposed to being faced with situations requiring a judgment call on the job that one is not sure how to handle. While often advocating placing a call to one's agency under such circumstances, it also brings awareness to student/new reporters that such scenarios even exist.

*Successful Freelance Court Reporting* teaches methods of conducting oneself that lead to positive relationships with the players encountered within the freelance reporting profession. This book speaks to the fears and concerns of student/beginner reporters and reminds them that every reporter walked in their shoes at one time. It shares personal anecdotes and feelings of the author with its readers as a means of expressing empathy for them as they journey into the field. It hands the experience of a senior reporter to beginner reporters on a silver platter to facilitate their transition from student or beginner to, eventually, senior reporter status.

## THE ORGANIZATION OF THIS TEXTBOOK

*Successful Freelance Court Reporting* contains a table of contents delineating the specific subject matters in each chapter. The book is divided into a number of chapters designed to introduce the reader to freelancing in a chronological fashion. It is written in non-Legalese; therefore, no formal education is required to understand it. Figures illustrating difficult concepts appear throughout the book. At the conclusion of each chapter, short-answer and true/false questions are provided for the reader to test his or her comprehension of key points. In addition, there is a discussion section that poses thought-provoking questions, encouraging dialog between the aspiring court reporter and the court reporting educator. Following the chapters is an alphabetical glossary of court reporting terminology found within the book. The terms in the glossary also appear with their definitions in the margins of the text throughout the book. Thanks are given to those who have contributed to the success of this book in the Acknowledgment section, and readers may learn more about the author in the About the Author section. Readers are also invited to visit Dana Chipkin's Web site at www.DanaChipkin.com.

### Chapter 1

Chapter 1, entitled "A Career in Freelance Court Reporting," addresses basic questions about the freelancing profession commonly asked by those wondering if they have what it takes. It describes the attributes one must possess to be a successful court reporter and why those attributes are required or recommended.

### Chapter 2

Chapter 2, "Court Reporting School," outlines the National Court Reporters Association's requirements of schools that offer training for court reporters. It then explains the path that court reporting students generally follow in order to achieve the speed necessary to enter into the field, as well as other recommendations for this period of the reporter's education, such as finding a mentor to help the student stay motivated, sitting in with working reporters, and joining court reporting associations. Chapter 2 also provides a listing of the states where it is mandatory for a court reporter to become a notary public prior to being permitted to work as a reporter.

### Chapter 3

Chapter 3, "Examinations and Certifications," lists the states that require court reporters to pass a statewide examination prior to entry into the field. It then informs the reader about various certifications offered by the National Court Reporters Association. Chapter 3 concludes with information about examinations taken to obtain employment in civil service and non–civil service entities as an alternative to freelancing.

### Chapter 4

Chapter 4, "Tools of the Trade," lets the reader know what methods of obtaining court reporting equipment are available and what specific equipment will be required of the freelance court reporter. It explains the importance of having equipment that is compatible to that of agencies and scopists (professionals who assist reporters in the preparation of transcripts) with whom reporters work. Maintenance and repair of equipment are outlined in Chapter 4, as are maintenance and support agreements for one's equipment.

Chapter 4 then itemizes the specific items that freelance reporters will need to perform their reporting functions and those items that are recommended but not mandatory. The inclusion of red correction markers in this chapter serves as a segue into an explanation of the more common proofreading symbols utilized by reporters and others in the field. Recommendations for the freelance reporter's personal reference library fall within the purview of tools of the trade, as does professional attire.

### Chapter 5

Chapter 5, entitled "How to Fill Out a Work Sheet," is devoted to teaching freelance reporters how to obtain information necessary to prepare a transcript and list it on a particular freelance agency's work sheet. It teaches the reader verification methods for accuracy and educates the reader on different scenarios that may be encountered in the process of completing one's work sheet.

### Chapter 6

Chapter 6, "Interviewing," covers all aspects of interviewing from when to interview, how to make initial contacts, preparing a resume, all the way through to the specific issues that reporters should address with freelance agency owners. It defines call-in time and educates the reader on billing practices employed by freelance agencies. Chapter 6 teaches the reader that prior work/life experience may carry over and contribute to one's success as a freelance reporter.

### Chapter 7

A key feature of this book is Chapter 7, "Different Types of Jobs Encountered." It explains material differences between depositions and other types of proceedings, such as hearings and arbitrations, in simple, easy-to-read language. By characterizing the general parties involved and their functions, it eliminates the fear that new reporters experience when told for the first time, "You have a med mal tomorrow" or "This is going to be a hearing." Chapter 7 covers the most common subject matters of depositions reported by freelance court reporters beyond the standard negligence dictations they are familiar with from court reporting school. It provides readers with a preview of the kinds of assignments they may expect to report.

### Chapter 8

Chapter 8, "Before the Deposition," focuses on methods of preparation for reporting a deposition prior to actually going on the record. It guides the new reporter to a comfort level when certain information is gleaned ahead of time, such as copying the caption and setting up job globals and speaker designations. Chapter 8 provides a beginner's checklist so that the new reporter will remember what to ask when starting out in the field.

### Chapter 9

Chapter 9, "Taking the Deposition," delineates for the reader the specific functions of a freelance court reporter during the actual deposition proceeding. It discusses such things as the use of parentheticals, marking exhibits, recording rulings, knowing when to physically go off the record, and performing readbacks. Chapter 9 lets the reader know that there is a lot more to freelancing than just writing on one's machine at 225 words per minute.

### Chapter 10

Chapter 10, "For Your Information," delves into freelancing in more detail. It instructs the reader on topics such as the recording of numbers, dates and times, objections, and quoted material. It also provides guidance on the do's and don'ts of preparing court reporting transripts.

### Chapter 11

Chapter 11, entitled "Freelancer Protocol," describes situations that may arise on the job and offers suggested methods of handling them. Scenarios such as being told by one attorney to go off the record while being told by another to stay on the record and dropping something that should be on the record are discussed.

Chapter 11 also addresses the freelancer's responsibility to remain neutral and maintain a stoic expression upon one's face. It cautions reporters from getting themselves into trouble by saying more than they should and discusses controversial subjects such as tape-recording the proceeding without the knowledge of the parties and encountering conflicts of interest.

### Chapter 12

Chapter 12, "Beyond the Deposition," states the types of decisions that freelance reporters are faced with at the conclusion of proceedings, such as:

- Whether to scope the job oneself or give it to a scopist to prepare
- Whether to proofread the job oneself or utilize a proofreader
- Methods of sending the job to the agency when the transcript is completed

Chapter 12 also provides the reader with a sample ledger sheet for organized recordkeeping and stresses the importance of continuing to build one's personal dictionary.

### Chapter 13

Chapter 13, "The Transcript," identifies the elements of a standard deposition transcript and references sample transcript elements for review by way of figures. It also identifies the types of items commonly requested by clients in addition to the standard transcript, such as a condensed transcript, keyword index, or ASCII disk. In addition, this chapter addresses nonstandard transcripts, such as excerpts, confidential excerpts/transcripts, transcripts wherein two reporters were involved, and booking the testimony of two witnesses together.

### Chapter 14

Chapter 14, "Being an Independent Contractor," covers the pros and cons of freelancing in terms of vacations, sick days, and maternity/paternity leave. A freelance court reporter's obligations to the taxing authorities are discussed, as is the home office as a tax deduction. Chapter 14 offers a rudimentary explanation of what it means to receive 1099s and how to estimate one's taxes each year. It also provides suggestions for money management.

### Chapter 15

Chapter 15, "Every Court Reporter's Nightmare," is an accounting of some of the author's personal anecdotes of negative experiences that taught the author her most valuable lessons. Chapter 15 is designed to remind the reader that even when encountering one's worst fears on the job (or after the job), a happy ending may be had, or you simply do the best you can given the circumstances.

### Chapter 16

*Successful Freelance Court Reporting* goes beyond the realm of standard books on freelance court reporting by allaying the fears of beginner reporters regarding switching agencies and by instructing beginner reporters on the methods utilized by freelancers to network. Chapter 16, entitled "Making Changes," helps readers to surpass the emotional baggage that accompanies job changes and inspires them to use the many means currently available to find work elsewhere.

### Chapter 17

Chapter 17, "Other Forums for Your Skills," outlines alternatives to freelance court reporting and jobs that can be done in conjunction with freelance court reporting. It discusses the many different avenues down which court reporting may lead. As the final chapter in this book, Chapter 17 leaves you with the knowledge that this is just the beginning.

Freelance court reporting is still a viable and lucrative profession shared by many people who do not view each assignment as just another workday but, rather, are empassioned by the opportunity to learn something new every day. My wish is for you to feel the kind of passion and pride that I and others experience while reporting even after a substantial number of years.

# ACKNOWLEDGMENTS


Deanna Baker, for her assistance regarding realtiming and closed captioning.

Betty Barfield, for questions answered and referrals to others as research sources.

Valerie Berg, principal, Admiral Reporting.

Ellen Birch, principal, Realtime Reporting.

Harriett Brenner, principal, Realtime Reporting, for being my mentor, role model, and friend, and for taking the time to answer so many questions.

Nancy Cavender, National Verbatim Reporters Association, for educating me about voice recognition.

Barry Cohn, financial advisor.

Rosanna Correra, Dalco Reporting & Legal Video.

Jan Cooper, National Verbatim Reporters Association.

Bill Davis, Esq., Scheichet & Davis, for his legal services and recommendation to submit my manuscript to West Legal Studies.

Medea Eder, for her friendship, support, and recommendations.

Lisa Flatley, for her patience and assistance in the publication process.

Joan Gill, for being the best editor a writer could hope to have.

Randy Gordon, for allowing me to share what I know with the students at Stenotopia Business School.

Susan Hanback, Deputy Chief Reporter, U.S. House of Representatives, for the generous amount of time expended to educate me on legislative reporting.

Nancy Hendell, Mindy Perlish, and Edie Berkowitz, for being phenomenal educators.

Stacey Hollander, for her friendship, encouragement, and support.

Linda Ireland, for her expertise at copyediting and proofreading.

Debra Levinson, principal, Dalco Reporting & Legal Video, DalcoTech veteran reporter and great sister-in-law, for suggesting court reporting to me as a career choice and encouraging me as a court reporting educator.

Barry Liebman, Esq., for his assistance regarding legal material, as well as friendship.

Donna Ann Liebman, for her support and undying faith in this book's success.

Jerry Linell, Chief Reporter, official reporters of debates, U.S. Senate, for the generous amount of time expended to educate me on legislative reporting.

Lana Magro, Dalco Reporting & Legal Video.

Mildred Mann, my mother, for not giving me a middle name at birth, knowing I was going to be a writer.

Lillian Morson, for sharing her time, knowledge, and encouragement.

The National Association for Female Executives.

The National Notary Association.

Mel Pfeferstein, CPA.

Marc Reinig and the staff at Reinig Reporting, Inc., for believing I was actually writing a book even though they saw no evidence of it for three years, with special thanks to:

- Lorie Brunjes, scopist extraordinaire and good friend
- Pamela Kanaris, scopist extraordinaire and good friend
- Barbara Ochen
- John Ryals

Rick Richolson, for information regarding *Campbell's List*.

Gary Robson, for his assistance regarding captioning.

Scott Rohr, typesetting assistance.

Sven Schirm, photographer.

Richard Sherman, for his guidance and expediency in responding to my many e-mails.

Stenograph Corporation, for assistance in my research.

Dr. William Stewart, AFM Steno Repair, for sharing his vast knowledge regarding equipment maintenance and repair.

Peter Wacht, Editor, NCRA, for his encouragement about the book's merits.

Antoinette L. Williams, Esq., for her assistance regarding legal terms.

## SPECIAL THANKS TO:

My husband, Kenny, for his editorial comments and suggestions, support, love, and understanding throughout this tremendous undertaking. I love you with all my heart. Always have.

My children, Julian and Lane, for giving up some "Mommy" time so that I could write this book. You are my inspiration.

To family members and friends, for understanding how distracted I have been the last few years while putting this together, working full-time and mothering my two boys, and for believing in my ability to make it happen. Your names are sporadically mentioned in examples of appearances throughout the book.

The classes I have taught at Stenotopia Business School and privately, for informing me about the educational needs of court reporting students and for your heartfelt feedback about my book.

The court reporting schools, for awareness of the educational needs of our ever-changing industry and amending your curriculum to accommodate them.

To past and future authors of court reporting–related material, for your participation in creating a grade of reporters that are better prepared for the marketplace.

The National Court Reporters Association and New York State Shorthand Reporters Association, of which I am proud to be a member, for their assistance in my research for the book and answering God knows how many questions. Extra thanks to Marshall Jorpland, Nancy Hodges, and Rhonda Claytor.

The National Verbatim Reporters Association.

A word of thanks also, to the reviewers who made valuable suggestions for improving this text:

Ms. Ruth Tossey
Academy of Court Reporting

Ms. Shirley Bechtel
Rasmussen College/Minnetonka

Mr. Glen Blazek
RAV Schools of Professional Studies

Ms. Marie Encianias
Metropolitan College of Court Reporting

Ms. Michelle Houston
Long Island Business Institute

Ms. Dawn Wilson
Brown Institute of Court Reporting

Please note the Internet resources are of a time sensitive nature and URL addresses may often change or be deleted.

**Contact us at www.westlegalstudies@delmar.com**

# ABOUT THE AUTHOR

In 1984, Dana Chipkin graduated from Georgetown University's School of Languages and Linguistics 6th out of a class of 114 with a major in the Arabic language and a business minor. Dissatisfied with other career opportunities, she decided to pursue a career in court reporting. She received a diploma from Stenotopia: A World of Court Reporting, located in Hicksville, New York, in 1988, a year and nine months after entering court reporting school.

Dana has freelanced in the state of New York from 1988 to the present. She is a Licensed Shorthand Reporter in the state of Connecticut. Dana is a notary public and has obtained and maintained RPR status continuously throughout her tenure as a court reporter. She is a member of the National Court Reporters Association, the New York State Shorthand Reporters Association, and the National Association for Female Executives; and she has been listed in *Who's Who in American Colleges and Universities and Two Thousand Notable Women.*

Dana has held staff positions with several prestigious court reporting agencies throughout the Metropolitan New York area. She has also reported in various courts on a per-diem basis. She has received overwhelming responses from court reporting students whom she has trained on the job. This led her to write the first draft of this book.

In 1998, she submitted *Freelance Court Reporting* to Randy Gordon, the owner of Stenotopia, for a professional critique. Randy was very impressed with the book and requested Dana's permission to test-market it with six volunteers from a high-speed class. The volunteers were equally enthusiastic and began to photocopy the book for other students in the class. Shortly thereafter, Dana was invited to teach the contents of the book in Stenotopia's Court Procedures class. It was extremely well received.

Dana then moved from Long Island to Holmes, New York, in 1999, where she resides with her husband and two young sons. She has continued her teaching through private seminars, which offer students an opportunity to sit in with Dana personally on freelance assignments. Dana serves as a mentor to the students throughout the seminars and well into their entry into the field by providing personal job placement assistance. Students receive continuing education units from NCRA for their participation in Dana's seminars. Dana has applied to become a Court Reporting Instructor through the NCRA. She is currently affiliated with Dalco Tech, a progressive court reporting school in Westchester, New York, and is freelancing within Dutchess/Putnam/ Westchester counties, as well as working on other educational projects for court reporters. Be on the lookout for her future publications.

# CHAPTER 1

# A Career in Freelance Court Reporting

## WHAT IS FREELANCE COURT REPORTING?

The profession of freelance court reporting in the legal environment involves the stenographic recording of proceedings and subsequent production of a verbatim transcript. Other duties of the **freelance court reporter** encompass timekeeping, the swearing/affirmation of witnesses, the reading of recorded testimony upon request, and the marking of exhibits. The bulk of proceedings reported are usually legal in nature; however, the freelance reporter may be hired for nonlegal matters as well, such as seminars or stockholder meetings. Although the freelance reporter is commonly referred to as a court reporter, the majority of assignments do not take place in a courthouse but, rather, in law offices and business offices. The crux of the freelancer's work is the recording of depositions, not trials. The freelancer's role in litigation is generally at the pretrial/presettlement phase.

## WHO ARE THOSE REPORTERS IN COURT?

Reporters who are employed by the court system are delineated **official court reporters.** Prior to becoming employed by the court full-time, they may be referred to as **provisional reporters.** In order to obtain an official position in court, certain criteria must be met regarding the passing of lower/higher court tests, certifications, and/or numbers of years' experience freelancing. Thus, freelancing is an integral step toward a career in the court system, if that is a goal.

Some courts have a designated area for depositions, which are reported by freelance reporters. In addition, freelancers may work in the courthouse on a per-diem basis on matters generally handled by official reporters. However, these **per-diem reporters** are not considered official court reporters; they are freelance reporters.

**Freelance court reporter:** May refer in general to a court reporter not employed full-time by an agency or court; may also refer to a freelance reporter who freelances among many agencies as opposed to being on staff with just one agency.

**Official court reporter:** A court reporter employed full-time by the court system or the United States House of Representatives. *Official reporter* may also refer to the reporter who provides the original transcript at a proceeding where two freelance reporters are present and who performs the requisite functions of the proceeding.

**Provisional reporter:** A reporter who works regularly in a courthouse who has not yet received an official reporter position.

**Per-diem reporter:** A reporter who works for an entity on random days as needed and is paid a flat fee for the day.

## WHY DO SOME PREFER FREELANCING TO OFFICIAL REPORTING?

Although official reporting is often viewed as the pinnacle of reporting, not every reporter aspires to work in the court system. Some prefer freelance reporting because:

- To work full-time in the court system, the reporter must pass certain court entrance examinations.
- Official reporting involves procedures and terms that freelancing does not encompass.
- Placement in a specific courthouse is dependent upon available positions.
- Working in the court system generally increases the number of players to designate in a proceeding.
- Deposition work gives the freelancer more control over the proceeding than when a judge is involved.
- Some reporters are intimidated by courtroom settings and find it easier to communicate their needs in a conference room environment.
- A freelancer's workday lasts only as long as the assignment. The freelance reporter is expected to arrive shortly prior to the time the proceeding is to begin and may leave when it is concluded.
- Freelancers do not have to work five days a week.
- The process of taking time off/vacations is a lot simpler.
- Freelancers may work in a different location each day and occasionally get to report internationally or abroad.
- Freelancers generally encounter different people from day to day, which lessens the likelihood of personality conflicts, petty jealousies, and so on.
- Freelancers do not have to physically go to their agency offices on a daily basis.
- Unless the freelance reporter is working on a continuing assignment, a modest business wardrobe can go a long way.
- In certain courts the proceedings are transcribed only upon request and often months or years after the proceeding takes place, but freelance proceedings are usually transcribed automatically. It is much easier to transcribe notes closer to the time they were written.
- Some reporters are intimidated by media involvement.
- There may be a lot of pressure associated with high-profile court cases.
- If a freelancer has a heavy writing day, a lighter job or a day off can be requested for the following day.

Other benefits of freelance reporting are:

- The opportunity to sit in with more experienced reporters in an agency prior to working in order to learn the ropes
- The provision by freelance agencies of format booklets to train new reporters as to transcript and procedural preferences
- Assistance from freelance agencies that stand behind reporters who follow agency directives when problems arise
- The classification of reporters by experience level in order to send them on assignments that are within their capabilities

- In-house personnel who assist in the preparation/proofreading of transcripts
- The opportunity to request that another reporter relieve the freelancer or be sent in his or her stead if the freelancer experiences difficulty on a continuing job
- Opportunities to increase one's value to agencies by acquiring additional skills or becoming known for reporting specific types of cases
- Rotation of the difficulty level of an agency's work to prevent reporter burnout
- The potential to earn in a single day enough to justify one's workweek
- The opportunity to claim a portion of one's home as a tax deduction

## WHAT TRAINING IS NECESSARY TO BECOME A FREELANCE REPORTER?

In order to enter the field of court reporting, you need to enroll in a court reporting/business school/community college where you will study a shorthand writing theory. After studying theory, you will pass through various speed classes in order to obtain the requisite speed to graduate from school: 225 words per minute (wpm). You must be able to process testimony at 225 wpm, jury charges at 200 wpm, and literary dictations at 180 wpm. Now, do not be frightened by these numbers. The keyboard of a court reporting machine is vastly different from that of a typewriter, and comparing typing speeds to court reporting speeds is like comparing apples and oranges. Speed classes entail receiving dictations, recording them, reading back some of the material, and transcribing stenographic notes into English. In addition to theory and speed classes, there are a number of academic courses that reporters may take, such as:

- Basic grammar for the court reporter
- Computer-Aided Transcription (CAT)
- Court reporting procedures
- Law
- Legal terminology
- Anatomy/Medical terminology
- Punctuation for the court reporter
- Technical terminology
- Keyboarding
- Current events

A particular school may deem certain courses optional.

Many schools offer internship programs for their students during which students sit in with working reporters and write alongside them. Depending upon the school, you may be required to sit in with a working reporter and prepare a transcript of the proceeding before being granted a diploma. This assures the school that not only have you achieved 225 wpm, but you also understand the components of a transcript and possess standard court reporting skills.

Besides obtaining a court reporting certificate or diploma, some states have additional requirements before a reporter can begin working. They may require freelance reporters to pass a state examination and/or require freelance reporters to be notary publics.

## Finding the Right School

Choosing a school to learn court reporting should not be determined solely by closest location to your home. Other factors to consider are:

- Reputation of the school
- Whether the programs offered match your needs
- Whether the school offers optional subjects of interest to you
- The actual amount of dictation time received
- Credentials of the academic staff
- Whether the school is approved by the National Court Reporters Association (NCRA)
- The school's ability to place its students with freelance agencies
- Number of complaints lodged against the school

Court reporting is even offered by some educational institutions via the Internet.

Just because a school's curriculum may deviate from **NCRA**'s approval guidelines does not necessarily cast dispersions on a particular school. There are a great many nonapproved schools with excellent reputations in the industry. However, rotten eggs exist in all walks of life, so it is essential to check out any possibly shady or illegal practices of a school by contacting:

- Working reporters/agency owners
- The Better Business Bureau
- The local sheriff's office

## How Long Does It Take to Complete Court Reporting School?

Unfortunately, there is no single answer to this question. The time required to complete school can range from anywhere between a little under a year to multiple years, depending on the individual student. Several factors that affect the length of one's court reporting education are:

- Dexterity of the student
- Practice time constraints
- Clean versus sloppy steno writing
- The ability to read one's steno notes
- The ability to transcribe steno notes
- The ability to punctuate
- The ability to process versus think
- Attendance
- Completing sitting-in requirements
- Completing mandatory class requirements
- Test-taking abilities
- Attending school full-time versus part-time
- Attending school during the day versus night school

Many people who work during the day choose to go to night school, which does not leave a great deal of time for practicing. This can slow down the process even further. But remember, once you become a reporter, it is relatively immaterial how long it took you to graduate from school. The point is that you did it.

**NCRA:** National Court Reporters Association

## What Is the Cost of Court Reporting School?

Costs of schooling will vary from school to school and fluctuate throughout the years. It is a good idea, when evaluating potential schools, to compare tuition costs and to weigh them against the contents of each program. Do not let that be the deciding factor, though, as it is not the best determinant of the value of your education. There are different ways of financing your court reporting education, such as:

- The Federal Pell grant, which an income-based grant that is applied for annually
- Federal government loan programs (Stafford loans), which are available throughout the country and may have certain enrollment-status requirements, such as being a full-time student versus a part-time student
- The Frank Sarli Memorial Scholarship offered by the National Court Reporters Foundation for students nearing graduation. A one-time randomly picked payment of $500 is awarded to a student who: is an NCRA student member, is enrolled in an NCRA-approved court reporting program, has passed at least one of the court reporting program's Q&A tests at 225 wpm, maintains a grade-point average (GPA) of 3.5 or more, has demonstrated a need for financial assistance, possesses all qualities exemplified by a professional court reporter (such as attitude, demeanor, dress, and motivation), and whose information has been confirmed and verified by the submitting court reporting program. This scholarship may be applied for via nomination by the court reporting program prior to a specified date (usually toward the end of February of each year) and is awarded annually
- State association scholarships—consult your state court reporting association to see if this applies. Some states offer a lump-sum payment to several students who meet the standards set forth by the state court reporting association involving enrollment in a licensed court reporting school, attendance schedule and/or record, speed level and GPA requirements, and/or financial aid restrictions
- State-offered grants/tuition assistance programs applied for annually
- Applications for student members, printed in NCRA's spring *Journal of Court Reporting*, whereby NCRA awards $500 to six applicants chosen randomly in a lottery-type procedure. The only criteria are that the court reporting student is a member of NCRA
- Funding offered for Vietnam veterans or family members thereof toward education
- Scholarships offered by state law enforcement/correction, fire, or police associations to disabled members or family members of disabled/deceased employees
- Scholarships offered by fraternal organizations to their members and their families
- Bank loans
- Loans from friends/relatives

Most schools work on a pay-as-you-go basis, since there is no set time frame for your education to be completed. That in itself may serve as a motivating force to work harder and finish sooner.

## WHAT ATTRIBUTES DO SUCCESSFUL REPORTERS POSSESS?

There are three categories of attributes that are necessary for court reporters: physical traits, personal qualities, and indicators of success.

### Physical Traits

***Good Hearing*** Since the primary role of the reporter is to process the spoken word, if you cannot hear it, you cannot record it. Obviously there will be times when reporters with even the sharpest ears will not hear something, which can be compensated for by asking for a repeat of what was said, but if you suffer from any hearing impairments, reporting is not recommended.

***Dexterity*** Court reporters must have the ability to stroke keys with both hands at a high-speed level. If you type rapidly, play a musical instrument, or add ferociously with a calculator, you may be a likely candidate for the reporting profession.

***Good Physical Condition*** Unless the job is a continuation from the previous day and the reporter's equipment was left there overnight, the freelancer must tote equipment to and from jobs. A reporter must also bring a writer for rulings before a judge if the assignment takes place in a courthouse. Therefore, average strength is required of reporters. Also, medications can affect one's processing/writing abilities, so physical conditions that require medication should be a consideration in your career choice.

***Stamina*** The duration of freelance assignments is highly unpredictable and can last anywhere from a few minutes to multiple hours with minimal breaks. Therefore, a reporter must have a lot of stamina for sitting for long periods of time and writing for many hours. Not all parties are generous with lunch and bathroom breaks, so the reporter must be able to perform the reporter's functions with relatively little reprieve.

### Personal Qualities

***Dedication*** The court reporting student must have the mindset that no matter how long it takes to graduate, the student will prevail. In order to traverse through the various speed levels to arrive at 225 words per minute, the reporter must practice, practice, practice. Since there is no taskmaster standing over you with a whip, if you are not a self-motivated person, you may plateau at a speed, get discouraged, lose sight of your goals, and eventually quit school. Court reporting schools, compared with other types of schools, have extremely high dropout rates for this very reason.

Dedication has a slightly different meaning to working reporters. They must be dedicated to providing verbatim transcripts in a timely manner, as well as keeping abreast of changes in legislation and current events in the industry.

***A Good Command of the English Language*** Even though reporters are responsible for recording the speech of others, they must be able to distinguish between soundalikes and homonyms such as *and* and *in, affect* and *effect,* as well as record phonetically unfamiliar words. If a reporter, while writing, gets thrown by just one word, the distraction may cause a loss of subsequent words.

Therefore, a person possessing excellent English skills brings a tremendous advantage to a court reporting career.

That is not to say that you need a college education to be a court reporter. There are many successful reporters who applied themselves in court reporting schools to learning grammar, punctuation, and various terminologies for reporting and sought continuing education through reporting-related books and seminars to raise their levels of knowledge. Excelling in English can actually be something of a hindrance, as court reporting involves punctuating the spoken word. Punctuating in this context requires a completely different set of rules from those taught in standard English classes. You may need to "forget" some of what you already know in order to comprehend court reporting principles.

If you have a knack for spelling, this talent will be a tremendous aid to you. Poor spellers may not have the capability of detecting typographical errors when copying information. This may result in the misspelling of a word throughout an entire transcript if the error is not noticed during proofreading/spell-checking. Reporters who are proficient in spelling are more inclined to double-check spellings with attorneys or witnesses before leaving a job.

***Professionalism*** A great degree of professionalism is required of freelance reporters, as they are the liaison between court reporting agencies and their clientele. Maintaining or losing clients can be as dependent upon the demeanor of a reporter present at a proceeding and the quality of transcript subsequently delivered as the page rate that the agency is charging the client. Therefore, reporters must take their roles as professionals seriously if they want to continue being treated as professionals. This applies to virtually all aspects of reporting: punctuality on assignments, appearance, performance of job functions, responses to questions/requests, interaction with attorneys and witnesses at the proceeding, methods of handling stressful situations that occur, and so on. Now, no one expects you to necessarily have an innate sense of professionalism; it can be a learned trait, and one of the purposes of this book is to teach you how to appear professional even though you may be reporting your very first deposition.

***Ability to Shoulder Responsibilities*** Freelance reporters must be able to handle responsibility, since there are quite a few responsibilities inherent to freelance reporting. They encompass:

- Educational training
- Interviewing honestly about one's education, experience, qualifications, capabilities
- Obtaining and maintaining reporting equipment
- Punctuality
- Calling for/accepting/canceling assignments
- Obtaining information regarding:

  —Parties present at the proceeding
  —The legal process utilized to arrange the proceeding
  —The stipulations the proceeding is pursuant to
  —Delivery of the transcripts
  —Billing for the transcripts

- Notifying parties of potential conflicts of interest

- Impartiality
- Noting the time that the proceeding began/ended and when breaks were taken
- Administering oaths/affirmations to witnesses
- Verbatim reporting
- Marking/maintaining/copying exhibits
- Reading back portions of the record upon request
- Stopping proceedings that are unreportable
- Requesting repeats/clarifications, when necessary
- Reflecting nonverbal activities
- Aiding to avoid confusions on the record
- Approaching work-related/client information as confidential
- Preparing/proofreading/correcting/spell-checking/delivering transcripts
- Certifying the accuracy of the transcript
- Providing additional materials requested
- Maintaining a backup of each job
- Billing agencies for completed jobs
- Recording job information/payment information
- Reporting freelance income to federal/state tax authorities

Do not become overwhelmed by the length of this list. After court reporting schooling, a little work experience, and reading this book, these responsibilities will all become second nature to you.

***Assertiveness*** There can be difficulties in recording a verbatim transcript. For instance, a reporter may encounter persons who unconsciously place their hands over their mouths while speaking, resulting in the reporter straining to hear what they are saying. The reporter must be able to forego any momentary embarrassment and communicate difficulties in order to rectify the situation.

## Indicators of Success

Success will surely follow if you possess the following attributes.

***Inquisitiveness*** Knowing how to elicit information in a professional manner can save hours of research after the job ends. Do not be afraid to seek clarification while it is most accessible—at the proceeding. Attempt to be a reporter who views each day as a learning experience and not only processes but also understands, at least to a minimal degree, the subject matter recorded.

***Perfectionism*** Do not give just the bare minimum of yourself. Be a perfectionist. Rather than place "(phonetic)" or "(ph.)" after the name of a city or town that you do not have the spelling of, utilize reference materials and do not give up until you have tapped all of your resources. Or if an attorney makes a special request of you, seek clarification until the request is crystal clear. Going the extra yard is what earns reporters good reputations.

***Congeniality and Respect for Others*** Freelance court reporters are largely dependent upon freelance agencies for work. Therefore, cultivating and maintaining pleasant relationships with agency personnel is integral to the success of a reporter. You will be interacting with:

- Agency owners
- Office managers/administrative assistants

- Secretaries
- Scopists (see Chapter 2)
- Computer personnel
- Billing personnel
- Filing clerks
- Proofreaders
- Messengers

Congeniality and respect should be shown to everyone involved in the reporting process. They are all participants in the development of a successful reputation. Be a team player, because at various times their assistance may prove invaluable.

On the job, freelance reporters encounter different players, such as:

- Receptionists
- Witnesses
- Attorneys
- Judges
- Arbitrators
- Hearing officers
- Videographers
- Interpreters
- Other reporters

Freelance court reporters must be able to enter a room full of people they have never met and interact with them in a professional manner. There are many situations that call for the reporter to put aside personal feelings toward someone and remain pleasant and respectful.

***Good Memorization Skills*** When reporters come across an unusual name or word that is cumbersome to write, they often devise outlines that enable them to not get thrown each time the word is repeated. Usually the first syllable of the word is written twice, if it does not conflict with another word, phrase, or speaker designation that is written the same way. When asked by an attorney to read a portion of the testimony, the reporter must be able to remember what the stenographic outline represented in order to deliver a good readback. Sometimes a reporter will struggle to keep up with a fast-paced proceeding and the reporter's notes will be sloppier than usual. Having good memorization skills helps you to look at sloppy notes and know what you were writing.

## HOW MUCH MONEY DO FREELANCERS EARN?

Payment for freelance assignments in the legal setting is generally determined by the number of transcript pages produced. Therefore, an assignment where 200 pages are written over several hours will earn the reporter more than a job that yields a 30-page manuscript and lasts 40 minutes. Certain geographic locations/agencies pay reporters appearance fees in addition to a page rate. These are flat fees determined by the reporter's presence during specific time frames of the day/evening. Reporters who work for agencies that do contract work for the government or the court system may be remunerated on a flat-fee basis.

Page rates vary from state to state and agency to agency. They also fluctuate due to:

- Type of proceeding reported
- Amount of transcript copies ordered
- Turnaround time for delivery of the transcript
- Level of experience of the reporter
- Whether the reporter is on staff with the agency
- Additional reporting skills that the reporter possesses

Therefore, there is no uniform answer to the question of how much freelancers earn. However, it is safe to say that freelance court reporting is a profession in which you can potentially earn in a single day what some would consider their weekly salary. It is also safe to say that the financial gains you derive from reporting reflect the amount of dedication that you devote to your career. Likewise, it is safe to say that *Successful Freelance Court Reporting* will guide you from paying your dues as a beginner reporter to taking your place beside the top reporters in the field.

## SHORT-ANSWER QUESTIONS

1. The profession of _________ court reporting in the legal environment involves the stenographic recording of proceedings and subsequent production of a verbatim transcript.
2. The bulk of proceedings reported by freelance court reporters are usually _____ in nature.
3. Freelance reporters must be able to distinguish between ________ such as *affect* and *effect*.
4. Students nearing graduation may apply to the National Court Reporters Foundation for a scholarship known as the _____ _____ ________ ___________.
5. A reporter employed full-time in the court system is referred to as an ___________ reporter.
6. A _________ reporter's stenographic notes are transcribed shortly after a job, while an ________ reporter's stenographic notes are transcribed upon request.
7. Reporters must be able to record and transcribe testimony at the speed of _________ words per minute, jury charges at _________ words per minute, and literary/current events dictations at ________ words per minute.
8. The four physical traits necessary to be a reporter are _________, ____________, __________ and _________.
9. Prior to becoming an official reporter in the court system, reporters working in the court system are referred to as _____________ reporters.
10. Punctuality on assignments, your appearance, and how you conduct yourself on the job are elements of _______________.

## TRUE/FALSE QUESTIONS

1. All proceedings recorded by freelance reporters are legal proceedings.
2. The only duty of a freelance reporter is stenographically recording the proceeding.
3. The majority of freelance assignments are reporting depositions rather than trials.
4. Most of the proceedings reported by freelance reporters take place in a courthouse.
5. Freelance reporters are referred to as official reporters.
6. The procedures and terms utilized in depositions and trials are the same.
7. Trials generally involve more speakers to designate than depositions.
8. Freelancers must work five days a week.
9. If a freelance reporter finds a job beyond his or her capabilities, the reporter may request that another reporter be sent to cover the job.
10. NCRA-recommented court reporting training involves theory, speed, and academic courses.
11. Court reporting schools must be approved by the National Court Reporters Association.
12. The time spent trying to attain 225 wpm in court reporting school varies from student to student.
13. A student's dexterity, practice habits, and ability to punctuate are three factors that can affect the length of a student's court reporting education.
14. You must possess a college degree to become a reporter.
15. Freelancers are paid a rate per page transcribed unless they are doing contract work for the government or the court system.
16. Turnaround time for delivery of a transcript can affect the page rate paid to the reporter.

## DISCUSSION QUESTIONS

1. State three ways in which freelancing differs from official reporting.
2. List five academic courses that reporters are required to take.
3. What are three ways to investigate complaints about a court reporting school in which you are interested?
4. List five responsibilities of a freelance reporter.
5. State three categories of people that may be encountered at a freelance assignment.
6. List the indicators of success.
7. What are six things that can affect the page rate paid to a freelance reporter?

# CHAPTER 2

# Court Reporting School

## NATIONAL COURT REPORTERS ASSOCIATION (NCRA) REQUIREMENTS

Effective August 1, 2000, NCRA's council on approved student education published its general requirements and minimum standards to obtain NCRA approval of a court reporter education program. It stated that:

> The approved court reporter education program shall offer at least the following instruction: machine shorthand, keyboarding, English, law, legal terminology, anatomy and/or medical terminology, court reporting procedures, technology, current events, and internship.

The following is NCRA's breakdown of what each course should entail:

**A. Machine Shorthand**

**Institutional Standards:**

Machine shorthand classes shall include:

1. Instruction in writing the spoken word with punctuation by means of a conflict-free reporting theory as approved by NCRA to provide instantaneous translation.
2. Theory instruction shall include the use of tutorial and/or realtime technology and teacher interaction.
3. Speed and accuracy development.
4. Live practice dictation. The dictation shall include but shall not be limited to two-voice and multi-voice testimony (including medical and technical material), literary, jury charge, and current events. Two-voice dictation should be delivered by two people; multi-voice should be delivered by multiple people.
5. Testing at incremental speeds on unfamiliar material. The same test shall not be dictated more than once every six (6) months to the same student.
6. Readback and analysis of shorthand notes.

7. Once-a-week transcription by all students from their shorthand notes under institutional supervision. This may include tests, homework notes, projects, and so forth.
8. All tests transcribed on site, monitored, and timed by an institutional supervisor. When tests are completed using the computer, all copies (hard disk, RAM, floppy diskettes, etc.) of the tests shall be deleted immediately in order to maintain test integrity.
9. Minimum grading criteria shall be the RPR guide, "What Is An Error?"
10. A simulated RPR skills test at the following speeds: 225 wpm testimony (2-voice), 200 wpm jury charge, and 180 wpm literary with no more than three and a half hours of transcription time. Transcription may take place outside normal classroom time.
11. A simulated Certified Realtime Reporter (CRR) test at a speed of 180–200 wpm literary for 5 minutes.

**Outcomes:**

Students shall be able to:

1. Write a conflict-free shorthand system.
2. Read aloud from shorthand notes, quickly locating portions to be read, maintaining composure while reading, reading distinctly and with authority to the satisfaction of the instructor.
3. Transcribe a minimum of three 5-minute, 2-voice testimony tests with a minimum of 95% accuracy dictated at a minimum of 225 wpm.
4. Transcribe a minimum of three 5-minute jury charge tests with a minimum of 95% accuracy dictated at a minimum of 200 wpm.
5. Transcribe a minimum of three 5-minute literary tests with a minimum of 95% accuracy dictated at a minimum of 180 wpm.
6. Transcribe a simulated RPR skills test at RPR speed levels in 3.5 hours.
7. Write a simulated CRR skills test at a speed of 180–200 wpm literary for 5 minutes.

**B. Keyboarding**

**Institutional Standards:**

Keyboarding class instruction shall include:

1. Instruction on a typewriter and/or computer.
2. Speed and accuracy development which will enable a student to achieve a minimum of 60 gross words per minute for five (5) minutes with a maximum of five (5) errors.

Tutorial programs may be utilized.

**Outcomes:**

Students shall be able to:

1. Pass a minimum of two 5-minute timed writings at a minimum of 60 gross words per minute with a maximum of 5 errors. Correction of errors may be permitted during the 5-minute testing period.

**C. English**

**Institutional Standards:**

English shall include instruction in:

1. Basic rules of English grammar, spelling, punctuation, and capitalization.
2. Vocabulary (word knowledge).

3. Activities or exercises through which students develop their spelling and vocabulary skills.
   (Inclusion of English instruction in a shorthand dictation course does not meet the standard.)

**Outcomes:**
Students shall be able to demonstrate ability to apply the rules of grammar, spelling, punctuation, and capitalization to sentences, paragraphs, and transcripts through systematic testing and/or projects.

**D. Law and Legal Terminology**
**Institutional Standards:**
Law and Legal Terminology shall include classroom instruction in:

1. Civil Law.
2. Criminal Law.
3. The judicial system (discovery, trial, and appellate processes).
4. Legal terminologies.
5. Methods of researching legal citations.
   (Inclusion of law and legal terminology in shorthand dictation classes does not meet the standard.)

**Outcomes:**
Students shall be able to demonstrate an understanding and application of law and legal terminology.

**E. Medical Terminology and/or Anatomy**
**Institutional Standards:**
Medical Terminology and/or Anatomy shall include classroom instruction in:

1. The body systems and functions.
2. Psychological and physical diseases and drugs.
3. Methods of researching medical information such as names and descriptions of diseases and drugs, etc.
   (Inclusion of anatomy and/or medical terminology in shorthand dictation classes does not meet the standard.)

**Outcomes:**
Students shall be able to demonstrate understanding and application of medical terminology and/or anatomy.

**F. Court Reporting Procedures**
**Institutional Standards:**
Court Reporting Procedures shall include classroom instruction in:

1. Role of the reporter in trials, depositions (i.e., telephonic, discovery, perpetuation/evidentiary, and in aid of execution), and administrative hearings.
2. Marking and handling of exhibits.
3. Indexing and storage of notes.
4. Reporting techniques, which shall include but not be limited to, when and/or how to:
   - interrupt a speaker.
   - obtain spellings of proper names.
   - identify speakers in a multi-speaker situation.
   - swear or affirm witnesses and interpreters.
   - handle discussions off the record.
   - indicate nonverbal actions.
   - certify questions.

- report with an interpreter.
- sidebar discussions.
- handle reading and signing of depositions.

5. Transcript preparation and production.
6. Library and reference materials used in transcript production.
7. The profession and related job opportunities.
8. How to report and transcribe voir dire of the jury and witnesses and the polling of the jury.
9. Proofreading skills.
10. Ethics including the distribution of the NCRA Code of Professional Ethics.
11. Knowledge of and involvement in professional associations.
12. The importance of continuing education and life-long learning.
13. Professional image and dress.
14. Development of portfolios and/or resumes.

**Outcomes:**

1. Students shall be able to assume the role of the court reporter through simulated trials and depositions in performing the following functions:
   a. administering an oath/affirmation.
   b. marking and handling exhibits.
   c. exercising responsibility for reporting the proceeding.
   d. indexing and storing notes.
   e. interrupting a speaker.
   f. obtaining spellings of proper names.
   g. identifying speakers in a multi-speaker situation.
   h. handling discussions off the record and sidebar.
   i. indicating nonverbal actions.
   j. certifying questions.
   k. reporting interpreted proceedings.
   l. handling, reading, and signing depositions.
2. Students shall be able to apply the NCRA Code of Professional Ethics in simulated situations and case studies.
3. Students shall be able to identify the appropriate reference sources used in transcript preparation.

**G. Technology**

All NCRA-approved court reporter education programs must have on-site computer-aided realtime transcription systems dedicated to classroom instructional purposes. Equipment utilized by students in classroom instruction shall be maintained in good working order.

**Institutional Standards:**

1. Technology classes shall include hands-on instruction in:
   a. Computer-Aided Transcription
      (1) Instruction in operating a computer-aided transcription system.
      (2) Instruction in the basic care and maintenance of the computer hardware data input device.
      (3) Instruction in system support (customer service, software support, etc.).
      (4) Understanding of computer-aided transcription terminology.
      (5) Application of computer functions:

(a) Producing a transcript: reading, translating, editing, printing, using parentheticals and include files.
(b) Dictionary management to include editing of entries, adding new entries, and archival of dictionary files.

2. Instruction in the following may include: lecture, videotape, or hands-on instruction to provide familiarity in:
   a. Computer Operating Systems/Computer Literacy
      (1) Disk Operating System (DOS).
      (2) Windows.
      (3) Creating an ASCII disk.
      (4) Understanding computer terminology.
      (5) Overview of Internet applications.
   b. Realtime Application.
      (1) Instruction in operating a realtime translation system.
      (2) Instruction in setting up and operating realtime-related hardware.
      (3) Role of the realtime reporter in proceedings:
         (a) Speaker identification
         (b) Realtime transcript, composition, and formatting.
      (4) Utilizing all available resource material to prepare for writing realtime.
      (5) Psychology of writing realtime.
      (6) Realtime reporting in the Computer-Integrated Courtroom (CIC) environment:
         (a) Available realtime and litigation support technology.
         (b) Procedures to train attorneys, paralegals, court personnel, etc.
         (c) System management.
         (d) Case management (what, where, and why).
         (e) Indexing/conversion of software programs.
         (f) Optical scanning of documents, exhibits, building a litigation database.
         (g) Interacting with court computer systems.
         (h) Lexis, Westlaw, etc.
         (i) Case tracking.
         (j) Word processing.
         (k) File storage-archival/retrieval computer systems.
         (l) Coordinating activities with court administrators on CIC matters.
         (m) Telecommunications.
         (n) Public relations.
         (o) Distribution of transcripts, ASCII diskettes, etc.
      (7) Realtime Reporting in the Deposition Environment:
         (a) Available hardware and software technology.
         (b) Equipment setup.
         (c) Telecommunications.
         (d) Participants' needs.
         (e) Litigation support.
         (f) Public relations.
      (8) Realtime Reporting in the Classroom Environment:
         (a) Available hardware and software.

(b) Equipment setup.
(c) Participants' needs.
(d) Public relations.
(e) Interacting with faculty and students.
(f) Sign language/deaf culture.

(9) Realtime Reporting for Seminars/Conferences/Conventions:
(a) Available hardware and software.
(b) Equipment setup.
(c) Ancillary (audio, video, etc.) personnel participants' needs.
(d) Public relations.
(e) Coordinating support staff.

(10) Realtime Reporting in the Broadcast Environment:
(a) Ancillary (engineers) personnel.
(b) Coordinating support staff.
(c) Available hardware and software technology.
(d) Newsroom systems/interfaces.
(e) Public relations.
(f) Prenews/program preparation.
(g) Quality control.
(h) Off-line/post production.
(i) Broadcast industry.
(j) Broadcast production format and materials.
(k) Current events.
(l) Broadcast/news production equipment.
(m) Audience.

c. Litigation Support
(1) An overview of litigation support such as ASCII disks, keyword indexing, etc.
(2) An overview of the role of litigation support in the judicial system.
(3) An overview of the reporter's role in litigation support.

d. Videotaping
(1) An overview of the use of video equipment in trials and depositions.
(2) An overview of NCRA's Certified Legal Video Specialist program.

e. Information on related software packages, such as spreadsheets, word processing, scheduling, and job tracking.

**Outcomes:**

1. The student shall be able to produce salable transcripts of at least ten pages on a computer-aided transcription system from the student's own stenographic notes, including:
   a. title page.
   b. index.
   c. jury charge/opening and/or closing statements if applicable.
   d. direct and cross-examination.
   e. parentheticals.
   f. colloquy.
   g. certification page.
   h. such other entries as may appear in a given case, i.e., signature page.

2. Student shall be able to produce a five-page, first-pass transcript with a goal of 95% translation rate.
3. Student shall be able to demonstrate knowledge of basic hardware care, maintenance, and setup of a realtime system.
4. Student shall be able to demonstrate understanding and application of the body of knowledge required in technology through systematic testing and/or projects.

**H. Current Events**

**Classroom instruction in:**

1. Local events.
2. National events.
3. International events.
4. Geography.
5. Cultural diversity.

Inclusion of current events instruction in a machine shorthand dictation class(es) does meet the standard.

**Outcomes:**

Demonstration of student's understanding of current events.

**I. Internship**

The objective of the internship program is that the student spend some time in a freelance office, a courtroom, and a realtime environment, observing and participating in the role of the court reporter using machine shorthand technology in the judicial or educational process.

**Institutional Standards:**

1. Internship shall not commence until a student completes the institution's 180 wpm testimony requirements.
2. The institution is responsible for assisting the student in arranging the internship experience.
3. The internship shall include official, freelance, and realtime reporting experience where possible.
4. The student shall not serve in the capacity of the actual reporter during participation in this internship period.
5. Internship shall include a minimum of 40 hours of actual writing time under the supervision of a practicing court reporter using machine shorthand technology. This must be verified in writing by the reporter(s) under whom the internship is being completed.
6. A transcript shall be produced for educational and grading purposes only and shall not be sold.
7. Records must be maintained to verify the internship experience, including:
   a. internship verification form.
   b. narrative report.
   c. transcript of internship experience.

**Outcomes:**

The student shall:

1. Submit a written narrative report summarizing the internship experience. The written narrative shall include such things as a diary, new terminology encountered, new experiences, and activities/processes observed.

2. Prepare 40 pages of salable transcript for course evaluation taken from the freelance, the official, or the realtime reporting internship.
3. Submit the signed internship verification form.

As stated earlier, not all court reporting schools are NCRA approved, but most should offer a similar curriculum. Also, these standards apply to full-time day programs. Night school programs may not be as extensive.

## SHORTHAND THEORIES

The first course that you will take upon entering a court reporting school is **machine shorthand theory** (described in the previous section). In this course, you will learn the letters of the court reporting machine keyboard and how **stroking** one key or a combination of keys results in a word or phrase. This is where memorization comes into play. You will need to memorize, by stroking, a whole stenographic language. Although this knowledge is imparted via textbook, there are classroom and homework exercises that can be performed only on a steno machine. Therefore, at this stage in the game, you will need to have obtained a steno machine. If you can borrow one from a friend or someone in the field who has a spare, that is recommended, as new ones are costly and you may subsequently decide that reporting is not for you.

## CONFLICT-FREE WRITING

Shorthand theories taught in court reporting schools focus on **conflict-free writing. Conflicts** occur when the reporter strokes two words or phrases the same exact way. When transcribing stenographic notes into English, either word or phrase may fit into the context of the sentence and it may be impossible to discern which of the two to choose. That is why it is of prime importance to take the time while in school to practice conflict-free writing. Practicing writing a word over and over slowly enables the reporter to form good writing habits so that when **pushing** for speed comes into play (struggling to write beyond one's comfortable speed level), the reporter is able to go on automatic, freeing the mind and allowing the fingers to perform by rote.

## Q&As, JURY CHARGES, AND LITERARY MATTER/CURRENT EVENTS

After completing their theory class, reporters progress through a series of speed classes where they write while receiving dictations from an instructor at various speed levels. The material dictated falls into the categories of Q&A, jury charges, and literary matter/current events.

### Q&As

**Q&A** stands for the question and answer format, which is a format found in legal proceedings. Once the reporter has designated who is doing the questioning and who the witness is, the reporter can simply strike the Question bar by

**Machine shorthand theory:** A method of writing on a stenographic machine that enables the reporter to attain higher levels of speed than if the reporter were writing by pen or typing.

**Stroke:** The pressing of one key or a combination of keys on a steno machine to write a number, letter, word, or phrase.

**Conflict-free writing:** Following a shorthand theory or principles that provide the reporter a method of writing words and phrases so as to avoid conflicts.

**Conflict:** Two words/phrases written exactly the same way that requires the computer, reporter, or scopist to figure out which of the two should be selected.

**Push:** To attempt to report at a writing speed that the reporter is not comfortable at or that is beyond the reporter's capabilities.

**Q&A (question and answer):** The format by which the examination of a witness is recorded stenographically. Reporters are tested at different levels of Q&A to obtain a court reporting school diploma and various certifications.

pressing the keys *STPH* and *SKWR* simultaneously and then record the question. When the question is answered, the reporter strikes the Answer bar by pressing the keys *FPLT* and *RBGS* simultaneously and records the answer. Q&As also may include **colloquy,** which occurs when the examining attorney or the witness speaks to anyone else on the record or when anyone in the room other than the examining attorney and witness speaks on the record. The reporter gives each person a separate designation in preparation for colloquy before the proceeding begins.

Q&A is designed to build speed while acquainting the student with terminologies standard to cases involving negligence, medical malpractice, patent/copyright infringement, bankruptcies, and so on.

### Jury Charges

**Jury charges** are straight matter dictated by the class instructor simulating a judge charging (instructing) a jury during a trial before the jury deliberates on the case. The instructor is not designated on the record as a judge; the student reporter just begins writing the straight matter. Jury charges familiarize the student reporter with language utilized in the courts, and also prepares the student reporter for tests in the field, which contain a jury charge section.

### Literary Matter/Current Events

Lastly, speed classes provide dictations (at slower speeds than Q&As and jury charges) from straight **literary** matter or current event articles to introduce student reporters to writing unfamiliar words and terminologies. Straight matter also aids in training reporters to record material that is quoted from during proceedings.

## DEVELOPING SPEED

Students record the dictated material and then the instructor asks for a volunteer to read a portion of it back. Then new material is dictated and the process is repeated. Students are tested weekly on the aforementioned subject matters by taking their stenographic notes and **transcribing** them into English. The examination is generally reviewed in a subsequent class, where the instructor redictates the material and the students follow along with their transcriptions in front of them, circling errors. Examinations are handed in to the instructor, who grades them at a later time.

Students lose points for:

- Words that were **dropped** (not written in steno notes)
- Spelling errors
- Punctuation errors
- Adding words not in the dictation
- Number errors
- Allocating text to the wrong speaker

The number of permissible errors may vary from school to school, but is generally based on a 95 percent accuracy rate. Students are encouraged to

**Colloquy:** A method of recording text on the record outside of Q&A that reflects: the witness speaking to someone other than the examining attorney, the examining attorney speaking to someone other than the witness, or speaking by anyone else present at the proceeding.

**Jury charge:** A judge's instruction to a jury during a trial before the jury deliberates on the case. Examinations in court reporting schools, as well as state and national examinations, include dictations whereby straight matter is dictated simulating a judge's charge to a jury to assess reporters' skills at specific speed levels.

**Literary:** Straight matter containing content of a literary or current events nature. *Literaries* are dictated to court reporters at various speed levels to assess their skills during court reporting school examinations and state and national examinations.

**Transcribe:** To translate steno notes into English.

**Drop:** To fail to record spoken text that should be on the record.

tape-record each day's dictations to create a personal library of tapes to practice against. The tape recorders are turned off during examination dictations.

There are a number of methods of increasing one's speed. They include:

- Practicing against tapes of dictations from your speed class at school
- Placing your tape recorder in a higher-speed class and practicing against a higher speed than you are used to
- Practicing against speed and stamina tapes advertised in NCRA's *Journal of Court Reporting,* state association magazines, and vendor catalogs
- Practicing against television programs/radio talk shows
- Doing finger exercises to increase the rapidity of finger movement and build stamina
- Sitting in on actual proceedings with other reporters
- Practicing **arbitraries** (alternate methods of writing difficult or lengthy words), also referred to as **briefs** or **short forms**
- Practicing numbers

Once students complete the mandatory academic classes and pass two Q&A tests at 225 words per minute, a jury charge test at 200 words per minute, and a literary test at 180 words per minute, they are deemed to have the necessary skills to graduate from school. In addition, some schools may require student reporters to pass a note test of a Q&A at a lower speed to ensure that their notes are legible and that the student is punctuating properly.

## BUILDING A DICTIONARY

The advantage of using a computerized stenographic writer in school is that it enables you to take your day's dictations and transfer them to the school's computer and create a main, or personal, **dictionary** of how you write. You define steno strokes with the words or phrases that they represent. The more words you are able to define in your dictionary, the easier it will be for a scopist to **scope** your work when you enter the field. **Scopists** are people knowledgeable of court reporting theories who prepare a **transcript** for you to proofread from a copy of your steno notes. They plug in information obtained from a work sheet that you provide and place the testimony in the proper format, place the proper parentheticals into the transcript to reflect nonverbal activities, and transcribe your untranslates. **Untranslates** are words that either have not been previously defined in your dictionary, are misstroked, are represented by an outline (such as *AK/AK* for acquisition), or are unique to a case, requiring someone to decipher the steno and replace it with its English counterpart.

When you interview with certain freelance agencies, some agency owners, referred to as **principals,** look at your number of untranslates on a job to determine your level as a reporter. A reporter with an untranslate level of 5 percent or lower is considered a good writer. An untranslate level of 5 percent reflects that 95 percent of the transcript was translated into English after being **tranned** against your dictionary. Of course, difficult jobs can increase one's untranslate level and are taken into account by principals. Conflicts may fall into the category of untranslates. The conflicting words/phrases may be

**Arbitrary:** A singular stroke that represents multiple words; synonymous with *brief* or *short form.*

**Brief:** A singular stroke that represents a commonly used word or phrase.

**Short form:** A brief, abbreviated method of writing an otherwise multiple-stroke outline, such as *SDOEFR* instead of *DIS/KOF/RAOE.*

**Dictionary:** A file that reporters program to define words. Main, or personal, dictionaries are all-inclusive; job dictionaries are used for globals pertaining to a specific case.

**Scope:** The process of editing rough steno notes, adding in parentheticals and include files, and setting commands to distinguish colloquy from Q&A.

**Scopist:** A professional knowledgeable in steno theory who assists reporters in the preparation of a transcript.

**Transcript:** A document prepared by a court reporter (and/or scopist), which is certified by the court reporter, consisting of a verbatim recording of a proceeding and parentheticals describing nonverbal occurences.

**Untranslate:** Undefined steno words after steno notes have been tranned against a reporter's personal (main) dictionary and/or job dictionary.

**Principal:** An owner of a feelance court reporting agency.

**Tran:** To run electronic steno notes through a personal dictionary, a job dictionary, if applicable, and an agency's edit style sheet.

programmed into one's dictionary to come up in English with an indication that they are conflicts, but the potential for error exists if the scopist selects the wrong word/phrase.

If a reporter has built a dictionary on one type of court reporting software system that is not compatible with that of an agency or a scopist, for a fee, court reporting software vendors can convert the entire dictionary onto compatible disks.

In addition to a main dictionary, in which reporters **(G) global** words/phrases, words particular to a specific case may be **globalled,** or programmed, into what is called a job dictionary. This may be done in your steno writer and/or software. It eliminates the need to redefine your short forms, outlines, and possibly speaker designations every time you work on a specific case.

## SCOPING WHILE STILL IN SCHOOL

If you are interested in part-time work during your court reporting training, working for a freelance court reporting agency can be beneficial on many levels. If you obtain a job scoping for an agency, you will learn how transcripts are prepared. You will develop speed scoping so that if you choose to scope your jobs when you are a working reporter, it will not be as time-consuming as it would be for someone who had never done it before. A scoping job will teach you some of the legal terminology that you will encounter on the job. Working for a freelance court reporting agency will probably ensure you a job when you graduate from school, which will eliminate much of the anxiety you now have about the interviewing process. And lastly, it will enable you to develop relationships with reporters and principals.

## MAINTAINING RELATIONSHIPS WITH FELLOW STUDENTS AND SCHOOL STAFF

While still in school, you should be working on developing good relationships with fellow students and school staff. These relationships do not necessarily end when you graduate. You should view fellow court reporting students as a support system rather than as competition because maintaining contact with people in the field is very beneficial. When a freelancing agency is busy, reporters are often asked if they know of any other reporters who may be able to cover assignments the following day. Giving telephone numbers of colleagues to the agency can introduce colleagues to your agency without them having to cold-call the principal of the agency at a later time looking for work. And what goes around comes around; they may do the same for you. If you keep in touch with your classmates, you can assist one another to find scopists, answer reporting questions, or just have people in your life who relate to your lifestyle.

Likewise, relationships with school staff should be cultivated and valued. Your placement with an agency may largely depend upon the school staff's recommendation. These relationships will benefit you post-graduation when you need advice or answers to questions.

Good relationships with fellow students and staff also lead to positive encounters at court reporting seminars, courthouses, and so forth.

**(G) global:** To define a steno outline permanently in one's main (personal) dictionary.

**Global:** To define steno outlines in English.

## FINDING A MENTOR

While attending court reporting school, reporters usually reach a certain speed level and plateau there for a period of time. This is very conducive to discouragement and oftentimes leads to a reporter's decision to drop out of school. It is at this point that the student needs to find a mentor, someone in the field who can offer some words of encouragement and lift the student's spirits. Just knowing that someone else remembers what it was like to be in your shoes is a form of empathy that family and friends may be incapable of offering. In your search for a mentor, you might want to consider:

- Signing up online with NCRA's Virtual Mentors Program at www.ncraonline.org/vmp, which pairs you with an experienced person in the field.
- Communicating with others online in forums such as the NCRA Online forum at www.ncraonline.org, the Reporter Central forum at www.reportercentral.com, and court reporting–related Web sites such as the author's site at www.danachipkin.com.
- Asking friends and family if they know a reporter you can contact
- Cultivating relationships with school personnel
- If you have ever attended a deposition, trying to locate the reporter by calling the reporter's agency
- Calling freelance agencies and asking if they can recommend a reporter who might be willing to take a few minutes to speak with a prospective reporter
- Attending court reporting seminars and making friends
- Contacting authors of books/articles in the field
- Arranging to sit in with other reporters

## SITTING IN

If you are nearing the completion of your court reporting schooling, you should be **sitting in** with working reporters to get the practical hands-on experience that you will need in the field. Most schools provide programs for their students to sit in at a nearby courthouse, either in a courtroom setting or deposition setting. If your school has some such arrangement, the school staff will give you the name of the person to speak to at the courthouse who will direct you to where you will be sitting in on trials.

Some courthouses permit you to go to the location in the courthouse where depositions are held, befriend a fellow reporter, and ask to sit in on the reporter's job outside of an internship arrangement with your school. It is important to contact the Court Clerk, prior to going to the courthouse, to see if this is acceptable practice at that particular courthouse. Schools usually require the reporter to fill out a form that indicates information about the case, lists who was present, and is signed by the reporter that the student sat in with. Although deposition schedules are variable, the most frequent deposition times are 10:00 A.M. and 2:00 P.M., so arrive around 9:30 to find a reporter with whom to sit in on a 10:00 deposition and around 1:30 to find a reporter with whom to sit in on a 2:00 deposition.

**Sitting In:** When a court reporting student attends a proceeding as a learning experience and sits next to the reporter assigned to report the proceeding, prepares a work sheet, reports the proceeding unofficially, and transcribes a few pages of the transcript for a review by a court reporting school or a freelance court reporting agency.

If you are at the job-interviewing stage, you can ask agencies if you can sit in with their reporters until you feel comfortable enough to begin working. When sitting in with a reporter of a prospective freelance agency, usually you are expected to fill out a work sheet and transcribe several pages, if not all, of the transcript. The reporter or agency with whom you want to sit in should get the acquiescence of the attorneys prior to your sitting in. If the attorneys do not mind, you will sit in a corner of the room, usually to one side of the official court reporter, and report alongside the reporter.

Although the term *official court reporter* is used to identify stenographers who are employed full-time in the court system, it has another meaning on the freelance level. It is used to describe the reporter who will provide the original transcript of the proceedings for the witness/witnesses to sign, as well as mark exhibits and read back testimony, if asked, during the proceeding, in cases where a second reporter is present.

When you sit in, the protocol is that you are not to say anything during the proceedings or to interrupt if you do not hear something. Do not be upset with yourself if you do not hear something that is said, because when you begin to work, you will be in a position to ask people to either speak up or repeat what was said or to ask that only one person at a time speak, and you will be sitting in a better location to hear than when you are just sitting in.

This sitting-in procedure is essential to learning about court reporting outside the classroom because you can learn many, many things by just watching the official reporter. You can observe how the official reporter:

- Obtains the information necessary to fill out a work sheet
- Obtains witness and attorney information
- Determines who the examining attorney will be
- Swears in/affirms the witness and/or interpreter
- Performs the court reporting functions
- Handles situations that arise
- Obtains billing and transcript delivery information

Sitting in is also a way to befriend working reporters and, if they are amenable to it, find a mentor to help you through this stage of your court reporting career. Ask for the reporter's business card and home telephone number. Inquire about the nature of the agency's work, how long the reporter has worked for that agency, and the names of the principal/principals/office manager. Be sure to give the reporter your name and telephone number so that the reporter may tell his or her principal to expect a call from you.

## JOINING COURT REPORTING ASSOCIATIONS

Before graduating from court reporting school, you should join court reporting associations at both the state and national level. When you become a member, you receive magazines that offer:

- Current events/updates on legislation in the field
- Information on changing requirements of aspects of the reporting profession

- Dates of certification tests
- Certification maintenance requirements and updates
- Dates and locations of upcoming seminars/activities
- Information on court reporting equipment and supplies
- Classifieds regarding equipment, scoping, and positions available
- Feature articles pertinent to reporting
- Methods of broadening your knowledge of language
- Steno brief suggestions
- Speed contest information
- Computer information and assistance
- A catalog of reporter reference materials and recommendations
- Student reporter tips/articles
- Articles and information regarding fellow members/reporters
- Articles pertaining to scoping
- Court reporting–related book reviews
- Suggestions for volunteer work
- Letters to the editor

The associations enable the student reporter to feel a part of the profession prior to completing school. They offer members various service discounts in areas such as long-distance call rates, insurance, and so on. Group membership may entitle you to participate in a retirement plan. Associations sponsor seminars/conventions that are of interest to both students and working reporters. Certain events provide the opportunity to meet court reporting vendors and demo and discuss the equipment/products, meet equipment repair companies, and check out new reference materials/court reporting–related books. There also may be raffles of reporting-related door prizes.

Students are given a discount on membership in the associations and at their respective seminars and often find both very motivating.

The National Court Reporters Association (NCRA) may be contacted by writing to: 8224 Old Courthouse Road, Vienna, VA 22182-3808; calling (703) 556-6272 or the 800 number from your area; faxing (703) 556-6291; or e-mailing the NCRA Web site at http://www.verbatimreporters.com. The 800 number is the NCRA's member service number that is available to members during business hours for court reporting–related inquiries.

## BECOMING A NOTARY PUBLIC

The requirement to be a notary public in order to freelance court report varies from state to state. In states where being a notary is mandatory, it is strongly recommended that reporters attempt to become notaries while still in school. As of the date of publication of this book, the specific states that mandate that the freelance reporter be a notary are:

- Alaska
- Arizona
- Colorado
- District of Columbia
- Florida
- Indiana

- Kentucky
- Maryland
- Massachusetts
- Mississippi
- Montana
- New Hampshire
- New Jersey
- Rhode Island
- South Carolina
- Vermont
- Washington

One becomes a notary by passing an examination. Some schools offer courses that prepare the reporter to become a notary. They are not mandatory, but they can be helpful. If your school does not offer a notary course, you can call the County Clerk or Department of State in your area and obtain an address to write to for an application to take the notary examination. They will send you an application form and a study booklet. Upon receipt of the application, the date and location of the examination will be identified via mail. You will take the test on the specified date and later receive in the mail a notice of having passed or failed. If you have passed, you will send in an application with the requested filing fee, and within a short period of time, usually eight to twelve weeks, a notary public card will be mailed to you with your notary number on it. You may then wish to have a notary stamp made up at a print shop. The stamp should have the following information: the name of the reporter, the state in which the reporter is a notary, the reporter's notary number, the county the reporter received his or her notary from, and the date on which the reporter's commission expires. A sample stamp is as follows:

ALICE SMITH
Notary Public, State of New York
No. 1234567
Qualified in Nassau County
Commission Expires January 1, 2003

If you fail the notary examination, providing you pay the required fee, you can take the examination as often as you wish until you pass it. In some states, the test is offered once a week, twice a day. You can take it twice on the same day, if you so desire.

Once you become a notary, you must renew your notary every two years, which involves a renewal fee. The County Clerk's office where your notary is filed will usually send you a reminder card that it is time to renew. You will fill out the renewal form and return it with a renewal fee via mail. Most states require the notary to be a resident of that state or have a business address in that state.

It is very rare that a freelance reporter is asked to notarize a document on the job, since many lawyers are notaries and can do it themselves. Notarizing documents is not a required function of a freelance reporting assignment. In states where being a notary public is mandatory for court reporters, freelancers must be notaries in order to perform freelancing functions related to swearing/affirming a witness and/or certifying that the record of the proceeding is accurate.

Court reporting schools and state associations should be updated on notary qualifications in your state. For further information, you can contact the National Notary Association at P.O. Box 2402, Chatsworth, CA 91313; telephone number (818) 739-4000; fax number (818) 700-1830; and Web site address www.nationalnotary.org. Call information for the 800 number applicable from your area.

## SHORT-ANSWER QUESTIONS

1. The NCRA-recommended speeds to begin court reporting are: Q&A at ______ words per minute, jury charges at _______ words per minute, and literary/current event dictations at _______ words per minute.
2. The class entitled ______ or __________ __________ familiarizes the reporter with body systems and functions, psychological and physical diseases and drugs, and how to research medical information.
3. The academic class that teaches reporters how to mark exhibits and swear/affirm witnesses and that familiarizes the reporter with other reporting techniques is called _____ _________.
4. An ___________ provides the student with an opportunity to spend time in a hands-on reporting environment.
5. According to NCRA-recommended guidelines, students should intern for at least _____ hours in preparation for reporting.
6. The first course a court reporting student will take is __________ ___________ to learn about the court reporting machine's functions and how to write conflict-free.
7. A question symbol appears when the reporter strokes the keys ______ and ________ simultaneously, and an answer symbol appears when the reporter strokes the keys _________ and ________ simultaneously.
8. _______ __________ simulate a judge instructing a jury before its deliberation on a case.
9. A person who is knowledgeable about court reporting theories and who prepares transcripts for reporters is known as a ___________.
10. A ___________ dictionary is created by a reporter to define how he or she normally writes words.
11. A ___________ dictionary is created by a reporter to define short forms, outlines, and speaker designations for a particular case.
12. The term _______ _________ refers to the reporter who is ordered by the attorney examining the witness first, who will perform readbacks when asked and who will mark exhibits when two reporters are present in a freelance setting, as well as to a reporter employed full time in the court system.
13. Some states require freelance reporters to be a __________ _______ in order to swear/affirm witnesses and/or certify that the record of the proceeding is accurate.

## TRUE/FALSE QUESTIONS

1. The NCRA recommends that reporters take only theory and speed classes to prepare for a career in reporting.
2. Reporters must practice readback of stenographic notes as part of their training.
3. Training with a typewriter/computer is a component of one's court reporting education.
4. Court reporting students are tested on 20-minute dictations weekly.
5. Court reporting students must pass dictation examinations with a 95 percent translation rate.
6. Students are expected to prepare a transcript (or a portion thereof) from internship experiences.
7. Conflicts are two steno outlines written exactly the same way.
8. If a reporter records a word in steno and spells it inaccurately on a transcription exam, an instructor will mark it as an error.
9. Reporting students lose points on dictation exams when words are dropped (missing from the record).
10. Putting a comma where a period belongs on a transcription exam will be counted as an error.
11. It is important for a student reporter to build his or her dictionary while in court reporting school.
12. A large dictionary will facilitate the scoping of jobs.
13. A reporter should global speaker designations in his or her main dictionary, for example, *SNAO* as *MR. COHEN.*
14. Only working reporters may join state and national court reporting associations.
15. Every state requires its reporters to be notary publics.
16. Notaries must renew their notary status every two years for a fee.

## DISCUSSION QUESTIONS

1. How do court reporting schools differ from traditional higher-education facilities?
2. State three reasons why a student reporter will lose points on a dictation examination.
3. State four methods of increasing one's reporting speed.
4. Why are knowledge of and dictations of current events important for court reporting students?
5. State three benefits of scoping for a freelance agency while attending court reporting school.
6. State five methods of finding a mentor while in court reporting school.
7. Does your state require reporters to be notary publics?

CHAPTER

3

# Examinations and Certifications

In addition to notary requirements, in certain states reporters cannot begin working until they have met other examination requirements. Since your speed is at or near 225 wpm, there is no better time than near the end of school to take these exams.

## CERTIFIED SHORTHAND REPORTER (CSR) AND CERTIFIED COURT REPORTER (CCR) EXAMINATIONS

On the state level, some states require their freelance reporters to pass either a **CSR** exam, which stands for Certified Shorthand Reporter, or a **CCR** exam, which stands for Certified Court Reporter and is the equivalent of the CSR exam in certain states. As of the date of publication of this book, it is mandatory to sit for all or part of the CSR/CCR exam in order to freelance in:

- Arkansas
- California
- Connecticut
- Georgia
- Idaho
- Illinois
- Iowa
- Kansas
- Louisiana
- Mississippi (by the reporter's first 18 months of working)
- Nevada
- New Hampshire
- New Jersey
- Oklahoma
- Texas
- Utah (unless reporter is an RPR)
- Washington

**CSR:** (Certified Shorthand Reporter) A state certification in certain states.

**CCR:** (Certified Court Reporter) A state certification in certain states.

In other states, the CSR/CCR certification is voluntary. The exceptions to the list are: the Canadian province of Alberta, where private practice requires an examiner's license or working for a person/entity that has one, and Rhode Island, where in lieu of the CSR/CCR exam, there is a state court skills test that freelance reporters must pass in order to work in the state.

Certain states may grant the reporter CSR/CCR reciprocity if the reporter is an **RPR** (Registered Professional Reporter), which means that the reporter can work in that state without taking an additional exam. These states are:

- Alabama
- Canadian province of Alberta
- Canadian province of Ontario
- Georgia
- Kansas
- Louisiana
- Nebraska
- New Hampshire
- Tennessee
- Utah
- Washington
- West Virginia

Some states may grant CSR/CCR reciprocity if the reporter has the equivalent credential in another state or is an RPR and meets additional conditions, such as continuing education credits, passing a portion of the state exam, number of years of experience, or has recently passed the RPR exam within a specific number of years prior to application for CSR/CCR status. These states are:

- Hawaii
- Illinois
- Indiana
- Iowa
- Michigan
- Mississippi
- Nebraska
- New Hampshire
- New Mexico
- Oklahoma
- Oregon
- Tennessee

In other states, legislation is pending or committees or task forces are currently in progress to make the CSR/CCR exam mandatory. For clarification regarding a specific state, you may contact its Department of Education or the state court reporting association, or request a copy of NCRA's "State Certification and Other Testing Information (Including Alberta and Ontario, Canada)."

**RPR:** (Registered Professional Reporter) A certification offered by the NCRA.

Although it varies from state to state, most states offer the CSR/CCR exam once a year at various locations. The number of locations is dependent upon applicant turnout and varies from state to state. CSR/CCR exams consist of both a skills test and a written knowledge test determined by the state's Department of Education. Applications must be in by a specified date or the reporter must wait until the exam is offered again. Certain states attach conditions to eligibility for the CSR/CCR exam, such as the reporter must:

- Be 21 or older
- Be a U.S. citizen
- Be a graduate of high school or hold a GED
- Have a minimum amount of years of freelancing experience

There is a fee determined by the state upon registration for the exam. CSR/CCR exams may entail:

- Transcribing for a set amount of minutes at varying speeds
- Reading back part of the dictation
- Transcribing medical testimony for a specified amount of time at a set speed
- Passing a written knowledge test consisting of legal/medical terminology and reporting procedures
- Passing a written knowledge test designed to evaluate the reporter's knowledge of English as it relates to principles of court reporting grammar and punctuation

Many states provide a live dictation for the skills portion of the exam. Depending on the state, if a reporter passes portions of the exam and not others, the state may credit the reporter with the **legs** passed and the reporter may only have to sit for the failed legs of the exam at a later date. Grades are generally mailed to the reporter within 60 days or so of the test date, indicating P for "pass" or F for "fail." One can request the actual numerical score if it is within 10 points of a passing grade. Those who fail the CSR/CCR exam may reapply to take it at a lower fee than the initial application fee.

When a reporter passes the CSR/CCR, the state usually mails the reporter a certificate and a registration card with a certification number. The reporter must then renew the CSR/CCR certification every three years thereafter for a fee. Some states do not require reporters to sit for the exam a second time if they fail to renew their certification in a timely manner.

## REGISTERED PROFESSIONAL REPORTER (RPR) EXAMINATION

The only state that requires working reporters to be Registered Professional Reporters (RPRs) is Hawaii. In all other states, the RPR is a voluntary examination. The National Court Reporters Association (NCRA) offers the test to become an RPR twice annually, the first Saturday in May and the first Saturday in November. The NCRA sells study guides for reporters to prepare for all of its exams. The RPR exam is conducted via an audiotape, the same administered simultaneously to all states, and it is comprised of a written portion that tests knowledge in areas pertinent to court reporting, as well as a skills portion. The written knowledge test gives the reporter an hour and a half to respond to 100 questions generally focused on reporting, transcript production, operating and professional issues, and continuing education. To pass, the reporter must score 70 or above. The skills portion of the RPR exam allows the reporter three and a half hours to warm up against a practice dictation; then the reporter must

**Leg:** One of the three elements comprising the skills portion of a court reporting examination; that is, Q&A, jury charge, or literary.

record three dictations—a literary at 180 words per minute, a jury charge at 200 words per minute, and a two-voice Q&A at 225 words per minute—and transcribe each dictation with 95 percent accuracy. To sit for the RPR exam, NCRA requires the reporter to be a member of NCRA with dues paid in full as of December 31 of the prior year. There is an application fee for the RPR exam.

After taking the RPR examination, reporters are notified of their grades via mail within about six to eight weeks. The results of the written knowledge test indicate P for "pass" or F for "fail" with the actual test score, while the results of the skills portion are broken down by category of dictation—literary, jury charge, Q&A—with a P or an F next to each. For a fee, the reporter may request specific scores on the skills portion of the RPR exam.

Do not feel discouraged if you do not pass the entire RPR examination on the first sitting, because if you pass any leg, or portion, of the exam—the written knowledge test or a leg of the skills section—you need only sit for the balance of the exam the next time you take the test. As prepared as I felt I was, the first time I sat for the RPR exam, the reporter seated to my left experienced a paper jam during the skills portion and let out an exasperated sigh, which distracted me to the point of breaking my concentration, causing me to drop some testimony. I, therefore, did not pass the skills portion and had to take it a second time. It was actually less stressful the second time around, having already passed the written knowledge portion of the RPR and just sitting for the skills segment, which I then passed.

Test conditions on exams, like in real-life reporting, are not always perfect. If you experience any difficulty during an exam, you should internalize it. Otherwise you risk jeopardizing someone else's chances for passing. Additionally, it is important not to get caught up in the "pass/fail" mentality, but rather to realize that the field supports the "If at first you don't succeed, try, try again" philosophy.

Once a reporter has passed the RPR exam, to maintain this credential, the reporter must remain a member in good standing of the National Court Reporters Association and must obtain 3.0 continuing education units (CEUs) every three years. Each CEU is equivalent to 10 hours of continuing education instruction. There are a variety of ways to achieve these units. Reporters may:

- Take quizzes offered in NCRA's *Journal of Court Reporting*
- Participate in the Home Study program, which allows reporters to obtain CEUs by passing a test following the reading of an NCRA-approved book or series of articles
- Physically attend NCRA- and state-sponsored court reporting seminars
- Participate in seminars via telephone or on the Internet
- Attend courses, such as CPR/First Aid courses, college courses, or adult education courses offered by NCRA-approved sponsors
- Author an article for the *Journal of Court Reporting* on a researched topic—an outline of the article must first be submitted to NCRA for approval

Reporters will lose their RPR status if they do not comply with CEU or membership maintenance requirements and will have to take the RPR exam over again.

The NCRA acknowledges RPRs by mailing them a hand-lettered certificate and listing them in NCRA's magazine, *The Journal of Court Reporting,* NCRA's

*Sourcebook,* and on NCRA's Web site. A number of colleges and universities grant the RPR an automatic 21 semester hours upon this achievement.

## OTHER EXAMINATIONS/CERTIFICATIONS

There are a number of certifications that may be further down the road for court reporting students as they may require freelancing experience or membership in NCRA for an allotted period of time, be contingent upon having first obtained other certifications, or require skills taught outside one's court reporting school. Although court reporting students may not be ready to sit for these exams, they should be knowledgeable about them. They include the RMR, the RDR, the CRR, and the CLVS.

### Registered Merit Reporter (RMR) Certification

The **RMR** credential stands for Registered Merit Reporter. It has replaced what used to be known as the **CM,** Certificate of Merit. The RMR is not mandatory in any state. It is a meritorious credential based on a very rigorous high-speed test, which one would normally take after many years of freelancing, rather than at the beginning of one's court reporting career. It is conducted via audiotape and is offered at the same time as the RPR exam—the first Saturday of May and the first Saturday of November of each year—by the National Court Reporters Association. There is an application fee for the exam. Similar to the RPR, the RMR tests the reporter's written knowledge of reporting, transcript production, administration and professional issues, and continuing education via 100 questions over a one-and-a-half-hour period. The reporter must score 70 or above. The skills portion, however, is at higher-speed levels. It consists of a literary at 200 words per minute, a jury charge at 240 words per minute, and two-voice Q&A at 260 words per minute. Reporters have one and one-fourth hours to transcribe each leg of the skills portion of the RMR exam. To pass any leg of the skills segment, the reporter's transcription must be 95 percent accurate.

The NCRA credits the reporter for passing any portion of the RMR exam. The reporter is credited with passing a single leg of the skills portion: literary, jury charge, or Q&A. Therefore, the reporter may pass, for instance, the written knowledge and the literary and jury charge portions in one sitting and return the next time the exam is offered to take only the two-voice Q&A portion.

To sit for the written segment of the RMR exam, reporters must meet one of the following criteria:

- The reporter has been an RPR for three continuous years
- The reporter has been a member of NCRA for four continuous years
- The reporter has six continuous years of reporting experience
- The reporter holds a bachelor's degree

To sit for the skills segment, the requirements are that you must be an RPR and a member in good standing of the NCRA with dues paid in full.

The RMR results are received in the same manner as those for the RPR exam within about six to eight weeks of taking the test. The NCRA acknowledges this achievement by sending the reporter a hand-lettered certificate in the mail and listing the reporter's accomplishment in the *Journal of Court*

**RMR:** (Registered Merit Reporter) A meritorious certification offered by the NCRA.

**CM:** (Certificate of Merit) A national reporting certification now replaced by the RMR certification.

*Reporting,* NCRA's *Sourcebook,* and on NCRA's Web site. Additionally, obtaining an RMR certification earns the reporter three semester hours in a number of colleges and universities.

RMRs, like RPRs, must remain members of NCRA and obtain 3.0 continuing education units over each successive three-year period in order to maintain their RMR certification. If reporters do not comply, they will lose their RMR status and have to reapply for the RMR exam.

## Registered Diplomate Reporter (RDR) Certification

The **RDR,** or Registered Diplomate Reporter, credential is a nonmandatory, even more meritorious credential than the RMR. The National Court Reporters Association, the first Saturday in May and the first Saturday in November of each year, offers the RDR exam. The examination consists solely of a written knowledge test with 100 multiple-choice questions focusing on: reporting, management, marketing, transcript production, education, and professional issues. The reporter must score 70 or above. Requirements to apply for the RDR exam are:

- The reporter has been an RMR for five continuous years
- The reporter holds a bachelor's degree
- The reporter has two of the following certifications: CMRS (Certified Manager of Reporting Services), CRR (Certified Realtime Reporter), CLVS (Certified Legal Video Specialist), CRI (Certified Reporter Instructor), MCRI (Master Certified Reporter Instructor), CPE (Certified Program Evaluator)

Aside from the CRR and the CLVS, the other certifications in this list pertain more to educators/administrators in the court reporting field.

There is an application fee determined by the NCRA for the RMR, as with the other tests. The test score is sent via mail to the reporter within about six to eight weeks after the exam date with a P/F and numerical score. The NCRA acknowledges this achievement by sending the reporter a hand-lettered certificate and by listing the reporter in the *Journal of Court Reporting,* NCRA's *Sourcebook,* and on NCRA's Web site.

To maintain the RDR certification, reporters must remain a member in good standing of NCRA with dues paid in full and obtain 3.0 continuing education units over each successive three-year period. Otherwise, RDRs will lose their RDR status and will have to reapply for the exam.

**RDR:** (Registered Diplomate Reporter) A meritorious certification offered by the NCRA.

**Realtiming:** The process whereby reporters provide instantaneous translation of the proceedings on a computer screen.

**CIC reporting:** Realtiming in a courtroom when there are multiple hook-ups for participants of the proceeding to observe.

**CRR:** (Certified Realtime Reporter) A voluntary certification offered by the NCRA for reporters who perform realtime.

## Certified Realtime Reporter (CRR) Examination

**Realtiming** is a court reporting skill that allows for instantaneous translation of a proceeding to appear on a notebook computer screen. **Computer-integrated courtroom (CIC) reporting** involves integrating computers so that all or most participants in the proceedings can see on a computer what you are writing as you are writing it. This is particularly helpful in depositions of deaf witnesses or attorneys and in high-profile cases that the media is covering. Realtime reporters become certified in realtiming by passing the **CRR,** or Certified Realtime Reporter, examination. This exam is offered by the National Court Reporters Association four times a year: usually at the time of their spring symposium in April, the first Saturday in May, at the time of their annual convention (generally held in July or August), and the first Saturday in November. Eligibility to take the exam requires the reporter to be a member of NCRA and an RPR.

The CRR credential is a voluntary credential. It is obtained by passing an exam that tests the reporter's ability to set up the realtime equipment properly, write realtime accurately for five minutes from a literary or legal opinion dictation via audiotape at speeds ranging between 180 and 200 words per minute, and then to convert this material to an **ASCII** disk, which is a disk that is compatible to all computer software. The reporter must achieve a combined score of 96 percent for all of these functions. Reporters are responsible for bringing all the equipment needed for the exam. A pass/fail notification is sent to the reporter within six to eight weeks of the test.

Upon passing the CRR exam, the reporter will:

- Receive a hand-written certificate in the mail from NCRA
- Have the accomplishment listed in the *Journal of Court Reporting,* NCRA's *Sourcebook,* in the *Directory of Certified Realtime Reporters,* and on NCRA's Web site
- Have obtained five hours toward continuing education units

To maintain the CRR credential, reporters must maintain their RPR credential and remain a member in good standing of NCRA; otherwise, they will have to reapply for the exam.

## Certified Legal Video Specialist (CLVS) Certification

The **CLVS,** or Certified Legal Video Specialist, certification is not exclusive to reporters. The CLVS is a voluntary certification for videotaping proceedings and is comprised of a three-step process:

1. Attending a seminar offered by the NCRA entitled "Videotape in the Legal Environment," which is offered in March and September in certain cities, and completing it by a specified date
2. Passing a one-and-a-half-hour written knowledge test consisting of 100 multiple-choice questions regarding video recording production, post-production, legal and judicial procedures, office procedures and operating practices, and professional development and ethics, which is offered the first Saturday of May and the first Saturday of November of each year, and scoring 70 percent or higher
3. Passing a production exam where you are given 30 minutes to become familiar with NCRA's video equipment and then given 5 to 10 minutes to video a mock deposition via audiotape

Each step in the process must be completed in the order of this list or the applicant is not eligible to move to the next step. Six to eight weeks after taking the written test, grades are received in the mail. After passing the production portion of the exam, a hand-lettered certificate is awarded by the NCRA via mail. Although no continuing education credits are required of a CLVS, the CLVS is awarded 24 credits for having attended the seminar and an additional 5 credits for completing the written knowledge test and production test. The CLVS certification is granted for a one-year period and is renewed by the NCRA annually each October for a fee. If the renewal fee is not paid and the CLVS certification

**ASCII:** (American Standard Code for Information Interchange) A standard type of file that is compatible to most computers and software.

**CLVS:** (Certified Legal Video Specialist) A voluntary certification offered by the NCRA for legal videographers.

lapses, one must again attend the seminar and pass the production exam. It is not necessary to take the written knowledge test over.

## CIVIL SERVICE EXAMINATIONS

If you aspire to work in the court system and you have met the eligibility requirements regarding a court reporting school diploma, any state exam certification, and freelancing experience, the next step is to take **civil service** examinations. If you are a member of your state's court reporting association, you will be sent notification regarding when statewide civil service exams are offered and a brief mention of specific eligibility requirements. The tests encompass both written and skills legs, the content of which may vary from court to court and state to state. State associations and court reporting schools generally offer practice dictation sessions to prepare you for the exams. In the state of New York, a magazine called *The Chief,* which provides civil service examination information, is available at newsstands in close proximity to courthouses. Perhaps your state offers a similar-type magazine.

**Civil service:** An adjective pertaining to working for an administrative service of the state or United States Government—*i.e.,* official reporting and legislative reporting.

**Non–civil service:** An adjective pertaining to nongovernment or state agencies.

## NON–CIVIL SERVICE EXAMINATIONS

For information regarding **non–civil service** examinations, which are examinations for entities outside the court system, you can call the individual entity that you are interested in working for and inquire about its specific requirements. Freelance agencies often contract with non–civil service entities and assign reporters to jobs on a per-diem basis.

Workers'/Workmen's Compensation is a wonderful training ground for new reporters, since the material reported often contains heavy medical content and the positions include benefits. You can call the Workers'/Workmen's Compensation board near you to obtain full-time job information.

## SHORT-ANSWER QUESTIONS

1. ________ ________ is the only state where reporters must pass a state skills exam in lieu of a CSR/CCR exam.
2. The ________/________ exam is a state certification that must be renewed every three years for a fee.
3. The __________ exam is offered by the NCRA, which consists of a written knowledge test and a skills exam that tests the reporter's literary/current event dictation speed at 180 words per minute, jury charge speed at 200 words per minute, and Q&A speed at 225 words per minute.
4. It is mandatory to be an RPR in __________ in order to freelance.
5. RPRs and ________ must obtain ________ continuing education units every three years to maintain their certifications.

6. The NCRA offers a ________ ___________ program for reporters to obtain continuing education units through quizzes, book reports, and courses.
7. The _________ tests reporters' skills via a literary dictation at 200 words per minute, a jury charge at 240 words per minute, and a Q&A at 260 words per minute as well as a written knowledge exam.
8. The _________ exam consists only of a written knowledge test with 100 multiple-choice questions.
9. To become a certified realtime writer, a reporter must obtain the _________ certification.
10. _____________ is a skill that enables participants in a proceeding to see on a computer what the reporter is writing as the proceeding is taking place.
11. The _________ is a voluntary certification for the videotaping of proceedings.
12. ________ __________ is a good training ground for new reporters, as reporters report hearings with heavy medical content and receive benefits.

## TRUE/FALSE QUESTIONS

1. It is mandatory in every state for reporters to pass a state exam known as a CSR or CCR in order to freelance.
2. If you freelance for an agency in the Canadian province of Alberta whose principal has a CSR/CCR certification, you may work without a CSR/CCR certification.
3. Some states grant reciprocity to an RPR so that he or she does not have to take the CSR/CCR exam in order to freelance.
4. The NCRA credits reporters for passing single legs of the skills portion of the RPR exam.
5. The RMR is a mandatory certification.
6. If you are not an RPR for three continuous years, are not a member of the NCRA, have not reported for six continuous years, and do not hold a bachelor's degree, you cannot sit for the RMR exam.
7. Reporters must pass all legs of the skills section of the RMR exam in one sitting.
8. The NCRA acknowledges reporters' certification accomplishments by sending reporters a hand-lettered certification and listing it in the *Journal of Court Reporting,* NCRA's *Sourcebook,* and on NCRA's Web site.
9. RMRs do not have to obtain 3.0 continuing education units every three years to maintain their certification.
10. You must be an RMR for five continuous years to sit for the RDR exam.
11. State associations notify member reporters about civil service exams.

## DISCUSSION QUESTIONS

1. Is the CSR/CCR certification mandatory to freelance in your state?
2. Even if a CSR/CCR certification is not required, what are the benefits of obtaining it?
3. Does a mandatory state certification help to raise the quality of reporters within that state?

4. State the five continuing education units in which RPRs must obtain six credits in every three-year successive period.
5. What are some of the methods by which the National Court Reporters Association enables reporters to maintain the continuing education units?
6. What benefits do you believe possessing certain certifications may yield?

CHAPTER

4

# Tools of the Trade

## REPORTING EQUIPMENT

Obviously, you need to have a court reporting machine to attend court reporting school. You may want to borrow a spare machine from someone you know, if possible, prior to investing in one in order to make sure reporting is for you. For school, it need not be the newest technology, and it need not be computerized; it just must possess the capability to write machine shorthand. There are some advantages, however, of having up-to-date equipment during school. They are:

- Getting familiar with the workings of computerized equipment before entering the field
- Receiving a student/group discount on equipment
- Building a dictionary with it (although many schools lend you a computerized writer when you are going to work on your dictionary)
- Practicing realtime writing

Although court reporting equipment vendors sell student models of current writers, some students may wish to go ahead and purchase/lease a current writer on the market.

Before graduating from court reporting school, reporters should investigate thoroughly the equipment that is currently on the market so that they can begin their new career with technology that will earn them an edge in a freelance agency. Realtime is the wave of the future for reporters. Beginner reporters who enter the workforce writing realtime may be more in demand than experienced writers who are not realtime-ready.

### Deciding Upon Which Writer/Software

Reporters may decide to purchase software compatible with their writing machines, which eliminates the need for assistance by outside sources. Court reporting software is classified as programs specifically designed for court reporters to perform the functions required of them. This is referred to in court reporting terminology as a **CAT system,** or Computer-Aided Transcription system. CAT systems enable reporters to:

**CAT system:** (Computer-Aided Transcription system) Court reporting software that enables reporters to create transcripts from electronic steno writers.

- Read steno notes into the computer
- Telecommunicate—send information via modem to other computers through telephone lines
- Translate steno notes into English
- Create **edit styles**—set up the transcript parameters preferred by each agency so that a transcript will appear in that agency's format
- Perform realtime functions
- Do **AICR (Artificial Intelligence-Conflict Resolution)**—select a menu option that assists the reporter in identifying and resolving conflicts
- Create job dictionaries for ongoing jobs
- Edit a job dictionary
- Edit a **job file**
- Spell check and identify duplicate words in a job file
- Merge transcripts together
- Create ASCII files
- Edit ASCII files
- Print transcripts
- Print **keyword indexes**—enabling the reporter to index examinations by different parties, exhibits, requests, inserts, rulings, etc.
- Print keyword lists—create a list of each word in the transcript and its corresponding page and line number
- Build a dictionary by adding outlines from a word list
- Modify and create word lists for dictionary building
- Edit one's dictionary
- Make copies of one's dictionary
- Go to a DOS prompt while in the software program
- Delete/copy job files in the software program

By the time you are reading this, modern technology will probably offer additional functions.

As court reporting equipment is expensive, a thorough investigation is warranted prior to entering into a purchase/lease agreement. Methods of familiarizing yourself with products currently on the market include:

- Speaking to vendors when they come to your court reporting school, obtaining promotional material, and sampling the equipment
- Asking staff at your court reporting school/reporters/agencies for personal recommendations
- Joining state and national court reporting associations, which have newsletters and magazines that advertise court reporting related equipment, occasionally contain articles about the equipment, and list used equipment for sale/lease assignment in their magazines
- Attending court reporting seminars, which gives reporters an opportunity to speak to vendors, obtain promotional material, and sample the equipment
- Calling the vendor directly and speaking to the sales representative in your area
- Visiting vendor Web sites

The purchase of a new product would be done directly through the vendor. One major advantage to buying new equipment from a vendor is that the

**Edit style:** Transcript-formatting parameters applicable to a particular freelance court reporting agency that take a reporter's rough steno notes and place them into a chosen format.

**AICR:** (Artificial Intelligence-Conflict Resolution) A method by which CAT software attempts to resolve conflicts for reporters.

**Job file:** A file on one's steno writer or CAT software containing steno and English notes of a proceeding.

**Keyword index:** An alphabetical listing of each word in a transcript that provides page and line numbers where the word is found; synonymous with *concordance*.

reporter receives a one-year warranty for parts and labor. Another advantage is that vendors offer complimentary **technical support** regarding difficulties with writers during the warranty period.

### Leasing Equipment

Another option available to the reporter is to lease equipment. Leasing equipment:

- Results in a smaller down payment by the reporter
- Results in a lower monthly payment than when purchasing
- Gives the reporter a longer-term tax deduction
- Allows the reporter the benefit of upgrading the equipment at the end of the lease if a more technologically advanced product has superseded the equipment

Companies that offer leases in the court reporting industry make themselves known at court reporting seminars/conventions, in trade magazines, and through the equipment vendors.

### Purchasing Used Equipment

A third option is to purchase used equipment, which is advertised regularly in the court reporting schools, trade magazines, on courthouse bulletin boards, and online. You must, however, be aware that software is licensed, so certain paperwork much change hands to properly transfer the license. If this is not done and if you need technical support or a software device replacement, you will encounter problems. Proper paperwork is also necessary to claim this purchase as a business expense, such as a receipt for the purchase that states the names of the seller and the buyer, the date of the transaction, and the amount paid for the equipment. Certain states require the reporter to pay sales tax on the purchase price.

When buying used equipment, you also need to know in advance about the compatibility of the product. For instance, if you are purchasing used software, is it compatible with your writer? If you are purchasing a used writer, is it compatible with: your software, your scopist's software, your agency's software?

It is important to obtain the complete documentation that goes with software and any updates that have been made to the software that help you to better understand the equipment. Find out if it is still possible to get updates on the software to enable it to attain current software status.

Court reporting software programs generally come with a **key** that attaches to the reporter's computer hardware. Without the key, the program cannot work. This key prevents the **pirating,** or copying, of software systems. If the key is lost, the vendor will charge a substantial fee for issuance of another key. When purchasing used software that may no longer be sold by equipment vendors, find out if it is possible to obtain a key for the program should this circumstance arise. With the advent of the Millennium, reporters are witnessing the emergence of keyless software systems.

If purchasing a used writer, inquire about whether it is still possible to obtain writer parts. Court reporting vending companies may merge, be bought out, or go out of business, and it is essential to know that another company will be available to you for technical support and the purchase of parts for your equipment.

**Technical support:** Service provided by a court reporting equipment vendor to answer questions or troubleshoot problems regarding equipment.

**Key:** A device that attaches to computer hardware and prevents pirating, or copying, of CAT software systems.

**Pirating:** The illegal copying of CAT software.

### Selling Used Equipment

If you are interested in selling equipment, you are required to transfer your software license to the new owner. You also should be aware that the Internal Revenue Service considers the sale of the equipment income. You have a responsibility to find out if your current software support contract agreement is transferable.

It is a good idea to purchase a service contract on your equipment because technical support can be quite costly on a problem-by-problem basis. Also, it is reassuring to know that if difficulties occur, you will have someone available to you to walk you through them. Equipment vendors bill annually for service contracts.

## COMPATIBILITY

Educated consumers must be knowledgeable about compatibility issues. The most common issues of compatibility as it relates to court reporting are:

- Dictionary compatibility
- Writer compatibility to one's software
- Writer compatibility to scopist software
- Writer compatibility to agency software
- Software compatibility to agency software
- Software compatibility to the reporter's computer hardware

### Dictionary Compatibility

When the student reporter builds a dictionary in school, upon graduation, he or she receives the dictionary on a disk/set of disks. This dictionary may only be compatible with the software that is utilized in the school. If the reporter then attempts, when working for any agency with a different software program, to be scoped by that entity, the reporter may encounter dictionary incompatibility and must call the vendor who sells the software of the agency and request a **dictionary conversion.** Dictionary conversions are in the several-hundred-dollar range and take some time to be performed.

**Dictionary conversion:** When the vendor of software different from that which the reporter's dictionary is programmed on takes the reporter's dictionary and makes it compatible to its CAT software.

### Writer Compatibility to One's Software

The software program purchased or leased must be compatible with the reporter's writer. Otherwise the reporter may be dependent upon others in the disk-formatting and/or transcript-production process.

### Writer Compatibility to Scopist Software

A reporter who freelances among many agencies and does not own/lease a software program is reliant upon the services of an independent scopist. Therefore, the reporter will be more apt to purchase a writer that is compatible with his or her scopist's software program.

### Writer Compatibility to Agency Software

It is always advantageous for a reporter's writer to be compatible with an agency's software. For a reporter who has a software program and does his or her own scoping or utilizes an independent scopist, compatibility is not generally an issue. However, suppose a job goes daily (which means that the transcript must be delivered the next day), the job is lengthy, and the reporter's regular scopist is unavailable. If the agency has an in-house scopist who can assist the reporter to turn the work out on time, compatibility saves the day.

### Software Compatibility to Agency Software

Reporters whose software is compatible with an agency's software often can simply produce the finished transcript on a disk for the agency or modem their jobs directly to the agency. Reporters whose software is incompatible with that of an agency will have to produce a printed copy of each transcript. Therefore, those reporters must purchase/lease professional laser printers. Delivering a printed copy of the transcript may result in:

- Postage fees
- Transcripts that are lost in the mail
- Timeliness issues
- Wasted postage and time if an error that needs to be corrected is discovered in the transcript prior to delivery
- Expenses for printer repair and maintenance
- Being dependent upon others to format disks if the reporter's software system and writer are not compatible

Reporters who have incompatible software to an agency's may modem their jobs online into the agency, but they will need to have purchased a modem and have an online provider with the capacity to do so.

### Software Compatibility to Reporter's Computer Hardware

If a reporter decides to purchase a laptop computer, for example, the laptop's hard drive must meet certain specs in order to run the reporter's court reporting software on it. Otherwise the reporter may have to purchase supplemental computer aids to ensure compatibility or may risk having the system crash.

## WRITER MAINTENANCE

Your writer is a precision instrument that requires special care. Recommendations for maintenance of your writer include:

- Thoroughly reading through and following the instructions in your writer's instruction manual
- Placing a cover over your machine when not in use to eliminate dust accumulation
- Making sure your writer resides in a padded case
- Double-checking that your writer is on a stable tripod

- Keeping your writer away from food/liquids
- Charging your batteries daily and alternating batteries
- Cycle-charging batteries, if applicable, once a month
- Washing your hands before each use to lessen transfer of body oil to the key pads
- Cleaning your **LCD screen** with a soft cloth and Windex. Windex should be applied to the cloth, not sprayed directly onto the LCD screen
- Cleaning the plastic on the writer with plastic polish applied to a soft cloth
- Protecting the writer from abrasive materials, water, and alcohol
- Limiting your writer's exposure to extreme weather conditions. Never leave your writer in the car overnight or for long periods of time in extreme weather, as extreme heat may cause the lubricants to liquefy/run out, extreme cold may cause solidification of the lubricants, and condensation on electronic parts creates problems
- Having your writer overhauled at least once every two years or as needed

The word **overhaul** is used in court reporting terminology to refer to a process performed by service technicians, which generally entails:

- Taking the writer apart
- Cleaning its parts and the body of the writer with solvent to remove paper dust, dirt, grease, and grime
- Air-drying
- Re-greasing/re-oiling
- Replacing the ribbon with a new ribbon
- Replacing old pads/platen with new pads/platen, if necessary
- Greasing the pads/platen
- Writing with the machine
- Testing its performance on a computer
- Returning the writer to the reporter

Reporters should retain technicians trained in reporting equipment to perform overhauls/writer repair. A service technician may be an independent service technician or a technician employed by a vendor. Independent service technicians should be certified by the vendor of your equipment. Certification ensures familiarity with and approved ability to work on your specific machine. To check whether a technician is so certified, you can simply call the vendor, which should have his or her name on a list. Aside from court reporting equipment vendors, there are a number of independent people/companies that perform overhaul/repair services. Many advertise in association magazines and attend court reporting seminars. Some get your name from state or national associations and send you flyers in the mail. Recommendations also may be obtained from agencies, schools, and/or fellow reporters.

Proximity to the reporter's home/office may be a factor in deciding which service technician to use. However, many reporters mail their equipment to service technicians. Equipment vendors and some independents offer loaner writers while they have your writer so that you do not lose time at work. Those who do not provide loaners are amenable to working out arrangements with reporters

**LCD screen:** A small liquid crystal display screen found on electronic steno writers that enables reporters to view a portion of what they are writing in English or steno, program J globals, set the writer's date and time, adjust steno note spacing, and so forth.

**Overhaul:** A process that is recommended to be performed on a steno writer as part of equipment maintenance once every two years or as needed.

to expedite things. If there is no urgent problem, you might send your machine in over a holiday or when you are taking a vacation. You may choose to send it on a Friday, for instance, and request that it be returned by Monday or Tuesday.

Reporters are encouraged to lubricate their writers as per the writer's instruction manual. However, they should exercise care not to over oil or over grease their machines or oil/grease the wrong parts, which then may necessitate replacement of those parts.

The term overhaul is often used interchangeably by vendors with the term **refurbishment.** A vendor refurbishment generally includes overhauling the writer, as well as routinely replacing old parts with new parts and updating parts. Most vendors do not recommend the refurbishment of new equipment until a certain period of time elapses, which is usually after the one-year warranty has expired. Therefore, a reporter may purchase a maintenance agreement from the vendor that may include replacement/updating of writer parts and replacement of the writer's battery.

## MAINTENANCE AGREEMENTS

Maintenance agreements for writing machines are offered by court reporting equipment vendors. It is like an extended warranty on the writer. Although they generally cost in the several-hundred-dollar range, benefits of a maintenance agreement *may* include:

- Parts and labor
- A refurbishment
- Use of a loaner writer while your writer is being worked on so there is no loss of work time
- The option of sending your writer to the vendor directly or to a local vendor-certified technician
- Covered shipping costs to vendor or to a vendor-authorized service provider

In essence, the maintenance agreement is an insurance plan for your writer. Misuse and abuse of the writer is not covered, for example, coffee spilling into your machine, a car backing up and running over your machine.

## SUPPORT AGREEMENTS

As pertains to court reporting software, reporters may choose to enter into a support agreement with a vendor. The advantages of such an agreement are:

- The assistance of a skilled department that is available to the reporter 24 hours a day
- Priority status over those without support agreements in getting a response from the support department
- Software-enhancement updates
- Immediate response if problems arise on a job

**Refurbishment:** The process whereby a steno writer is overhauled and old parts are replaced with new or updated parts.

## EQUIPMENT ACCESSORIES

### Writer Carrying Cases

Upon the purchase of a new writer, the reporter receives a case to transport it in. New writers used to be sold with hard cases; now they usually come in soft cases. Court reporting equipment is relatively heavy, and carrying it around is difficult for some reporters. Therefore, many reporters purchase cases with wheels attached. These can be procured through court reporting vendors or at your local office supply or luggage store. Products sold by the vendor are designed specifically for reporting equipment, whereas generic luggage carriers should be padded properly to ensure a snug fit for your writer and protection from external sources. Manufacturer or brand name is a matter of personal preference.

Be prepared for the court reporter reflex. It is the loud gasp that court reporters let out while driving peacefully to work and thinking for a moment that they left their writer at home, followed by the sudden turning of the head toward the back seat of the car to double-check.

### Tripod and Paper Tray

The purchase of a new writer always includes a tripod and a paper tray. The tripod is the metal piece of equipment that your writer sits upon, which may be positioned to accommodate the height of your chair. It is important that the reporter place the writer at an ergonomically correct level—where wrists are level with the writer, not at an upward or downward tilt—as a deterrent to disabilities such as carpal tunnel syndrome. Carpal tunnel syndrome occurs as a result of long-term repetetive hand motions and is evidenced by tingling, numbness, and often pain in the fingers and wrists. Varying the height of one's writer on lengthy jobs may alleviate physical discomfort. Tilting tripods and other ergonomically designed products are available through court reporting product vendors for special needs.

The paper tray is designed to attach to your model writer. Replacement paper trays are sold through court reporting product vendors.

### Spare Batteries

Writer batteries have a life span of about two years, if maintained properly. Reporters may forget to replace them with new ones in a timely manner or may forget to **cycle-charge** their batteries monthly or to charge them the night before a job. Freelance reporters should always have a spare (charged) battery in case they experience difficulties with their writer's battery. Batteries can be purchased through the vendor of the equipment that you possess.

### Chargers

Likewise, chargers have life spans. Reporters should have two chargers at all times. If a reporter's charger expires and he or she has no spare, the writer's battery cannot be charged for work the following day. Vendors are wonderful about expediting chargers to you, but even then there is a minimum of a day without charging capabilities.

**Cycle-charging:** A method of charging one's electronic steno writer's battery to increase its longevity.

Reporters should always bring their chargers to work with them in case their writer's battery expires.

## Extension Cords

When a reporter's writer battery is not charged, the reporter must rely on a spare battery. If the spare is not charged or the reporter does not have a spare, then the reporter should use a charger. In order to utilize the charger, the reporter must have access to an electrical outlet. Oftentimes, an outlet is not available or is in an inconvenient location in the room. An extension cord enables the reporter to utilize the charger wherever the reporter is seated. Similarly, extension cords are often needed for laptop (notebook) computers and realtiming. Extension cords may be purchased through reporting vendors or at local hardware/office supply stores or supermarkets.

## Extra Ribbons

If a writer ribbon tears or creates illegible notes, the reporter should have a spare ribbon handy in order to change it on a moment's notice. Service technicians will check the status of your ribbon when working on your writer and may suggest or automatically do a replacement. Writer ribbons may be purchased from equipment vendors or service technicians.

## Ink

Some of the older machines utilize ink to darken the print on the reporter's steno notes. If you are writing with this type of equipment, you should never be without a spare bottle of ink. One of the reasons for the updated ribbons that do not require inking is the messiness involved in the inking process and the likelihood of ink spills in your bag. Therefore, if you need to carry ink with you, be sure to close the lid tightly, wrap the bottle in something thick, and keep it in a place far away from your writer.

## Preformatted Disks

Reporters may have multiple disk needs. A reporter may need different types of disks to:

- Utilize in their writer
- Utilize in their software program
- Send to a scopist
- Send a job to be scoped or a completed transcript to an agency
- Create an ASCII disk for an agency or a client—ASCII disks are disks that are compatible with most software programs
- Back up finished jobs to archive

Therefore, upon purchase or lease of equipment, the reporter should review disk specifications so that he or she can then purchase the appropriate disks. Disk purchases may be made through reporting vendors or at your local computer/office supply store.

Even though it only takes a few minutes to **format** disks for one's writer, do not rely on having time before a proceeding begins to format a disk. Sometimes

**Format:** A process done on an electronic steno writer or CAT software that clears a floppy disk and prepares it for use in an electronic steno writer; also may refer to the manner or style of transcripts produced by freelance agencies.

you can feel the pressure to get the proceeding in progress practically before your writer is out of its case. Therefore, it is wise to keep a supply of preformatted disks in your work bag.

Check your disk supply regularly. I like to create a week-long supply each weekend so that I do not run out of disks and have a panic attack on the job. If you are in a courthouse, other reporters can help you out if you need a disk. If not, you may have to write diskless and pray that nothing happens to your writer until you dump the job onto a software program; if something does happen, that job will have to be rewritten or noteread. You may wish to purchase a disk case so that after a job you can protect the disk you have written on. These may be purchased at local computer/office supply stores. Rotate your daily job disks and throw out old disks periodically.

When using disks as a **backup** of finished transcripts, do a directory check and verify that the job is indeed on the disk before deleting it from your software program. Keep the disks in a fireproof box.

## REALTIME NECESSITIES

In order to perform realtime, freelance reporters must have:

- A writer
- The writer's charger
- A laptop
- A socket I/O card (for laptops with only one serial port)
- A cable connecting the reporter's writer to the laptop
- A cable connecting the reporter's laptop to the laptops of other participants requesting realtime services
- Extension cords

## ADDITIONAL TOOLS

Freelance reporters should also bring to a job:

- Their job diary
- An address book
- Work sheets
- Business cards
- Three packs of steno paper
- A Post-it™ pad
- A note pad
- Pens
- Exhibit stickers or an exhibit stamp
- A mini-stapler/staples
- Paper clips
- Transcript order forms (if applicable)
- Rubber bands
- A beeper
- A cellular phone
- A notebook computer

**Backup:** May refer to having a copy of a file/job in case anything happens to the original or may refer to having extra equipment in case one's equipment fails to operate properly.

- Materials to read during downtime
- Red correction markers

A reporter's home office will benefit from:

- A modem
- Access to a fax machine
- Access to a copy machine
- A telephone-answering machine

Reporter-specific items are purchased through court reporting vendors, while some of the more generic items may be purchased at your local stationery/office supply store. The gift certificate at the end of this book (see Figure 4–1) from NCRA entitles you to $15 off any item in the NCRA Store catalog.

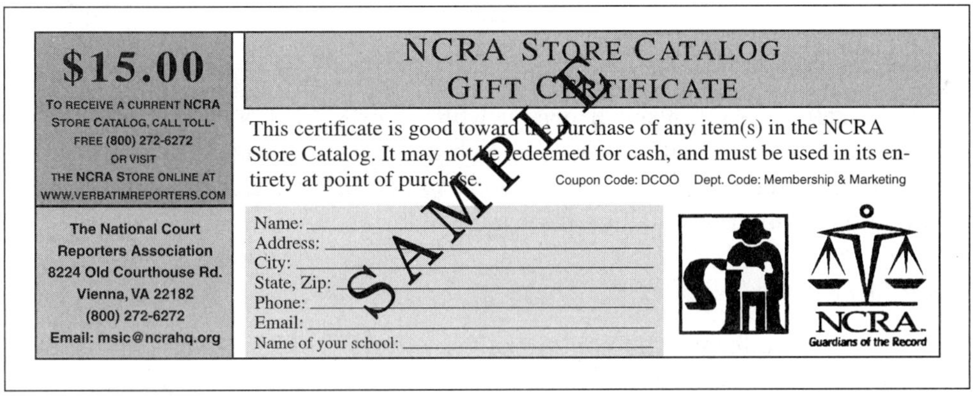
$15.00

TO RECEIVE A CURRENT NCRA STORE CATALOG, CALL TOLL-FREE (800) 272-6272 OR VISIT THE NCRA STORE ONLINE AT WWW.VERBATIMREPORTERS.COM

The National Court Reporters Association
8224 Old Courthouse Rd.
Vienna, VA 22182
(800) 272-6272
Email: msic@ncrahq.org

NCRA STORE CATALOG
GIFT CERTIFICATE

This certificate is good toward the purchase of any item(s) in the NCRA Store Catalog. It may not be redeemed for cash, and must be used in its entirety at point of purchase. Coupon Code: DCOO Dept. Code: Membership & Marketing

Name:
Address:
City:
State, Zip:
Phone:
Email:
Name of your school:

SAMPLE

NCRA
Guardians of the Record

**FIGURE 4–1**
NCRA Store Catalog Gift Certificate *(see end of book for gift certificate)*

## Job Diaries

It is recommended that freelance reporters annually purchase job diaries spacious enough to write next to each date:

- Which agency the job is for
- The agency job number, if applicable
- The time the job is to begin
- The location of the job
- A contact person at the job location, if applicable
- The telephone number where the proceeding is to be held
- The name of the client
- The name of the attorney who will appear on behalf of the client, if known
- The client's file number, if known
- A summarized caption name
- The witness's name, if known

The reporter may also need room to jot down directions or cross streets. That way if the reporter must return to the same location at a later date, this information will be at the reporter's disposal. The reporter checks this information en route to the job destination. The reporter should check it again before greeting and properly introducing himself or herself to the receptionist at the job location. At **call-in time,** the reporter must have the job diary handy to record the next day's assignment.

**Call-in time:** A specific time of the day that a freelance court reporting agency has reporters call for job assignments.

The best time to purchase large job diaries is at the end of each year, November to December, when supplies for the new year are stocked. Large office supply stores seem to offer the best selection and prices.

## Address Book

A freelance reporter should carry an address book replete with the telephone numbers of all the agencies for which the reporter works. When looking for work at call-in time, a reporter who freelances among many agencies may have to make several calls before receiving an assignment. Address books that provide blank spaces, either in the front or back, where the reporter can list agencies either alphabetically or in order of call-in priority, are recommended. These may be purchased at any stationery or local office supply store.

Although on-staffers may call their agency at call-in time from the room where the proceeding is held, freelancers may prefer to find a private telephone. Freelancers do not necessarily want the attorneys to know that they don't work regularly for the agency that sent them, nor do they want to make numerous telephone calls in front of the attorneys who are present. Likewise, the reporter should not make personal calls in a room with attorneys present. It is unprofessional, as is using an attorney's telephone to call information to obtain a telephone number and then making a second call.

## Work Sheets

**Work sheets** are forms that contain information necessary to prepare a transcript of the proceeding. Work sheets are referred to by a variety of names. I have yet to come across anyone knowledgeable about the etiology of any of these names. Depending upon your area, it may be called a dog sheet, poop sheet, dope sheet, job card, or information sheet. Each freelance agency provides work sheets of its own design, but most work sheets are comprised of spaces for the reporter to fill in:

- The date the job is taken
- The agency's internal job number, if applicable
- The reporter's name
- The scopist's name, if applicable
- The date the job is due in the office
- The location of the proceeding
- What classification the proceeding falls under
- What stipulations, if any, the proceeding is pursuant to
- Whether the proceeding is pursuant to notice, order, stipulation, subpoena, or agreement of the parties
- How many appearance fees the reporter is to be paid for
- The venue of the case
- The caption of the case
- The index/civil action/criminal action/case number
- The starting page number of the transcript
- Whether the job is a continuation, and if so, the date the job is continued from and the continuing page number the transcript should begin with
- If continuing at another time, the continuation date scheduled
- The number of witnesses

**Work sheet:** A sheet provided by a freelance court reporting agency to reporters for the recording of pertinent data necessary for preparation of the transcript of a proceeding.

- The names and addresses of the witnesses
- The time the testimony of each witness began and ended
- The names and addresses of the attorneys present/not present, if known
- File or claim numbers for each law firm
- The names of additional persons present during the proceeding

The work sheet may also include spaces for:

- The reporter's telephone number
- The scopist's telephone number, if applicable
- The party/parties to bill for the transcript and copies of the transcript
- Whether the job is requested regular, expedited, daily, or immediate delivery
- The party/parties to deliver the transcript to
- The date of loss or accident, if applicable
- **Exhibit** information
- **Speaker designations**
- Identification of the level of difficulty of the job
- Arbitraries or **outlines** used by the reporter
- An alphabetical **glossary**

See Figures 4–2 and 4–3 for sample work sheets.

## Work Sheet Supplies

Reporters should always keep a supply of work sheets on hand, in their bag or writer case, as opposed to just one work sheet for the assignment covered that day. Suppose the job **busts,** which, in court reporting terminology means gets cancelled. In such a case, you call an agency and ask them to assign you a second job for that same day. You will need a new work sheet for the next assignment. Or, if you finish a morning job for one agency and then a second agency offers you an afternoon job, you do not want to show up and write the name of the second agency over the first agency's name on your work sheet. Moreover, if an attorney requests the agency's address or telephone number, if you have the work sheet of the company on the table in front of you, you can recite it without hesitation.

This advice does not pertain only to reporters who freelance among many agencies. On-staff reporters (freelancers who give a first-call commitment to one agency) will give first call to their agency to pick up a second job for the day. If their agency has nothing for them, they are free to call other agencies. If another agency gives the reporter an assignment, the reporter should have that agency's materials on hand.

## Business Cards

The reporter should always carry a supply of business cards. At the beginning of each proceeding, the reporter is usually asked to provide his or her name and the name of the company he or she is from. Even though you may freelance among many agencies, handing out an agency's business card with your name on it connotes a sense of experience and permanence to attorneys. In addition, attorneys often ask for the agency's address and/or telephone number. If the

**Exhibit:** Material marked for identification at legal proceedings that may be used as evidence at the time of trial. Not all material so marked is admissible in evidence.

**Speaker designation:** An outline ascribed to each speaker in a proceeding for identification during a proceeding.

**Outline:** The steno that represents an English word or phrase.

**Glossary:** A sheet on which a reporter lists words and names alphabetically to assist a scopist in preparing a transcript.

**Bust:** Cancellation of a proceeding for which a reporter receives a minimum fee; may only apply in certain localities/agencies.

**FIGURE 4–2**
Sample Work Sheet

ARISTA COURT REPORTING CO.
192 LEXINGTON AVENUE
NEW YORK, NY 10016
(212) 684-6100
FAX: (212) 684-4360

JOB NO. ____________

Court ____________
County ____________

Reporter ____________
Date ____________
Held at ____________

Deposition ( )
Hearing ( )
Arbitration ( )

Stipulations:
Usual ( )
Federal ( )
Other ( )

Pursuant to ____________
Appearance: AM _____ PM _____

DATE OF ACCIDENT ____________

APPEARANCES

ATTN. FOR PLAINTIFF
Name ____________
Address ____________
Zip ____________
By: ____________
File # ____________

Name ____________
Address ____________
Zip ____________
By: ____________
File # ____________

Name ____________
Address ____________
Zip ____________
By: ____________
File # ____________

Name ____________
Address ____________
Zip ____________
By: ____________
File # ____________

WITNESS #1
Name ____________
Address ____________
Time started ____________
Time ended ____________

WITNESS #2
Name ____________
Address ____________
Time started ____________
Time ended ____________

WITNESS #3
Name ____________
Address ____________
Time started ____________
Time ended ____________

ALSO PRESENT:

DELIVERY INSTRUCTIONS
BILL 0+2: ____________
COPIES: ____________
SPLIT: YES NO
DELIVERY DATE: ____________
Other instructions:

agency is not one that you frequently work for, you do not want to hesitate before answering and then read the information from the work sheet. It is much more professional to say, "Let me give you my card."

Although some agencies supply business cards for their on-staff reporters, reporters usually have to buy their own. To order business cards, ask for a sample card of the agency you are working for and take it to a printer. If you work for a multitude of companies, this can become costly. Some agencies have cards with a blank space for new reporters to type/write their name in; however, a typewritten name appears more professional.

If you do not have a card with you on a job and it is requested of you, an acceptable response would be, "I just ran out and haven't replaced them yet. Let me give you my information." Then you would proceed to state your name and the agency you work for. If an attorney needs the agency's address or telephone number, he or she will ask you for it.

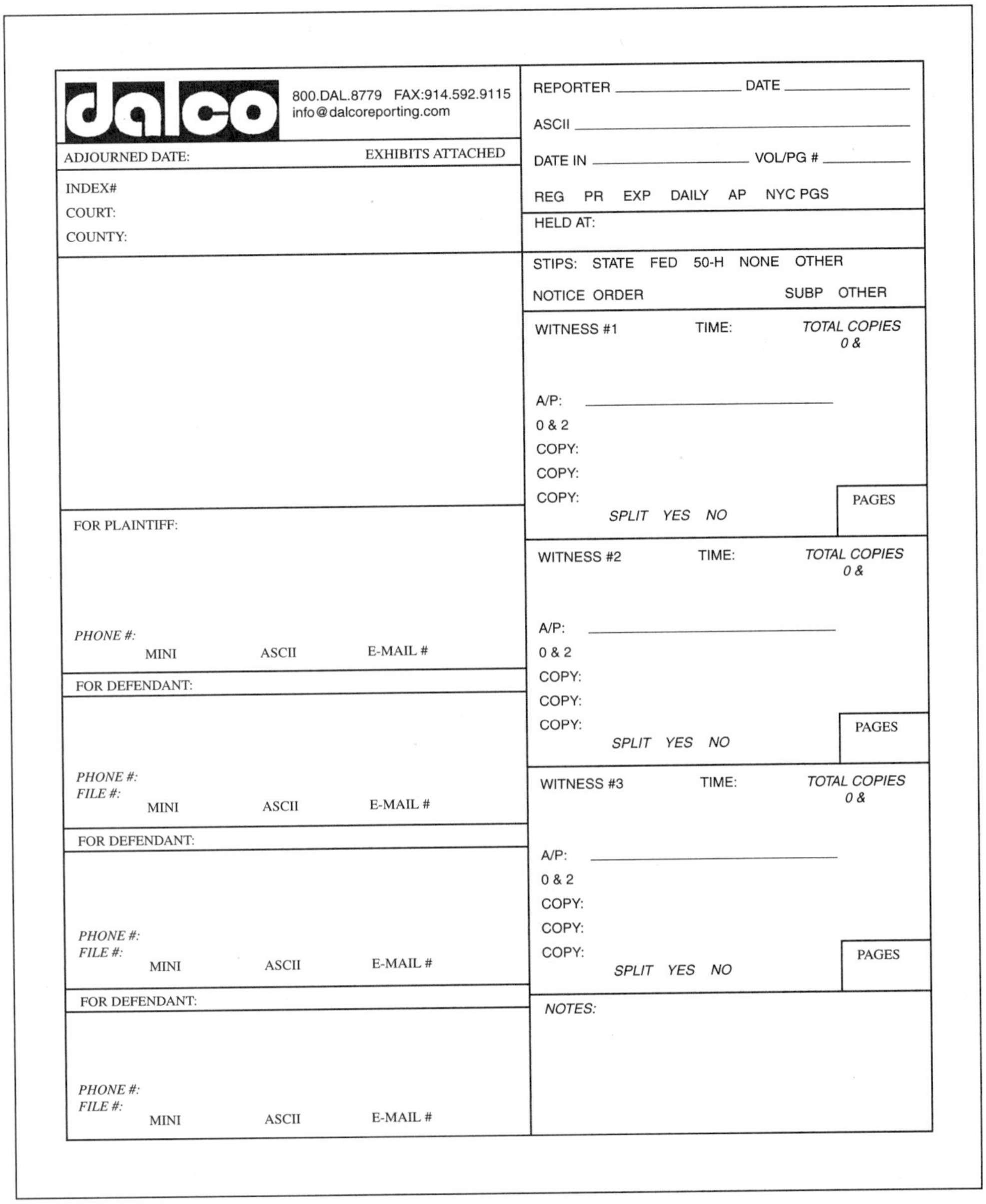
dalco 800.DAL.8779 FAX:914.592.9115 info@dalcoreporting.com

ADJOURNED DATE: EXHIBITS ATTACHED

INDEX#
COURT:
COUNTY:

FOR PLAINTIFF:
PHONE #: MINI ASCII E-MAIL #

FOR DEFENDANT:
PHONE #:
FILE #: MINI ASCII E-MAIL #

FOR DEFENDANT:
PHONE #:
FILE #: MINI ASCII E-MAIL #

FOR DEFENDANT:
PHONE #:
FILE #: MINI ASCII E-MAIL #

REPORTER ______ DATE ______
ASCII ______
DATE IN ______ VOL/PG # ______
REG PR EXP DAILY AP NYC PGS
HELD AT:
STIPS: STATE FED 50-H NONE OTHER
NOTICE ORDER SUBP OTHER

WITNESS #1 TIME: TOTAL COPIES 0 &
A/P: ______
0 & 2
COPY:
COPY:
COPY: SPLIT YES NO PAGES

WITNESS #2 TIME: TOTAL COPIES 0 &
A/P: ______
0 & 2
COPY:
COPY:
COPY: SPLIT YES NO PAGES

WITNESS #3 TIME: TOTAL COPIES 0 &
A/P: ______
0 & 2
COPY:
COPY:
COPY: SPLIT YES NO PAGES

NOTES:

**FIGURE 4–3**
Sample Work Sheet

## Steno Paper

Reporters should carry about three packs of steno paper. Generally, a pack is equivalent to a hundred transcript pages, although this can vary depending upon how you set the spacing on your writer. You may write a lot in three hours and then pick up an afternoon job and write a lot at that job also. It is better to be safe than sorry.

## Post-it™ Pads

Post-it™ pads are often used by reporters to create seating charts and to note attorney designations in multiple-attorney proceedings. The reporter simulates the shape of the table and places attorney designations and corresponding names in the respective seating positions. At the end of the job, the reporter should retain the seating chart with her job information.

**FIGURE 4–3**
(continued)

| | |
|---|---|
| FOR DEFENDANT:<br><br>*PHONE #:*<br>*FILE #:*<br>MINI ASCII E-MAIL # | WITNESS #4 TIME: *TOTAL COPIES 0 &*<br><br>A/P: __________<br>0 & 2<br>COPY:<br>COPY:<br>COPY:<br>*SPLIT YES NO* |
| FOR DEFENDANT:<br><br>*PHONE #:*<br>*FILE #:*<br>MINI ASCII E-MAIL # | |

| | | |
|---|---|---|
| A | B | C |
| D | E | F |
| G | H-I | J-K |
| L | M | N |
| O-P | Q-R | S |
| T-U | V-W | X-Y-Z |

## Notepads

Yellow, lined notepads seem to be the preferred choice of freelance reporters. Reporters keep a notepad in front of them so that they can keep a running list of exhibits marked and jot down notes to themselves. These notes generally involve writing down text that warrants a clarification or a name or word that warrants a spelling check. Reporters make notes when there is a pause in the proceeding.

At the beginning of the proceeding, the reporter should date the notepad. Having the date on the notepad facilitates the exhibit-marking process, as you must include the date on each exhibit. At the conclusion of the proceeding, the notepad notes—together with the work sheet, completed transcript order forms (if applicable), copies of documents quoted from, exhibits, the seating chart, and any business cards obtained—are wrapped around the reporter's steno notes with a rubber band.

### Pens

A supply of pens comes in handy, as your pen may run out of ink or an attorney may forget to bring a pen and ask to borrow one. You will need a pen to fill in your work sheet, to mark and keep a running list of exhibits, and to jot down notes on your notepad.

### Transcript Order Forms

Some freelance agencies require transcript order forms to be filled out by any attorney ordering a copy of the transcript who is not a client of the agency. Others may require their clients to also fill one out. Carry a supply of these order forms and request that attorneys ordering copies fill them out. If an attorney refuses, then you have made the attempt and you simply tell that to the agency.

### Rubber Bands

Another necessity is rubber bands, with which you will bind your steno notes upon completion of the job. Wrapped around it will be your work sheet, your legal pad notes, a seating chart with attorney designations, any copies of documents obtained, and any business cards that were given to you.

### Beepers

Beepers are a must for a freelance court reporter. A few scenarios that frequently occur are:

- An agency receives a spot call, which is a call to send a reporter to a proceeding immediately, and they need to find out if you are free or will soon be free to cover it.
- An agency wishes to let you know they are going to be busy the following day and to ask whether you are available.
- Attorneys for a previous job need the transcript expedited and the agency wants to make arrangements for its completion and delivery with you.
- A family emergency occurs

A beeper is the most effective means of being contacted at any time. However, the beeper should be in the "vibrate" mode to avoid disrupting the proceeding with loud beeps. I prefer to keep my beeper on the table in front of me with its screen facing me. This enables me to determine whether an immediate response is required or whether a return call may be made at the next break in the proceeding. If it is an emergency, you may notify the examining attorney and request a break.

If you are in the habit of attaching your beeper to your work bag, be sure to remember to switch your beeper from "vibrate" mode to "audio" when the assignment has ended. Otherwise, the beeper is rendered useless if you fail to notice incoming information that warrants an immediate callback.

Many reporters devise codes with their families/agencies that represent the nature of the beep. An agency may add 911 after their phone number to request an immediate callback. Often this happens when the agency wants to see if you can cover a spot call or an assignment later in the day. If you are at a proceeding that is expected to go all day, obviously you cannot. Most of the time, reporters cannot predict the duration of the assignment. If contacted for a spot call or later assignment, you may, on a break, inquire of the attorneys as to how long they expect to go and state the reason for your inquiry. If they are unsure, it is always best to recommend that the agency try to cover the spot call with another reporter.

## Cellular Telephones

Another invaluable tool of the trade is a cellular telephone. Common scenarios with freelancers are:

- You are in transit at call-in time
- You are in transit and get beeped on your beeper
- You are in a conference room and there is no telephone available
- You do not have your address book with you and a person's/agency's number is preprogrammed into your cell phone directory

## Notebook Computers

Having a **notebook computer** is practically a must for freelance reporters. One cannot perform realtime writing without a notebook computer or writer with a notebook attachment. Possessing a notebook computer also enables the reporter to scope/proofread his or her work during downtime. Freelance reporters experience a great deal of downtime commuting to and from an assignment, on a lunch break, or simply waiting for the job to begin. A common occurrence in the freelancing field is that many times you will arrive at a proceeding and be told that:

- The witness or an attorney is going to be late
- The start time of the proceeding was moved
- The start time the agency gave you was incorrect
- Both sides will be examined that day, but the attorney for the other side has ordered a reporter to record the witness's examination that he will be taking

In the last scenario, which reporter writes first depends upon which **party** in the caption their agency's client represents. For instance, say the attorney for the plaintiff ordered you and the other reporter was ordered by the attorney for the defendant. Generally, examinations of witnesses are taken in the order the parties are named in the caption, so the examination of the plaintiff would precede the examination of the defendant. Since defendant examinations are often much shorter than plaintiff examinations, sometimes the attorneys will not make the defendant wait for hours to be deposed and will switch the order.

Now, here is the tricky part. At depositions, attorneys do not examine their own client; they examine the other parties. However, if they need clarification on a few matters, they may question briefly in colloquy or question upon the conclusion of the other parties' examination of their witness, which is called cross-examination. Depositions do not always specifically refer to cross-examinations by an attorney; *EXAMINATION BY* and the examining attorney's name generally convey change of examining attorney. Generally, the

**Notebook computer:** A portable, or laptop, computer that is programmed with CAT software which enables reporters to perform realtime or transcription functions anywhere.

**Party:** A person or entity named in a caption.

attorney for the plaintiff will examine the defendant and the attorney for the defendant will examine the plaintiff. Since the attorney for the plaintiff hired you and he will be examining the defendant after the plaintiff's testimony is concluded, you will have some time to kill.

You may attempt to obtain your work sheet information along with the other reporter in an unobtrusive manner, if possible, or get it when your examination is to begin. You will then wait outside of the conference room until notified that the first proceeding has concluded. Since the reporters are ordered for separate examinations, it is unnecessary to list the name of the other reporter under *ALSO PRESENT*.

While waiting, you can pull out your **laptop computer** and scope/proofread previous jobs rather than wishing you were at home getting something done. When it is your turn to go on the record, you will enter the conference room and set up.

## Reading Materials

As downtime is often part and parcel of the freelance reporter's day, you are advised to carry in your work bag:

- A transcript to proofread
- A copy of the *Journal of Court Reporting* or your state association's magazine
- A book or magazine
- Mail

## Red Correction Markers

Many reporters, to correct transcript errors while proofreading, utilize red correction markers. Often they circle the page number on pages containing corrections that need to be made. They may draw a slanted line over the printed line number at the left margin of the transcript page to indicate that a correction needs to be made on that line. The ¶ symbol is used by the reporter to indicate a new paragraph. When a new paragraph was begun and should not have been, place a ~ symbol to bring the two paragraphs together. The infinity symbol (∞) may be used to indicate that the order of two letters or words needs to be reversed. To move something to the right, use ]; to the left, use [ . A carat symbol (^) may be used to indicate that something should be inserted. Reporters are asked to circle things that should be deleted from the transcript upon correction, such as duplicate words or plural words with the letter *s* written twice. A giant circle or X may indicate that a huge amount of text should be deleted, such as a reporter's rewriting a quotation on a break or a reporter's note to himself or herself. Two lines are drawn under a letter to indicate (a) if it is uppercase (capitalized), it should be lowercase, or (b) if it is lowercase, it should be uppercase. An alternate method of reflecting uppercase versus lowercase letters is to place two lines beneath a letter that should be uppercase and only one line under a letter that should be lowercase. Whatever your method of choice, be consistent. Write *DS* if the lines should be double-spaced; *SS* if they should be single-spaced. To insert a space in text, add # between the words/letters. To bring text together as one word, place a ⁀ between the words.

**Laptop computer:** Portable hardware programmed with CAT software that enables reporters to perform realtime or transcription functions anywhere; synonymous with *notebook computer*.

## Modems

Modeming is sending information electronically directly through a telephone line, much like a fax machine, without an Internet e-mail account. A modem is necessary if you want to send your job to your agency or to your scopist from a job location immediately, such as when reporting a daily. A **daily** exists when the attorneys request the transcript the following (business) day. A modem is also a necessity in order to e-mail information. E-mailing jobs to scopists and agencies saves time, which in the court reporting field is always an important issue, as well as money spent on postage. When your scopist is done scoping your job, he or she can e-mail it to you. If you have an expedited job and your agency is going to scope it in-house, then it is best to have a means available to send it to the agency quickly, especially if you do not live near the agency.

To go online, you must engage an online service provider. Put e-mail addresses of agencies and scopists in your Internet address book. Finished jobs can also be sent via e-mail, rather than by regular mail, with your work sheet faxed into the office.

## Fax Machine Access

Access to a fax machine may enable the reporter to bypass the cost of mailing work sheets and glossaries to scopists and agencies. Having a fax machine in your home office facilitates the receipt of captions and glossaries from agencies on continuing assignments or cases, as well as material from attorneys that may aid in transcript preparation. Some fax machines can also make copies, eliminating your need to purchase a copy machine. Therefore, a fax machine might be a worthy investment. Be aware, however, that the print on certain fax copies may fade over time, so ask salespeople about this before purchasing one.

## Copy Machine Access

Having a copy machine or access to a copy machine allows the reporter to copy documents prior to sending them to a scopist or agency. If anything gets lost in the mail or is undeliverable, the reporter will have a backup. While on-staffers may feel comfortable asking to use an agency's copy machine, freelancers may not. Therefore, having your own copy machine might be beneficial, but it is not mandatory.

## Telephone-Answering Machines

Freelance reporters should own telephone-answering machines. In addition to trying to contact a reporter by beeper, many agencies leave messages for reporters on their telephone-answering machines. Therefore, at least once during the workday, the reporter should check these messages. The reporter's outgoing message on the machine should be brief and professional. Avoid the temptation to have lengthy, loud, or cutesy messages that perhaps feature your children.

**Daily:** A term used to indicate delivery of the final edited transcript the (business) day following the proceeding.

## Reference Books

When beginning your court reporting career, you should invest in a few reference books. An up-to-date dictionary is the primary necessity, as new words are added annually. You will also need a good medical dictionary, such as *Taber's*

*Cyclopedical Medical Dictionary* (Davis Co.) or *Stedman's Medical Dictionary* (Williams & Wilkins Co.). In addition, you may want to purchase a drug handbook, such as *American Drug Index* (J. P. Lippincott Co.), or a PDR—*Physicians' Desk Reference* (Medical Economics Co.) The PDR lists generic names of drugs as well as brand names and manufacturers. A PDR, which is published annually, sometimes can be obtained from a physician who is updating his or her reference books. A book of legal terminology, such as *Black's Law Dictionary* (West Publishing Co.), is also useful. Finally, a book of chemical listings may come in handy, such as:

- *Hack's Chemical Dictionary*
- *Academic Press Dictionary of Science and Technology*
- *McGraw-Hill Dictionary of Chemistry*
- *McGraw-Hill Dictionary of Scientific and Technical Terms*
- *A Dictionary of Chemistry*
- *The Merck Index: An Encyclopedia of Chemicals, Drugs and Biologicals*
- *Hawley's Condensed Chemical Dictionary*
- *Gardner's Chemical Synonyms and Trade Names*

If you have access to the Internet, you may locate chemical references at:

- Pubs.acs.org/chemcy (Chemcyclopedia Online)
- www.chemie.de/tools/acronym.php3?language=e (Acronym Database)
- www.epa.gov/enviro/html/emci/chemref/index.html (The Chemical References Web pages)
- www.chemie.de/tools/dictionary/?language=e (Chemistry Science Dictionary)
- www.chemfinder.com (Cambridge Soft ChemFinder)
- www.sourcerer.co.uk/asp/english/onlineeen.asp (Sourcerer Chemical Dictionary)

Other recommendations include:

- An architectural reference book—*Architecture, Design & Construction Word Finder* (Prentice-Hall)
- A zip code book—*ZIP Code Directory* (Post Office Department, Washington, DC)
- A book on slang—*Slang! The Topic-by-Topic Dictionary of Contemporary American Lingoes* (Pocket Books)
- *Familiar Quotations* (Little, Brown)
- *One Word, Two Words, Hyphen-ated?* (NCRA press)

These books may be found at any large bookstore or in NCRA/vendor catalogs. Some may be found on the Internet. Also, keep your old Yellow Pages and White Pages, since you may need to check the spelling of a company or person listed, as well as a telephone number.

Some major cities sell avenue or cross street reference guides that assist reporters in finding city buildings by number. These types of aids may be purchased at city newsstands, subway stations, or street vendors. You can contact the Chamber of Commerce in your state for geographic guides and maps sold at a nominal fee. Certain software programs offer the same type of information, or you can go online to a popular search engine, like Yahoo, and check the header for maps. In addition, some agencies may have this type of material to hand out to their reporters.

## PROFESSIONAL ATTIRE

Professional attire is a necessity for court reporters. Since the legal profession is a somewhat conservative profession, dressing conservatively is recommended. For both men and women, suits are the best way to go. Remember that when you walk into a deposition room, you have to exude confidence, since these people do not know anything about you and your skills or level of education. All they know is what they see; and if they see a professional entering the room who appears confident, they will think that you are an experienced reporter, even though it might be your first deposition.

In the summertime, you may want to wear something a little more casual, especially if you are commuting, but wearing a jacket is still preferred. You can always take it off once you make that first impression. Also, many times you will be in an air-conditioned room. Sexy, sleeveless blouses or casual slacks are not very professional looking. Anything exposing your midsection is also frowned upon.

Male reporters should appear in suits with ties, making sure their shirts are not extremely creased or hanging out of their pants. Male reporters sporting earrings and/or ponytails are looked at unfavorably in the legal field.

For women, pant suits are more acceptable these days in the legal field, especially since the courts have deemed it acceptable for female attorneys to now wear them in court. When reporting, women may feel more comfortable in pants than skirts or dresses because of the usual position of our writers. The key is to look professional, clean, and neat.

This applies to your hair and nails as well. Hair should be on the conservative side, both in color and style. Clean fingernails get noticed, as attorneys' eyes turn toward you as you are marking exhibits. Nail polish colors should be subtle and conservative. Although your sense of freedom of expression may be reflected in your appearance, you do not want to be remembered or referred to as "the guy with the pink hair," or "the girl with the black nail polish." Female reporters should be cautious about the length of their nails; long nails may affect their writing.

Jewelry and accessory choices also should be on the conservative side. Reporters may opt to leave expensive jewelry at home, especially when reporting in lower-income areas. Wearing tight wristbands or bulky rings can impede one's ability to write. Although you may like the warmth afforded by a fur coat in the wintertime, it may be inappropriate when working with the indigent at The Legal Aid Society. If reporting in a prison environment, reporters should dress down.

Do not walk into a proceeding chewing bubble gum or wearing sneakers. Many reporters commute in sneakers and carry a pair of shoes with them. You can always find a place to change your shoes before entering the job location. If not, you can walk in, introduce yourself to the receptionist, and ask where the nearest restroom is—then get yourself together before the attorney is told you are there. For female reporters, if you are reporting while you are pregnant, maternity shops sell professional maternity clothing. Even purchasing one or two black skirts with multiple blouses can provide a sufficient maternity wardrobe.

Since the attorney is not getting the transcript until after the proceeding, what they know of you is what they see; if they see a professional, they will assume you are one. Imagine that you need brain surgery. Who would instill more confidence in you, the surgeon who enters the room in shorts with a bandana tied around his forehead or the surgeon who enters the room in a conservative, button-down shirt with a tie?

## SHORT-ANSWER QUESTIONS

1. Beginner reporters who write ________ may be more in demand than experienced reporters who are not _________-ready.
2. Software that enables court reporters to perform court reporting functions on a computer after reporting an assignment is called a __________ system.
3. An _________ style sets up a job file within an agency's specific transcript format guidelines.
4. __________ is an acronym for Artificial Intelligence-Conflict Resolution.
5. __________ equipment usually involves a smaller down payment, a lower monthly payment, and a longer-term tax deduction.
6. Certain paperwork must change hands to properly transfer the license for _________ equipment.
7. Many court reporting software programs require a __________ that attaches to the reporter's hardware in order for the software to function.
8. A court reporting software vendor may perform a ____________ ____________ if the reporter wishes to be compatible with a different software program than the one the dictionary was created on.
9. ___________ of your writer involves such things as covering your machine when not in use to eliminate dust accumulation, keeping your writer away from food/liquids, cleaning your writer, having it overhauled at least once every two years, and limiting its exposure to extreme weather conditions.
10. Extreme ____________ can cause solidification of the lubricants in your writer.
11. Extreme ____________ can cause your writer's lubricants to liquefy/run out.
12. An ________ involves taking a writer apart, cleaning it, air-drying it, re-greasing/re-oiling it, replacing parts, greasing the new pads/platen, and testing its performance.
13. A _____________ generally includes an overhaul of a writer, a replacement of old parts with new parts, and an updating of parts.
14. Dog sheet, poop sheet, dope sheet, job card, and information sheet are synonyms for a _______ ________.
15. A ___________ refers to a job cancellation.
16. ___________ agreements with vendors may include replacement/updating of writer parts, replacement of the writer's battery, use of a loaner writer, and covered shipping costs for delivery to and from the vendor or vendor-authorized service provider.
17. Among the benefits of ___________ agreements with vendors are 24-hour assistance, priority over those without such agreements, and software-enhancement updates.

18. _____________, or notebook, computers enable reporters to write realtime or scope during downtime on jobs.
19. Rather than mail your transcript to an agency, if you are online, you may __________, or modem it, and then ____________ the work sheet.
20. The _______________ lists generic names of drugs as well as brand names and manufacturers.

## TRUE/FALSE QUESTIONS

1. Vendors offer court reporting students student/group discounts on equipment.
2. It is not recommended for reporters to purchase/lease software compatible with their steno writer.
3. Artificial Intelligence Conflict-Resolution assists reporters in identifying and resolving conflicts.
4. Reporters build job dictionaries on CAT systems.
5. Steno machines may be purchased at local computer stores.
6. Used equipment for sale may be advertised at court reporting schools, in trade magazines, on courthouse bulletin boards, and online.
7. Sales tax is never added to the purchase price of used equipment.
8. A reporter may not be permitted to claim the purchase of used equipment as a tax deduction in the event of an audit if he or she cannot provide paperwork evidencing the transaction.
9. Software vendors will provide technical support for used software that is unlicensed by that vendor.
10. A reporter may easily obtain a key for unlicensed software.
11. Writer parts may be unattainable for used equipment if the equipment is outdated or the equipment vendor no longer exists.
12. The IRS considers money received for selling used equipment as income.
13. Compatibility is not an issue in the reporter's selection of a scopist.
14. Reporters should get their writers overhauled every five years.
15. Reporters should bring their writer charger to work in case their writer battery dies.
16. When on a job and beeped by an agency to cover a second job that same day, an on-staff reporter should call the agency he or she is on staff with to see if they need her services prior to accepting the job from the agency that has beeped her.
17. Reporters should always bring six packs of paper with them to jobs.
18. Generally, parties are deposed in the order of the caption in multiple-witness scenarios.
19. Attorneys examine the parties they represent in depositions and sometimes examine the other side.
20. Courts have now deemed it acceptable for female attorneys to wear pant suits.

## DISCUSSION QUESTIONS

1. What are the advantages of having up-to-date equipment while attending court reporting school?
2. What functions can a reporter perform with a CAT system?
3. What advantages are there to possessing a CAT system?
4. What are some methods of investigating the purchase/lease of court reporting equipment?
5. Why is compatibility a key factor in a reporter's decision regarding equipment?
6. What are recommended methods of maintenance for court reporting writers?
7. What are the advantages of having maintenance and support agreements?
8. Why are beepers, cellular telephones and telephone-answering machines recommended for today's freelance court reporter?

# CHAPTER 5

# How to Fill Out a Work Sheet

## WORK SHEET REQUIREMENTS

Although each agency has individual preferences regarding filling out its work sheet, there are some basic guidelines to follow.

## VENUE AND CAPTION

**Caption:** The title or name of a legal action filed with a court that lists the court and county the action is filed in, the parties in the suit and their classifications, and the case number assigned the action by the court. When speaking about closed captioning, a caption would refer to words superimposed onto a visual media, such as a television program.

**Venue:** The court and county in which a legal action is filed.

**Uppercase:** Capital letters.

**Lowercase:** Small or noncapital letters of the alphabet.

**Initial capped:** When only the first letter of a word is capitalized (uppercase), such as in English

At the job location, the reporter usually requests and is given what is referred to as a **caption.** In lay terms, the caption is the name of the case. Above it is what is called the **venue,** which identifies the jurisdiction (court and county) where the case is filed.

The reporter is given something from which to copy the caption. You should not add any punctuation to the information you are copying. You are responsible for copying it exactly as it appears, **uppercase** letters where there are uppercase letters, **lowercase** letters where there are lowercase letters. Student reporters are sometimes in the habit of capitalizing everything; this may lead to problems distinguishing what should be uppercase versus lowercase when preparing the transcript.

The venue is to be entirely uppercase. In the caption, the names of the parties are uppercase, *-against-* or *vs.* is lowercase, and classification of the parties—that is, *Plaintiff/Defendant*—is **initial capped** only. Reporters must be consistent with singulars and plurals. If there are three plaintiffs listed, for example, the work sheet must reflect *Plaintiffs,* not *Plaintiff,* in the caption. Do not add apostrophes where they do not belong, for example, *Attorneys' for Plaintiffs.*

### Case Numbers

When you are copying information from a caption, you should also note the *case number.* This is the number given to an action upon its being filed in a particular jurisdiction. The case number is referred to by different names, depending on the court and type of action. You will encounter captions that contain **Index No., Civil (Civ.) Action No., Criminal Action No., Case No.,** and so on. Supreme and lower courts use *Index No.* Federal courts use *Civil Action No., Criminal Action No.,* or simply *Case No.* If the information that you are given does not contain a case number, ask the attorneys present if they can locate it for you. If the work sheet does not provide a specific space for the case number, write it to the right of the caption, still within the caption box. That is how it will appear on the transcript. If there is no room to the right of the caption, you may write it on the bottom left of the caption box, but you should remember to add it into its proper place (to the right of the caption) when preparing the transcript.

## Multiple Captions

There may be more than one caption to copy. The venue of the subsequent caption(s) may be:

- The same as the first caption's venue and, therefore, not included
- The same as the first caption's venue yet needs to be repeated
- Different from the first caption's venue and will, therefore, need to be indicated

The captions may be differentiated by Action No. 1, Action No. 2, and so on, and they may or may not contain different case numbers. Copy them exactly as shown.

## Caption Abbreviations

Captions may include abbreviations that you are not familiar with, such as:

- *S/h/a*—sued herein as
- *A/k/a*—also known as
- *F/k/a*—formerly known as
- *D/b/a*—doing business as
- *D/b/u*—doing business under
- *A/s/o*—as subrogee of
- *N/k/a*—now known as

If such an abbreviation is found within a caption, it is to be copied exactly as it appears. If the reporter learns that a party is named incorrectly in the caption, the correction may be made on the title page and/or the appearance page. For instance, say the **named party** in the caption is ABC Co. and the correct name of the company is ABC, Inc. If the witness being deposed is on behalf of this company, the title page will reflect *Deposition of ABC, INC., s/h/a ABC CO., by ABIGAIL TAYLOR,* and under the company's attorney's appearance on the appearance page, it will reflect something like:

SUSAN PEETRY, ESQ.
Attorney for Defendant - ABC, INC. s/h/a ABC CO.
113 Mathews Place
Washington, D.C. 12345

**Index number:** Identification number assigned by the court clerk to an action in state or lower court. It is the equivalent of a case number (Civil Action No./Criminal Action No.) in federal court

**Civil (Civ.) Action Number:** The docket or identification number assigned to a civil action by a federal court. It is the equivalent of an index number, or case number, in state/lower courts.

**Criminal Action No.:** The docket or identification number assigned to a criminal action by a federal court. It is the equivalent of an index number, or case number, in state/lower courts.

**Case number:** The number given to an action upon its being filed in a particular jurisdiction.

**Named party:** A person listed individually or appearing on behalf of an entity listed in a caption.

## APPEARANCE SECTION

In the appearance section of the work sheet, the reporter is to list all present attorneys/law firms representing a party or a witness. The order of attorney appearances listed on a work sheet should correspond to the order of the parties named in the caption.

The order of the specific information for an individual attorney/law firm may vary. Some agencies/states list the law firm name first, whom they represent, the address of the law firm, and then the attorney, while others list the attorney's name, followed by the law firm name, whom they represent, and law firm address. The firm name and attorney's name generally are uppercase but may vary due to agency preference. Obtaining the attorney's business card enables the reporter to double-check the accuracy of the information copied down. If no business card is available and the attorney provides his or her information verbally, repeat the information back to the attorney for verification. Ask for the attorney's middle initial, if applicable. If the attorney introduces himself or herself with a nickname or shortened version of a formal name, inquire as to which name should appear on the transcript—for example, *Bill/William, Hank/Henry, Bob/Robert, Jeff/Jeffrey.* Always confirm the spelling of names, as it is not uncommon to spell *John* as *Jon, Jeffrey* as *Geoffrey, Lori* as *Laurie/Lorie,* and so forth. The same applies to names that are mentioned on the record.

On multiple-attorney cases, the reporter may choose to ask attorneys to write on their business cards whom they represent and applicable file or claim numbers. An attorney may draw a pi sign ($\pi$) in lieu of writing *plaintiff* or a small triangle ($\Delta$) in lieu of writing *defendant.* New reporters, however, should write out whom the attorney represents rather than give a work sheet with symbols on it to an agency.

When a reporter asks an attorney for his or her file number, the reporter is looking for the firm's interoffice file number to identify the case for billing purposes. Some firms do not use such numbers. New attorneys may erroneously respond by giving you the index number of the case.

If you previously received and copied onto your work sheet caption and appearance information, search out the appearance information and note whom each attorney/firm represents. Verify this information for accuracy.

### Representation of a Party with Different Classifications

When a party is named in the caption with different classifications, such as being both a plaintiff and a third-party plaintiff, the appearance of the firm or attorney representing the party would be written on your work sheet as:

SMITH & LAVEZZOLI, ESQS.
Attorneys for Plaintiff/Third-Party Plaintiff—JOSEPH COOK
    88 Marilyn Plaza
    Jodi, AZ 98765
BY: DARA RACHELS, ESQ.

Note that the order of the appearance information may vary according to agency preference.

## Representation of Multiple Parties

In scenarios where one law firm or a **solo practitioner** represents parties with different names and classifications, the appearance on your work sheet would appear as follows:

> SMITH & LAVEZZOLI, ESQS.
> Attorneys for Plaintiff JOSEPH COOK and Third-Party
> Defendant XYZ COMPANY
>     88 Marilyn Plaza
>     Jodi, AZ  98765
> BY: DARA RACHELS, ESQ.

Note that the order of the appearance information may vary according to agency preference.

## Multiple-Name Law Firms

The reporter should put ampersands *(&)* where they belong, *AND* if a firm name so appears, and commas/periods only if the firm name utilizes them. It is a current trend for multiple-name law firms to eliminate commas between the names and to eliminate periods if the firm is a *PC* (professional corporation), *LLP* (limited liability partnership), or *LLC* (limited liability corporation). Following the name of a multiple-name law firm, for example, *SMITH, SMITH & JONES,* if there is no P.C., L.L.P., or L.L.C., the reporter should put *ESQS.*, which is an abbreviation for *Esquires,* a synonym for *Attorneys.*

The next line usually identifies whom the firm is representing. It would be reflected as *Attorneys for the Plaintiff, Attorneys for the Plaintiffs, Attorneys for the Defendant, Attorneys for the Defendants,* and so on. The word *Attorneys* will be plural and should be initial capped. Depending upon your agency's preference, those whom the attorney represents—*Plaintiff/Plaintiffs/Defendant/Defendants,* and so on—may or may not be initial capped.

The subsequent line will list the law firm's street address and suite/floor number. Reporters are discouraged from putting down a P.O. Box number, as many messenger services, when delivering the transcript, require an actual street address. Ask the attorney for the street address. The street address is initial capped only, as is the word *suite* or *floor.* Delivery or messenger services may charge the sender for the omission of a suite or room number.

The next line states the city, state, and zip code of the law firm. The city is initial capped. A comma separates the city from the state, which is also only initial capped and is written out completely, not abbreviated. Therefore, you would write out *Rhode Island* instead of *RI.* Two spaces are usually left between the state name and the zip code. Zip codes within the transcript may follow this format as well, depending on agency preference.

The last line (or first line, depending on your state/agency practice) gives the name of the attorney who physically appeared at the proceeding that day. It is preceded by the word *BY,* in uppercase letters, a colon, a space (where to tab depends upon agency preference), and the full name of the attorney, generally in uppercase letters, followed by a comma and then *ESQ.*, unless the attorney tells you he or she is not yet admitted to the bar. Here is a sample appearance:

**Solo practitioner:** An attorney in private practice who is not a member of a multiple-name law firm.

SMITH, SMITH & DAVID, ESQS.
Attorneys for the Plaintiff
    123 Appletree Lane - Suite 226
    Mineola, New York 11501
BY: DIANA SMITH, ESQ.

Depending upon agency preference, there may be a space between the line for the city, state, and zip code and the last line, unless your agency lists the name of the attorney as the first line of the appearance.

If there is more than one attorney appearing on behalf of a law firm, the way to reflect this is to list each, giving priority to the attorney who:

1. Is doing the examining of the witness
2. Is a partner—if both are partners, then give priority to the first-name partner in the law firm's name
3. Speaks more than the other

Be sure to ask the attorney for a file/claim number and list that on the work sheet as well.

## Solo Practitioners

Lawyers who are in private practice may physically appear at the proceeding themselves or send an attorney in their stead. If a solo practitioner appears, then the work sheet should list the full name of the attorney, completely uppercase, followed by a comma and *ESQ*. Note that it is not *ESQS.*, as it is only one attorney. The subsequent line identifies whom he or she represents. Note that the word *Attorney* is singular, reflecting that he or she is not a part of a law firm but, rather, a singular attorney. The next two lines will reflect the attorney's business address, exactly as described with a multiple-name law firm. The only words that are initial capped are the street name, city, and state. There is no need to put *BY:*, a space, and then write the attorney's name a second time followed by a comma and *ESQ.*, since we already have it in lieu of a law firm name. An example would be:

JESSICA SMITH, ESQ.
Attorney for the Defendant
    456 Main Street
    Killingworth, Connecticut 12345

An exception to this rule is when the solo practitioner's business is incorporated or a limited liability partnership. Then *P.C., L.L.P., or L.L.C.* following the attorney's name will indicate this. When you see any of those, your work sheet should list:

- The attorney's name in uppercase letters, a comma, and *P.C., L.L.P., or L.L.C.* in lieu of *ESQ.*
- The attorney's business address in the following two lines as described previously
- *BY:*, a space, the name of the attorney in uppercase letters, and a comma, followed by *ESQ.*

For example:

JESSICA SMITH, P.C.
Attorney for the Defendant
456 Main Street
Killingworth, Connecticut 12345
BY: JESSICA SMITH, ESQ.

Another exception occurs when another attorney is sent on behalf of the solo practitioner. Then your work sheet should list:

- The attorney's name in all caps, a comma, followed by *ESQ., P.C., L.L.P., or L.L.C.,* whichever applies
- The attorney's business address in the following two lines as previously described
- *BY:,* a space, and the completely uppercase name of the attorney who physically appeared at the proceeding, a comma, followed by *ESQ.*

For example:

JOHN SMITH, ESQ.
Attorney for the Defendant
456 Main Street
Killingworth, Connecticut 12345
BY: ELLIOT T. MURPHY, ESQ.

## Esquire of Counsel

Sometimes an attorney will tell you that he or she is appearing **of counsel.** This means that the law firm the attorney is appearing on behalf of does not employ the attorney; the attorney is just covering the job for that firm on this particular day. In this case, the aforementioned rules would apply, except that after listing the name of the attorney physically present at the deposition in uppercase letters, you would put a comma, then *ESQ.,* all in uppercase letters, another comma, then *of Counsel,* with only the word *Counsel* initial capped. An example would be:

SMITH, KENNY & JUSTIN, ESQS.
Attorneys for the Defendant
123 Julian Lane
Holmes, New York 12531
BY: NICHOLAS R. MULLINS, ESQ., of Counsel

While many freelance agencies subscribe to this definition of an attorney who is of counsel, there are agencies that believe that any lawyer not named as a partner of the law firm should automatically be considered of counsel. For example:

SMITH, SMITH & JONES, ESQS.
Attorneys for the Defendant
123 Appletree Lane
Mineola, New York 11501
BY: IRA L. GOLD, ESQ., of Counsel

In addition, some agencies list the attorney's name followed by *ESQ.*, on one line, and then *of Counsel* on the next line. Check with each agency about its preference.

## Not Present

Sometimes you will note that parties in the caption are represented by law firms that are not present at the proceeding. Inquire as to whether or not they still represent that party, whether they are expected to attend the proceeding, and whether or not anyone has heard from them regarding ordering a copy of the transcript.

If they still represent a party but choose not to attend, most agencies want the court reporter to list the law firm on the appearance page of the transcript with *(Not Present)* or *NOT PRESENT* above or below the law firm's name and address. Other agencies may discourage the listing of a nonpresent law firm, as there are cases where a particular party is no longer in the suit but the caption has not yet been amended to reflect the change. Whether or not *(Not Present)* or *NOT PRESENT* should be included in your transcript is at the agency's discretion, and whether it will appear initial capped, completely in uppercase letters, in parentheses, or underlined is also a matter of agency preference.

## Also Present

When listing those present at a deposition on your work sheet, sometimes you will encounter a person who is neither the witness currently testifying nor an attorney representing a party to the action. This person may be:

- An interpreter
- A videographer
- Another working freelance court reporter
- A student/beginner court reporter
- A party to the action who is not testifying but is just sitting in on the deposition to hear the testimony
- A witness who was examined at the same proceeding just prior to the current witness's examination
- A witness who will be examined subsequent to the current witness's examination
- An intern of the law firm where the proceeding is being held
- An attorney who is not yet admitted to the bar who is auditing the proceeding
- A company's in-house counsel who is not counsel of record for the company but is just auditing the proceeding
- An attorney's child (believe me, it happens!)
- A family member of the witness
- A friend of the witness
- The witness's caretaker/aid

Interpreters and videographers have functions to perform pertinent to the proceeding. The reporter should list on the work sheet under *ALSO PRESENT* their names, a comma, their functions (for example, *Interpreter, Videographer*), and perhaps their agency name, depending upon the reporter's agency's preference for their appearance.

The presence of a second reporter occurs when:

- One party in the case has a contract that requires the party to obtain transcripts only from reporters of the contracted agency
- Two law firms have gotten their signals crossed and each has ordered a reporter but they agree to let the reporters write side by side and deliver a transcript to the respective firms that ordered them

The reporter whose client is the first attorney examining is generally designated as the official reporter. The official reporter in this instance will swear/affirm the witness, read back testimony (if applicable) mark exhibits (if applicable), and deliver the original transcript of the proceeding and a copy to his or her client. The official reporter will list the nonofficial reporter under *ALSO PRESENT* by name, comma, *Court Reporter,* and perhaps the name of the nonofficial reporter's agency. Agency preference dictates the specific format. The nonofficial reporter's work sheet will list the name of the official reporter under *ALSO PRESENT,* followed by a comma, then the words *Official Reporter* or the official reporter's agency, depending upon the preference of the nonofficial's agency. Student reporters who sit in with a reporter should be listed under *ALSO PRESENT* by name, comma, then *Student Court Reporter.* No further explanation is necessary.

Parties to the case should be listed under *ALSO PRESENT* by name only. It is *not* necessary to classify them, for instance, as *JOE KING, Defendant.* Their classification is obvious from the caption. Similarly, other witnesses who are testifying at a deposition before or after the current witness and who sit in on the proceeding are to be listed under *ALSO PRESENT* by name only. At hearings and arbitrations, witnesses who are examined during the proceeding are not listed under *ALSO PRESENT;* only those witnesses who attend but are not examined are listed. Legal interns and the like, when attending a legal proceeding, are listed under *ALSO PRESENT* by name only.

In the case of multiple witnesses, it is recommended to place next to each name listed under *ALSO PRESENT* on your work sheet the number of the witness whose examination was attended. One person listed under *ALSO PRESENT* may sit in on two other witnesses' examinations, while another person may sit in on only one examination. An example:

#1 - ELIZA JACOBS
BILL BANNO
#2 - ELIZA JACOBS

If no one attended Witness #1's deposition, for example, then there is no need to place a *#1* followed by a zero, meaning no one was also present. Simply list the number of the witness the person was present for when applicable. For example:

#2 - ELIZA JACOBS

This serves as a reminder, when you are preparing each witness's transcript, to properly list who was present for each specific witness's examination. I suggest highlighting the number of the witness on your work sheet to draw your attention to the *ALSO PRESENT* information lest it gets overlooked upon preparation of the transcript.

As some people who would be categorized as *ALSO PRESENT* are not parties in the case, many times they are not permitted to attend the proceeding; they have to wait outside the conference room or are given an estimated return time. In circumstances where they are allowed attendance privileges, you would simply list their names on your work sheet under *ALSO PRESENT.*

## WITNESS INFORMATION

Work sheets usually have spaces or boxes for multiple-witness information. If there are multiple witnesses on a particular job and the work sheet does not delineate an information area for each witness as *Witness #1, Witness #2, Witness #3* or *Witness A, Witness B, Witness C,* and so on, you should so mark the work sheet to keep the witness data separate and distinct.

To obtain witness information, the reporter simply asks the witness for his or her full name and address. This generally is done at the conference room table before the proceeding commences. Even if the witness's name is in the caption before you, always double-check the spelling, as typographical errors in the caption are a possibility. If the witness has an Italian last name, check capitalization preferences—for example, *LoBianco, DiBenesse*—as well as whether or not a space should be left in such last names between the initial letters *Di, De, Lo, Le* and what follows. Write the witness's name in uppercase letters. The witness's address would not be completely uppercase.

Sometimes witnesses will decline to give you a home address if they are representing, for instance, a governmental body or a business entity—or for a variety of other reasons. In that case, you should ask the attorneys present if using the business address will be sufficient. If they agree to it, then you take the witness's business address and specify on your work sheet that it is a business address. In the transcript, the first two questions, which pertain to the witness's name and address, should be amended to reflect that the address is a business address, not a home address, if the attorneys do not make a comment to this effect in colloquy on the record.

The next step is to classify the witness, for example, *plaintiff, defendant, nonparty witness, expert witness.* After asking the witness for his or her name, check the caption to see if the witness is a named party in the action. If not, it is important to inquire of either the examining attorney or the witness's attorney whether the witness is appearing on behalf of a company that may be listed as a party to the suit or is a nonparty or expert witness. If the witness is representing a company named in the caption, the work sheet information should state:

- The classification of the company—*Plaintiff, Defendant,* and so on—initial capped only
- The full and accurate name of the company in uppercase letters
- The word *by* in lowercase letters
- The full name of the witness in uppercase letters

For example:

Plaintiff ABC COMPANY, INC. by ALAN PERLA

A witness may be appearing on behalf of more than one company listed in the caption. It is important that you ask the examining attorney if the wording on the cover page of the transcript should reflect that the witness is representing both or all of the companies. Attorneys will tell you their preference. An example of how you would reflect this on your work sheet is:

Defendants XYZ, INC. and LMN CORPORATION by RAQUEL GONZALEZ

Another scenario that may occur is where the witness represents one company that is listed in different classifications in the caption. An example would be:

Defendant/Third-Party Plaintiff RST, LTD. by PERCY ARDEL

### Expert Witnesses

An **expert witness** is a witness called to give testimony regarding a subject matter in which he or she has expertise. Expert witnesses are generally asked to review the elements of the case; to state their education, experience, and publications; and then to render opinions on questions posed by counsel and cite authoritative texts that support their opinions. Counsel for any party may question an expert witness, although the attorney who arranged for the court reporter will probably question the witness first. Your work sheet should read:

**Expert Witness SAMUEL BURNS**

or

**SAMUEL BURNS, an expert witness herein,**

A **nonparty witness** is a witness not named in the caption or presently working for a named party in the caption. Nonparty witnesses may be examined by any of the attorneys present. Your work sheet should reflect the words *Nonparty Witness,* with the name of the witness in uppercase letters. For example:

**Nonparty Witness ELEANOR SIMMONS**

or

**ELEANOR SIMMONS, a Nonparty Witness herein,**

Agency preference dictates whether or not *Nonparty Witness* is initial capped. However, if the attorney representing a named party tells you that the witness is being produced on behalf of the named party but that the witness no longer works for them, the work sheet should reflect:

- The classification of the company, initial capped only
- The company's name in uppercase letters
- The word *by* in lowercase letters
- The name of the witness in uppercase letters

For example:

Defendant PRR CORPORATION by SAMUEL SCHWEITZER

After the classification and name of the witness, you will list the witness's address. Generally following that you will see *Time Started* and *Time Ended,* with spaces for you to insert the time that *each* witness's testimony began and ended. You must be sure to note the beginning time of the proceeding as soon as you obtain all of your work sheet information and are ready to swear or affirm the witness. When the testimony ends, the reporter should write *Time Noted:*

**Expert witness:** A witness who, by virtue of education, work experience, and/or publications in a specific field, is asked to give testimony on particular subject matter. This term has specific definitions in state and local practice that normally imply that such a witness is testifying regarding subject matter that is beyond the ken of normal or ordinary understanding.

**Nonparty witness:** A witness who is not individually named or appearing on behalf of an entity listed in a caption.

and the corresponding time into the steno notes and then, with a pen, note the ending time on the work sheet. Reporters should always ask nonparty witnesses whether they are waiving their signature or wish to review and sign the transcript.

### Multiple Witnesses

If there are multiple witnesses at a proceeding, remember to note the time that the testimony of *each* witness begins and ends, as well as listing a witness present at another witness's examination under *ALSO PRESENT* on your work sheet. An exception is made to this rule when recording the testimony of witnesses who have parent-child or husband-wife relationships where the parties reside at the same address and the testimony of the second witness consists of just a few questions. When the second witness's testimony is lengthy, separate transcripts are usually created. Another criteria in booking testimony together is that each witness is present during the other's examination. Rather than reflect a husband and wife or parent and child as *Witness #1* and *Witness #2* or *Witness A* and *Witness B,* by the area designated *Witness #1,* the reporter should fill in the space with both names and the beginning time of the first witness's testimony and the ending time of the second witness's testimony. For example:

> Plaintiffs HAROLD SMITH and MARY SMITH
> Time started: 10:05 a.m.
> Time ended: 4:48 p.m.

Even in these circumstances, however, some agencies prefer to keep the transcripts separate. For instance, say the father's testimony is requested via expedited delivery and the child's is not. Or say the husband has two classifications in a combined caption (plaintiff and third-party defendant) and the wife has only one classification (plaintiff). Attorneys at the proceeding may request a copy of the husband's testimony and not the wife's. In these types of cases, you would list each witness's name and address separately, list the beginning and ending times of each, and list each witness under *ALSO PRESENT* while the other witness testifies. Always check with the agency and follow its directive.

No matter the agency's preference, in this scenario, I always like to play by the better-safe-than-sorry rule and note the beginning and ending time of each witness into my steno notes and just delete it upon preparation of the transcript in cases where witnesses are booked together.

## OTHER WORK SHEET GUIDELINES

A lot of the other information to be filled out on a work sheet is self-explanatory, such as reporter name, date of the job, and so on. Many agencies require the reporter to just list the street, city, state, and (depending on agency preference) zip code of the location where the job is held, while others include the name of the law firm/company/courthouse, if applicable. If the work sheet delineates only two lines for the location of the job, then you can assume it is the standard address-only information that is to be written in. Many reporters do not know the actual street address of a local courthouse. Just ask the agency that assigned you the job. Even though you should get the zip code of the location of the proceeding, usually the zip code does not appear on the cover page of the transcript. If the location of the proceeding is the office of one of the law firms/attorneys representing a party/witness in the case, the zip code will appear with the attorney's information on the appearance page of the transcript.

There is usually a check-off section of the work sheet to classify the proceeding, for example, *deposition, hearing, arbitration.* The reporter is generally told by the agency the nature of the proceeding before accepting the job if it is not a standard deposition. Sometimes the reporter learns the nature of the proceeding on the job.

There may also be a check-off section of the work sheet to identify the stipulations that the proceeding is governed by if stipulations apply in your state. Stipulations are agreements between and among the attorneys made prior to the proceeding. These stipulations fall into the category of *usual/state, federal, other,* and *none.*

## STIPULATIONS

**Usual (state) stipulations** apply in most nonfederal courts. An indication that the case may be pursuant to usual/state stipulations is the presence of an index number. In some states, these stipulations are referred to as state stipulations, whereas in others—for example, New York—they are referred to more as usual stipulations, or usual stips. If the job is pursuant to usual/state stipulations, a usual/state stipulation page is placed in the transcript. The specific stipulations vary from state to state. The wording of a state's usual/state stipulations varies from agency to agency.

**Federal stipulations** apply to cases involving a venue in a federal court. A tip-off that a court is a federal court is, as mentioned previously, the words *UNITED STATES* in the venue, for example, *UNITED STATES DISTRICT COURT.* Another indication that a court is a federal court is the presence of a civil action or case number as opposed to an index number. If a job is pursuant to federal stipulations, a federal stipulation page is placed in the transcript. There exists both a long form of federal stips and a short form. Your agency should know which to advise you to place into the transcript. Federal stipulations maintain that it is stipulated and agreed by the attorneys for the respective parties that the filing, sealing, and certification of the transcript of the deposition be waived and that all objections except as to the form of the question are reserved to the time of the trial. Depending upon the freelance reporter notary requirements in your state, the federal stipulations will contain wording as to whether the witness may sign and swear to the transcript before the reporter who reported the job or before any notary.

The *other stipulations* category is generally reserved for stipulations pursuant to laws of jurisdictions outside the state where the proceeding is being held or specific stipulations stated orally on the record by counsel at the proceeding. Say the proceeding is being held in New York, for example, and out-of-town attorneys tell you that it is pursuant to Michigan Rules of Practice. If they do not have a copy of the Michigan Rules of Practice to give to you to copy into

**Usual (state) stipulations:** Stipulations agreed to by and amongst counsel regarding how they will conduct an examination before trial of a witness for a case venued in a state or local civil court.

**Federal stipulations:** Stipulations applicable to actions venued in federal courts.

your transcript, you can simply state on the transcript's cover page *pursuant to Michigan Rules of Practice,* rather than inserting a stipulations page. You could also ask for assistance from your agency to obtain the actual Michigan Rules of Practice. Consult the agency in either case regarding its preference.

If the attorneys dictate specific stipulation wording into the record, no stipulation page is added. You would just reflect who said what in colloquy. Attorneys tend to rattle this information off rapidly. Slow them down if you are having difficulty or ask for a copy of the stipulations, if read into the record.

The reporter checks the *none* category of the stipulations section of the work sheet when no stipulation page is to be placed into a transcript. This may occur when:

- A named party witness is pro se—meaning the witness is appearing without representation by an attorney—and there is not a second attorney present to enter into a stipulation with the attorney that is present
- The job is a continuation of the witness's examination on a prior date and the stipulations agreed to at the beginning of the witness's testimony do not have to be repeated; they still apply. In this case, usual/state or federal stipulations might be checked off; this is a matter of agency preference
- The nature of the proceeding is one that does not involve stipulations
- You are reporting in a state that does not insert stipulation pages, for example, New Jersey.

Aside from the types of proceedings that do not involve stipulations, which we will discuss in a later chapter, it is among the responsibilities of a reporter to verify whether stipulations apply, and if so, which stipulations apply. The reporter does not want to assume the responsibility of being incorrect.

I recommend carrying a copy of each agency's usual and federal stipulations in your work bag so that when asking if the case is pursuant to the usual stipulations or federal stipulations, if an attorney responds, for example, "What are the usual stipulations?" you can offer the attorney the copy to look over.

## PURSUANT TO NOTICE, ORDER, STIPULATION, SUBPOENA, OR AGREEMENT

The *Pursuant to* section of the work sheet requires the reporter to find out and subsequently fill in whether the witness is appearing via:

- Notice
- Order
- Stipulation
- Subpoena
- Agreement of counsel

Most commonly depositions are pursuant to notice or order. When filling out the work sheet prior to commencement of the proceeding, the reporter should ask the examining attorney, "Pursuant to notice or order?" If the job is pursuant to stipulation, subpoena, or agreement of counsel, the reporter will be told which. Subpoenas are a common method of bringing a nonparty witness in to testify. If possible, get the date that the subpoena was issued. A subpoena duces tecum is a subpoena that requests that the witness produce certain materials/documents at the proceeding.

If you are handed a notice to copy your information from, note the date of the notice. If you are told orally that the job is pursuant to notice, ask for the date of the notice. If the attorneys do not know the date, writing on your work sheet that the job is pursuant to notice is sufficient.

If the proceeding is pursuant to an order, always ask the judge's name. Many times you will be given only the judge's last name. You should ask for his or her first name as well. If you sense resistance or if no one knows it, there are lists of names of judges that you can obtain from a variety of books. For names of federal judges, there is a book called the *Federal Judiciary Almanac.* For names of judges in the United States, you could consult *The American Bench.* A directory of federal, state, county, and city court judges can be obtained from a book called *The New York Lawyers Diary and Manual,* which provides the full name of each judge and tells which court he or she is in. This is particularly helpful for situations where, for instance, you are looking up the first name of Judge Bartels and find that there are two Judge Bartels listed and one presides in the Supreme Court in one county and one presides in the Supreme Court in another county. By the caption venue on your work sheet, you can identify which judge's order it is pursuant to. Having a copy of this type of reference aid at your disposal is a plus.

## WORK SHEET LEGIBILITY

Unless the agency is scoping the reporter's work in-house, the original work sheet is given to an agency with the completed transcript. The agency then retains the work sheet for its files. Since the work sheet is the basis for the accuracy of the transcript, it is essential that the reporter submit a clear and legible work sheet to an agency. When filling out a work sheet, a new reporter should write everything out rather than attempting to abbreviate, as this may result in the reporter's or the agency's inability to decipher the abbreviations at a later time.

Sometimes the information given to the reporter to copy is inaccurate or has changed. This results in cross-outs, changes with correction fluid, arrows pointing to the correct information, and so forth. Therefore, many reporters rewrite their work sheets before handing them in to the agency. Photocopying multiple copies of an agency's work sheet enables the reporter to have a large supply to use as first drafts, so to speak. Some reporters prefer to utilize a notebook to write the information into and later transpose it onto their work sheet.

Remember, when filling out a work sheet, these are just general principles. Have the agency review its work sheet preferences with you and follow the agency's directives.

## SHORT-ANSWER QUESTIONS

1. The _______ is the name or title of the case.
2. The _____ indicates the court and county where the case is filed.
3. A _____ ______ or ________ ______ number indicates the jurisdiction of the case is a federal court.
4. An _____ number indicates the jurisdiction of the case is a state or supreme court.
5. _/_/_ is an abbreviation for doing business as.
6. _/_/_ is an abbreviation for also known as.
7. _/_/_ is an abbreviation for as subrogee of.
8. _/_/_ is an abbreviation for now known as.
9. _/_/_ is an abbreviation for formerly known as.
10. _/_/_ is an abbreviation for sued herein as.
11. _____ is an abbreviation for professional corporation.
12. ______ is an abbreviation for limited liability corporation.
13. ______ is an abbreviation for limited liability partnership.
14. _______ is a synonym for *attorneys.*
15. If an attorney appears at a proceeding to cover it for a law firm but is not a partner or associate of the law firm, ___, __ _______ follows the attorney's appearance.
16. The words *UNITED STATES DISTRICT COURT* in a venue tip you off that the proceeding may be pursuant to _______ stipulations.
17. ___ ________ _____ is an up-to-date listing of judges in the United States.
18. A _________ witness is a witness not named in the caption or appearing on behalf of a named party in the caption.
19. An ______ witness is called to give testimony on a subject in which he or she has expertise.
20. A witness who audits another witness's examination should be listed on your work sheet and in the transcript under ____ _______.
21. Witnesses with _______-____ or ______-_____ relationships may have their transcripts booked together.

## TRUE/FALSE QUESTIONS

1. The venue is written entirely in uppercase letters.
2. The caption should be entirely in uppercase letters.
3. Ampersands *(&)* and the word *and* are interchangeable when copying the name of a law firm onto your work sheet.
4. If no *P.C., L.L.C., or L.L.P.* follows the name of a multiple-name law firm, *Esqs.* should be placed after the name of the firm.
5. If a solo practitioner attorney representing someone related to the case appears personally at a proceeding, it is not necessary to list the lawyer's name twice in the appearance unless *P.C., L.L.C., or L.L.P.* follows the attorney's name.
6. If a lawyer who has not yet been admitted to the bar attends the deposition, he or she should be listed under *ALSO PRESENT.*

7. Reporters should list an interpreter's agency and agency address under *ALSO PRESENT* on both the work sheet and transcript.
8. A party to a case who is not being deposed but, rather, is auditing the proceeding should be listed by name and classification on your work sheet and transcript, for example, *Amy Fintz, Plaintiff.*
9. The title page of a transcript always includes the zip code of the location where the proceeding took place.
10. A witness not named in the caption is always a nonparty witness.

## DISCUSSION QUESTIONS

1. Why do reporters ask attorneys for their office's street address as opposed to P.O. Box numbers?
2. What types of people present at a proceeding are listed under *ALSO PRESENT?*
3. For what reasons might two reporters show up to report the same job?
4. When two reporters report the same proceeding, how is it determined who the official reporter of record will be?
5. How will the appearance of the official reporter be listed on the nonofficial reporter's work sheet and transcript?
6. How will the appearance of the nonofficial reporter be listed on the official reporter's work sheet and transcript?
7. In what scenarios would there be no stipulations?
8. In what cases might you book the testimony of a parent/child or husband/wife separately?

CHAPTER

# 6

# Interviewing

## WHEN TO INTERVIEW

The best time to start interviewing is when you are getting ready to pass your last tests in court reporting school. By this time, you should have sat in on a few proceedings to learn the ropes. If your state mandates that you must be a CSR/CCR to report, you should be preparing to take the examination. You should also take some time to answer the following questions:

- Do I aspire to be a freelance reporter or an official court reporter or work for a non–civil service entity, such as Workers'/Workmen's Compensation?
- If I choose to be a freelance reporter, do I want to be on staff with one agency or freelance among many agencies?
- How does my prior experience or education enhance my value as a court reporter?
- Do I have any special needs or work restrictions that must be communicated to an agency?
- Do I have any special skills/knowledge that other reporters do not have?

## NON–CIVIL SERVICE ENTITIES

Since freelance court reporting on both the on-staff and freelance level cannot guarantee a set income and does not generally offer benefits, some reporters prefer to work for non–civil service entities, such as Workers'/Workmen's Compensation. Each entity has its own specific requirements, so it is best to contact the entity to discuss application requirements and information regarding job availability. Requirements may include:

- A court-reporting school diploma or number of years' work experience verified by an agency in lieu of a diploma
- Having passed a state exam or an exam given by the individual entity
- A high school education or equivalent

Ask for the person to speak to regarding employment, find out the steps necessary to obtain the position you desire, and map out a plan.

## FREELANCING VERSUS BEING ON STAFF WITH AN AGENCY

At the commencement of your court reporting career, often you are just happy to be working, but as you come to understand the mechanics of the industry, you will find that agencies have different types of work. The nature of this work defines an agency's reporter requirements. Also at this time, reporters develop a sense of their personal reporting preferences. As with any relationship, there must be a certain level of compatibility between the reporter and the agency. Finding a compatible match is not always achieved right out of school. While one reporter may prefer to freelance among many agencies, another reporter may prefer to be on staff with one agency.

Although the word *freelancer* has been utilized to draw a distinction between reporters working outside the court system and official reporters of the courts, there is a second definition of the word in court reporting terminology. The word *freelancer* may also refer to reporters who work for multiple agencies as opposed to freelance reporters who go on staff with one agency.

Being **on staff** entails giving what is known as **first call** to an agency. First call means that each day at call-in time you will call this agency first for an assignment. If the agency has no assignment for you, then you are free to call another agency. If the agency you are on staff with does have an assignment for you, then you are expected to accept work from that agency rather than from another agency that may have already contacted you for a job. There are advantages and disadvantages to both. Some considerations that may factor into a reporter's decision are:

1. Reporters who freelance can work as many days a week as they choose, provided work is available, while on-staff reporters may be expected/required to work on a more regular basis
2. Reporters who freelance can take vacations or days off whenever they choose, whereas on-staffers must give advance notice and obtain consent
3. New reporters without connections in the field may prefer to be on staff, since they have not yet established a reputation or work experience, while seasoned reporters are more in demand for freelance work
4. Reporters who are on staff get first priority over freelance reporters for work, while freelancers tend to be at the bottom of the totem pole
5. Since on-staffers get first priority for jobs, although never guaranteed, their income is generally more reliable than that of a reporter who freelances
6. On-staff reporters generally have only one phone call to make at call-in time. If there is no work, they are free to call other agencies. Reporters who freelance may have to make a number of calls before obtaining work
7. On-staff reporters have the advantage of only having to familiarize themselves with one agency's format, while reporters who freelance must learn the format of each agency they work for and may become confused or overwhelmed

**On staff:** When a freelance court reporter has a first-call agreement with one agency.

**First call:** A reporter's giving first priority to a freelance court reporting agency over other agencies for assignments at designated call-in times.

8. On-staffers are more familiar with the agency's clientele and may, therefore, get requested for jobs, while those who freelance generally appear on a one-time basis
9. On-staffers are paid on a specified payment schedule, whereas the payment schedule may differ for freelancers
10. On-staffers may enjoy certain agency perks and incentives not offered to freelancers
11. Freelancers may work for any agency they choose, while on-staffers may be restricted from working for competitor agencies and may encounter loyalty issues
12. On-staffers are considered part of an office, whereas reporters who freelance may not be known by office personnel and may have to identify themselves each time they call for a job
13. Since they know office staff personally, on-staffers may feel more comfortable seeking assistance than reporters who freelance among many agencies
14. On-staffers may not need to purchase court reporting software if their writer is compatible with their agency's software and/or the agency scopes all of their jobs in-house, while reporters who freelance may need to purchase software if their writer is not compatible with the software of the agencies the freelancer works for
15. On-staff reporters may be more apt to buy software compatible to that of their agency, while freelancers may choose any software that appeals to them

When you interview with an agency, you must state clearly your intention to be on staff or not.

Many agencies prefer new reporters to be on staff because it takes a while to train the new reporter and teach him or her agency protocol and preferences. Agencies prefer experienced reporters to be on staff because they can be sent on different types of proceedings, many of which new reporters will not encounter until they have proved themselves. Agencies will try to retain as many reporters as they can keep comfortably busy. Busier agencies tend to like more on-staffers.

## FREELANCER VERSUS OFFICIAL REPORTER

If your goal is to make freelancing your profession, then you have options regarding:

- Whether to freelance or go on staff with an agency
- Attaining and maintaining reporter certifications
- Developing skills (e.g., realtime writing, closed captioning) that will increase your value as a reporter
- Opening up your own freelance agency

If your goal is to become an official reporter, then you should research the court system and query officials so you can zero in on what level of the court system you ultimately aspire to work in. Since you must first gain freelance experience, pass certain examinations, and then gain experience in the lower courts, you should map out a plan for yourself. You may begin by applying for the lower court exams and contacting courthouses to offer your reporting services on a per-diem or provisional basis. Then sit for the higher court exams, gain experience as an official in the lower courts, and keep yourself educated about available positions in the higher courts. Based on the grade you receive on these exams, your name is placed on a waiting list until a position opens and interviews commence.

## SPECIAL NEEDS AND WORK RESTRICTIONS

In addition to what freelance agencies need from their reporters, reporters may have special needs and/or work restrictions. You should identify what your needs are prior to interviewing and think of articulate ways to communicate these needs during the interviewing process.

Can you work three or more days a week? Reporting full-time can result in an enormous workload, especially if you are also scoping your own work and then proofreading each job. To turn out your transcripts in a timely manner, you must be aware of the workload that you are capable of handling.

Can you work beyond 5 P.M. if necessary? An agency must be apprised of any day care or baby-sitter restrictions that prevent you from staying late on a job when requested. Most freelance reporters understand the unpredictable element of the job regarding time and arrange for backup coverage should the situation present itself.

People observing the Sabbath on Friday evenings must be home before sundown. As a freelancer, there are no guarantees that a job will end by a certain time. Therefore, observers of the Sabbath may be able to accept on Fridays only those jobs that the agency is told are morning-only (a.m.) jobs. But what if the proceeding goes overtime? The agency should be prepared to send a reporter to relieve you. This is a matter that should be discussed with the agency at the interviewing stage.

Are you able to handle dailies and expedited jobs? While regular delivery is about two to three weeks—it varies from agency to agency—a daily requires the transcript to be provided to the attorneys the next day. Expedited jobs usually have a turnaround time of three to five days. If it is a lengthy job or if you do not have the equipment to scope your jobs yourself, the timing element can put you in a precarious situation. This is something that also needs to be worked out between you and the agency.

Are you willing to travel to all job locations? Some reporters, especially females, have reservations about working in areas reputed to be less than safe. Rather than getting stressed out every time you are assigned a job in the area, you should communicate this to the agency. Also on the subject of travel, some agencies have work that warrants travel outside your state. Your value to an agency can be greatly increased if you are in a position to accept such jobs. Those with young children at home or a fear of flying may not be candidates for these assignments.

Travel to certain local job locations may be impeded by physical limitations of the reporter. A reporter may have difficulty carrying equipment up and down a staircase in a nonelevator building. In such cases, the reporter may seek assistance from a bystander. If no one is available, the reporter may buzz the office and ask for assistance or, if no buzzer is available, leave the equipment at the bottom of the stairway and request assistance upon entering the office.

Some reporters prefer driving to job locations to taking public transportation for physical reasons. Therefore, they may wish to voice a preference for jobs closer to their homes. Additionally, finding a parking spot may be difficult, if not impossible, at certain locations. The reporter must communicate with the agency about these matters, but sometimes an alternate job is not available and the reporter is given the choice of either accepting the job and making do or not working.

Reporters who have a medical condition that might result in the necessity to take periodic breaks during the proceeding, such as pregnancy, hypoglycemia, diabetes, back problems, and so on, should communicate this to the agency. The agency will generally try to select assignments for the reporter that are more amenable to periodic breaks or that may not be as physically demanding as others. Before the proceeding begins, the reporter should also communicate to the examining attorney the possibility of breaks for medical reasons so that he is more understanding of the reporter's needs. I have fond memories of reporting while pregnant, as it assured me a definite lunch break!

## EXPERIENCE AND EDUCATION

Although it is not imperative, preparing a resume that highlights any work experience and education that you bring to your court reporting career is usually very well-received. Familiarization with a specific terminology—legal, medical, maritime, architectural, insurance, or chemical—is noteworthy, as is a background in proofreading, scoping, or typing. Court reporting certifications are always impressive. List educational highlights, college degrees, awards, and memberships. Even if you do not hold any educational degrees and have no real employment to speak of, there are ways of wording the resume to focus on your court reporting school accomplishments and personal attributes to present a positive picture. The NCRA offered a sample resume in their December 1997 edition of the *Journal of Court Reporting* (see Figure 6–1).

## TOP-NOTCH REPORTERS

If you have a propensity for a specific terminology (legal, medical, chemical, insurance, architectual, chemical), this will facilitate your reporting in certain types of proceedings. As cases involving these terminologies are generally given to seasoned reporters, knowledge of any of the vernacular in a particular field will move you up a notch in the hierarchy of reporters. If you become known for handling specific types of jobs, your value to the principal will increase.

Similarly, knowledge of a language or culture that a case encompasses is a plus. It is much easier for a reporter familiar with ethnic names and terms to write them into steno than it is for a reporter who has never heard them before.

Experience with realtiming, CIC reporting, performing **CART** (communication access realtime translation) and/or closed captioning, enhances a court reporter's value to an agency. Realtime is the immediate translation during a proceeding displayed on a computer screen. Computer-integrated courtroom

**CART:** (Communication Access Realtime Translation) A realtime service that is provided for people with hearing/learning disabilities or whose native language is not English.

**FIGURE 6–1**
NCRA Sample Resume

**JANE DOE**
Home address: 225 Wordsworth Avenue
Hometown, Illinois 61111
(000) 555-1234

**PERSONAL DATA:**
Date of Birth: July 1, 1977
Marital Status: Single

**CAREER OBJECTIVE:**
To obtain a position as a freelance reporter with an established court reporting firm.

**EDUCATION:**
Associate of Science Degree in Court Reporting. Graduated December 1997.
Court Reporting University, Hometown, Illinois.
G.P.A.: 3.27/4.00.
Hometown High School, Hometown, Illinois. Graduated 1995.

**RELATED COURSE WORK AND SKILLS:**
Machine Shorthand (225 wpm)
Typing (60 wpm)
Medical Terminology
Legal Terminology
Transcript Typing
Use of Reference Materials
Computer-Aided Transcription (StenoCAT)
Word Processing (Microsoft Word)
40 hours internship (freelance and official)
Mock deposition at School of Law
Mock trials at School of Law

**ACTIVITIES AND HONORS:**
Passed officialship test, 1/97.
Dean's List, Spring Semester 1996 to present.
National Dean's List, Fall Semester 1996 to present.

**EMPLOYMENT:**
Retail Sales. The Dress Shop, University Mall, Hometown, Illinois. August 1995 to Present.
Duties: selling to customers, operating cash register, stock and inventory.

**PERSONAL TRAITS AND INTERESTS:**
Dependable, good attendance, punctual, proper attire, considerate of others, responsible.
Hobbies include boating, fishing, traveling, sewing and shopping.

**REFERENCES AVAILABLE UPON REQUEST**

(CIC) reporting is realtiming in a courtroom when there are multiple hook-ups for participants of the proceeding to observe. Communication access realtime translation (CART) involves utilizing reporting skills to provide services for the deaf/hard-of-hearing community. Closed captioning is a skill whereby a realtime caption is superimposed onto a visual media. These skills earn reporters remuneration above and beyond regular reporting fare. Reporters who have attained high-speed certifications, such as the RMR, or have won speed contests obviously have no trouble finding work.

When an agency interviews numerous reporters, those who bring something special to the table stand head and shoulders among the rest.

## FINDING OUT WHO IS HIRING

The first step in finding out which agencies are looking for reporters is to ask the owner/staff of your court reporting school. They may be in touch with many principals and generally know who is in need of reporters or who is amenable to training new reporters. You should then ask reporters with whom you are acquainted who they work for and if they could put in a good word for you. This includes people that you sit in with, which is why it is so important to request and maintain their business cards. A recommendation to their boss about you might be all it takes.

Agencies often advertise for reporters in trade magazines, so that is another good reason why it is essential to be a member of both your state association and the NCRA. Agencies may also advertise on bulletin boards of courthouses or court reporting schools, as well as online. For those reporters who have worked for freelance reporting agencies while attending court reporting school or who have friends or relatives in the business, making contacts with agency principals will be fairly effortless as compared to those who have to cold-call. However, the cold-calling process is relatively straightforward. Agency personnel, if uninterested, will often give you suggestions or leads for finding work elsewhere.

## INITIAL CONTACT

If you can find out the name of the agency's principal in advance, it is a feather in your cap. The owner of your court reporting school should be familiar with local agency owners. If not, call the agency directly and ask. You might say, "Hi. I'm getting ready to graduate/a recent graduate of (the name of your school) and I wanted to find out the name of your agency's principal." Upon obtaining the name, thank the person. In case the person then asks if you would like to speak with the principal, be prepared in advance. Before making the call, do a practice run in your mind.

Most agency principals are too busy to answer the phones, so the first person you will probably speak to is the secretary or the office manager. Oftentimes, these are the people who give the assignments to the reporters at call-in time and channel information through to the principal, so it is important to make a good impression on them as well.

Make the call in the late morning. You want to give the principal time to get settled in the office, and you want to avoid the late afternoon, when the principal and office staff are busy preparing for call-in time. When you reach the agency, identify yourself. Say something like, "Hello. My name is _______. I'm about to graduate/a recent graduate of (the name of your school). I would like to speak to Mr./Ms. *(principal's name)* regarding an interview." Expect one of the following scenarios:

- The principal will be unavailable and you will be told to call back. Inquire about the best time to call back
- The principal will be unavailable and your name and telephone number will be taken so that the principal can call you back
- The office manager will do a preliminary telephone interview, set up an appointment, and relay your information to the principal at a later time.
- You will be transferred to the principal
- The speaker will identify himself/herself as the principal

If the office manager conducts a telephone interview, speak to that person as you would the principal. Be sure to note the office manager's name down

**FIGURE 6–2**
Reporter Utilizing Beeper and Cell Phone at Call-In Time

somewhere. Be flexible in arranging for an interview time. Do not present yourself as too busy to interview. Remember, this is your career. Take it seriously. If you are told that the information will be given to the principal, wait a few days and then make a follow-up call. Ask for the office manager, identify yourself, and inquire if the person has had the opportunity to speak with the principal about you. If not, ask if this is a good time to speak to the principal personally or whether you should wait for a callback.

If and when you speak to the principal on the telephone:

- State your name
- State your graduation/work status
- Give an approximation of how much sitting in you have done
- Mention who referred you
- Mention the names of reporters you know who work for the agency
- State whether you are seeking to go on staff with the agency or not

The principal should suggest at this point that you meet at the agency for an interview. Be flexible with the date and time, and ask directions if you are unfamiliar with the area.

The principal may decide to conduct an interview by telephone. Have all of the questions you would like to ask written out on a sheet of paper in front of you. If the principal answers a question before you have an opportunity to ask it, jot down the information on your sheet so that you do not reask it. If all goes well and the principal does not suggest an in-person interview, you should. Again, be flexible, and ask for directions if necessary.

## IN-PERSON INTERVIEW

Now it is time for your interview. Dress professionally, as you would for an actual court reporting job. Wear a suit; do not wear sneakers. Be neat and conservatively dressed. Do not chew bubble gum. Show up early. Since the agency owner does not know you personally, he or she can only assess how clients will view you when you enter the proceeding in the same manner. If you arrive early to the interview, the principal can assume you will be early or on time to jobs as well.

Upon entering the office for the interview, acknowledge the office personnel. You will probably have more dealings with them in the future than with the principal. Good relationships begin here. Try to remember names. When introduced to the principal, shake his or her hand firmly. A firm, confident handshake will probably be noted by the principal. Look confident, be personable, speak intelligently, and be honest about your work experience.

Speak well of your school. Respect for others reflects well on the reporter. Do not badmouth anyone you know in the field; the court reporting community is a tight-knit community, and principals often know local school owners and reporting agencies.

It is always nice to mention something positive about the agency—that you have heard of their excellent reputation, that they have a nice office or a nice view of the city, and so forth. Also be sure to mention who referred you or the names of reporters that you know who work for that agency. If you have family members/friends who are lawyers that you can refer to the company as clients, that is always a plus.

Listen to everything the principal wants to explain about the agency, and then ask questions regarding subjects not covered. State again whether or not you are looking for a staff position. On-staffers will be expected to give the agency first call. This means that each day at call-in time, you will call this agency first for an assignment the following day. If they have nothing available for you, then you are free to call another agency in search of work. However, if they have work for you, you are expected to accept work with the agency, even if another agency has already contacted you for an assignment.

Freelancers may call in on a less frequent basis, as they have other agencies that provide assignments to them. Or the agency may call freelancers only when there are more jobs in the job diary than there are on-staff reporters available. Freelancers may get preferential treatment if:

- Requested specifically by the attorneys on a case
- The client was introduced to the agency by the freelance reporter
- The case is a continuation of one that the freelancer has already taken and the attorneys prefer to keep the same reporter throughout
- The freelancer possesses knowledge of the terminology utilized in the case
- The freelancer possesses special skills required for the assignment

## CALL-IN TIME

You should ask about the call-in time for each company you interview with, as it may differ. Agencies with later call-in times may be a lower priority for reporters who freelance among many agencies because if the reporter calls for an assignment and there is none, other agencies may have already completed their job-assignment process.

## The Call

At the agency's specified call-in time, not before or after, you call for your assignment for the following day. Calling too early will result in being told that the jobs are not all confirmed yet and that you should call back later; calling too late may result in all of the assignments having been given out already. When you call, have your job diary open and a pen or pencil handy, and be ready to write. (See Figure 6–2.) When someone from the agency answers the phone, identify yourself and state that you are calling in for the next day's assignment. Either the person on the phone or someone else will check the office's job **calendar** and give you an assignment or tell you that one is unavailable.

If you are on the record or going to be unavailable at call-in time, notify the agency and ask if they can leave your assignment on your telephone-answering machine. Tell them that you will confirm that you have received it shortly thereafter, and be sure to do so.

## Job Diary Entries

You should possess a job diary with room enough for you to write in:

- The name of the agency that gave you the assignment
- The interoffice job number, if applicable
- The time the job is to begin
- The location of the job
- A contact person at the job location, if applicable
- The telephone number where the proceeding is to be held
- The name of the client
- The name of the attorney who will appear on behalf of the client, if known
- The client's file number, if known
- A summarized caption name
- The witness's name, if known

## When There Is No Work

One of the things that you must get used to is that when it is a slow time, you cannot take it personally that there is no work. You may ask in a nice way if it is slow, but do not moan and groan about how you need to work. Do not bother speaking to the principal about it unless you are off several days in a row. If it is not a genuinely slow time of year, no work for several days may be an indication that a) the office feels that you are backlogged and need some time to catch up, or (b) the office is dissatisfied with your work. If you are backlogged, it is time for you to employ a scopist to help you with your workload. If the agency communicates dissatisfaction with your work, ask for guidance and spend some time with in-house personnel. Do not be defensive of agency criticism; no one is perfect. Show an open-mindedness to combatting your weaknesses. Ask for recommendations for ways to improve. Take classes, attend seminars, and read articles and books to better yourself.

**Calendar:** The book in which freelance agencies record jobs that are subsequently assigned to reporters.

It is a good idea to establish relationships with other agencies in order to pick up jobs when your first-call agency has nothing for you. Unfortunately, when one agency is slow, other agencies may be as well, but if you put the word out to a number of agencies that you are available, you may be able to find something.

There are organizations that reporters may call to notify of their availability by leaving their:

- Name
- Home phone number
- Beeper number
- Cellular telephone number
- Information regarding a.m., p.m., or all-day availability for the following day
- Locations where the reporter will or will not work
- Names of agencies the reporter will not accept work for, which is kept confidential

If these organizations are contacted by an entity requiring reporting services for the following day, they will contact the reporter. These organizations also send mailings to working reporters. Similar organizations may be found online. Surf "Court Reporting" on the Internet and contact court reporting–related Web sites. You never know what information you will come across. If you really want to work, these are some of the methods to employ.

Be aware that freelance agencies tend to be slow around holiday times. Many people take vacation on holidays, and therefore, attorneys have a difficult time arranging for all of the parties and witnesses to attend the proceeding. Reporters can expect slow periods to begin a day or two before a holiday and last for a day or so after the holiday.

### Agency Holiday Schedules

In addition to the fact that attendees of proceedings are often unavailable around holidays, agencies may close early the day before a holiday and may be closed the day of the holiday itself. Reporters should purchase job diaries that list holidays so that they can check with the agency ahead of time to know when to call in for jobs. If an agency is closing early the day before a holiday, they may tell you to call by noon or 1:00 P.M. for jobs, or they may inform you that if they have something for you, you will be contacted. If they are open until their regular closing time, call-in time will be at its usual time.

## PAGE RATES

Freelance reporters are usually paid a **page rate** times the amount of pages written. There are exceptions, such as per-diem contracted assignments which pay a flat fee; but generally, the more pages you write, the more you earn. Therefore, it is necessary to find out what the agency's page rate is. As a beginner reporter, you do not usually have much negotiating power here, since you are more or less at the bottom of the totem pole when it comes to the company's reporters.

**Page rate:** The amount that a freelance court reporting agency will pay a reporter per transcript page.

During the interviewing process, the principal will speak about page rate in terms of scoped and unscoped rates. The **scoped page rate** is the rate you will charge if you scope your own work. The **unscoped page rate** will be a lower page rate than the scoped rate. This is because an amount is deducted per page from the scoped page rate to pay an in-house scopist, if the office provides such services.

As previously mentioned, scoping involves:

- Putting a transcript together in the agency's format
- Adding include files (the title page, appearance page, stipulation page, if applicable, sworn/affirmed parenthetical, jurat/acknowledgment page, index and certification page)
- Setting up the Q&A versus colloquy formats
- Inputting parentheticals (parentheticals being a word or several words in parentheses conveying a nonverbal occurrence)
- Marking of exhibits
- Punctuating
- Defining job globals
- Resolving conflicts
- Replacing untranslated steno with proper names and words unique to the job

A scopist is a person possessing these skills to whom you may give a job rather than scoping the job yourself. You are required to proofread transcripts scoped by others (unless you have them proofread by a **proofreader**), and either you or your scopist, depending on your individual arrangement, will do corrections. Frequently reporters do their own corrections. Scopists may charge an extra amount of cents per page to do corrections for you.

If you choose to hire an independent scopist to do your work, you will pay the scopist a fee out of the scoped page rate without recouping the cost from your agency. Scopists charge a set amount per page, which should be agreed upon prior to their accepting a job from the reporter.

Inquire about what software the office uses so that you know whether your software program is compatible to theirs.

## Copies

Certain agencies will pay the reporter an additional amount of cents per page for each copy ordered beyond the standard original transcript and examining attorney's copy. Reporters working for these agencies, therefore, will profit more from multiple-attorney jobs where the parties are ordering copies of the transcript than from jobs where only two attorneys are present. The amount to bill for additional copies should be discussed in the interviewing process.

## Evening Rates

Certain agencies may pay the reporter an additional amount of cents per page for pages written after 6 P.M. Not all agencies subscribe to this additional page rate, so it is important to inquire about it at the interview. If the agency does pay the reporter an evening rate, the reporter should make a notation in the steno notes when it is 6 P.M. so that he or she can make a determination, when preparing the transcript, as to the amount of pages beyond the notation that

**Scoped page rate:** The amount a freelance court reporting agency pays a reporter per page for a transcript that the reporter scopes himself or herself or pays an independent scopist to prepare.

**Unscoped page rate:** The page rate that a reporter receives from a freelance court reporting agency for pages scoped by an in-house scopist.

**Proofreader:** A professional who reads a reporter's scoped transcript for detection of errors and lists the errors on an errata sheet or on a copy of the transcript itself.

should be billed at the evening rate. When scoping and proofreading of the transcript are completed and the reporter is doing final corrections, the reporter should remember to delete the notation from the transcript.

If you are not working with a substantial amount of pages, consult with your agency. They may choose not to bill their client extra or to pay the reporter an evening page rate; the pages following the 6 P.M. notation may be billed at the regular page rate.

## Page Rates for Immediate/Daily/Expedited Delivery

Ask what you will be paid for immediate/daily/expedited delivery, even though agencies will probably send their more experienced reporters on these types of jobs. The rate for **immediate delivery** is the page rate received for handing the attorney(s) a disk at the conclusion of the proceeding. This pertains to reporters who are performing realtime or who give the attorney(s) what is referred to as a dirty daily. A dirty daily is an unedited or partially edited ASCII disk of the proceeding. This is the highest page-rate category, and the rate, obviously, varies from agency to agency.

The rate for *daily delivery* is the page rate received for delivering an edited (finished) transcript either the same day or the following day. Arrangements may be made with an agency to send/deliver a portion of the job to the agency during breaks so that an in-house scopist can prepare portions of the transcript while the reporter continues to write. Although this varies among agencies, reporters may be paid as much as double their regular page rate for dailies.

The rate for **expedited delivery** is the page rate received for delivering a finished transcript within an amount of days that the agency defines as expedited. Generally, it pertains to delivery within three to five days. Again, there is no universal rate; reporters are paid an amount of cents per page above their regular page rate for expedited transcripts.

Sometimes an attorney will request a transcript by a certain date. If the date falls just short of the turnaround period for regular delivery by a day or a couple of days, the reporter is usually paid the regular rate. If the transcript is requested within two days of the proceeding, for example, the reporter may be paid a page rate midway between the expedited and the daily page rate; again, these decisions are determined by the agency.

## Realtime Rates

Also covered in the interview should be questions concerning realtime, such as:

- Whether there is a large amount of realtime work in the agency
- How many reporters are currently writing realtime
- The page rate for realtime writing
- The page rate per attorney hookup

If there is a large amount of realtime work at the agency, they may expect you to become realtime-ready within a certain time span if your writing is good, your conflicts are few, and you have a substantial-size dictionary. Inquire about whether you would be expected to accept realtime assignments immediately or over a period of time, and inquire about what that period of time would be specifically.

**Immediate delivery:** Delivery of a transcript (usually via ASCII disk) at the conclusion of a proceeding.

**Expedited delivery:** A term used to indicate that delivery of a transcript must be made before the regular delivery date, usually within three to five days of the proceeding or by a specific date requested by an attorney.

Finding out how many reporters are currently writing realtime at the agency as compared to the percent of realtime jobs that the agency tends to have will give you an idea of what your status within the agency will be if you are not a realtime writer. You should be aware of the agency's page rate for writing realtime, since, as with expedited/daily delivery, reporters earn an extra amount per page for realtime. The reporter may also earn an extra amount per page for additional attorney hookups and/or delivery of ASCII disks. Find out the agency's payment policy for this as well.

### Weekend Page Rates

Although it is rare that reporters are asked to work on the weekend, occasionally an agency will need coverage and will recompense reporters who accept such assignments by paying them a weekend page rate.

## APPEARANCE FEES

If you report in an area where it is applicable, you will receive **appearance** fees in addition to the page rate. Agencies that offer them usually have one set amount for all their reporters. Many agencies determine how many appearance fees you will receive by what period of time you are at the job location. Reporters usually receive one for the morning and one for the afternoon. A reporter may be paid one appearance fee for attendance anytime in the morning until 1:00 P.M. and another for attendance from 1:00 through 6:00 P.M.

Some agencies will pay a third appearance fee for work done after 6 P.M. When the proceeding ends, the reporter will fill in on the work sheet the number of appearances accumulated. If the reporter forgets to do so, the 6 P.M. notation in the steno notes serves as a reminder. If the proceeding concludes at 6:05 or 6:15 P.M., the agency may view five or fifteen minutes as an inconsequential amount of time and not pay the reporter an extra appearance fee.

Let me reiterate that appearance fees may not apply to freelance reporting across the board.

## BUST FEES

Likewise, an agency's bust rate is important to know. A bust is the cancellation of a proceeding on the same day as the proceeding is to take place. You might be in transit when your agency is called and notified that the job has been cancelled. You may physically arrive to the assignment and find out that it was cancelled. You may even set up at the job location, obtain your work sheet information, and then find out the job has busted. After a period of time, at the discretion of the attorney who is present, you may be asked to record a brief statement before packing up, which will subsequently be transcribed. In these scenarios, the reporter will usually be paid a bust fee, also referred to as a **minimum** or per diem.

A bust fee is a minimal set amount that a reporter charges for busts and any jobs transcribed that amount to less than the bust fee. In other words, if the bust fee exceeds the total billed to the agency for the amount of pages transcribed

**Appearance:** A fee paid a reporter in some localities in addition to his or her page rate that is determined by the reporter's presence at a proceeding within specified time periods. *Appearance* may also be used synonymously with *bust fee, minimum,* or *per diem* to reflect a fee paid reporters by freelance agencies to compensate them for their time when the proceeding they are assigned to report does not take place.

**Minimum:** A fee that a reporter receives for his or her appearance when he or she arrives at an assignment and the proceeding does not take place (sometimes paid to reporters before their arrival to the job location); synonymous with *bust fee*. Reporters also receive the minimum fee when billing for a job that amounts to less than the minimum amount.

including an appearance fee (if applicable), then you would bill for the bust fee. Therefore, the reporter will not make less than the bust/minimum fee on any given day.

If the reporter is notified of a cancellation anytime between when the reporter accepts the assignment at call-in time and before the reporter leaves home to go to the job location, no bust fee is paid, and the reporter has lost a day's pay. However, if an agency is notified of a cancellation and the reporter cannot be reached before showing up at the proceeding, an agency may pay the reporter a bust fee out of its own pocket. Agency views differ on this, so check with the principal during the interview.

In the case of a bust, the reporter should write *BUST* in large, bold letters on the work sheet. The reporter should fill in as much information as possible on the work sheet to faciliate billing, since the agency's client or another party may be charged the fee to compensate the reporter for his or her time and effort. If the job busts after the reporter has arrived at the assignment location, the client that ordered the reporter usually pays for the bust. If the cancellation was a result of another party's failure to appear, the client may advise the reporter to bill the other party for the bust. The reporter should not only write this on the work sheet in large, bold letters, but also should notify the agency orally. Otherwise it will be assumed that the client that ordered the reporter will be billed for it.

## TURNAROUND TIME FOR TRANSCRIPTS

You will need to know the agency's policy for turning in transcripts for regular delivery. Agencies differ vastly on this. I have worked for agencies that require finished transcripts within one week, ten days, and two to three weeks.

Agencies that offer in-house scoping services may have a policy that jobs to be scoped must be in the office the day after they are taken. This may affect how freelancers prioritize the agencies they call for work. Shorter **turnaround times** may hinder the reporter's ability to work more days a week and deliver transcripts in a timely manner.

## BILLING AND PAYMENT SCHEDULES

Reporters are usually paid for bills containing all finished transcripts that were turned over to the agency by a specified date in the billing cycle. The reporter keeps track of each completed job within the billing cycle on a bill form for each agency and submits the bill on a given date. For instance, reporters of an agency may have to submit a bill by the Wednesday preceding the 15th and 30th of every month if the payment schedule of the agency is the 15th and 30th of every month. Another agency may require the reporters' bills be submitted on a designated payday. Yet another agency may pay reporters shortly after delivery of the transcript. Therefore, the agency's billing cycles should be discussed during the interview.

Some agencies have an arrangement with on-staffers whereby when you first begin working for them, your first month's earnings will be withheld for the first four weeks of employment, and then every two weeks or so after that

**Turnaround time:** The time between the reporter's recording of a proceeding and the court reporting agency's receipt of the transcript to prepare it for delivery to a client.

you will be paid regularly. Other agencies may pay weekly or on every second Friday. Ask the principal and take notes.

## NATURE OF AGENCY'S CLIENTELE

Although most freelance reporting agencies handle everything that court reporting entails, some have a commercial clientele, some have a large number of medical malpractice clients, government contracts, contracts with civil service/non–civil service entities, and so forth. As a beginner reporter, unless you have proven capability, you usually will not be sent out on:

- Commercial cases
- Medical/legal malpractice cases
- Technical cases
- Chemical cases
- Maritime cases
- Product liability cases
- Expert witness proceedings
- Convention reporting
- Realtime/closed captioning/CART assignments

If this is the crux of an agency's work, at some point down the road, this is the type of work you will be reporting. You should inquire about the nature of the company's work during the interview, but fellow reporters and court reporting schools tend to be the best sources of information in this regard.

If you are a new reporter, you should also ask if the agency has any policies regarding beginners as far as:

- Sitting in with the agency's more experienced reporters
- Beginner training by the principal/office manager
- Nature of jobs assigned
- Average amount of days a week beginners generally work

## SUBSIDIARIES

The reporter should also ask about subcompanies of the agency. Many freelance agencies have **subsidiaries** that they contract work for, which have a different clientele than that of the agency. If you are told that you will be working for one of the agency's subsidiaries, the agency will give you the name of that subsidiary and you will hand out a card on the job that has the subsidiary name on it, if you have one. If not, you will decline the request for a card by saying something like, "Sorry, I don't have one, but I will give you my information," and then proceed to state that you are from the subsidiary's name.

If you are using a work sheet from your agency and do not have an alternative work sheet with the subsidiary's name on it, delete the agency name and write in the subsidiary's name and telephone number so that if asked by an attorney, you can glance at the work sheet in front of you and recite it without hesitation. If you do not have an opportunity to delete the agency name, fold the top of the work sheet with the other agency's name on it so that it is not visible.

**Subsidiary:** A company that a freelance court reporting agency contracts work for and provides court reporters on behalf of, that has a separate clientele than that of the agency.

Whether you are scoping this job yourself or giving it to a scopist to do, you will need to tell the scopist to put the subsidiary's name and telephone number on the title page and footer of the transcript rather than the name of the agency that you usually work for. Also note whether or not the transcript format of the subsidiary differs from that of the agency.

## REPORTER INCENTIVES

Some agencies will offer reporters perks or incentives in the form of financial remuneration for:

- Clients the reporter brings to the company—The agency may pay the reporter $x$ cents per page on transcripts for the reporter's client referral regardless of whether the reporter reports it or another reporter covers the assignment
- Test taking—To induce reporters to obtain certain certifications, the agency may pay the reporter's application fee for exams
- Seminar attendance—To encourage reporters to learn about specific subjects, an agency may pay for the reporter's registration fee
- Reporter referrals—An agency may offer a bonus to a reporter who refers other reporters for full-time work to the agency if those reporters remain beyond a specified period
- Volume of pages written annually—An agency may award monetary bonuses at the end of the year to reporters who exceed writing a set amount of pages for the year

## AT THE CONCLUSION OF THE INTERVIEW

If the interview goes well, ask for work sheets for the company and any subsidiaries, as well as bills and business cards, if applicable, so that you have the supplies you need to begin working. Request a format booklet or sample transcript from the agency so you can learn its preferences. When working with different agencies, it is best to keep an organized file on each agency that includes a sample format booklet and information regarding the name of the principal, the name of the assignment contact person, and agency preference notations. Also ask for the telephone number to call at call-in time, what time to call, and who you should speak to about a job assignment. Find out the agency's e-mail address so you can send jobs into the office. Ask for the agency's fax number as well.

Before the interview ends, give the principal your:

- Home telephone number
- Cellular telephone number
- Beeper number
- Fax number
- Home address
- E-mail address
- Social Security number
- Personal dictionary (a copy) of the agency's software is compatible to yours.

Request to meet the office staff. Shake people's hands and remember their names. Thank the principal for taking the time to meet with you; smile and shake hands when saying good-bye. Also say good-bye to office personnel on your way out.

### Thank-You Notes

Follow up on the interview with a thank-you note stating how much you are looking forward to working with the principal and his or her agency.

## SHORT-ANSWER QUESTIONS

1. ________ ____________ is an example of a non–civil service entity.
2. A _________ court reporter may be someone who works for one court reporting agency on staff or for multiple agencies.
3. __ - _____ reporters work mainly for one agency and give that agency first call.
4. __________ time refers to the time between taking a job and delivering a scoped, proofread, and corrected transcript.
5. A _____ requires the transcript to be delivered the next day.
6. Preparing a ______ noting work experience and educational highlights is recommended for job interviews.
7. __________, ____ and ______ __________ are skills that enhance the value of a reporter.
8. ____ - __ time is the time designated by an agency for reporters to phone in for job assignments.
9. Reporters should purchase ___ _______ to record assignment information.
10. If you are __________ with your workload, an office may not give you work until you catch up.
11. Reporters can expect slow periods to begin a day or two before a _______ and last for a day or so after the _______.
12. The ______ page rate is the rate you charge an agency if you transcribe your own work.
13. A _______ is a person who prepares a transcript from a reporter's notes for a fee.
14. The _______ page rate may apply to jobs past 6 P.M.
15. _________ delivery involves giving an attorney a disk of the proceeding at the conclusion of the proceeding.
16. _____ delivery involves delivering a transcript the day following the proceeding.
17. _________ delivery involves, generally, a three- to five-day turnaround for delivery of the transcript.
18. An __________ fee may be charged by a reporter in addition to the page rate to recompense the reporter for his or her presence during certain time intervals.
19. A ____ is the cancellation of a proceeding on the same day as the proceeding is to take place.
20. A __________ is a company that an agency owns that has a different name, telephone number, different clients, and possibly, a different transcript format than the agency.

## TRUE/FALSE QUESTIONS

1. Freelancers who work for multiple agencies do not necessarily have a first-call commitment to any agency.
2. If you are on staff, you should call your agency prior to accepting a job from another agency.
3. Freelancers generally get priority over on-staff reporters during job assignments.
4. All agencies have the same transcript format.
5. Non–civil service entities may require a court reporting school diploma or a minimum amount of years' work experience, a state or entity exam certification, or a high school diploma or equivalent.
6. Freelance reporters never have to work beyond 5 P.M.
7. You should acknowledge office personnel when interviewing with an agency.
8. A freelancer may get priority over an on-staff reporter if specifically requested by an attorney or if the reporter possesses knowledge of terminology utilized or a special skill required for the assignment.
9. Call-in time is the best time to call an agency regarding an interview.
10. If an agency's call-in time is 4:30 P.M., calling at 4:00 will ensure that you get work.
11. If an agency has no work for you for the following day, it means they are dissatisfied with your work.
12. Freelance court reporting agencies always stay open on holidays.
13. Call-in time may be altered by an agency's early close the day before a holiday.
14. When one agency is slow, all agencies are slow, so it is not worth calling them for work.
15. There are organizations in existence that find reporters for entities requiring reporting services.
16. The unscoped page rate is lower than the scoped page rate.
17. If a scopist prepares your transcript, you do not have to proofread the transcript.
18. If you work until 6:05 P.M., you should charge an evening page rate for pages written beyond 6 P.M. and charge an extra appearance fee.
19. If a transcript is requested to be delivered within two days of the proceeding, the reporter may bill at a rate midway between the daily and expedited page rate.
20. Reporters earn extra for weekend assignments.
21. Reporters may earn an extra amount per page for transcript copies ordered beyond the original transcript and copy to the examining attorney.
22. If you write a five-page statement, you will bill the agency for five pages and an appearance fee, if applicable.
23. If you accept a job at call-in time and it is cancelled three hours later, you will not charge the agency for a bust.
24. The client who ordered the reporter always pays the bust fee.
25. Some agencies offer financial compensation to reporters who bring clients to the agency.
26. All agencies pay for their reporters' test registration fees.

## DISCUSSION QUESTIONS

1. What are the merits of freelancing among many agencies?
2. What are the merits of being on staff with one agency?
3. What steps can you take to find out who is looking for reporters?
4. Where might agencies advertise for reporters?
5. What methods could you use to find out about the nature of an agency's work?
6. If you forget your job assignment information at home, what should you do?
7. If your first-call agency has no work for you for the following day, what can you do to look for work?
8. If you suspect an agency is dissatisfied with your work, what should you do?
9. How should you respond to a client if asked for a business card that you do not possess?

CHAPTER

# 7

# Different Types of Jobs Encountered

## DEPOSITIONS

Depositions are probably the majority of assignments you will encounter as a freelancer. Witnesses are brought forth by various methods to testify under oath in what is referred to as the **disclosure/discovery,** or pretrial, phase of **litigation.** Depositions involve a party known as the *plaintiff(s),* which brings an action against another party, the *defendant(s).* There also may be combined or consolidated actions that are reflected by multiple captions, such as third-party impleader actions and joint trial actions.

### Multiple Captions

**Disclosure:** The exchange of relevant material prior to trial, as well as the exchange of material that may lead to the discovery of relevant material.

**Discovery:** A pretrial phase of litigation wherein pertinent information is procured or exchanged by the parties in preparation for trial; referred to as *disclosure* in New York civil practice.

**Litigation:** The legal process whereby parties seek the court's assistance in resolving disputes and awarding damages (financial rewards) for their grievances.

***Third-Party Impleader Actions*** If a defendant, in response to the action brought against it by a plaintiff, brings an action against a party not named in the first caption, an impleader action is created. Its caption will be placed right below the first caption. Since the defendant is bringing the action against a third party, the defendant is listed in this caption as the third-party plaintiff, and the third-party defendant is the new party brought into the action. Each caption will be listed chronologically. To the right of each caption, the index number is listed, as these captions have separate index numbers.

The venues of the captions subsequent to the first caption are usually the same as the first caption's and are not repeated above each caption. However, your job is to copy the captions as you see them, so if the captions are shown with venues above them, copy them verbatim.

If a named party is in any of the captions, the witness's classification on the title page after *DEPOSITION OF* must so reflect; for example, *Plaintiff, Defendant, Third-Party Plaintiff, Third-Party Defendant, Second Third-Party Plaintiff, Second Third-Party Defendant,* and so on. A witness representing multiple parties within the captions will have his or her classifications reflected on the title page with a slash or the word *and* between them; for example,

*Plaintiff/Second Third-Party Defendant XYZ CO. by MARY SMITH* or *Defendant and Third-Party Plaintiff XYZ CO. by MARY SMITH.*

On the appearance page of the transcript, the order of the attorneys would be as follows:

- Attorney(s) for the Plaintiff/Plaintiffs
- Attorney(s) for the Defendant/Defendants
- Attorney(s) for the Third-Party Plaintiff(s)
- Attorney(s) for the Third-Party Defendant(s)
- Attorney(s) for the Second Third-Party Plaintiff(s)
- Attorney(s) for the Second Third-Party Defendant(s)

All else follows the regular deposition format.

***Joint Trial Actions*** Sometimes actions with common issues and facts of law will join together, resulting in multiple captions. Each caption's venue must appear above the caption, even if the venues of the two captions are identical. However, if a caption venue is not reflected on the caption you are given to copy, then just copy it as it appears.

These separate captions are reflected by chronological action numbers to the right of the caption boxes, as Action No. 1 would have a plaintiff/plaintiffs (Party A) suing a defendant/defendants (Party B), and Action No. 2 would likewise have a plaintiff/plaintiffs (Party C) suing a defendant/defendants (Party D). Therefore, on the transcript's appearance page, the attorneys are listed in order of the named parties in the various captions; for example:

- Attorney(s) for the Plaintiff/Plaintiffs in Action No. 1
- Attorney(s) for the Defendant/Defendants in Action No. 1
- Attorney(s) for the Plaintiff/Plaintiffs in Action No. 2
- Attorney(s) for the Defendant/Defendants in Action No. 2

On the title page, the witness classification for a party named in the caption should also include the number action that the classification pertains to; for example, *DEPOSITION OF DENISE ASHLEY, the Plaintiff in Action No. 2.* All else follows the regular deposition format. It is not unusual that a party may acually be a plaintiff in one captioned action and a defendant in another. In this case, the witness's classification should be listed as such; for example, *Plaintiff in Action No. 1 and Defendant in Action No. 2.*

***Counterclaims*** When a defendant in an action turns around and makes a claim against the plaintiff(s) bringing the action, the claim is referred to as a counterclaim. In many jurisdictions, this does not result in a separate caption or index number; however, instead of just having *Attorney(s) for the Plaintiff(s)* and *Attorney(s) for the Defendant(s)* listed on the transcript's appearance page, there may be, additionally, *Attorney(s) for the Plaintiff(s) on the Counterclaim* and/or *Attorney(s) for the Defendant(s) on the Counterclaim.* The title page will reflect plaintiff or defendant only, not *DEPOSITION OF PLAINTIFF ON THE COUNTERCLAIM* or *DEPOSITION OF DEFENDANT ON THE COUNTER-CLAIM.* All else follows the regular deposition format.

***Cross Claims*** If one named defendant asserts a claim against a codefendant in the same action, this claim is referred to as a cross claim. This does not result in a separate action with a separate caption. The reporter ordered for either of the two actions will copy the information that is given to him or her. Whether you are reporting the initial action or the cross claim, the transcript copied will have one caption with one index/civil action number and will follow customary deposition guidelines. Attorneys representing a party on a cross claim, if present, will be reflected in the appearance section.

## General Deposition Information

The reporter obtains work sheet information, inquires about stipulations and what the deposition is pursuant to, notes the time, swears or affirms the witness, and begins writing. How to take a deposition will be covered more in depth in the next chapter.

Depositions are basically a question-and-answer session between the examining attorney(s) and the witness. Common elements of depositions include:

- An introduction by the examining attorney
- Questions seeking to elicit information about the witness's background (name, address, Social Security number, education, employment, and marital/parental status)
- Questions concerning a specified time period prior to the accident/incident that is the subject matter of the lawsuit
- Questions directly related to the accident/incident
- Questions concerning the aftermath of the accident/incident
- The marking of exhibits for review and questioning
- If the questioning is of a party bringing the action, a review of the complaint and allegations therein

After the attorney is through examining the witness, other attorneys present may question the witness. Many times the initial examining attorney will have follow-up questions after other attorney(s) examine the witness. Other attorneys may ask follow-up questions as well.

When questions are asked of a witness by the examining attorney, a Q&A (question and answer) format is used. While on the record, if the attorney speaks to anyone present in the room other than the witness or if the witness speaks to anyone other than the examining attorney, a colloquy format is used. A colloquy format is also utilized when other attorneys or people listed under *ALSO PRESENT* speak on the record.

During a deposition, the reporter may be asked to:

- Mark exhibits for identification
- Mark certain portions of the record for rulings
- Place inserts in the record for information to be filled in by a witness or the witness's attorney
- Read back testimony from the reporter's notes
- Reflect nonverbal activity through **parentheticals**
- Note break times

**Parenthetical:** A description of a nonverbal activity in a transcript, set in parentheses, that assists readers of the transcript in understanding what transpired during the proceeding.

At the conclusion of the deposition, the reporter will note the time and obtain billing and delivery instructions.

## EXAMINATIONS BEFORE TRIAL (NEW YORK)

While the word **deposition (depo)** is all-encompassing to freelancers in other states, freelance reporters in New York State use the word *deposition* to delineate a proceeding that is venued in a federal court and is pursuant to federal stipulations. Similarly, in New York, the term *disclosure* is used in state courts, and the term *discovery* is used in federal courts.

A proceeding venued in supreme or civil court that is pursuant to usual or state stipulations is called an *Examination Before Trial (EBT)* in New York State, and the transcript is so titled, even though the verbal reference to "deposition" is still used.

The Q&A/colloquy format and reporter functions are the same for an EBT as for a deposition. The main differences are (1) the use of the words *EXAMINATION BEFORE TRIAL* rather than *DEPOSITION* in the transcript on the title, stipulation, jurat, and certification pages; and (2) usual stips in New York may provide that a courtesy copy of the transcript be furnished to the witness's attorney by the examining attorney(s). It should be noted that in federal court, the stipulations differ from those used in a New York State examination before trial.

## MEDICAL MALPRACTICE CASES (MED MALS)

Medical malpractice cases, or **med mals,** are another type of proceeding with which the reporter should be familiar. In most cases, the agency knows up front that it is a med mal and will tell you when assigning you your job. Generally, your agency is told the case is a med mal so that it will send someone experienced in med mals to report it; therefore, you probably will not be doing these cases right out of school.

So how does one get experienced at med mals? Usually when you have proven your reporting skills to an agency and have worked for a period of time determined by the principal, or when you, yourself, feel ready to accept the challenge of a med mal, you will take one. Practicing against tapes comprising medical terminology is one way to prepare for this type of proceeding, as well as sitting in with other reporters on med mals and/or practicing against television programs with heavy medical content.

The two types of witnesses you encounter on a med mal are the medical-related party to the action and the expert witness. When a medical witness is a party to an action, you can expect the questioning to include a rundown of that person's resume, or curriculum vitae (CV), which consists of the person's training, experience, and any publications that he or she has been a part of, followed by a reading into the record of most, if not all, of the notes and medical information regarding the plaintiff in the case. Occasionally you may have a case where a doctor is being deposed and giving nonmedical testimony, such as suing his landlord for breaching their lease agreement.

An expert witness will be asked for curriculum vitae information as well, but rather than being asked to read through notes and/or hospital records, this witness will be asked to comment about standards of care in the medical field, his or her expert opinions regarding the care and treatment rendered to the

**Deposition/depo:** A process within the discovery phase of litigation whereby examinations are taken under oath and recorded by a stenograoher who subsequently provides a transcript of the proceeding.

**Med mal:** Examination of a medical-related party to an action or an expert medical witness.

plaintiff in the case, and authoritative publications that support those opinions. Expert witnesses are generally chosen for their wealth of knowledge on a particular subject matter, and these proceedings can be very difficult.

Arriving early when reporting on a medical malpractice case is recommended so that you can try to get a Bill of Particulars or Response To Interrogatories to familiarize yourself with the terminology involved in the case. It is important to ask for a copy of a curriculum vitae, if necessary, as well as any medical records quoted from that you may need, as people tend to read more quickly than they speak. If denied a copy of a medical record, ask the witness to go over with you the portion of the testimony that you had trouble with and rewrite it into your steno notes in a note to yourself or make notes on your notepad. I find it crucial not to leave a med mal without reviewing with the witness or attorneys any questions I may have regarding spellings or names mentioned. Reporters often rely on medical dictionaries to look up the name of a new surgery or acronym used in the medical field, only to discover that it cannot be found or that they wrote it in a way that makes it impossible for them to determine its spelling.

A good percentage of the doctors that you will encounter are foreigners, and adding an accent to already unfamiliar territory can be harrowing. Always speak up when you do not understand something that was said. Remember, a verbatim transcript is the most important part of the proceeding. Ask the agency for a sample format of how to organize the reading of a medical record in the transcript. Some agencies use quotations; others do not. Some use paragraphing; others use commas/periods.

Learning to read from medical records, if you are not medically trained, is quite an undertaking. Reporting and subsequently checking medical records against what you have written requires familiarity with medical notations. Figure 7–1 shows a list of prescription-related abbreviations taken from an article in the April 20, 1999, edition of *Woman's Day* magazine. Lists such as this one can aid you in becoming familiar with medical notations.

## LEGAL MALPRACTICE CASES (LEGAL MALS)

There are also legal malpractice cases, or **legal mals.** A legal mal is a proceeding where the witness being deposed is an attorney; therefore, more legal terminology may come up in this type of proceeding. Also, since attorneys already know the procedures followed in a deposition, the speed of the testimony may be faster than usual. Other than that, these proceedings are similar to regular depositions.

**Legal mal:** Examination of a witness who is an attorney.

**Maritime:** An examination where the subject matter involves navigation, commerce, or other happenings on the sea.

## MARITIME REPORTING

An area that some reporters choose to specialize in is **maritime** reporting. The format is the same as that of a regular deposition with the exception that the subject matter encompasses navigation, commerce, or other happenings on the sea. Since this area utilizes very specific terminology, beginner reporters generally will not be given these types of cases. At one time, NCRA offered a

**Decoding Prescriptions**

**Few of us recognize that "2 caps. p.o. t.i.d." simply means "Take two capsules by mouth three times a day." To avoid dangerous mixups, here's what those cryptic notations mean:**

| | |
|---|---|
| ***q.o.d.*** every other day | ***ut. dict.*** use as directed |
| ***q.d.*** every day | c̄ with |
| ***b.i.d.*** twice a day | s̄ without |
| ***t.i.d.*** three times a day | ***p.o.*** by mouth |
| ***q.i.d.*** four times a day | ***a.l.*** or ***a.s.*** left ear |
| ***q.h.*** every hour | ***a.d.*** right ear |
| ***p.r.n.*** as required | ***a.u.*** both ears |
| ***a.c.*** before meals | ***o.l.*** or ***o.s.*** left eye |
| ***p.c.*** after meals | ***o.d.*** right eye |
| ***h.s.*** at bedtime | ***o.u.*** both eyes |

© Sue Ellen Browder, originally appeared in *Woman's Day*.

**FIGURE 7–1**
Prescription-Related Abbreviations

certification for maritime reporters known as the All-Star Team, but currently no examinations for this certification are offered.

## BANKRUPTCIES

You may also encounter bankruptcy cases. These are basic depositions, but instead of plaintiffs and defendants, the parties to a bankruptcy are called *debtors* and *petitioners*. These cases are governed by federal law. *Debtors* are those who are seeking a discharge from certain debts, and *creditors/petitioners* are the parties petitioning the Court for judgments against debtors. Chapter 7, Chapter 11, and Chapter 13 are types of bankruptcies that are frequently referred to. It is a good idea to check figures against documents or ask the witness or attorney for verification and to continue practicing numbers. These cases generally involve a lot of numbers.

## MATRIMONIALS

Matrimonials are depositions that involve marital disputes; for example, separation agreements, divorce actions, and child custody matters. Basic deposition principles apply to matrimonials; however, one can expect to record information regarding:

- Prenuptial agreements
- The witness's employment
- Assets and liabilities of the witness
- Bank statement deposits, withdrawals, transfers
- Personal check register entries
- Statement of net worth listings
- Personal loans
- Child care expenses
- Inheritances

Therefore, be prepared to have a large number of proper nouns and figures thrown at you. In addition, since the soon-to-be ex-spouse often attends the proceeding, expect some adversarial behavior amongst the parties and/or their attorneys. Generally, matrimonials only involve two attorneys, one for the plaintiff and one for the defendant, since the most common type of matrimonial is a divorce action.

## ESTATE-RELATED CASES

Freelance court reporters are also utilized to record matters of controversy regarding a person's will or, if no will exists (the person dies intestate), his or her assets/liabilities. Parties may seek information regarding the possible whereabouts of a will, life insurance policy information, gifts given by the deceased to others during his or her lifetime, and so on. As opposed to *plaintiff* and *defendant* party classifications, the party bringing the action is referred to as the *petitioner,* and the party responding is called the *respondent.* Since these types of cases involve discussion about a decedent (person who has passed away), witnesses may get very emotional. Since they often involve parties disputing the distribution of funds and assets after someone's death, witnesses may evidence a great deal of hostility, and fights may erupt.

## CLASS ACTION SUITS

Class action suits are lawsuits where multiple plaintiffs sue one or more defendant(s) in one action rather than each plaintiff pursuing a separate action. The captions in these cases may be quite voluminous, and although they are, again, basic depositions, there may be many attorneys present at the proceeding and taking turns doing the questioning. Be sure to obtain the business card of everyone in the room with the party he/she represents and his or her firm's file number written on it. Try to get a photocopy of a prior transcript and appearance page in order to save the time of rewriting it all. Be sure to ask which attorneys present are ordering a copy of the transcript.

## CELEBRITY WITNESSES

Deposing celebrities can be an exciting aspect of the job. Protocol dictates that:

- You do not ask for an autograph
- You do not tell celebrities about your qualifications/desire to get into their business
- You do not tell anyone about your experience

Stage names may differ from celebrities' legal names, so reporters still have to ask the witness's name. You may get glares from either the attorneys or the witness, but saying something like, "Sorry, it's just a formality," should get you off the hook.

I once had an assignment where an actor was deposed in a rather informal setting, and he began to flirt with me on breaks. I remember the look on the attorneys' faces when he followed me out of the conference room and into the elevator. He asked if he could walk me to my car. As flattered as I was, my professional and ethical responsibilities were foremost in my mind, so I told him that it was nice to meet him and politely declined his offer.

## MUNICIPAL HEARINGS

A municipal hearing, such as a *50-h hearing* (in New York State), is similar to a deposition, but it is taken prior to the deposition stage in litigation. It is an initial inquiry of the party who files the notice of claim, known as the *claimant.* It is conducted by the party responding to the notice, known as the *respondent.*

The title page of a municipal hearing reads *EXAMINATION OF,* followed by the witness's name. The appearance page is the same as that of a regular deposition, but rather than listing the attorney for the plaintiff and the attorney for the defendant, it will list the attorney for the claimant followed by the attorney for the respondent.

The majority of municipal hearings are pursuant to general municipal law, so there are no stipulations. As a beginner reporter, this may be where you get your feet wet, so to speak.

## EXAMINATIONS UNDER OATH

An *Examination Under Oath (EUO)* is an **examination** taken by an insurance company regarding a questionable claim of an insured party. These proceedings are not pursuant to stipulations, and many times the witness appears pro se, without an attorney.

Examinations under oath may cover a listing of items stolen or damaged and can include very detailed descriptions of items by product brand, size, and so on. You can ask for a copy of the examining attorney's list of items at the end of the EUO, if necessary. Like municipal hearings, EUOs involve claimants and respondents and may only pertain to practice in certain states. See Figure 7–2 for a sample examination under oath transcript.

## INTERPRETER PROCEEDINGS

Some proceedings require the use of an interpreter because the witness cannot understand or speak English or feels more comfortable being examined in his or her native language. The reporter swears the interpreter in before the witness is sworn or affirmed. You would do this by asking the interpreter to raise his or her hand and then saying, "Do you solemnly swear to translate the questions posed from English to [witness's language] and the responses given from [witness's language] to English to the best of your ability, so help you God?" or similar wording. After the interpreter says yes, you might say, "Please ask the witness to raise his right hand," and then you would swear/affirm the witness as you normally would, and the interpreter will translate it.

Aside from the swearing-in process, which now must be amended to first swear in the interpreter, you would also list the interpreter under *ALSO PRESENT* on your work sheet and transcript appearance page by name, comma, the

**Examination:** The questioning of a witness under oath by parties seeking to elicit information pertaining to a legal action; also includes questioning of a witness at a trial, arbitration, and so on.

**FIGURE 7–2**
Sample Examination Under Oath Transcript

------------------------

IN THE MATTER OF THE
EXAMINATION UNDER OATH OF
PATRICIA WIGGINS,
TAKEN BY
ABC INSURANCE COMPANY.

------------------------

EXAMINATION UNDER OATH of the Respondent, PATRICIA WIGGINS, taken by the Claimant, held at the law offices of LAZARIDES & LAZARIDES, ESQS., 84 Tufts Place, Spring Grove, Virginia 23881, on June 9, 2005, commencing at 11:45 A.M., before Dana Chipkin, a Registered Professional Reporter and Notary Public within and for the State of New York.

REINIG REPORTING, INC.
192 Lexington Avenue
New York, New York 10016
(212) 684-7298

company he or she works for, followed by what language the interpreter is translating. For example:

ALSO PRESENT: Jose Perez, ABC Translations,
Spanish Interpreter

Consult the agency for its preference, as some agencies do not choose to list the interpreter's company. Agencies may also differ on whether or not to list the interpreter's name entirely in uppercase letters.

Usually the parenthetical regarding the swearing in of the interpreter, followed by the swearing in of the witness, conveys to the readers of the transcript

**FIGURE 7–2**
(continued)

APPEARANCES:

LAZARIDES & LAZARIDES, ESQS.
Attorneys for Claimant
84 Tufts Place
Spring Grove, Virginia 23881

BY: EVERETT LAZARIDES, ESQ.

PATRICIA WIGGINS, Pro Se Witness
76 Underhill Road
Deshier, Nebraska 68340

REINIG REPORTING, INC. (212) 684-7298

that all questions in English were posed to the witness in his or her native language and that the interpreter's response to the question was on behalf of the witness. However, some interpreters may speak in colloquy to the attorneys or to the court reporter regarding difficulties or questions that arise. Therefore, you should always have a separate designation for the interpreter when colloquy occurs.

Interpreters are supposed to speak in the first person. However, sometimes they will speak in the third person and say something like, "He says the accident occurred on XYZ Avenue" rather than "The accident occurred on XYZ Avenue." Therefore, since the interpreter is not translating directly, the

**FIGURE 7–2**
(continued)

PATRICIA WIGGINS, having
been duly sworn by a Notary Public
within and for the State of New York,
and having stated her address as
76 Underhill Road, Deshier, Nebraska
68340, was examined and testified under
oath as follows:

EXAMINATION BY MR. LAZARIDES:

REINIG REPORTING, INC. (212) 684-7298

response should be in colloquy. If this occurs more than once, the reporter may politely call attention to it during a pause in the proceedings and ask if the interpreter could respond in the first person.

Interpreters will either perform consecutive or simultaneous interpreting. Consecutive interpreting involves a pause after the examining attorney's question before translating it to the witness and a pause between the witness's response and the translation of the answer. Simultaneous interpreting involves an interpreter translating the question to the witness while the attorney is asking it and translating the answer as the witness is responding. The problem with simultaneous translation is that it may distract the reporter from hearing the attorney's question fully and clearly, since the interpreter is speaking at the same time. If this occurs, you should, by all means, politely request that the interpreter perform consecutive reporting.

Sight translation is interpretation of a document during the proceeding. If the interpreter is asked to translate a document on the record, it is the reporter's responsibility to record it. If the interpreter seems to be murmuring while perusing a document, it is the reporter's responsibility to request that the interpreter read aloud or read silently, depending on what the attorney has requested of the interpreter.

Another situation that may arise is that the witness, although instructed to speak through the interpreter at all times, may not do so. A witness who has a minimal understanding of English may answer in English rather than in his or her native language that the interpreter would then translate into English. This results in the reporter having to differentiate, with only a second's notice, between when the witness is speaking in his or her native language and when the witness is speaking in English. If the attorneys do not instruct the witness to speak only in his or her native language through the interpreter, you may speak up and request that the interpreter ask the witness to do so. The attorneys will appreciate your intervention for the clarity of the record, and your job should become easier after the witness is cautioned to follow these instructions.

When a witness forgets and responds in English, you hit the Answer bank, then an open paren, write *In English,* hit the closed paren, and then write the response. For example:

A (In English) I fell.

## VIDEO PROCEEDINGS

Video proceedings are the same as regular proceedings with the exception that a videographer is present. The video camera is aimed solely at the witness (if a multiple-camera shoot, then at the witness and attorneys) except for the initial introductions, so there is no need to feel uneasy in front of the camera. The witness, rather than the reporter, is positioned at the end of the table during video proceedings, and the reporter will sit adjacent to the witness. List the videographer's name on your work sheet under *ALSO PRESENT,* a comma, *Videographer,* and whether or not the videographer is a CLVS (Certified Legal Video Specialist).

The proceeding usually begins with the videographer announcing the date and time, giving a brief synopsis of the caption, and asking those present to identify themselves. Therefore, be sure to have a separate speaker designation for the videographer. Although you always record this introduction, some agencies do not wish it to be part of the transcript, so check with the agency about its preferences.

When the videographer speaks, it appears in your transcript as colloquy. When all present are asked to identify themselves, this includes you, the reporter. As I find it cumbersome to write in steno simultaneous to identifying myself, I take a moment to write into the record, for example, *KR-RPT/KR-RPT* twice, colon, *Dana Chipkin, XYZ Reporting,* and then verbalize it. Also, you should not swear in the witness until asked on the record to do so, as the videographer will request it of you. The videographer will be announcing the stopping time when asked to go off the record, as well as the time you go back on the record. Therefore, before the proceedings begin, it might be a good idea to synchronize your watch/clock with the videographer's.

Protocol dictates that you do not interrupt the proceedings unless there is sufficient cause. One time I was told by the attorneys where to sit, and when the proceeding began, I realized I could not hear the witness and had to interrupt the proceeding to move my seat. Obviously, that is an acceptable reason; however, the situation could have been averted by anticipating the problem beforehand. You must never be too embarrassed to communicate your needs as a reporter, especially if a threat to the accuracy of the transcript is posed.

Upon request, the videographer, who is usually contracted by the court reporting agency that sent you, will give you a courtesy copy of the audiocassette at the end of the proceeding. One reason this is helpful is that in nonvideo proceedings, you may automatically edit, or clean up, attorneys in their questioning by deleting false starts of five words or less and questions beginning with the words *and, but, so, now, well, by the way,* and *by any chance;* yet, when your transcript must correspond exactly to the video, every utterance must remain on the record. In a nonvideo proceeding, you might also interrupt a witness who nods his or her head or answers with an *Mm-hmm* or *Uh-huh* to verbalize his or her answer; but in a video proceeding, it is up to the attorney to recognize and remedy the situation, and you should just record whatever is said.

Although most agencies that I have worked for have requested the cleaning up of the attorneys, some agencies do not wish you to do this. Again, this is a matter of agency preference.

## TELEPHONIC PROCEEDINGS

Sometimes a reporter will record a proceeding where one or more people attend via telephone. This is called a telephonic proceeding. Even if the agency tells the reporter that the assignment will be a telephonic proceeding, the reporter must indicate it on the work sheet.

Although the position of the National Notary Association is that a notary cannot swear/affirm a witness who is not physically present, some states permit it. Prior to graduating from court reporting school, reporters should inquire of their court reporting school and the state's court reporting association as to practice in their state.

If an attorney is appearing telephonically, list the attorney's name, *(Via Telephone),* and then the attorney's address and telephone number on the work sheet. On the appearance page in the transcript, you would list the attorney's information followed by a line that reads *(Via Telephone),* or whatever wording the agency prefers.

If the witness is appearing telephonically, list on your work sheet the classification of the witness, for example, *Plaintiff,* the witness's name, *(Via Telephone),* and then the witness's address. The title page will read *TELEPHONIC DEPOSITION of,* followed by the witness's name. The sworn/affirmed parenthetical in the transcript will contain the witness's name, *via telephone, was duly sworn/affirmed* (if applicable), followed by the rest of the information that usually appears in the parentheticals.

Trying to identify multiple voices on a telephone is a painstaking process. Therefore, before the proceeding begins, it is important to request that each speaker state his or her name prior to speaking. Also, ask ahead of time for the witness to pause before answering questions so that any objections or colloquy will be heard. If the witness is present before you and an attorney or several attorneys, state up front that no gestures should be made to the witness before you, since the attorney(s) appearing telephonically would not be able to see them, and they may unduly influence the witness's response. Ask everyone to remain on the line at the end of the proceeding for spellings, billing, delivery information, and so on.

If a speaker starts to say something and gets cut off, write *(Telephone interruption.)* in your steno notes, communicate the problem, and request a repeat. When the proceeding concludes, remember to ask attorneys who have not examined the witness if they are ordering a copy, as well as if the witness is to receive the original transcript directly for reading and signing. Be sure to note all information on your work sheet.

## INTERROGATORIES

Interrogatories are another method of taking a deposition. Instead of an attorney calling a witness to physically appear to give testimony under oath, the witness is furnished the examination questions in a legal document known as an **interrogatory/interrogatories.** The witness then reads the questions and provides answers to the questions in a legal document entitled *Answers to Interrogatories,* which is usually prepared by the witness's attorney's office. The witness would proofread this document, make any corrections, and sign it before a notary public. However, in some states, a court reporter's services may be utilized to:

- Read the interrogatory questions to the witness and record his or her answers instead of, for example, preparing a Braille interrogatory for a blind witness
- Solely record the Answers to Interrogatories given by a witness; this is most common with pro se witnesses
- Read interrogatory questions to a witness, record the witness's answers, and record cross-questioning by opposing counsel present, the transcript of which will appear in legal document known as *Cross-Interrogatories* prepared either by the court reporter or the attorney's office
- Record cross-interrogatories only

The recording of interrogatories by court reporters is infrequent. The attorney who wishes to examine a witness through interrogatories in conjunction with a court reporter will be the party to bill.

In some localities, the reporter may be responsible for the entire interrogatory procedure and, therefore, must obtain a commission and a subpoena. This legalizes the reporter's appearance, properly informs the witness and opposing counsel of the proceeding, and enables the reporter to obtain additional documentation needed by the parties to proceed with the case. Commissions would be obtained by filling out a form provided by the clerk at the courthouse where the case is venued, which must then be approved by the Court. A notice is subsequently prepared and sent to opposing counsel, followed by the witness's

**Interrogatory/ interrogatories:** A question or number of questions set forth in a written document that are required to be answered under oath. Depending on the circumstances, the services of a court reporter may be used in lieu of an attorney's presence to read the questions to the witness and record the answers.

subpoena. State and federal cases have different guidelines for preparing notices. A freelance agency, your state association, or the clerk of the court may provide guidelines or samples for assistance in preparing and serving these documents.

The subpoena must be served by either the reporter or the local sheriff or constable within that state's mandatory time frame prior to the date of the proceeding. The reporter would pay for any expenses incurred in the serving of documents and would later be reimbursed by the party initiating the interrogatory procedure. After service of the subpoena is confirmed, the proceeding will take place. The reporter will bring the written interrogatories to the proceeding in addition to the usual work tools.

The reporter swears/affirms the witness as in a deposition. There would be no stipulations, since attorneys are not generally present. After writing *DIRECT INTERROGATORY NO.* and the number of the interrogatory, the reporter then reads the number of the interrogatory and the interrogatory to the witness. The Answer bank is then stroked, followed by the witness's response. If cross-interrogatories are taken, *CROSS-WRITTEN INTERROGATORIES* is written into the record, and each question is preceded by *Cross-Interrogatory No.* and the number of the cross-interrogatory, and is followed by the Answer bank and the witness's response. Whether *Direct Interrogatory No.* and *Cross-Interrogatory No.* appear entirely uppercase or initial capped in the transcript, and whether the witness's answer is preceded by *ANSWER* or *A* in the transcript, are matters of local practice or agency preference. Parentheticals may be added if integral to the witness's responses, such as *(Witness peruses document.)* The witness should be asked if he or she will be signing or waiving the signing of the interrogatories. The reporter may be requested to copy documents and return them with the interrogatories, and should double-check that everything is in his or her possession prior to leaving the proceeding.

The beginning and ending times of the proceeding are noted on the reporter's work sheet, but are not generally reflected on the interrogatories. The venue may appear at the top of the title page or to the right of the caption; local practice dictates. An index is necessary only if both direct and cross-interrogatories were recorded; it lists the page that each begins on. At the end of the interrogatories, the reporter prepares a signature line for the witness (if required) and a certificate page that the reporter signs. If required, the reporter would obtain the witness's signature and then file the original written interrogatories with the clerk of the court where the case is venued. If these are sent by mail, send a cover letter detailing what is being sent, referencing information regarding the caption, index or civil action number, and witness deposed, and use a reliable delivery service with tracking capabilities. If delivering them personally to the opposing sides, the reporter should have their offices sign something evidencing receipt of the document.

## DEFAULT STATEMENTS

**Opposing counsel:** Any attorney representing an adversary (opponent) in an action.

Sometimes you get to a job and it does not take place because an attorney or a witness does not show up and the **opposing counsel** wants to put a default statement on the record to let the Court know that the opposing party has defaulted in its obligation to appear. This is a very brief comment by an attorney stating the date and time, how the nonpresent party had been previously notified of what was to take place, where and when, and that they failed to appear.

There is a grace period of time given before you go on the record to write a default statement. It is usually about 45 minutes, but it can be shorter or longer, at the attorney's discretion. The reporter should attempt to get as much work sheet information as possible and should write *DEFAULT STATEMENT* in large, bold letters on the work sheet. Prior to going on the record, get the spelling of the name of the witness that was supposed to appear, since it will probably be mentioned on the record. While waiting for a party to appear, if you are notified that he or she may not show up, you can apprise agencies of the situation so that you may be able to procure a second job that day.

Default statements usually involve one attorney placing a statement on the record. The attorney's statement is recorded in colloquy. Before going on the record, you should synchronize your watch with the attorney's so your beginning and ending times correspond. Even though the attorney may state the time on the record, you are responsible to note the statement's beginning and ending time as well. Reporters should not consent to falsifying the statement's recording time in order to leave early; the missing party must be granted a reasonable grace period within which to arrive.

After you finish writing, you may leave. If you are not told, you should inquire as to who pays for the default statement, as it is often charged to the party who did not appear. See Figure 7–3 for a sample default statement title page.

The agency may have the words *DEFAULT STATEMENT* or simply *STATEMENT* on the title page. The agency may use the wording *Scheduled Deposition of,* followed by the witness's name in the paragraph on the title page; this is a matter of agency preference. The appearance page will usually reflect the appearance information of the attorney present and, if known, the information of the nonpresent attorneys, followed or preceded by a line that reads: *(Not Present)* or *NOT PRESENT.* Some agencies may prefer to list only the present attorney. Check with your agency.

There will be no stipulation page. There will be no jurat or acknowledgment page. There will be no need for an index unless the attorney present asks you to mark exhibits during the default statement. A special certification page will be added to the end of the transcript. Ask the agency for a copy of the certification it uses.

You may bill the agency for a bust fee after delivery of the default statement transcript, since the few pages written will probably result in a lesser amount than the bust fee/minimum/per diem.

## STATEMENTS

Statements may be put on the record when a proceeding does not take place for reasons other than a default on the part of one of the parties. Sometimes you will go to your assignment and learn that the deposition clerk (person in a law firm in charge of scheduling depositions) ordered you for the wrong date or some such scenario, and the attorney may wish to put a brief statement on the record to explain what has occurred.

**FIGURE 7–3**
Sample Default Statement Title Page

SUPREME COURT OF THE STATE OF NEW YORK
COUNTY OF WESTCHESTER
---------------------------
JANE SMITS,

Index No.
Plaintiff, 12345/98

–against–

EMERY SMITS and CARLOS VIEJO,

Defendants.

---------------------------

DEFAULT STATEMENT, held at
the law offices of JACKSON & O'SHAUGHNESSY, P.C., on
December 1, 1999, commencing at 10:46 A.M.,
before Dana Chipkin, a Registered Professional
Reporter and Notary Public within and for the
State of New York.

REINIG REPORTING, INC.
192 Lexington Avenue
New York, New York 10016
(212) 684-7298

The reporter should attempt to get as much information as possible to enter on the work sheet. In large print and uppercase letters, *STATEMENT* should be written. The attorney who is present should be listed, as well as the attorney(s) who are not present, with the notation *(Not Present)* or *NOT PRESENT,* if their information is known and that is the agency's preference.

The reporter should note the time the statement begins and ends. The statement will be written in colloquy. After recording the statement, you are free to leave. The party that made the statement usually pays for the statement.

The title page of the transcript will say *STATEMENT* or *STATEMENT FOR THE RECORD* on it; again, this is a matter of agency preference. The appearance page will usually reflect the appearance information of the attorney

**FIGURE 7–3**
(continued)

APPEARANCES:

JACKSON & O'SHAUGHNESSY, P.C.
Attorneys for Plaintiff
101 Burnside Place
Albany, New York 12345

BY: MARTIN I. VITALE, ESQ.

REINIG REPORTING, INC. (212) 684-7298

present and, if known, the information of the nonpresent attorney(s), followed or preceded by a line that reads: *(Not Present)* or *NOT PRESENT.* Some agencies may prefer to list only the present attorney. Check with the agency.

There will be no stipulation page. There will be no jurat or acknowledgment page. There will be no need for an index unless the attorney present asks you to mark exhibits during the statement. A special certification page will be added to the end of the transcript. Ask the agency for a copy of the certification they use. After you have turned in the transcript of the statement, you may bill the agency for a bust fee/minimum/per diem.

In addition to the type of statement that an attorney places on the record when a proceeding does not take place, reporters may be hired by other entities,

**FIGURE 7–3**
(continued)

MR. VITALE: It is now 10:46 a.m. The Defendant Emery Smits was noticed to be at the offices of Jackson & O'Shaughnessy, 101 Burnside Place, Albany, New York 12345, on December 1, 1999 at 10 a.m. for the taking of a deposition.

A subpoena was served upon him on October 4, 1999 and he has failed to appear.

I have also not received any of the requested documents from the Defendant Emery Smits. The Defendant Emery Smits, therefore, is in default of the subpoena.

(Time noted: 10:48 a.m.)

REINIG REPORTING, INC. (212) 684-7298

such as adjusting companies, insurance companies, and police departments to record statements. These may take place at their offices or you may be asked to accompany the interviewer to another location. If you have a moment before the statement begins, ask:

- For details about the case
- For the spelling of the location of the incident/accident
- If the interviewer would like you to swear the witness in
- When you should begin writing, since a casual dialog might ensue before questioning

**FIGURE 7–3**
(continued)

STATE OF NEW YORK )
) ss.:
COUNTY OF NEW YORK )

I, DANA CHIPKIN, a Registered Professional Reporter and Notary Public within and for the State of New York, do hereby certify:

THAT the record contained herein is a true record of the proceedings.

I further certify that I am not related to any of the parties to this action by blood or marriage and that I am in no way interested in the outcome of this matter.

IN WITNESS WHEREOF, I have hereunto set my hand this 1st day of December, 1999.

_____________
DANA CHIPKIN

REINIG REPORTING, INC. (212) 684-7298

See Figure 7–4 for a sample statement title page.

## STIPULATIONS

Sometimes you will arrive at your job and the parties will settle the case. They can do this without putting anything on the record, or they may put the stipulations of the settlement on the record. In the latter scenario, the word *stipulations* is used in a different context than it is when referring to the stipulations that a proceeding is pursuant to.

**FIGURE 7–4**
Sample Statement Title Page

SUPREME COURT OF THE STATE OF NEW YORK
COUNTY OF SUFFOLK
- - - - - - - - - - - - - - - - - - - - - - - - - - - -
MEDEA SALAMONE,

Plaintiff, Index No. 879/99

–against–

THOMAS RAILROAD STATION,

Defendant.
- - - - - - - - - - - - - - - - - - - - - - - - - - - -

<u>STATEMENT FOR THE RECORD,</u>

held at the law offices of CANDY CROWLEY, ESQ. on 33 Danielle Drive, Effingham, Illinois 62401, commencing at 10:00 A.M., on August 24, 1995, before Dana Chipkin, a Registered Professional Reporter and Notary Public within and for the State of New York.

REINIG REPORTING, INC.
192 Lexington Avenue
New York, New York 10016
(212) 684-7298

Stipulations in settlement of a case are written completely in colloquy. The transcript is treated similarly to a statement. There will just be a title page, a noted beginning time, the recorded stipulations, followed by the time that the reporter finished writing, and a (short) certification page. If any exhibits are marked, there will be an index page as well.

## HEARINGS AND ARBITRATIONS

A hearing or an arbitration is a proceeding in which the parties have agreed to submit their case to a third party—an administrative law judge, hearing officer, arbitrator or panel of arbitrators—to decide their case in lieu of taking it to

**FIGURE 7–4**
(continued)

APPEARANCES:

CANDY CROWLEY, ESQ.
Attorney for Plaintiff
33 Danielle Drive
Effingham, Illinois 62401

NOT PRESENT
MUCCI, DEVAUL, MOLINA, GOLBE & BURKE, ESQS.
Attorneys for Defendant
One Hollow Tree Boulevard
Holmes, New York 12531

REINING REPORTING, INC. (212) 684-7298

court. These proceedings are often held in multiday sessions but are not always held on consecutive days. Since hearings and arbitrations are a little more complex than depositions, these proceedings are generally assigned to experienced reporters.

The caption may read something like *In The Matter of ABC CO., Claimant, vs. XYZ CO., Respondent,* and the parties may be referred to as *claimant* and *respondent* rather than *plaintiff* and *defendant.* This information will appear on the title page of the transcript. In the appearance section of the work sheet and on the title page of the transcript, *BEFORE* is written, followed by a colon and then the name of the hearing officer/arbitrator(s), a comma, and corresponding title.

**FIGURE 7–4**
(continued)

MS. CROWLEY: It is now 10 a.m. on August 24, 1995. The defendant was scheduled to be deposed in the case of Salamone vs. Thomas Railroad Station at 9 a.m. this morning.

On August 17, 1995, defendant's counsel and I arranged for defendant's deposition to be taken this morning.

Last Friday, August 21, 1995, I had my secretary call defendant's counsel's office to confirm today's deposition and was told that it was in defense counsel's diary for this date and time.

As of today, August 24, 1999, I have not received any indication from the defendant or its counsel that they would not appear. We have waited an hour and no one has appeared.

We will make a motion to the Court for defendant to pay for the court reporter's appearance.

Thank you.

(Time noted: 10:02 a.m.)

REINIG REPORTING, INC. (212) 684-7298

When listing attorney appearances, you will write on your work sheet: *For The Claimant* or *For The Plaintiff,* and then list the attorney information, followed by *For The Respondent* or *For The Defendant* and the corresponding attorney information. Whether or not *For The Claimant/Plaintiff/Respondent/Defendant* is underlined is a matter of agency preference. You will then list anyone else present under *ALSO PRESENT.* If anyone listed under *ALSO PRESENT* turns out to be a witness during that day's proceedings, remove his or her name from *ALSO PRESENT* and list that person on your work sheet where spaces are provided for witness information. There are no stipulations involved in these proceedings.

**FIGURE 7–4**
(continued)

STATE OF NEW YORK )
) ss.:
COUNTY OF NEW YORK )

I, DANA CHIPKIN, a Registered Professional Reporter and Notary Public within and for the State of New York, do hereby certify:

THAT the record contained herein is a true record of the proceedings.

I further certify that I am not related to any of the parties to this action by blood or marriage and that I am in no way interested in the outcome of this matter.

IN WITNESS WHEREOF, I have hereunto set my hand this 25th day of August, 1995.

\-------------
DANA CHIPKIN

REINIG REPORTING, INC. (212) 684-7298

All parties are designated before the proceeding takes place. Judges/arbitrators/hearing officers generally open the proceeding, so be prepared for some colloquy. Then there may be what is referred to as housekeeping on the record. This is where the parties have a discussion with one another regarding details about the case.

The elements of an arbitration/hearing differ from that of a deposition. The order of the proceeding is:

- Opening statements
- Direct examination

- Cross-examination
- Redirect examination
- Recross-examination
- Further redirect examination
- Further recross-examination
- Rebuttal
- Surrebuttal
- Final arguments/closing statements
- A statement by the arbitrator/hearing officer

Not every arbitration or hearing contains each of these elements, but that is the general order of business. If you are reporting the continuation of a proceeding, the record may just begin with a statement by the judge/hearing officer/arbitrator and a continuation of the stage in the proceeding where the parties left off.

Opening statements begin with a statement by the party that brought the action speaking in colloquy, followed by the party/parties responding to the action, also in colloquy. They serve to describe what the dispute is about, what each side's position is, and what the parties will be attempting to prove during the proceeding. The header on these transcript pages is *PROCEEDINGS*.

Following opening statements is direct examination. There will usually be colloquy by the arbitrator/hearing officer to the effect that direct examination is to begin. Direct examination is where the attorney for each party calls witnesses to examine on behalf of his or her client. At this point, you should write in your notes *DIRECT EXAMINATION BY* and the name of the attorney examining, and then write in the Q&A format. A judge/arbitrator/hearing officer, rather than the reporter, may swear in the witness. If that is the case, be sure to reflect that in your steno notes. You may write *SWORN/SWORN BY ARBITRATOR;* you need not write the swearing of the witness verbatim. The sworn/affirmed parenthetical is placed immediately preceding the testimony of each witness rather than at the beginning of the record as seen in deposition transcripts. The names of witnesses are not listed on the title or appearance pages, nor do jurats/acknowledgment pages appear at the end of the transcript requiring individual witnesses' signatures. The index page will include which witnesses were examined and the page number(s) their examination(s) began/continued on. Do not start a new page for each witness; simply start a new line for the sworn/affirmed parenthetical. Change the header below it to reflect direct examination of the new witness; for example, *DIRECT EXAMINATION – SMOLEN* or *JOHN SMOLEN – DIRECT EXAMINATION,* depending on agency preference. Then place *DIRECT EXAMINATION BY* and the attorney's name starting on a new line (or two new lines if your agency prefers to use two). Name and address are not included as the first two questions unless the examining attorney or judge/hearing officer/arbitrator specifically asks for them to be on the record.

When opposing counsel examines this same witness, it is called cross-examination. Again, there is usually an indication in colloquy before cross-examination begins. You should write *CROSS-EXAMINATION BY* in your notes, the name of the attorney examining, a colon, and then proceed to write in the Q&A format. When the transcript is prepared, the page header should be changed to *CROSS-EXAMINATION,* a hyphen, and the last name of the witness. When the witness is excused, you may write the parenthetical *(Witness excused.),* or a similarly worded parenthetical.

Redirect examination may then take place. This occurs when the attorney who originally examined the witness has some follow-up questions after cross-examination. The judge/arbitrator/hearing officer will ask the attorney in colloquy if the attorney has any redirect. If so, you should write into your notes *REDIRECT EXAMINATION BY* and the attorney's name followed by a colon. The Q&A will begin on the next line.

Similarly, recross-examination may follow if opposing counsel then has follow-up questions. The judge/arbitrator/hearing officer will ask the attorney if he or she has any recross before recross begins. You should write in your notes *RECROSS-EXAMINATION BY,* the attorney's name, a colon, then the Q&A.

When preparing the transcript, the transcript header should be amended to reflect *REDIRECT EXAMINATION* or *RECROSS-EXAMINATION.* Further redirect and further recross-examination may follow. On the record, many reporters find it too fast-paced and confusing to classify the examination and just write in their notes *EXAMINATION BY* and the attorney's name. They will then classify the examination as direct, cross, redirect, recross, further redirect, further recross, rebuttal, or surrebuttal when preparing the transcript.

Oftentimes, the judge/arbitrator/hearing officer will mark the exhibits, not the reporter. You will still make your notation in the record of the marking. It is important to note whether the exhibit is marked for identification or in evidence. It may be submitted for identification first (unless marked for ID prior to the proceeding), then later accepted into evidence if there is no objection by opposing counsel. However, exhibits in hearings or arbitrations are generally marked in evidence only. A dialog in colloquy between the person in charge and attorneys should indicate whether the exhibit will be marked for identification or in evidence, as well as offer a description of the exhibit. If you are unsure as to the description, the judge/arbitrator/hearing officer will be keeping a running list of exhibit information. On a break, you can go over any questions you have regarding the exhibits.

If exhibits are marked for identification at depositions prior to the proceeding and now are received in evidence, the transcript parenthetical will reflect something like:

(Claimant's Exhibit 7, lease dated March 1, 1998, received in evidence, as of this date.)

If exhibits are both marked for identification and received in evidence in the same proceeding, you would not add a description of the exhibit to the received-in-evidence parenthetical, but would just indicate:

(Claimant's Exhibit 7, received in evidence, as of this date.)

During the hearing or arbitration, parties may object to a question. If an objection is valid and the person in charge agrees that the question should be rephrased, then the judge/hearing officer/arbitrator will say, *Sustained,* and an answer to the question will not be permitted. If the objection is not valid, the judge/hearing officer/arbitrator will say, *Overruled,* and an answer to the question will be permitted.

If an attorney makes an objection by saying, *Motion to strike,* it will either be granted or denied. The attorney who made the motion to strike or an objection may take exception to the ruling, noting it for use in a possible appeal of the decision. This pertains to hearings, as arbitrations are not usually appealable.

Note all break times and the times that the lunch recess began and ended. There may be a lunch parenthetical such as:

(Luncheon recess taken from 12:10 p.m. to 1:30 p.m.)

This parenthetical would be followed by:

AFTERNOON SESSION
(Time noted: ____p.m.)

Then the witness's name is inserted all in caps, followed by *resumed and testified as follows,* whether or not it is direct or cross-examination or a continuation of either direct or cross-examination, and the name of the examining attorney.

At the conclusion of the plaintiff's/claimant's case, the plaintiff/claimant will say it rests its case, and then defense counsel will have a chance to present evidence and call witnesses. When defense counsel examines his or her witness, it is called *direct examination.* When the plaintiff/claimant examines the defense's witness, it is called *cross-examination.* The same procedure described earlier may be repeated.

*Rebuttal* involves the plaintiff/claimant calling additional witnesses to testify as a means of disputing the defense's evidence/testimony. *Surrebuttal* follows, offering the defense an opportunity to question these additional witnesses. On the freelance level, proceedings rarely include rebuttal and surrrebuttal.

When both sides have rested (concluded testimony and exhibit marking), each party is asked if it would like to make a *final argument* or *closing statement.* Counsel for the defendant/respondent traditionally goes first in turn, followed by counsel for the plaintiff/claimant. This will be written in colloquy. The attorneys may speak very rapidly, but it is not recommended that the reporter interrupt the attorney during a final argument/closing statement. Rather, if you have difficulty, ask for clarification at a later time or for a copy of the attorney's statement, if obtainable.

The judge/arbitrator/hearing officer will usually make a brief statement on the record as to when the parties can expect a decision, as it is not common for a decision to be rendered on the spot.

The judge/arbitrator/hearing officer generally reviews the testimony and evidence presented and may or may not need to consult the transcript in his or her decision-making process. The judge/arbitrator/hearing officer will then make a statement that the proceeding has concluded or say, "We're off the record." The reporter will note the time and proceed to obtain billing information from the party that ordered the reporter. Unlike depositions, the original transcript does not go to witnesses to sign but, rather, to the judge/arbitrator /hearing officer.

When preparing the transcript, the judge/arbitrator/hearing officer is referred to in colloquy as *THE JUDGE, THE ARBITRATOR,* or *THE HEARING OFFICER.* If there is a panel, each person will be referred to in colloquy by the title and then his or her name; for example, *ARBITRATOR SMITH, ADMINISTRATIVE LAW JUDGE JONES.* There are no stipulation pages or jurats for hearings and arbitrations, and there is a shorter type of certificate page used. Since motions, directions, and rulings are generally dealt with on the record, you do not need to list them in the index; just index what stages of the proceeding took place that day and their corresponding page numbers. Reflect in the index the witness(es) who were examined and whether it was direct, cross, and so on; the attorney who did the examining; and the corresponding page numbers. List the exhibits, a brief description, whether they were marked for identification (ID) or in evidence (in evid.), and the corresponding page numbers. Consult your agency for its preference as to whether line numbers should be included as well. See Figure 7–5 for a sample arbitration transcript.

## REPORTING CONVENTIONS, SEMINARS, AND CONFERENCES

Conventions, seminars, and conferences are held to exchange viewpoints on one or more subject matters. The number of people present on the podium and in the audience may be intimidating to a new reporter. Therefore, these jobs are generally offered to seasoned reporters.

Find out in advance what costs are covered by the association hiring you, such as flight/travel expenses, hotel expenses, meal expenses, photocopy costs, and costs associated with returning documents to people. Also find out billing and delivery information in advance, if possible. Ask if there are any confidentiality guidelines. Obtain permission regarding tape-recording the proceeding for backup purposes, if necessary. Inquire as to whether or not the transcript or a portion thereof is saleable to the public.

If the location warrants travel arrangements, plan to travel the day/evening before the proceeding begins to reduce the stress of a late arrival. Have with you at all times your equipment and a suitable outfit in case your luggage is lost or delayed.

If checking into a hotel, identify yourself as the court reporter for the proceeding, and ask the front desk to locate your contact person so that you can get information about the proceeding in advance. Check in for the function, and let key personnel know your room number and where to reach you at all times. If there are going to be exhibits utilized during the proceeding or vendor display areas, familiarizing yourself with things such as technological words and brand and model names will be beneficial.

If the proceeding is local, plan to arrive about an hour before it is scheduled to begin. During this time, you should find your contact person, provided you were given the name of someone to speak to, and ask for an agenda, a list of names of scheduled speakers, and any printed material on the subject matter. Familiarize yourself in advance with the room where everything will take place.

If the proceeding is going to be videotaped, arrange to meet the videographer in advance of the proceeding to go over details. The reporter may opt to use earphones in conjunction with a mixer to facilitate hearing the proceeding. Be sure to get the videographer's information, and ask if you can get a courtesy copy of the audiotape when the proceeding is over.

Befriend the contact person or someone else whom you might be able to ask for a word list. If you cannot find such as assistant, make notes to yourself with your **StenoMark** or **NoteMarker** and ask for spellings or clarifications during the next available break.

**StenoMark or NoteMarker:** A buttonlike device found on a steno writer utilized by reporters to mark or flag spots within their steno notes.

Set up in a location where you can clearly see the nameplates of all speakers on the podium or dais, which usually will be in front of each panel member. If audience participation is expected, sitting to the right of the speaker setup gives

**FIGURE 7–5**
Sample Arbitration Transcript

AMERICAN ARBITRATION ASSOCIATION

------------------------------------------------x

IN THE MATTER OF,

MARY MARX and TREVOR MARX,

Claimants,

–against–

THE ABC INSURANCE CO.,

Respondent.

------------------------------------------------x

9000 Old Country Road
Mineola, New York 11501

March 7, 1989
10:05 a.m.

BEFORE:

MICHAEL MICHEL, ESQ.

EVAN TORTURRO, ESQ.

RONALD STEIN, ESQ.

Arbitrators.

REINIG REPORTING, INC.
192 Lexington Avenue
New York, New York 10016
(212) 684-7298

the reporter a view of the panelists as well as speakers from the audience. Do not let your contact person dictate where you should sit if your view or ability to hear is obstructed. Prepare a seating chart, and have a notepad ready to jot down notes to yourself.

If no confidentiality guidelines exist, find out where the closest copy machine is and who you can ask to assist you to make copies. If a document is read from or referred to, on a break, ask the speaker for a copy or for the document itself so that you may copy it. Double-check the page quoted from or referenced. Ask for a business card, as well as the person's room number, to ensure a prompt return of the document. If no business card is available, have a piece of scrap paper handy to obtain this information. Try to have someone copy the

**FIGURE 7–5**
(continued)

APPEARANCES:

LAW OFFICES OF RICHARD ENGEL, P.C.
Attorneys for Claimants
11 Poplar Street
Dix Hills, New York 11746
BY: RICHARD ENGEL, ESQ.

GOLDEN & GOLDEN, ESQS.
Attorneys for Respondent
Two World Trade Center - Suite 15000
New York, New York 10048
BY: BARRY WATERMAN, ESQ.

ALSO PRESENT:

MARY MARX

TREVOR MARX

DANA CHIPKIN, R.P.R., Stenographer

REINIG REPORTING, INC. (212) 684-7298

document for you during a break. If the proceeding is over, ask if you can mail the document back to the person. Photocopy it and return the original as soon as possible. Use a reliable mail service that offers tracking capabilities. If asked to insert copies of exhibits or a portion of a document into the record, make sure you know specifically the task at hand.

Note the time that the proceeding begins, breaks, and ends each day. A convention may begin with an invocation, which is a request for support regarding the given subject matter. This may go on for quite a while, so be prepared for some literary-type writing. Ask your contact person or a chairperson in advance if audience speakers need to be identified by name. If they do and they fail to identify themselves, you may request that they state their names.

**FIGURE 7–5**
(continued)

PROCEEDINGS

ARBITRATOR MICHEL: We will go on the record here now and – –

(Discussion is held off the record.)

ARBITRATOR MICHEL: On the record.

This is the matter of Mary and Trevor Marx against the ABC Insurance Company.

We have three arbitrators here who have filed their oaths with the American Arbitration Association.

We are ready to take testimony and receive evidence on this matter here before us.

We intend to go with liability today and medical as far as the claimants are concerned, and tomorrow we will go with the medical witnesses that are going to be examined.

At this particular point, I have received quite a bit of information from the parties.

Is there anything new to be

REINIG REPORTING, INC. (212) 684-7298

There may or may not be a panel of speakers on the podium at one time. It is much easier to report if there is only one speaker on stage at a time. However, sometimes there are multiple panel members who are asked questions randomly by audience members. The reporter, who has a predetermined designation for each speaker and who has a separate designation for Audience Voice or Unidentified Audience Voice, designates speakers in a colloquy format. The audience speaker may give his or her name before asking a question or making a comment, but it is often difficult for the reporter to hear the name clearly or to spell it. If a speaker says something or states his or her name and you cannot make it out, you may have to place a *(Name inaudible:)* or *(Inaudible:)* parenthetical in the record.

PROCEEDINGS

submitted at this time or has
everything been exchanged in the way of
documentary evidence?

MR. WATERMAN: We've submitted
everything.

MR. ENGEL: I believe we have
everything we need.

ARBITRATOR MICHEL: Do you wish
to do opening statements?

MR. ENGEL: No, sir.

MR. WATERMAN: No, sir.

ARBITRATOR MICHEL: Then let's
proceed with your first witness,
Mr. Engel.

Please raise your right hand.

BERNICE SOKOL, having been duly
sworn, was examined and testified under
oath as follows:

DIRECT EXAMINATION BY MR. ENGEL:

Q Good morning, Ms. Sokol.

A Good morning.

Q Please state your home address
for the record.

A RFD 3, Pawling, New York 12564.

REINIG REPORTING, INC. (212) 684-7298

**FIGURE 7–5** (continued)

Many reporters designate audience speakers as *Voice #1, Voice #2, Voice #3,* and so on. Use of the number bar may come in handy to designate either podium speakers or unidentified audience speakers. If you are going to use the number bar for podium speakers, verify that the numbering system you have set up corresponds to the correct speaker, as speaker order may vary from the preprinted agenda. Make notations on your seating chart or program. Descriptions by physical appearance may prove superior in a multipanel scenario.

Although agency preference determines the title page format, usually the name of the event and its location are centered on the title page. Below that are the date and the time of the conference. The appearance page should reflect the

**FIGURE 7–5**
(continued)

March 7, 1989

INDEX

WITNESSES

| WITNESSES | DIRECT | CROSS | REDIRECT | RECROSS |
|---|---|---|---|---|
| BERNICE SOKOL | 4 | 56 | 62 | 64 |
| MARY MARX | 66 | 117 | 133 | 137 |
| TREVOR MARX | 140 | 158 | 176 | 178 |

oOo

EXHIBITS

| CLAIMANTS' | | FOR IDENT. | IN EVID. |
|---|---|---|---|
| 1 | Insurance policy | | 8 |
| 2 | 1994 tax return | | 10 |
| 3 | X ray film | | 12 |
| 4 | Diagram | 13 | 14 |
| 5A-5E | Photographs | | 68 |

DOCUMENTS AND/OR INFORMATION REQUESTED

PAGE / LINE
123/4
239/22

oOo

REINIG REPORTING, INC. (212) 684-7298

names of all the people on the dais in alphabetical order and their corresponding titles or affiliations. An index should be included to reflect the elements of the proceeding and corresponding page numbers.

The transcript is prepared in a colloquy format with a header of:

- *PROCEEDINGS* or *PANEL DISCUSSIONS*
- The name of the person giving the speech
- The printed agenda heading for that segment

It contains no footer. Ask the contact person for his or her preference.

**FIGURE 7–5**
(continued)

STATE OF NEW YORK )
) ss.:
COUNTY OF NEW YORK )

I, DANA CHIPKIN, a Registered Professional Reporter and Notary Public within and for the State of New York, do hereby certify:

THAT the record contained herein is a true record of the proceedings.

I further certify that I am not related to any of the parties to this action by blood or marriage and that I am in no way interested in the outcome of this matter.

IN WITNESS WHEREOF, I have hereunto set my hand this 17th day of March, 1989.

\-------------
DANA CHIPKIN

REINIG REPORTING, INC. (212) 684-7298

## ROUNDTABLE DISCUSSIONS

Roundtable discussions generally involve a sharing of ideas on a certain subject matter that a group of people want memorialized in a transcript-type format. You would set up in a location where you can see everyone. I would suggest that you get some placards, write your speaker designations on them, and place them before each person present. Everything is written in colloquy. Although you can attempt to lay down some ground rules before going on the record, these types of proceedings are often very unorganized, and speakers jump in and interrupt frequently. It is practically impossible for the reporter to know who will speak next, so you must keep your eyes and ears open at all times. Agencies usually send their most experienced reporters to report roundtable discussions, as these reporters have experience with writing colloquy and communicating when difficulties arise.

## MISCELLANEOUS

Sometimes you are requested to report unusual types of proceedings. An agency I once worked for was hired by Warner Bros. to record a meeting to brainstorm the scenes for the screenplay of the film *Contact.* Present to plot out the film scene by scene were the author of the book *Contact,* Carl Sagan, the screenplay writer, and the producer and director. It took place in the very elegant penthouse of the Carlyle Hotel in New York City. When I saw the film years later, in some small way I felt I had contributed to its success.

The exciting thing about freelancing is that from day to day, you do not know what you will be walking into or the kinds of information that you will be privy to.

## SHORT-ANSWER QUESTIONS

1. A __-_ hearing is an initial inquiry of a party bringing an action prior to the deposition stage of litigation.
2. An __________ ______ _____, or ___, is an examination taken by an insurance company regarding a questionable claim by one of its insureds.
3. In a municipal hearing, a _______ brings the action, and a _________ responds to the action.
4. In a deposition caption, the party who brings the action is called the ________, and the party who responds to the action is called the ________.
5. When a plaintiff sues a defendant and the defendant then brings a claim against the plaintiff in the same action, the claim is called a ___________.
6. If a defendant in an action asserts a claim against a codefendant in the same action, this claim is called a _____ _____.
7. A _____ - _____ _________ action is created when a defendant in an action brings a subsequent action against a party not named in the first caption.
8. The majority of cases encountered by freelance court reporters are __________.
9. Interpreters are expected to translate witnesses' responses in the _____ person.
10. ___ ___ are depositions wherein medical-related parties to an action or expert medical witnesses give testimony under oath.
11. Rather than taking the deposition of a witness, an attorney may furnish the deposition questions in written _____________.
12. A _______ _________ is taken when the present party wishes to put something on the record for the Court stating that the opposing side has failed to appear.
13. When a witness provides responses to written interrogatories in writing, the document created is called _______ __ _____________.
14. _____ ___ are depositions of witnesses who are attorneys.

15. ________ reporting is the recording of proceedings involving navigation, commerce, or other occurrences on the sea.
16. _________ cases involve debtors and petitioners and testimony that includes a lot of numerical figures.
17. A ______ is the person in debt, and a ________ or _________ is the person who petitions the Court for judgments against the person in debt.
18. In estate-related cases, the party bringing the action is referred to as the _________, and the party responding is called the _________.
19. A ________ is taken when a party wishes to explain why a proceeding is not taking place for reasons other than a default on the part of one of the other parties.
20. A ________ may also refer to the recording of information at adjusting companies, insurance companies, and police departments.
21. Parties may settle their case off the record and simply ask the reporter to place the __________ of settlement on the record.
22. A ______ or __________ is a proceeding where the parties have agreed to submit their case to a third party in lieu of bringing the case to trial.
23. At the beginning of a hearing, the parties usually make _______ ________ to describe what the dispute is about, what each side's position is, and what they will be attempting to prove during the proceeding.
24. When a party examines a witness who is called on behalf of that party's client in a hearing/arbitration, the examination is known as a _____ __________.
25. When opposing counsel subsequently examines a witness called, the examination is referred to as _____ - __________.

## TRUE/FALSE QUESTIONS

1. A deposition is held after the court trial on an action has concluded.
2. Multiple captions are usually delineated as *Action No. 1, Action No. 2,* and so on.
3. When reporting an action with a counterclaim, attorneys for parties in the counterclaim should be listed under *ALSO PRESENT* on the appearance page.
4. A cross claim is a separate action with a separate caption from the initial action.
5. Interpreters are sworn/affirmed after the witness.
6. The parenthetical used for the swearing/affirming of an interpreter indicates to the reader of the transcript that all questions were posed to the witness in the witness's native language and that all answers given by the witness were translated from his or her native language into English on his or her behalf.
7. Reporters do not need speaker designations for interpreters or videographers.
8. Every utterance should remain in the record of a videotaped proceeding.
9. Reporters cannot administer oaths to witnesses via telephone in any state.
10. Reporters can expect medical records to be read or quoted from during depositions of doctors/nurses named in captions of med mal cases.
11. Reporters are discouraged from asking celebrity witnesses for their full name and address at depositions.
12. Parties in municipal hearings are referred to as *plaintiffs* and *defendants.*
13. Parties in EUOs are referred to as *claimants* and *respondents.*

14. A court reporter's services may be utilized to read interrogatory questions to a blind witness.
15. Pro se witnesses may hire a court reporter to prepare Answers to Interrogatories.
16. In localities where the reporter is responsible for the entire interrogatory procedure, obtaining a commission and subpoena are unnecessary.
17. In localities where the reporter is responsible for the entire interrogatory procedure, the reporter initially absorbs all expenses related to an interrogatory procedure but is eventually reimbursed.
18. The reporter should ask the witness if he or she will be signing or waiving the signing of the Answers to Interrogatories.
19. The average grace period for a party to appear at a proceeding is 45 minutes.
20. Statements/default statements are recorded in colloquy.
21. There are no stips, jurats, or acknowledgment pages in default statement transcripts.
22. The party making a statement is usually the party billed for it.
23. Reporters bill by the page for statements/default statements.
24. Hearings/arbitrations may have a panel of people deciding the case as opposed to just one person.
25. There are no stipulation pages in hearing/arbitration transcripts.
26. Reporters usually swear in witnesses at hearings/arbitrations.
27. The sworn/affirmed parenthetical in a hearing/arbitration is placed immediately prior to the witness's testimony rather than at the beginning of the transcript.
28. Headers read *PROCEEDINGS* all throughout hearing/arbitration transcripts.
29. Exhibits are always marked in evidence at a hearing/arbitration.
30. Hearing/arbitration indexes list the page that each stage of the hearing and/or each witness's examination begins on.

## DISCUSSION QUESTIONS

1. What can be done if an interpreter continually translates in the third person?
2. What should you do if a witness sworn to testify through an interpreter testifies partially in his or her native language and partially in English?
3. What would you do if you could not hear something said during a videotaped deposition?
4. How can reporters prepare for med mal reporting?
5. How can reporters best prepare for reporting a bankruptcy case?
6. What should you not do when reporting a case involving a celebrity witness?
7. Under what circumstances might a reporter's services be utilized for a witness's response to written interrogatories?
8. What steps are taken when advised that a default statement will be placed on the record?
9. What are the elements of a hearing/arbitration?
10. How do hearing/arbitration transcripts differ from deposition transcripts?

CHAPTER

8

# Before the Deposition

## BEGINNER ANXIETY

When you begin to accept your first few assignments, you may experience a lot of anxiety even if you have sat in with a reporter a number of times. Now it is time to prove yourself with the freelance agency with which you have interviewed. The reporter you sat in with is no longer beside you to answer questions. The attorneys are relying upon you for a verbatim transcript. You are trying to appear confident and relaxed, but you have so much to think about! Just remember that all reporters were walking in your shoes at one time or another and felt the very same way you do.

When I first started reporting, I had stomachaches before each job for two months straight. I had to carry a bottle of Pepto-Bismol in my work bag. I would arrive to the job all nervous, take a deep breath, introduce myself to the receptionist, then ask where the ladies' room was. By the time the questioning began, I was fine. I kept telling myself to see it out. After those two months, the fear and anxiety subsided.

There were some steps I took to ease the transition from student to reporter, which I would like to share with you.

## PRACTICE

The first thing that you want to do is practice regularly your first few months out in the field. Warm up the night before a job and also for a few minutes on the morning of a job so that your mind and fingers are working. On Sunday nights, this is especially important because Monday morning to a new reporter is like taking one's first job all over again. This applies even to experienced reporters who take a long hiatus from reporting. Liken yourself to a concert pianist. Do you think the pianist would go back on tour after a two-month break and not practice before a performance? Practicing to a dictation tape at a high speed, such as 225 or 240, will get you ready for action. Do not concern yourself with what you are dropping. This is merely an exercise for your brain and hands. You may also want to listen to a high-speed dictation cassette en route to your assignment to get yourself into the reporting mindset.

## EAT A GOOD BREAKFAST

On the day of a job, you should eat a good breakfast because you do not always know that you will get a lunch break or, if you do, at what time it will be. If your job is scheduled to begin, say, at 11:30 or 12:00, you should eat a late breakfast or mid-morning snack, because oftentimes you will not be getting a lunch break. It is always a good idea to pack a snack and/or lunch in case you end up working late in the day with no lunch break. Then at least you can eat something on a five- or ten-minute break or have something to eat when you finish the job rather than having to go search for a place to buy lunch.

## BE PREPARED

Successful reporters form habits such as having court reporting machines charged immediately upon returning from a job so that they do not go to a proceeding the next day and suddenly realize that they have an uncharged machine. After each job, you should check that you have an adequate supply of:

- Work sheets
- Business cards
- Steno paper
- Disks
- Notepaper
- Exhibit labels

Upon accepting a job from an agency at call-in time, you can begin to fill out your work sheet by filling in:

- Your name
- The interoffice job number, if applicable
- The date of the job
- The location of the job

At this point, it is also a good practice to date your notepad so that when your job begins the next day and you are asked to mark exhibits, you do not forget the date and end up looking unprofessional. Another helpful step in preparing for the job in advance is to call the office where the assignment will take place for directions. Some reporters feel that the most stressful part of the job is finding the job location.

## ARRIVE EARLY

Be early to the job. Arriving 15 to 20 minutes before the deposition is recommended in order to:

- Obtain a caption or a Bill of Particulars—the Bill of Particulars will give details about the case and pertinent names and terms that will probably be mentioned on the job
- Set up
- Go the bathroom—who knows when your next opportunity will be
- Get a cup of coffee

- Schmooze with the attorney who ordered you and find out what the case is about, if he or she is in a talkative mood
- Obtain a word list, if possible, so that you can preglobal words that would not be found within your personal dictionary
- Check that your equipment is functioning properly and that you have adequate work supplies

## GREETING THE RECEPTIONIST

When you enter the office where the deposition is to take place, greet the receptionist warmly. You should say something like, "Hi. I'm the court reporter for the Smith vs. Jones case at ten o'clock." If you know which attorney from the firm is handling the deposition, ask for the attorney by name. You will probably be told to have a seat, and then the receptionist will contact the attorney who is handling the deposition.

## OBTAINING CAPTION INFORMATION

You may ask the receptionist if it is possible to get a caption or Bill of Particulars. The Bill of Particulars is much more detailed than just a caption. It generally provides:

- The date of the accident or loss
- Dates of hospitalization
- The location of the accident or loss
- Other addresses that might be mentioned
- Names of hospitals and health-care providers
- A description of the medical/surgical subject of the litigation, if applicable

You will be more apt to write medical words accurately if you have seen them in advance and written them down on your notepad.

If you do not obtain a copy of the caption or Bill of Particulars from the receptionist, another attorney on the case may show up from whom you may be able to get it while you are waiting to set up. To save time later, you may also ask for business cards and file numbers of attorneys who arrive on the same case.

## PREGLOBALLING

Also from the caption you are handed, you can decide upon the globalling system that you are going to use on the job. Modern steno machines have the capability of globalling words to create a dictionary specifically for an individual job. If you see from the caption that the plaintiff's name, for instance, has four syllables, you can take the first syllable of the name and **J (job) global** it, if you have time, into your machine by writing it twice and defining it as the plaintiff's name. Then it will appear on your LCD screen correctly for readbacks so that you do not have to struggle to read through the steno or write it out completely throughout the job.

**J (job) global:** To define outlines from steno to English for definitions utilized for a specific job that will not be programmed into the reporter's main (personal) dictionary.

Do not use job globals to represent more than two or three words; many times, attorneys will only use the first couple of words and not the whole phrase, and the globals might throw you off. Also, do not use globalling excessively unless you have a good memory and can think quickly in a readback situation. If you are using a machine with an LCD screen to read back from and you have pregloballed most of your words, then this should not be a problem; but if your machine does not have this capability, then when asked to read back, you could fumble while trying to remember what your arbitrary, or J global, represented. This is why it is important to always write down on your notepad, during a pause or break, what your global refers to and to keep the notepad within eye's view.

If you have time before the examination begins, steno into your notes a brief intro of the case. Identify attorney designations. Write in a summarized name of the case and the date of the proceeding. Write *EXAMINATION OF,* followed by the witness's name, *TAKEN BY,* and the examining attorney's name. If there is not enough time to do this, it is of no consequence, as you will be writing this information physically in pen on your steno notes at the end of the deposition, and you will have previously written the information on your work sheet.

## SETTING UP

Ask the receptionist if you can set up early. Sometimes an attorney will be prepping, or preparing, his client in the conference room and will not want you to set up in advance of the deposition. If that is communicated to you, you should politely say something like, "No problem," and wait until you are told to enter the conference room.

When you are permitted to enter the room, note where the closest outlet is in case you need to use it. Be sure to sit in a practical place. The reporter usually sits at the end of the conference table, catty-corner to the witness on one side and the examining attorney on the other. If the attorneys have a preference for where you should sit and it enables you to see and hear well, set up as directed. If the location is not conducive to performing your functions, speak up and suggest a better location, but do so in a courteous manner. Place on the table before you:

- Your business cards
- One or two spare packs of paper (unless you know you are recording a brief statement for the record, you should always start with a fresh pack of paper so that you do not run out of paper minutes after the proceeding begins)
- Your work sheet
- Your notepad
- A pen
- Exhibit stickers—stickers for the party that the examining attorney represents go on top; for example, the plaintiff's attorney will be marking exhibits as Plaintiff's Exhibit _____
- Paper clips, if applicable

- The seating chart, if there are multiple attorneys (you can place this somewhere on your writer or on the conference table in front of you)
- A stapler

If you get a dry throat or have a cold, having a bottle/glass of water and cough drops or throat lozenges in front of you is advisable. But be prepared; you may go into a coughing fit, and the attorneys, if on a roll, will keep on speaking. There is not always time to ask for a break while it is happening, and you may have to continue writing until you cannot write anymore. You may also want to have a small pack of tissues handy, even though you cannot blow your nose and write at the same time. If you know that you are not well the day before, do not accept work for the following day. Do not attempt to experiment with cold medications before a job, even if they purport to be nondrowsy, because they may affect your writing capabilities.

## COURTHOUSE DEPOSITIONS

Things work a little differently with depositions conducted at courthouses. The agency will generally instruct you as to the number of the room or floor where depositions are to be held. Depending upon the courthouse, there may be a clerk with whom you can check in and who can tell you what room your case is assigned to, or you may have to walk up and down a corridor lined with people, shouting out your case name, in an attempt to identify the participants in your deposition. Once you have identified an attorney on your case, attempt to get a caption.

Many courthouses require all parties to be present before assigning a room or table. When everyone appears, due to the shortage of rooms or tables, there may be a waiting period until other depositions have finished before yours can begin. This waiting period may last a long time. Be prepared for a change of location if this occurs. Many freelance agencies rent space in locales near courthouses so that the reporter can suggest moving the location of the deposition there to expedite matters. Attorneys also may suggest changing the location to one of their offices or even to a nearby restaurant or just directly outside of the courthouse, if weather allows. Be flexible. If you report at a courthouse, anticipate a less-than-perfect hearing environment. Some courthouses have one large deposition room where all of the depositions are taken, and people come in and shout out the name of their case while you are taking testimony. Others have private rooms.

When you are finished with your deposition, tell the clerk on your way out that your room/table is free for the next group.

## AS THE PARTIES ARRIVE

As the parties enter the room, they will seat themselves. They may then introduce themselves. If a caption has not been given to the reporter by this time, the reporter should identify the attorney who ordered the reporter and request one. Then the reporter should begin to copy the information onto the work sheet and obtain from the attorneys:

- The name of the law firms they represent
- The address of the law firms
- Representation information (whether that attorney/law firm is the Attorney for Plaintiff, Attorney for Defendant, and so on)
- The attorneys' names
- File or claim numbers—plaintiffs' attorneys generally do no use inter-office file numbers but, rather, locate actions by the plaintiffs' names

The reporter should inquire of the examining attorney whether a law firm or solo practitioner who is not in attendance should be listed as *(Not Present)* or *NOT PRESENT.* The reporter asks the witness for his or her full name and address and enters this information onto the work sheet. Then the reporter obtains the names of others in the room and lists them under *ALSO PRESENT.*

## RESISTANCE FROM ATTORNEYS

Some attorneys respond negatively to being asked a lot of questions, so if you sense any resistance at all, just be polite and let it go, since your agency can assist you later on in finding out any missing pertinent information. However, you must never leave a proceeding without the names of the people present, who they represent, and caption information.

I once worked for an attorney who was so anxious to begin the proceeding, he would not even give me an opportunity to get appearances or to see the caption. It was a multiple-attorney case, and I knew I needed appearances in order to designate everyone and a caption to see the names of the parties in the case, so I stood my ground and told him, "This is what I need to do my job or I can't go forward." He gave in, and I was more relaxed and, in turn, provided him with an excellent transcript.

If you are told that there exists a more updated or consolidated caption, request the more complete version of the caption. Do not settle for a caption reading, for example, *BARBARA BAINES, Plaintiff, vs. DAWN RICH, et al., Defendants.* If the complete caption is not available, you can get it faxed to your office at a later time.

## SPEAKER DESIGNATIONS

Prior to the commencement of the deposition, the reporter gives a speaker designation to each person in the room. When designating the attorneys present, many reporters write *SNAO* for the plaintiff's attorney and *SKWRAO* for the defendant's attorney. If there are more than two attorneys, the other attorneys may be designated *IFPLT, IRBGS,* or by the first syllable of their last name stroked twice. The latter method only works if the first syllable of the attorney's name, when written twice, is not a conflict. For instance, *MARK/MARK* could not be used for Mr. Markowitz, as it would conflict with the universal outline indicating the marking of an exhibit. If more than four attorneys are present, some reporters hit *AO* plus the Question bank for an attorney and *EU* plus the Answer bank for another. You can also use the number bar in conjunction with the Question or Answer bank for additional attorneys.

There are reporters who determine their speaker designations by the location of the attorneys. The drawback to designating this way is that you might find yourself in a position where a break is taken and the attorneys return to depose a new witness and change seats. When colloquy occurs, you may get confused. Therefore, writing the first syllable of the attorney's last name twice is the preferred method in multiple-attorney situations.

If two attorneys present have the same first syllable in their last name, choose the second syllable to be written twice for one attorney's designation. If the first syllable of each attorney's name is, for example, *SIL,* as in Silverstein and Silber, write *BER/BER* for Mr. Silber or *STEIN/STEIN* for Mr. Silverstein. Or you could invert the letters of the first syllable of Silverstein by writing *SLIV/SLIV.* You also could select an outstanding feature and write it twice, such as *BLUE/BLUE* for the attorney wearing the blue suit. Be careful with adjectives like *BALD/BALD* or *RUDE/RUDE* because sometimes attorneys glance at your writer's LCD screen. One time an attorney who was married to a court reporter glanced at my LCD screen to see his designation, saying that he was curious whether he was going to be SNAO'd or SKWRAO'd during the deposition!

## SHORT-ANSWER QUESTIONS

1. It is important to ______________ even after graduating from school.
2. ____________ your notepad in advance of a job will aid you in the exhibit-marking process.
3. A _______ _______ ___________ gives details about the case and pertinent names and terms that will probably be mentioned on the job.
4. ___________ is the process of defining a steno outline with a desired translation in English.
5. ______ ________ defines steno outlines with a desired translation in English for an individual job.
6. If an attorney is __________ his or her client in the conference room, you may not be able to set up early.
7. A law firm representing a party in the caption may be listed as _______ ___________ if they do not attend the deposition.
8. *SNAO, SKWRAO, IFPLT,* and *IRBGS* are examples of _______ ___________.
9. ___________ is the designation generally used by reporters to refer to the plaintiff's attorney.
10. __________ is the designation generally used by reporters to refer to the defendant's attorney.

## TRUE/FALSE QUESTIONS

1. Once you graduate from court reporting school, there is no reason to practice writing steno.
2. It is a good habit to charge your machine after each assignment.
3. You can enter certain information onto your work sheet prior to a job, such as your name, interoffice job number, and the date and location of the job.

4. Calling the office where a job is to be held to obtain directions may facilitate finding a job location.
5. Reporters should always arrive an hour before the proceeding is to begin.
6. Names of health-care providers and medical/surgical terms may be found within a Bill of Particulars.
7. Job globals should be written on your notepad and kept within eye's view during a job.
8. Reporters generally sit at the end of the deposition table, catty-corner to the witness on one side and the examining attorney on the other.
9. If you are given a caption that is not updated to reflect changes that have occurred, it is sufficient for preparing your transcript.
10. A reporter can write the first syllable of an attorney's name twice as a speaker designation if it does not conflict with anything else in the reporter's steno theory.

## DISCUSSION QUESTIONS

1. What work materials should you check daily to make sure you have an adequate supply of?
2. What benefits are there to arriving early to the job location?
3. What are the benefits to a reporter of job globalling?
4. What are the problems that a reporter may face as a result of job globalling?
5. What should you do if you are told to set up in a location where you are having difficulty hearing?
6. What supplies should be on the table before you during a deposition?
7. What information is asked of attorneys by reporters before the deposition begins?
8. What information is asked of witnesses by reporters before the deposition begins?
9. What are the drawbacks of designating attorneys by location?
10. If there were 10 attorneys on a case, how would you designate them?

CHAPTER 9

# Taking the Deposition

## BEGINNER'S CHECKLIST

For my first few assignments, I had a checklist on my notepad to remind me of the order of my responsibilities. The items listed were:

- Stipulations?
- Continuation?
- Pursuant to?
- Note time deposition begins
- Swear/affirm witness
- First two questions
- Note break times
- Note time deposition ends
- Billing information
- Delivery information
- Litigation support

The first seven of these items are discussed in detail in the following text. The last four items are discussed in detail later in the chapter under the main heading "Beginner's Checklist—Continued."

### Stipulations

We have already discussed finding out what stipulations the deposition is pursuant to when filling out the work sheet. It may be pursuant to state/usual stipulations, federal stipulations, no stipulations, or other stipulations. Stipulations should be agreed to by the attorneys prior to going on the record.

If you forget to ask about the stipulations and remember during the deposition, notify the attorneys at a pause or on a break. You may then write a note to yourself in your steno notes so that if you forget to check it off on your work sheet, it will serve as a reminder when preparing the transcript. Even though you may have asked what stipulations the deposition was pursuant to after the deposition began, if there is to be a stipulation page, it will be inserted in the usual place, the page before testimony begins in the transcript, not in the spot where the information was obtained.

It is an embarrassment when you have forgotten to ask about stips and midway during the deposition one of the attorneys asks, "We're operating under the usual stipulations?" and another attorney answers, "No, I don't believe we agreed to any stipulations." Even though, if you forgot to ask, the attorneys should have remembered to specify the stipulations under which they are operating, it is best to make a note to yourself to ask before the proceeding begins.

There may be no stipulations in a transcript if the proceeding is a continuation of the witness's prior testimony, as a particular agency may contend that the stipulations abided by in the first session of the proceeding pertain throughout all subsequent sessions. This is a matter of agency preference; some agencies will include a stipulation page anyway. Attorneys may neglect to tell you that the job is a continuation or you may forget to ask, and the transcript may be prepared as a first session, inclusive of a stipulation page.

## Continuations

After inquiring about stipulations, you should ask if the deposition is a **continuation**. Your agency may know in advance and tell you about it, but this is not always the case. Sometimes the examining attorney will tell you, but not always. It is a no-brainer if the questioning begins with, "When we left off at your last session . . ."; however, you should confirm it anyway.

If the job is a continuation of a witness's testimony and the witness has been sworn or affirmed in the first session, you can raise your right hand, ask the witness to raise his or her right hand, and say, "Let me remind you that you are still under oath."

For continuing testimony, before testimony begins in the transcript, a parenthetical is placed to the effect of:

> J I M S M I T H, recalled as a witness, having previously been sworn/affirmed by a Notary Public, was reminded of his oath and was examined and testified further as follows:

It is unnecessary to put the witness's name and address in the record as the first two questions on a continuation, as it already exists in the transcript of the first session of the witness's testimony. If you are asked to reswear the witness, the transcript will read something to the effect of:

> J I M S M I T H, called as a witness, having been resworn by a Notary Public, was examined and testified further as follows:

If the proceeding is a continuation, you should ask to see the transcript of the last session. Make sure that it is, indeed, a transcript of the last session and not a transcript of an interim session. Note the ending page number of the last session's transcript. Your transcript will begin with the subsequent page number. If, for instance, the job is continuing from the previous day and the reporter who took that testimony down obviously has not yet completed his or her transcript, then you should communicate to the agency that you will need the starting page number for your transcript when that reporter finishes the transcript. You should also make a note on your work sheet for yourself and/or for your scopist that you will start with a page number other than page 1. If you are

**Continuation/continuance:** When a proceeding is adjourned and resumes on a subsequent day.

unsure about the starting page number at the time of the deposition, put on the work sheet, Start page No. ___. This will remind you to put it in later. If continuing a job, you should also note the last exhibit number from the previous session so that you may continue in succession. If you were asked to retain exhibits from the prior session(s), bring them with you to the continutation, as they may need to be reviewed further.

Bringing the glossary and a copy of the work sheet from the last session will facilitate things, as well as making you look more efficient. If you were the reporter from the previous session, look up the information in your archived jobs. If another reporter was present, ask your office to obtain the last page number and exhibit number. Or, when you get to the job, ask the attorneys if they have a copy of the prior transcript so that you can obtain this information.

If a new witness is to be deposed in a case that you have previously been assigned to, look up the case in your archived files and print out the caption and appearance page. Bring your notepad notes to the job. This will expedite the process of obtaining appearances and you will have an edge as to the terminology and names specific to the case.

As opposed to looking at the final page number of a noncontinuing job and billing an agency for that number of pages, when billing an agency for a continuation, the formula is to subtract the beginning (title) page number from the final page number and add one page. Therefore, if your continuing job started on page 244 and concluded on page 387, you would subtract 244 from 387, which gives you 143 pages, and add a page, thus billing the agency for 144 pages.

### Pursuant To

The next item on the checklist, *Pursuant To,* will remind you to ask whether the job is pursuant to notice, order, stipulation, subpoena, or agreement. You will ask, "Is this pursuant to notice or order?" and be told if it is pursuant to anything else. (See Chapter 5 for more details.)

### Noting Time Deposition Begins

Reporters are responsible for noting the time that a proceeding begins and ends. It is very easy to get sidetracked from noting the beginning time, as things move pretty rapidly after the witness is sworn/affirmed. That is why it is recommended to note the time just before administering an oath.

If you have more than one witness, you must remember to note the time that the testimony of each witness begins and ends.

### Swearing/Affirming Witnesses

At this point, you would write into your steno notes *SWORN/SWORN* if the witness has been sworn or *FAIRMD/FAIRMD* if the witness has been affirmed. This will bring up an include file, which is a generic file previously set up by your scopist or yourself that will place the correct parenthetical into the transcript.

**Swear:** To have a witness raise his or her right hand and vow to tell the truth during the examination. This procedure involves mention of the word *God* as opposed to affirming, which does not.

The difference between swearing and affirming is the mention of the word *God*. When **swearing** in a witness, the reporter says, "Would you raise your right hand, please. Do you solemnly swear to tell the truth, the whole truth, and nothing but the truth, so help you God?" or a variation thereof.

Members of certain religious affiliations prefer to be **affirmed** rather than sworn. A yarmulke or a Muslim name is an indication that a person may wish to affirm rather than be sworn in. If you suspect that this is the case, ask the person, before you begin swearing him or her in, about his or her preference. To affirm someone, simply ask, "Do you affirm to tell the truth, the whole truth, and nothing but the truth under the pains and penalties of perjury?" When affirming rather than swearing in, it is important to change the wording in the jurat/acknowledgment page and certificate page to reflect the affirmation.

If you forget to swear in or affirm someone and remember during the proceeding, you can, at a pause or a break, mention this to the questioning attorney and then say to the witness, "Please raise your right hand. Do you swear/affirm that the testimony previously given and that you are about to give is the truth, the whole truth, and nothing but the truth?" You can also do this at the end of the job by saying, "Do you swear/affirm that the testimony given herein was the truth, the whole truth, and nothing but the truth?" Then write it in your steno notes. You do not want to be responsible for the testimony being contested at a later date by an attorney because the witness was not sworn/affirmed. No matter when the witness is sworn/affirmed at a deposition, it is reflected in a parenthetical in the transcript before the record of the proceeding begins.

One reporter shared with me her embarrassment when, as per her routine, she asked the witness to raise his right hand and then realized that he was a quadriplegic. It is very important to be as observant as possible and alter the rules as needed. A simple, "Let me swear the witness in. Do you swear to tell the truth, the whole truth, and nothing but the truth?" without any mention of the witness raising his right hand could have spared the reporter some discomfort.

***Administering the Oath to an Interpreter*** There is a different process of administering an oath to a witness when an interpreter is present at the deposition. The first thing you do is ask the interpreter to raise his or her right hand, and then you ask, "Do you solemnly swear to translate from English to [language being interpreted] and [language being interpreted] to English to the best of your ability, so help you God?"*SWORN/SWORN/INTERPRETER* is noted in your steno notes. Once the interpreter responds affirmatively, you will say something like, "Please ask the witness to raise his/her right hand." At this point, the interpreter will translate this to the witness, the witness will raise his or her right hand, and you will say, "Do you solemnly swear/affirm to tell the truth, the whole truth, and nothing but the truth?" The interpreter will then translate it to the witness. *SWORN/SWORN/WITNESS* is noted in your steno notes as well.

## First Two Questions

It is standard for the first two questions of the deposition to be as follows (or some variation of these):

Q Please state your name for the record.
A -*.
Q What is your address?
A -*.

**Affirmed:** To have a witness who prefers not to be sworn attest that he or she is telling the truth under pains and penalties of perjury without mention of the word *God*.

Sometimes the attorney will forget to ask these questions and will assume that the reporter placed them into the record automatically, having obtained the witness's information for the work sheet previously. However, some agencies do not feel it is the reporter's responsibility to do so if it is not properly on the record. Therefore, after administering the oath to the witness, the reporter should ask the attorney, "First two questions?" One of three things may then occur:

- The attorney will respond in the affirmative, and the reporter will automatically place it into the record when later preparing the transcript
- The attorney will respond affirmatively but will then ask for the same information on the record, in which case the reporter should keep the record as it is, with whatever the attorney asks the witness, not adding in anything
- The attorney will respond negatively, and the reporter will not insert anything and will only place on the record what the attorney asks the witness in this regard, if he or she chooses to do so

By asking, "First two questions?" the reporter has protected him- or herself when working for an agency that advocates placing name and address into the record automatically against an attorney who refutes having acquiesced to it.

When the reporter turns on his or her machine, he or she may write in *TITLE/TITLE,* which will be programmed to bring up an include file for the title page, appearance page, stipulation page, if applicable, sworn/affirmed parenthetical, *EXAMINATION BY -*:,* the command for the transcript header, which is discussed later, as well as the first two questions (name and address). The reporter then fills in the information furnished by the witness that is written on the reporter's work sheet.

If there is time before you begin, it is best to write the name and address questions and answers completely into your steno notes; but you can always insert these when the transcript is prepared, since you have the information on your work sheet. A quick notation such as *(NAME AND ADDRESS)* will suffice at this time.

When you ask the attorney, "First two questions?" if the attorney answers yes, you can say, "I already have it in the record," or you may ask them of the witness aloud. You would turn to the witness and say, "Please state your name for the record." You will record the question and answer, and then ask, "What is your address?" and record the question and answer. As most reporters find it hard to write and speak simultaneously, it is much easier to say you already have it in the record and then look at the work sheet and read the attorney the witness's name and address. You can insert it into the transcript later.

## Noting Break Times

There are some agencies that want you to note the time that all breaks begin and end. Others may require this information only upon the request of a specific client.

Luncheon recess beginning and ending times should be noted in the record. One agency may choose to have a simple parenthetical such as:

(Luncheon recess taken.)

Another may prefer the parenthetical to read something like:

(Whereupon, a luncheon recess was taken from 12:00 p.m. to 12:45 p.m.)

Some agencies will use a parenthetical noting only the beginning time of the luncheon recess in the transcript followed by:

A F T E R N O O N   S E S S I O N

(Time noted: _____p.m.)

Then the reporter notes the time that the afternoon session began. Agencies may also require an additional parenthetical concerning the resumed session, stating who began the examination after the luncheon recess. For example:

AFTERNOON SESSION

B A R B A R A   J O H A N S E N, resumed the stand and testified further as follows:

EXAMINATION (cont'd) BY MR. PAPPAS:

Check with the agency to see what its preference is regarding this issue. On the job, write whatever parenthetical or **blurb** conveys the information. Subsequent to the job, you can correct it. Remember, you can always delete, but you cannot add something that does not exist into your transcript.

## CHANGE OF EXAMINING ATTORNEY

A change of examining attorney often takes place on the job, and you usually have less than a second to note this in the record. Simply writing *EXAMINATION BY* and the attorney's name or designation will suffice to indicate what has occurred. In a pinch, stroking *EXAMINATION* twice and then the attorney's name or designation will do.

If you fail to put this in the record, you may luck out if the attorney now examining introduces himself or herself on the record by saying something like, "Hi. My name is Tim Brooks, and I represent the defendant in this matter. I'll be asking you some questions about the accident that occurred on June 10, 1994." This will tip you off that there was a change of questioning attorney; however, you should not rely on this happening, since some attorneys just start off with a question and no introduction.

If a change of attorney examining takes place during an attorney's examination and it is a brief exchange, keep the testimony in colloquy. If it goes just beyond a few Q&As, indicate *EXAMINATION BY MR./MS.* -* in the record, and use the Q&A format. Be sure to note if and when the testimony reverts back to the previous attorney examining the witness.

## MARKING EXHIBITS

**Blurb:** A parenthetical conveying information to the reader of a transcript.

Exhibits are items of evidence to be utilized during a court trial. Oftentimes, they are delineated as exhibits in the discovery stage of litigation, which occurs prior to trial, that is, during depositions. Although the usual system regarding the marking of exhibits is that plaintiffs' exhibits are marked numerically and defendants' exhibits are marked alphabetically, sometimes attorneys will have a preference to do just the opposite or will erroneously request the opposite. You have the option to either say, for instance, *"Did you mean Plaintiff's 1 rather than Plaintiff's A?"* or just write it as the attorney requested it. This applies only when you are beginning to mark exhibits. If a defendant's attorney has had his or her exhibits marked as Defendant's Exhibit 1-25, just continue this methodology.

Exhibits are marked for identification during depositions. Hearings/arbitrations may involve both the marking of exhibits for identification and in evidence, but generally exhibits are marked for identification during the depositions preceding a hearing/arbitration, and the exhibits previously marked for identification in those settings are then marked in evidence. The marking process is the same, but instead of writing *FOR ID* on the exhibit sticker, you would write *IN EVID.*

Although official reporters in certain states may be requested by the Court to utilize a specific color for exhibit stickers, freelance reporters may generally choose whatever colors strike their fancy. It is recommended, however, regarding whatever colors you choose, that a separate and distinct color be used for plaintiffs' as opposed to defendants' exhibit stickers or claimants' as opposed to respondents' exhibit stickers.

When marking an exhibit at a deposition, choose the correct exhibit sticker. The plaintiff's attorney's exhibits will be marked Plaintiff's Exhibit 1, 2, 3, and so on, and the defendant's attorney's exhibits will be marked Defendant's Exhibit A, B, C, and so on, unless you are specifically requested to deviate from the standard. When in doubt, ask.

You will keep a running log on your notepad as to the number/letter of the exhibit followed by a brief description of the exhibit. Then you will write the number/letter of the exhibit on the exhibit sticker, followed by the abbreviation *for ID,* meaning for identification, and your initials. Black ink pens are preferred for the marking function. See the sample exhibit stickers in Figure 9–1.

If you have marked Plaintiff's Exhibit 1 through 10 already and then the attorney asks you to mark Plaintiff's 10 and you know that it should be Plaintiff's 11, in a courteous way, you can ask, "Plaintiff's 11?" The attorney should then correct himself on the record. One of your responsibilities is to aid the attorney in making an accurate record, but in doing so, you must be professional in your behavior so as not to embarrass the attorney in any way. By keeping a log on your notepad of exhibits, if the attorney makes a mistake, you will be able to correct it without confusing the record.

If an attorney representing the defendant, for example, asks you to mark an exhibit as Plaintiff's 1 rather than Defendant's A, unless the plaintiff's attorney asked the defendant's attorney to mark the exhibit for him or her, you should

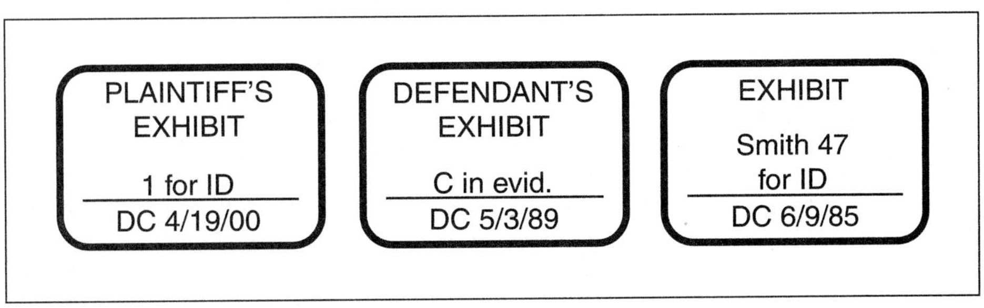


**FIGURE 9–1**
Sample Exhibit Stickers

correct the attorney politely by asking, "Did you mean Defendant's A?" This will give the attorney an opportunity to correct himself or herself. This colloquy between the reporter and the examining attorney need not be on the record, and you may correct the examining attorney's original request to reflect the accurate method of marking the exhibit. In cases where another attorney suggests something be marked, for example, the plaintiff's attorney wants an exhibit marked and the defendant's attorney is examining, the defendant's attorney may choose to mark it as a defendant's exhibit or a plaintiff's exhibit while he or she is examining.

Reporters may be asked during the deposition to mark exhibits. Anything can be marked as an exhibit, not just documents. Other types of items marked may be:

- Photographs—reporters usually put the exhibit sticker or stamp on the back of a photograph
- X-rays—it may be best to find blackened spots on which to place your exhibit stickers or to ask the examining attorney to place the exhibit sticker on these for you
- Forms—reporters find a blank space on the front to put the exhibit sticker or place it on the back
- Cassette tapes, videos, CDs
- Food items
- Fabrics

Exhibits may be kept in a plastic bag or manila envelope. You should note the enclosure that the exhibit is contained within as well as the exhibit item. You may be asked to place the exhibit sticker or stamp on the enclosure.

If you are unclear as to what a particular exhibit is and the examining attorney and witness do not identify it on the record, you should put a question mark next to the exhibit number on your notepad and ask the examining attorney at the next break for a description for your index.

The marking of an exhibit may be reflected in the transcript as:

(Document marked Defendant's A for identification, as of this date.)

Or the transcript may describe the exhibit marked in more detail:

(Contract between ABC Corp. and XYZ Co., dated November 20, 1962, is marked Defendant's A for identification, as of this date.)

Agency preference will dictate.

If multiple exhibits are marked simultaneously, a notation in your record like *MARK/MARK Plaintiff's Exhibits 1 through 3* is sufficient. However, you would note on your notepad a description of each exhibit individually. If all of the exhibits were sheets containing one photograph, for example, you might write on your notepad *Plf's 1-3—sheets containing one photograph,* but if Plaintiff's Exhibit 1 was a sheet containing two photographs rather than only one photograph, you would write *Plf's 1—sheet containing two photographs.* As far as the transcript goes, if two to three exhibits are marked simultaneously, many agencies prefer you to group them together. For example:

(Lease dated January 1, 1988, rider to lease, and letter dated March 22, 1988 are marked Plaintiff's Exhibits 1 through 3, respectively, for identification, as of this date.)

Some agencies may advise you to condense the parenthetical for the marking of two to three exhibits to:

(Documents marked Plaintiff's Exhibits 1 through 3, respectively, for identification, as of this date.)

Then you would just delineate the exhibits individually on the **index** page.

Any more than three exhibits marked simultaneously would be reflected in separate parentheticals. For example:

(Lease dated January 1, 1988 marked Plaintiff's Exhibit 1 for identification, as of this date.)
(Rider to lease marked Plaintiff's Exhibit 2 for identification, as of this date.)
(Letter dated March 22, 1988 marked Plaintiff's Exhibit 3 for identification, as of this date.)
(Letter dated March 23, 1988 marked Plaintiff's Exhibit 4 for identification, as of this date.)

Depending on agency preference, you may be advised to use the blanket parenthetical *(Documents marked Plaintiff's Exhibits 1 through 4 for identification, as of this date.)* and describe each exhibit on the index page.

Sometimes the attorneys request that you deem an exhibit marked for identification. In this case, you should write in steno *DEEM/DEEM Plaintiff's Exhibit 15.* The parenthetical in the transcript will include a description of the exhibit **deemed marked.** For example:

(Lease dated March 1, 1998 deemed marked Plaintiff's Exhibit 7 for identification, as of this date.)

Generally, when deeming that an exhibit be marked for identification, there will be a description of it on the record. Be sure to make a note on your notepad of the exhibit deemed marked and ask the examining attorney at the next break if he or she would like it physically marked at that time. He or she may decline. If instructed to physically mark it, note it in your steno notes.

A variety of scenarios can occur regarding the retaining and/or copying of exhibits marked during a proceeding. Sometimes there are no exhibits marked, and therefore, the reporter has no responsibility regarding this matter. Sometimes there are exhibits marked and the attorney decides to retain them. Sometimes the reporter is asked to have his or her agency temporarily retain the exhibits and bind them at the end of the original transcript, bind original exhibits to the original transcript and attach photocopies of the exhibits to the transcript copies, or bind the exhibits separately. Sometimes the agency is requested to permanently retain the exhibits marked. In some states, the reporter is asked to personally retain the exhibits. If you are asked to maintain or copy the exhibits, double-check that you have all of them before leaving the proceeding. Be sure to maintain them in a protected environment, that is, away from young children, pets, and food/liquids.

If you temporarily require the exhibits for spelling assistance, quotations read, or names mentioned during the proceeding, you may request them of the attorney who asked you to mark them. You can offer to send them back within a day or two—giving you a chance to glean what you need from them or photocopy them—or to mail them back with the transcript. If you sense any resistance, do not pursue the matter, but try to see the document or documents

**Index:** A page in a transcript that indicates the page numbers that each witness's testimony began on, page numbers that each attorney's examination of each witness began/continued on, and information regarding requests, inserts, rulings, and exhibits marked or deemed marked during a proceeding. Indexes sometimes include directions not to answer and motions, depending upon the agency.

**Deem marked:** To identify an exhibit on the record without physically marking it. It has the same effect as if the exhibit had been physically marked and is listed on the index page of the transcript.

needed before you leave the proceeding and either write the information into the record in a note to yourself, jot a spelling down on your notepad, or get a copy at that time.

Students often ask me how reporters can mark exhibits when their hands are supposed to be on their machines reporting. When a reporter is asked to mark an exhibit, all present are supposed to stop speaking so that the reporter may do so. However, there are occasions where the examining attorney forgets to give the reporter time to mark an exhibit or where the witness, unaware of the reporter's specific functions, will begin to speak while the reporter is trying to mark an exhibit. These situations require that the reporter speak up and inform the parties present that he or she is not on the record. Saying something like, "Let me just mark this before we go back on the record," should get the point across. Otherwise, you may indicate in your steno notes that an exhibit is being marked; but if someone starts speaking and you return your hands to your machine and start writing, you may either (a) forget to physically mark the exhibit altogether or (b) mark it at a later point in the record nowhere near the request for that exhibit to be marked.

Another problem occurs regarding the time allotted the reporter to do the actual marking of the exhibit. As reporters are responsible for an index page description of the document in more detail than just *Document marked . . .*, ample time should be taken to jot down a brief description of the exhibit. My recommendation is to first indicate the marking in your steno notes, even if you are being handed the exhibit by the questioning attorney, because things move quickly from that point on. After writing *MARK/MARK* and the classification of the exhibit *(Defendant's Exhibit A, Plaintiffs' Exhibit 54),* take a second to describe the exhibit on your notepad, and then physically mark the exhibit. If you hand the exhibit back to the examining attorney, he or she will often jump into the next question before you have a second to return your hands to your writer. If you hand it to the witness, he or she may begin to answer before you can get back to your writer. Therefore, I like to place the exhibit on the conference table midway between the questioning attorney and the witness so that I am assured the few seconds I need while either party picks up the exhibit before speaking.

## USE OF PARENTHETICALS

Parentheticals, descriptions in transcripts of nonverbal activities that are set in parentheses, assist readers of the transcript in understanding what transpired during the proceeding. There are a number of parentheticals deemed relevant enough to include in a transcript. Some of the standard or common steno outlines for parentheticals are:

> *RECESS/RECESS* or *BREAK/BREAK* when a recess/break is taken, which will bring up the parenthetical *(Recess taken.)* or whatever wording is preferred by an agency. Some agencies require reporters to note the time of each break as well. Reference as to the length of the break should not be noted; beginning and ending times of the break will suffice. Brief pauses are not generally noted (unless specifically requested), as there are many pauses during a proceeding and they only serve to

clutter the record. If a moment is taken by only one person at the proceeding, *(Pause.)* may be warranted. Lengthy pauses are noted as breaks.

*CONFER/CONFER* when the witness and his or her counsel speak privately, which will bring up the parenthetical *(Witness and counsel confer.)* or whatever wording the agency prefers.

*INSERT/INSERT* followed by a line (or several if the information requested is lengthy) when asked to leave a blank space for information to be filled in.

*PERUSE/PERUSE* when the witness is perusing a document for more than a moment or two, which will bring up the parenthetical *(Witness perusing/peruses document.)* or *(Pause while witness peruses document.).*

*NOD/NOD* when someone nods rather than responds verbally, which will bring up the parenthetical *(Nodding.)* or *(Witness nods.)* The reporter may also write in steno the Question/Answer bank or colloquy speaker designation followed by *(Shaking head.).*

*EXCUSE/EXCUSE* when a witness is excused during a hearing or arbitration, which will bring up the parenthetical *(Witness excused.).*

*COMPLY/COMPLY* when the witness is complying to a nonverbal request, which will bring up the parenthetical *(Witness complying.)* or *(Witness complies.).* The witness's compliance may be reflected as an answer:

Q Would you turn your head to the left for us.
A (Witness complying.)

Or it may be reflected as a nonverbal gesture prior to the answer:

Q Would you turn your head to the left for us.
(Witness complies.)
A Do you need me to show you again?

*DOCUMENT/DOCUMENT* when the reporter needs to refer to a document for accuracy regarding a quotation or spelling when preparing the transcript.

*NOTE/NOTE* when making notes to oneself regarding corrections in the record or other matters, which will bring up the parenthetical *(Note to myself:),* once programmed into one's personal dictionary.

Just be sure that your parenthetical outlines do not conflict with outlines utilized on a job.

If a witness responds physically rather than verbally on the record, for example, by crying, and no one describes the action on the record, generally reporters are not expected to reflect that in the record. However, if what follows verbally makes reference to the action, such as the attorney of a crying witness, in colloquy, requesting of the examining attorney to take a break, it may be necessary in some cases to make such a notation. Since reporters cannot know at the time of the action what will follow it, a note on the record may be made and later deleted while scoping/proofreading. If such a notation is integral to what follows, seek agency guidance as to the wording of the parenthetical.

Generally reporters are not expected to reflect actions of attorneys on the record; however, there may be occasions where it is warranted. Say, for example, two attorneys are arguing on the record and the first points at the second and the second responds by saying, "Stop pointing your finger at me." Therein, an indication of the action, such as *MR. SMITH: (Pointing.)* preceding the comment may be required. If you did not witness the actual action, do not add it in when preparing the transcript. You do not want to put yourself in a precarious position if the action was merely an embellishment by one of the parties.

Sounds made during a proceeding are not recorded by reporters. Things such as coughing, an *Excuse me* after a sneeze, a telephone ringing, and so on, need not be noted unless reference is made to the sound on the record following it. If it is anything of import, it is the responsibility of the attorney(s) present to reference it on the record.

Most agencies limit a reporter's use of parentheticals to a select few. It is best to check with the agency as to whether or not a parenthetical is necessary in a given spot and to ask for guidance as to the proper wording of the parenthetical.

## PART-TIME PRESENCE AT PROCEEDING

Indicate in your steno notes when someone enters the deposition after it has begun. Make sure to get the person's appearance at the next break in the proceeding. The agency may want you to indicate the person's appearance on the appearance page of the transcript followed by *(part-time)* or may simply have you indicate the person's appearance on the appearance page as if the person were present throughout the deposition with no parenthetical within the transcript as to the time the person entered the deposition.

Note also when someone leaves the deposition. Similarly, an agency may have you list that person's appearance on the appearance page of the transcript with or without *(part-time),* and with or without a parenthetical as to the person's departure within the transcript.

## NONVERBAL ANSWERS

*KA*IG* may be programmed into your dictionary to bring up the *(Indicating)* or *(The witness indicated.)* parenthetical. This parenthetical is used when a witness makes a gesture during a proceeding and the action is not accompanied by a verbal exchange that reflects that the action is occurring. For example:

Q Did you fall forwards, backwards, on your side?
A (Indicating.)
Then I fell forward.

or

Q Which car in the photograph is yours?
A (Indicating.)

When words accompany the action that indicate that an action is occurring, reporters usually do not add an *(indicating)* or *(The witness indicated.)* parenthetical. Some reporters choose to, but agencies tend to discourage this practice.

The *(Handing)* parenthetical is utilized when:

- Someone is requested or directed to hand something to another person and then does so on the record without speaking
- Something is handed to someone with no verbal reference made on the record that then changes the course of what is said on the record and requires mention

Since documents are handed routinely during the course of legal proceedings, placing *(handing)* within sentences where it is obvious something is being handed over would clutter the record extraneously. When reference is made to the item being passed, it is unnecessary to use the *(handing)* parenthetical. Some examples:

Q I'm handing you Defendants' Exhibit D.

Q I'm showing you what's been marked as Plaintiff's Exhibit 8.

Q Would you take a look at Exhibit 4.

*HA*ND/-G, (H*AG),* or whatever your shorthand theory teaches, is written when an object is handed to someone with no verbal exchange. The Question/Answer bank or the speaker designation is stroked, and then *(HA*ND/-G).* It is reflected in the transcript as:

Q (Handing.)

or

A (Handing.)

or

MR. SMITH: (Handing.)

If an object is handed to someone in conjunction with a verbal exchange, a parenthetical is not usually added. For example:

Q Which invoices fall into that category?
A This is all I have.

Paragraphing may be used in lieu of the *(handing)* parenthetical to reflect something being handed to someone. For example:

Q I show you Exhibit 5.
Is that your signature?

When no verbal exchange takes place, the Question or Answer bank or colloquy speaker designation is stroked, the parenthetical is written, and a period is placed before the closed parenthesis, not after the closed parenthesis, as follows:

A (Indicating.)

or

A (Handing.)

Particular agencies may eliminate the period within a parenthetical. Also, note that the first letter of a standalone parenthetical is uppercase. If a parenthetical such as *(handling)* or *(indicating)* accompanies a verbal exchange, the first letter of the parenthetical is lowercase, and punctuation for the exchange is written at the conclusion of the exchange (after the closed parenthesis). Parentheticals may be deemed unnecessary when an attorney follows up the action with a comment in colloquy, such as:

Q Did you fall to your left, to your right, forward, backward?
A I fell this way.
MR. SMITH: Indicating to his left.

Agencies have different preferences regarding the use and placement of the *(Handing.)* and *(Indicating.)* parentheticals and should be consulted upon preparation of the transcript.

Other requests that result in nonverbal communications occur when witnesses are asked to demonstrate an action or to write something. In those circumstances, parentheticals may be used. For example:

Q Please show us how he swung at you.
A (The witness demonstrated.)

or

Q Would you place a circle around the post in Defendant's A which your car hit.
A (The witness marked Defendant's Exhibit A.)

or

A (The witness complies.)

## DISCUSSIONS OFF THE RECORD

*OFF/OFF* is written to reflect that there was a discussion held off the record. One of the attorneys will say something like "Off the record" to you to indicate that you should stop writing. The attorney's indication will be in colloquy on the record, followed by the parenthetical. Many times, however, nothing is said, and the attorneys will go on to make jokes or comments that should not be on the record. An experienced reporter usually knows when to stop writing, but as a beginner, you should keep writing until told that something was off the record. You can always delete something, but you cannot add it. If you are told that you should not be writing or you are off the record, just make a note to yourself like *(Delete - that was off the record starting with . . .)* and write an indication of what is to be deleted.

When told to go off the record, keep your hands in view of the attorneys so they know you have followed their directive. They get very perturbed if they think you are still writing. Many times they forget to tell you to go back on the record. If you suspect that this is the case, inquire politely, "Is this on the record?"

If a witness requests to go off the record, let the witness know that you only go off the record at the request of the attorneys, and let the attorneys then direct you.

## READBACKS

Before reading back, note that you did so with a readback parenthetical. If you wait until after you have given a **readback,** the attorneys may go back on the record right away, depriving you of the opportunity to write the parenthetical. Common readback parentheticals are:

> *READ/READ* when asked to read back a portion of the record, which may be programmed to bring up the parenthetical *(Record read.)* or *(The record was read back by the reporter.)*
> *KWERD* when asked to read back a question only, which may be programmed to bring up the parenthetical *(Question read.)* or *(The question was read back by the reporter.)*
> *A*ERD* when asked to read back an answer only, which may be programmed to bring up the parenthetical *(Answer read.)* or *(The answer was read back by the reporter.)*
> *KWAERD* when asked to read back both the previous question and answer, which may be programmed to bring up the parenthetical *(Question and answer read.)* or *(The question and answer were read back by the reporter.)*

Outlines may vary from steno theory to steno theory. Parentheticals are subject to agency wording preferences. One agency may prefer a generic *(Record read.)* for all readbacks, while another may want the reporter to specify what was read back.

You can use any steno outline that works for you, such as:

- *READ/READ question* or *answer*
- *READ/READ penultimate question*
- *READ/READ next-to-last question and answer*
- *READ/READ last sentence of the answer*

You should try to be as specific as possible as to what was read back. If various material was read back and you cannot recall specifically what was read, *(Record read.)* may be placed into the record. If various questions were read before a judge for a ruling, your parenthetical might read:

> (The following questions were read as follows:
> "Q What is your Social Security number?
> "Q Who did you speak to at the company about it?
> "Q What did your attorney tell you?")

The words *The following testimony* or *The following answers* would be substituted for *The following questions* depending upon the content of the material read back.

If you are requested to read back the last question, just read back the last question. If the last question is meaningless without the context of the question prior to it, state, "Let me read the prior question also, for the sake of context," and then proceed to do so. Likewise, if you are asked to read back the last answer, read back only the last answer.

**Readback:** Reiteration of the record at a proceeding by a reporter as requested by a judge, a jury, an attorney, or a witness.

When you are asked for the last Q&A, if there is colloquy in between, read back the colloquy as well. A seating chart within eye's view will assist you with your colloquy speaker designations. If the attorneys are not interested in the inclusion of colloquy in a readback, they will tell you so.

When reading back, you should say, *Question,* and then read back the question, *Answer,* and then read back the answer. Your voice should be loud enough for all to hear, your readback should be at a relaxed pace that everyone can follow, and you should read matter-of-factly, without self-imposed inflection. If you read something back incorrectly or in an unconfident manner, you can be sure that the attorneys will ask you for readbacks continuously throughout the job to satisfy themselves that you are getting everything.

Sometimes you will be asked to search far back into the record for something. Modern steno machines are superior in that they have the capability of searching on the computer key words in both steno and English, which saves reporters a lot of time. If you search back and subsequently read a requested question or answer specifically, upon preparation of the transcript, you may want to reflect the actual question or answer in your readback parenthetical. An example:

> (The answer was read as follows:
> "A I've never been to Nevada in my whole life.")

As long as it is not a conflict with anything else in your shorthand theory, any method that you devise for yourself to communicate nonverbal actions is acceptable. Just find out the agency's preference on whether or not it is an essential parenthetical and how the agency chooses to word it in the transcript.

In cases where a nod or gesture is given and there is no verbal response from a witness and the attorneys do not pick up on it, you should say something like, "I need a verbal response for the record." A transcript replete with *(Indicating.)* or *(Witness nodding.)* notations is not going to do the attorneys much good before a judge or jury, and they may not have the foresight to realize it at the time of the deposition. If you do not get a chance to speak up, simply place *(No verbal response.)* in the record. You may mention it to the examining attorney on a break, who may request a reread of the question and then elicit an answer from the witness on the record.

## DIRECTIONS NOT TO ANSWER

During a deposition, the witness may be directed by his or her attorney not to answer the question posed. The instruction is recorded by the reporter in colloquy. Some agency transcripts asterisk directions not to answer for inclusion in the transcript's index page; others do not. If an agency does include it, the asterisk is placed at the left margin next to the attorney's colloquy concerning the direction and may or may not be deleted upon preparation of the index page; this is a matter of agency preference.

## RULINGS

When attorneys are in dispute over an issue and cannot resolve it themselves, they may contact a judge for guidance. The attorneys introduce themselves, then the judge hears each side's story, renders a decision, and directs the attorneys how to proceed. This is called a ruling.

During the course of a proceeding, a ruling may be recorded in person (if the proceeding takes place in a courthouse) or over the telephone before a judge, law clerk, or law secretary. At this point, it is important to write in steno *RULING/ RULING,* which you may preprogram into your dictionary to bring up the ruling parenthetical. You should note the time that the ruling begins and the name of the judge, law clerk, or law secretary. Agencies vary on their wording, but the ruling parenthetical will be similar to

> (At 10:55 a.m., the following ruling took place before Law Secretary Alan Smith:)

If I do not know in advance the name of the person giving the ruling, I simply stroke the full bank (both the Question and Answer bank) as his or her designation—and then get the person's name and title afterward. Rulings are written in a colloquy format. The reporter is responsible for noting the time that the ruling ends.

Rulings usually entail the reporter being asked to read to the judge, law clerk, or law secretary a question or line of questioning that is in dispute, so search the questions out and be prepared to read them. If you are in a courthouse and you are not specifically told to accompany the attorneys before the judge, ask whether they would like you to go for the ruling or stay in the deposition room. Sometimes they will have the reporter read the question(s) verbatim for the ruling. Other times they may just choose to get a ruling on whether or not a type of question or line of questioning may be permitted and do not require the reporter's attendance.

To physically mark where rulings are requested, you can use your StenoMark or NoteMarker, a paper clip, a business card, or a note on your notepad indicating the numbered page of your steno paper (a good reason to purchase numbered steno paper), or you can tear your steno paper slightly or fold your steno paper. Modern electronic stenographic writers have searching devices that allow you to search for the steno outline *RAOULG,* for example, and easily locate the text to be read for the ruling. However, with multiple requests for rulings, it may be quicker to physically mark the locations.

If there is no one available to give a ruling and you are asked to mark something for a ruling, a subsequent colloquy among the attorneys may take place. This may be followed by a request for a readback of the question so that the examining attorney may think of a way to rephrase the question to avoid it being objected to and subsequently ruled upon.

You may be asked later during the day to read all requests for rulings—*Mark it for a ruling*—to a judge or the judge's law clerk or law secretary. If not, you will note the rulings in your index upon preparation of the transcript so that the attorneys may have it ruled upon following receipt of the transcript. Many times attorneys just say, *Mark that,* in which case you should provide the page and line number of the question or comment in dispute under *Rulings* on the index page.

When scoping or proofreading the transcript, the reporter may place an **RL* at the left margin of the question marked for a ruling to flag the page and line number where it appears in the transcript so that they are noted in the index. The **RL* may or may not be subsequently deleted from the transcript; this is a matter of agency preference.

## MOTIONS

A motion is an application to a judge for specific relief. The most common form of motion encountered by reporters on depositions is a *motion to strike.* This is an attempt by an attorney in colloquy to have testimony physically stricken from the record by the Court at a later time.

Frequently heard motions are: *move to strike that portion of the answer that is not responsive to the question, move to strike as nonresponsive,* or simply *move to strike.* When preparing a transcript, motions may or may not be included in the index, and *MO* may or may not be placed at the left margin of the colloquy of the attorney making the motion; this is a matter of agency preference.

Attorneys may move to strike a reference to an insurance company because if the case should go to trial, juries may be more sympathetic to witnesses who have no insurance coverage regarding damages, thus creating juror impartiality.

## REQUESTS FOR DOCUMENTS OR OTHER INFORMATION

Attorneys may make requests on the record for documents and other items that were not provided at the time of the deposition. If the request is directed at an attorney, the request is written in colloquy. If the request is directed at the witness, it may be in a Q&A format, depending upon agency preference. The reporter simply writes the request into the record during the deposition. When scoping and/or proofreading the transcript, the reporter should flag the requests by placing an **RQ* or **REQ* at the left margin of the request so that the request itself and the page number are placed into the index. The **RQ* or **REQ* may or may not be subsequently deleted from the transcript; this is a matter of agency preference.

## INSERTS

Blank lines are placed into the record for information to be inserted into the transcript at a later date by the witness (or his or her attorney). A single line is placed into the transcript for information that can fit into one line. Several lines are placed for responses requiring more than one line. Some agencies put the word *INSERT* with a colon before the (first) line, while others simply place a solid line without the word *INSERT.* An asterisk or the word *INSERT* calls attention to the fact that the insert's page number should be listed in the index with a brief description of the information to be inserted. The asterisk may or may not be deleted from the transcript after this is done; this is a matter of agency preference.

## BREAKS

Reporters may request a five-minute break every hour or hour and a half during depositions to use a rest room, shake out their hands, or grab a snack or a drink. Try to request a break when there is a pause in the proceeding. Do not interrupt a steady flow in a line of questioning. It is always best to ask specifically for a rest room break, as they are rarely denied to a reporter. An attorney may try to finish a line of questioning before the break is taken, so try not to ask to go to the rest room when you are at your breaking point; try to ask a few moments before. If the attorney forgets about your request, wait for another pause in the questioning and remind the attorney.

During breaks, the reporter should always check the paper tray. It is better to throw out a quarter inch of steno paper than to go back on the record after a break and run out of paper minutes later. At the conclusion of the break, notify the examining attorney if there was a pending question prior to the break. Be prepared to read it back at the attorney's request.

Lunch breaks are usually given on all-day jobs, but when they are taken and if they are taken are determined by the attorneys present. Many times everyone in the room will order lunch and expect you to keep writing while they eat. Not only is it difficult to hear while people are chewing, slurping, opening and closing bags, and popping cans open, but it is not fair to the reporter, who also needs to eat. You must be assertive and say that you need a break as well. You may want to phrase the request by telling the attorneys that you have not yet mastered the art of reporting and eating simultaneously. That is generally good for a chuckle and reminds them that you are a person, not a machine.

On jobs that are not all-day jobs, many attorneys feel that if they skip taking a lunch break, everyone can get out of the deposition sooner. Although this practice is good in theory, oftentimes their promise that "It should only be another hour" is broken, and "another hour" turns into two or three hours.

Requesting a lunch break when everyone else wants to continue without one is a precarious situation. You may have to "feel out" the attorneys and weigh your impressions against your ability to keep writing without a lunch break. You do not want to appear as obstructive to the continuation of the deposition, but at the same time, you are entitled to a lunch break. It is in these situations that my earlier recommendation of bringing lunch or a snack with you comes into play. You can always say, "I'm sorry, but I just need five or ten minutes to eat something before I can continue"; they will not deny you that, because no one wants a court reporter who cannot concentrate. In most cases, they will respond by calling a lunch break. Sometimes you will feel like the bad guy when you request a lunch break, but lunch is important to your health and concentration. Many witnesses and attorneys present have approached me after my request for a lunch break and thanked me because they, too, felt like they were starving or needed a break.

You may want to speak to the examining attorney privately about any health problems or conditions you have that require you to eat at certain times. However, it is better to mention such things before the deposition begins.

Again, if you sense opposition to the idea of a break or if it is only a matter of a short while to conclude the deposition, be professional and agree to continue writing.

Prior to call-in time, let the attorney know when you will need to call your office for your next day's assignment. Do not let the attorney deter you, as that could mean the difference between work and no work the following day.

## BEGINNER'S CHECKLIST—CONTINUED

### Noting Time Deposition Ends

Getting back to the beginner's checklist, upon the conclusion of the deposition, the reporter is responsible for noting the time that it ends. The reporter does this by writing *Time noted:* and the time in parentheses.

If the attorneys choose to go back on the record after you note the ending time of the deposition, you can simply continue writing, note the time the deposition finally concludes, and delete the first *Time noted:* parenthetical from the transcript when scoping/proofreading. If you have closed out the file in which you were writing the deposition and the attorneys decide to go back on the record, open a new file and continue writing. Be sure to note on your notepad and your work sheet that the job is on two files so that you do not see the first *Time noted:* and forget about the second file.

### Billing Information

After the deposition concludes and before the attorneys leave, the reporter is responsible for obtaining information regarding whom to bill for the transcripts. The examining attorney generally pays for the original transcript (the transcript that the witness must sign and have notarized) and his or her copy of the transcript. You must confirm with other attorneys present if they are ordering copies of the transcript. Some agencies may ask you to have the attorneys who are not the agency's client sign a transcript order form or initial on your work sheet that they are ordering a copy of the transcript.

You should make a notation on your work sheet as to which attorneys are to be billed for copies of the transcript. Reporters often use **O+1** to refer to the original transcript and one copy, O+2 for original plus two copies, and so on. The abbreviation *1cc* is used to refer to a copy of the transcript.

In the state of New York, an examining attorney operating under state, or usual, stipulations pursuant to the Civil Practice Laws and Rules is required to provide a copy of the transcript to a party witness's attorney at the examining attorney's expense. Therefore, an O+2 is standard billing when two attorneys are present.

### Delivery Information

The reporter is responsible for obtaining delivery information for the transcripts. This includes ascertaining whether the examining attorney is to receive:

- The original transcript and his or her copy
- The original transcript and multiple copies of the transcript for himself or herself and other attorneys ordering copies, whom he or she will then mail the additional copies to
- Simply a copy, with the original sent directly to the witness

**O+1:** The original transcript and one copy. (O+2 indicates the original plus two copies, and so on.)

In cases where an attorney is appearing as esquire of counsel, he or she will probably request that you deliver the transcript(s) to the law firm that he or she is representing rather than to his or her own address. Do not assume, however; confirm the address.

The original transcript may be delivered directly to a witness:

- When the witness is appearing pro se—without legal representation—or is a nonparty witness
- For expediency of the execution (signing) of the trancript by a witness
- In states where that is the practice

Certain states require the witness to sign the original transcript before the reporter who took the deposition, while other states permit the witness to sign the original transcript before any notary public. Ask your court reporting school instructors, your state association, or reporters/agencies/online reporting forums about practice in your state. The executed (signed) transcript is then returned to the freelance agency, which will file it with the appropriate court.

The reporter also has to ascertain when the transcript is to be delivered: regular delivery, expedited delivery, or daily delivery. If you are on a job that requires immediate delivery and you are performing realtime, you know this up front. Many jobs require expedited or daily delivery, and the reporter knows this up front as well. Other situations, however, can determine the need for expediency, such as:

- The discovery of unexpected information that aids in the litigation process
- The need to meet some sort of Court deadline
- The preference to have the transcript before another deposition is held in the case
- The need to have certain issues ruled upon by the Court

If an expedited transcript is requested, ask in how many days it is needed or what specific date it is needed by and agree to it. Then notify the agency immediately so that scoping arrangements may be made, if necessary, and the agency can note that the transcript must be out of the office and in the attorney's hands by that date.

Many times the reporter is told that the transcript can be regular delivery and then an attorney calls the agency at a later time to request the transcript sooner. Be forewarned.

### Litigation Support

While obtaining billing and delivery information, reporters should inquire of attorneys as to their needs for **litigation support,** such as ASCII disks, condensed transcripts, e-mailed transcripts, and so on. These items are discussed in further detail in Chapter 13.

**Litigation support:** Tools that assist attorneys in litigation, such as ASCII disks, that enable attorneys to search information on their laptop computers that was given at previous depositions for use during an examination without having to physically carry multiple transcripts to the examination.

## THE FINAL FRONTIER

After noting the ending time of the proceeding and obtaining billing and delivery information, there are still some things that the reporter needs to do.

## Clearing Job Globals

If you have programmed job globals into your writer for use on the job, at the conclusion of the proceeding, you should delete them. If you forget, you may go to your next assignment, begin writing, use the same outlines, and have the previous assignment's globals come up. Each writer has a different method of removing job globals. Refer to your writer's instruction manual for details.

If the job is continuing the following day and you will be returning, obviously you should keep the job globals in your writer so that you do not have to take the time to reglobal them.

## Continuation Information

Sometimes after a brief discussion of continuation dates, which may be on or off the record, you will record the continuation information in colloquy at the end of the proceeding. If the attorneys cannot agree on a continuation date, your agency's client will call the agency at a later date with the information.

If the attorneys do not choose to place the continuation information on the record, ask the attorneys for the continuation date, where the proceeding will be taking place, and the time it will begin. Record this information in a noticeable place on your work sheet and call it in to your office as well.

***Reporter/Agency Allegiances*** It may be that your agency's client was the examining attorney on this job but that at the next session, another attorney will begin the questioning. This other attorney may choose to order a reporter from an agency that his or her firm uses. Although most attorneys prefer to keep the same reporter while deposing a single witness, since the reporter is already familiar with the names and terms unique to the case, many law firms have allegiances to certain court reporting agencies and will hire their own reporter.

If your agency's client will be continuing to examine the witness, writing the continuation information on your work sheet and calling it in to the agency will increase the chances that you will be the reporter sent for the continuation.

***Requested Reporters*** One of the best indications to a freelance agency that a reporter is good at the job is requests by its clients for an individual reporter. Even more indicative of a reporter's proficiency is when the other side requests the same reporter and the agency obtains a new client. That is why handing out your business card is so important.

There are usually three components to being a reporter who is frequently requested. They are:

- A pleasant personality
- Compliance with the attorneys' requests on a job
- Delivery of a good transcript

Requests for a reporter lead to gaining favor in the eyes of the principal and agency personnel. Strive to be requested!

## Entitling Your Steno Notes

After the deposition, you should write on the cover page of your steno notes in pen:

- The name of the agency you are working for
- The agency's internal job number, if applicable
- A brief summary of the caption name
- The date the proceeding was reported
- The name of the witness being examined
- Whether or not the job was a continuation

If there was more than one witness and the witnesses' testimony was not to be booked together (as is sometimes done with husband-wife testimony/parent-child testimony), you should tear the steno paper between witnesses so that a separate set of notes is created for the subsequent witness. You also should number each set of steno notes chronologically whether there are multiple witnesses or simply multiple packs of paper utilized for a single witness.

### Wrapping Up Your Notes

The next thing the reporter does is wrap the steno notes up in his or her work sheet notes and notepad notes, together with the seating chart or attorney-designation information, photocopies of material quoted from or marked as an exhibit, and any business cards obtained. A rubber band is then placed around the notes to keep all of the information together.

If you have been requested to maintain the exhibits or have them copied, place the exhibits in a flat, protected environment free of pen marks, correction fluid leaks, and so on.

## STORAGE OF NOTES

After photocopying the work sheet and sending the original to the freelance agency or keeping the original and faxing a copy to the freelance agency, the reporter wraps the photocopied work sheet with his or her notes. Then they write the date of the job with a dark marker on the tip of their steno notes and stand the notes in an upright manner with the date of the job visible. This storage method helps to expedite steno note retrieval. Many reporters utilize the boxes that the cases of steno paper are delivered in to store their steno notes. As each box is filled, they write on the box the beginning and ending dates of jobs contained within it, and place it in a waterproof location. (See Figure 9–2.)

## RESPONSIBILITY TO MAINTAIN NOTES

As far as filing is concerned, you are legally responsible for maintaining the actual steno notes or an ASCII disk for each job for a period of five years, although some reporters play it safe and hold onto them for seven years. The required time frame may vary from state to state, so check with your state association as to practice in your state.

Many agencies will also archive your jobs as a backup. However, disks may get displaced in an office, so you should keep backup copies of jobs on disks in a fireproof box as well. The backup disks should be labeled to indicate job date (including the year), the agency that the job was for, the interoffice job number, if applicable, and the last name of the witness(es). Organize them chronologically

**FIGURE 9–2**
Note Storage

so that if you are searching for a job taken on October 12, 1998, for instance, once you get to the disks that contain October/November 1998 jobs, you will only have a few disks to search through.

Since reporters are permitted to maintain disks of finished jobs in lieu of the actual steno notes, you may wish to place your dog sheet, yellow-pad notes, and any other paperwork from a job into a looseleaf notebook in chronological order. A three-hole punch may be purchased at a local stationery/office supply store. For those with limited storage space, this may be an alternative to the traditional method of storing jobs.

## SHORT-ANSWER QUESTIONS

1. A ___________ occurs when a witness's testimony was not completed in a previous examination and the witness returns for further examination.
2. The difference between _______ and _______ is the mention of the word *God.*
3. If present, an __________ must be sworn in prior to administering the oath to the witness.
4. The _____ ___ ________ refers to asking the witness's name and address.
5. Writing _____/_____ will bring up your title page, appearance page, stipulation page, if applicable, sworn/affirmed parenthetical, *EXAMINATION BY* -*:, the command for the transcript header, as well as the first two questions.
6. Reporters are responsible for noting the time a proceeding ______ and ______.
7. A deposition may be pursuant to usual/state or federal ___________ or may be pursuant to specified or no ___________.
8. Photographs and X-rays may be marked as _______ as well as documents.
9. _________ exhibits are marked numerically, while _________ exhibits are marked alphabetically.
10. At depositions, exhibits are marked ___ _____________.
11. An exhibit might be marked ___ _____________ or __ ________ at a hearing/arbitration.
12. _____________ are used to reflect nonverbal actions in a transcript.
13. ___/___ is written in steno to reflect an off-the-record discussion.
14. ____/____ is written in steno to reflect a readback by the reporter.

15. _____ may be written to reflect the readback of a question only.
16. The reporter should say ________ before reading back a question and ______ before reading back an answer.
17. When attorneys cannot resolve a dispute amongst themselves, they may seek a ______ before a judge, law clerk, or law secretary.
18. ___ may be placed in the transcript while scoping/proofreading is done to flag the page and line numbers of rulings for inclusion on the index page of the transcript under *Rulings*.
19. ___ or ___ may be placed in the transcript while scoping/proofreading is done to flag the page and line numbers of requests for inclusion on the index page of the transcript under *Requests*.
20. _______ are blank lines placed within a transcript upon request for information to be physically filled in by a witness.
21. Reporters may request a ____- minute break every hour or hour and a half on all-day jobs.
22. ____ _____ _ is written by a reporter into his or her steno notes, along with the ending time of a proceeding, at the conclusion of the job.
23. _ + _ refers to the original transcript and one copy.
24. ___ refers to a copy of the transcript.
25. A witness who appears without legal representation is a ___ __ witness.
26. _______ for a specific reporter are a positive indication to an agency.
27. The agency name and job number, the date the proceeding is reported, a brief summary of the caption name, the witness's name, and whether or not the job was a continuation should be written in your _____ _____.
28. Each set of steno notes should be ________ chronologically whether there are multiple witnesses or simply multiple packs of paper utilized for a single witness.
29. A ______ ____ is placed around a reporter's steno notes with the work sheet, notepad notes, seating charts, photocopies of quotations or exhibits, and business cards.
30. Reporters are legally responsible for maintaining steno notes or an ASCII disk for each job for a period of ____ years.

## TRUE/FALSE QUESTIONS

1. The transcript on a continuation should begin with the next consecutive number after the ending page number on the previous session's transcript.
2. Stipulations are agreed to by the attorneys at the conclusion of a proceeding.
3. If stipulations apply, a stipulation page will always be placed prior to the beginning of testimony in a transcript.
4. There may not be a stipulation page added into transcripts of continuing depositions, since certain agencies contend the stipulations agreed to in the first session of the witness's testimony apply throughout all continuing sessions.
5. On a continuation, reporters may remind the witness that the witness is still under oath or may reswear the witness upon request.
6. If a continuing job begins on page 145 and concludes on page 290, you will bill the agency for 290 pages.
7. When a witness is affirmed rather than sworn, no changes need to be made within the standard transcript format.
8. A witness wearing a yarmulke may prefer to be affirmed rather than sworn.

9. The sworn/affirmed parenthetical always appears in a deposition transcript just prior to the record of the proceeding.
10. Beginning and ending times of breaks must always be noted by reporters.
11. Reporters place the first two questions (name and address) in a continuing deposition transcript.
12. Reporters need not note a change of attorney in their steno notes, as the attorney always introduces himself or herself on the record before questioning.
13. Ten Q&As by an attorney other than the examining attorney should by reflected as *EXAMINATION BY,* the attorney's name, a colon, and Q&A rather than colloquy.
14. After a substantial number of questions by an attorney other than the examining attorney during the examining attorney's questioning, if the reporter writes it in a Q&A format, the reporter need not note when the examination of the second attorney ended and the proceeding reverted to questioning by the examining attorney, as it is readily apparent.
15. Reporters always maintain exhibits after a proceeding.
16. The placing of *(part-time)* next to a person's name on the appearance page of a transcript varies from agency to agency.
17. The first letter of a parenthetical is uppercase if no verbal exchange accompanies it.
18. It is recommended that reporters keep their hands where attorneys can see them when asked to go off the record.
19. If asked to read back an answer, the reporter should read back the question that precedes it.
20. Reporters should not include colloquy in their readbacks.
21. Reporters should request a verbal response when one is not given.
22. Rulings are written in colloquy.
23. It is not necessary to note the time a ruling begins or ends during a deposition.
24. Reporters must always go with the attorneys for a ruling in a courthouse.
25. If an attorney just says to the reporter, *Mark that,* the reporter should list the page and line numbers of the material being referenced under *Rulings* on the index page of the transcript.
26. A request by the examining attorney to the witness may be written in a Q&A format, depending upon agency preference.
27. Reporters are always given a lunch break.
28. Freelance reporters are generally responsible for obtaining billing and delivery information.
29. All states require the witness to sign the original transcript before the reporter that reported the proceeding.
30. Reporters should clear out job globals at the conclusion of each job unless continuing on the same case the following day.

## DISCUSSION QUESTIONS

1. If a job is a continuation, what is done differently in regard to the swearing/affirming process? The transcript?
2. What information can be gleaned from an archived deposition if you are assigned to report a continuation of the witness's testimony? The testimony of a different witness on the same case?
3. If a witness does not have a right hand or cannot raise it, how would you swear the witness in?
4. Practice swearing/affirming an interpreter and witness in.
5. If an attorney agrees to the first two questions but subsequently asks them on the record, what should you do?

6. If an attorney requests that an exhibit be marked with the same number or letter as a previous exhibit, what should you say?
7. If an attorney requests that an exhibit be marked as a letter rather than a number, or vice versa, what should you say?
8. When an exhibit is deemed marked, how is it reflected in your steno notes? In the transcript?
9. If you do not know how to identify an exhibit for your index, what should you do?
10. What should you do if an attorney forgot to tell you to go back on the record and you suspect you should be on the record again?
11. How would you ask for a lunch break? If you encounter resistance from the attorney, what would you say?
12. How can you remind yourself that you closed out your job file and then the attorneys went back on the record and you continued writing in another job file?
13. What is common billing practice in your state? Common delivery practice?
14. How does a reporter reflect billing/delivery information on his or her work sheet?
15. Why might attorneys request an expedited transcript?
16. What are the most common components to a reporter being requested by attorneys?

CHAPTER

10

# For Your Information

## CHILD WITNESSES AND VOIR DIRES

Occasionally you will encounter the examination of a child. This may include a brief **voir dire,** or prequestioning session, to determine whether or not the child knows the difference between right and wrong, lying and telling the truth, and to state that there is punishment for not telling the truth. You may be asked to swear the child in after this voir dire is concluded.

Similar voir dires may be conducted when the witness is aged, is known to be suffering from some type of mental deficit, or has taken medication that may affect the witness's testimony.

Another type of voir dire that occurs in deposition settings is an examination of a witness by an attorney other than the examining attorney during the examining attorney's questioning of the witness. It is directed at a specific issue, such as capacity to testify, foundation for other evidence, and so on. It is usually preceded by some sort of colloquy by the attorney requesting the voir dire, which may be on or off the record. The reporter should write *(VOIR DIRE EXAMINATION BY MR./MS . -*:)* in his or her steno notes before the voir dire begins, identifying who is taking the voir dire, and then proceed with a Q&A format.

When the voir dire is over, be sure to write in your steno notes *(EXAMINATION BY MR./MS. -*:),* the name of the attorney questioning prior to the voir dire, and continue with the examination in Q&A format. A deposition voir dire is not usually referenced in the index page of a transcript.

**Voir dire:** Questioning of a witness by an attorney to find out whether or not the witness is competent to testify. Most commonly done with child witnesses, aged or ailing witnesses, or those whose testimony may be affected by medication. A second meaning is a brief examination by an opposing party to determine whether or not the witness is the proper witness to bring in evidence versus another witness or to determine if a witness is qualified to provide testimony on a specific subject, or if a sufficient foundation has been laid in order to offer a document or testimony into evidence at a trial.

## SPELLING WORDS AND NAMES

When a word is spelled on the record, you would stroke each letter on the left bank of your machine in conjunction with the asterisk key. As spelling tends to break the Q&A-writing rhythm, reporters tend to record spellings inaccurately. It is always prudent to double-check the word/name spelled on the record before leaving the proceeding.

Depending on the agency's preference, spellings on the record may be written entirely in uppercase letters in the transcript: for example, R-U-P-E-R-T, or initial capped/lowercase, depending upon the word, for example, p-r-o-t-u-b-e-re-n-c-e. Some agencies like their reporters to always use uppercase letters while others do not. Inquire within the agency how spellings should appear. Always verify the spelling if you can. If the speaker spelled the word incorrectly, *[sic]* is placed after the spelling in the transcript. If the reporter spelled the word incorrectly in his or her own steno notes, it may be changed to reflect the accurate spelling.

## RECORDING NUMBERS

Taking down numbers tends to be difficult for reporters. Reporters may either record numbers by utilization of the number bar or by writing the number as an actual word, for example, *NAOIN* for 9. Fewer errors seem to be made when a number is written out as a word, since misstrokes of words are more decipherable, while a misstroked number on the number bar may result in the recording of a different number.

Often speakers will rattle off numbers like *1444444* instead of saying *one million, four hundred and forty-four thousand, four hundred and forty-four.* Later, when scoping or proofreading the transcript, numerous errors can occur if the reporter takes it upon himself or herself to make assumptions about where commas and decimal points should be. Therefore, when you notice this occurring on an assignment, be quick to request that the speakers use the words *billion, million, thousand, hundred, dollars, cents,* and perhaps *point* to reflect the decimal point.

## RULES REGARDING NUMBERS

Transcripts generally reflect the numbers one through ten as words and 11 and above as figures. The number 10 can go either way, depending on the numerical content and location of the number.

### Numerals as Figures

There are some exceptions, cases in which figures are always used. They include:

- Units of measurement
- Measurements of time
- Measurements of distance or speed
- Percentages
- Ages—for example, *She had her 2-year-old niece living with her.*
- Dates
- Numbers of pages, sections, paragraphs
- Numbers listed in a series
- Decimals numbers
- Ratios
- Proportions
- References to scores

It is more important to be consistent within the transcript than to follow the rules explicitly, since mixing words and figures may lead to ambiguities and choppy reading of a transcript. For example, if a witness answers, "I paid between six and 17,000 in taxes last year," most likely the witness did not pay between $6 and $17,000 but, rather, between $6,000 and $17,000. Therefore, the recommended method of reflecting this response in a transcript would be, "I paid between six and seventeen thousand in taxes last year." However, if the text reads without ambiguity and words and figures are mixed within a sentence, convert the words to figures to keep a sense of consistency. If the first number begins the sentence, convert everything to words for consistency (save the exceptions listed earlier).

## Roman Numerals

If you are privy to documents being referenced and note that numbers referenced in the documents are Roman numerals (I, II, III, IV, V, and so on) rather than Arabic numerals (1, 2, 3, 4, 5, and so on), you may replace the Arabic numeral with the appropriate Roman numeral upon preparation of the transcript. However, there are many times when you do not have access to said documents and, therefore, write the number in Arabic numerals, and this is entirely acceptable.

There are many occasions where a speaker references on the record a Roman numeral, such as *Roman numeral two.* This may be written either as *Roman numeral 2* or *Roman numeral II,* depending upon your preference. Many reporters like to use Arabic numerals after the words *Roman numeral* because writing the words *Roman numeral* and then the actual Roman numeral seems a bit redundant.

In addition, certain Roman numerals may prove to be conflicts, such as the Roman numeral four (IV), which may be confused with the abbreviation for intravenous (IV), or the Roman numeral ten (X), which conflicts with the letter *X.* Therefore, by writing the Arabic numeral—*Roman numeral 4* or *Roman numeral 10*—you avoid a conflict. You may also choose to global the abbreviation for intravenous (I.V.) using periods.

## Ordinals

The rule regarding ordinal numbers is that *first, second, third, fourth, fifth, sixth, seventh, eighth, ninth* and *tenth* are written as words. Numerals are used for $11^{th}$ and up; the number is written as a numeral followed by *st, rd, nd* or *th;* for example, $31^{st}$, $43^{rd}$, $80^{th}$.

When ordinal numbers below 10 appear in a series with ordinal numbers above 10, all would be written as the numeral followed by *st, nd, rd,* or *th;* for example, *We had our* $1^{st-}$, $12^{th-}$ *and* $15^{th}$*-year Christmas parties at this restaurant.*

Oftentimes street names that are ordinal numbers are spelled out rather than written as numerals, for example, *She works over on Third Avenue;* however, if the street is unknown to you, double-check.

There are also some rules regarding dates and ordinal numbers. As previously mentioned, if a date is stated in its entirety, uttered as *April* $4^{th}$*, 1967,* the *th* following the *4* is deleted when writing or preparing the transcript, and the transcript will read *April 4, 1967.* However, if a speaker cites a month and day without a year, for example, *November* $20^{th}$ *is his birthday,* the day remains an ordinal number. This applies as well to when the day appears prior to the month, for example, *the 9th of June 1962.* If a speaker cites a date without the ordinal number, for example, *December 30 is my mother's birthday,* do not add *th* to the *30,* but leave it as it was said.

## Dollar Figures

Dollar figures that do not include cents do not require decimal points. Commas should be utilized for numbers in the thousands and above.

## A Hundred Versus 100

If the speaker says *one hundred* rather than *a hundred,* generally it is written as 100. For example:

A I own 100 pairs of shoes at least.

When the word *a* precedes the word *hundred,* generally it is reflected as *a hundred.* For example:

Q You don't seem a hundred percent sure. Are you guessing?

Context may lead to exceptions to the rule, so if in doubt, seek guidance from the agency.

## Million/Billion

Round numbers followed by the word *million* or *billion* are written as figures with the word *million* or *billion* after the number, regardless of whether the word *dollars* or the dollar symbol accompanies it. For example:

She made $700 million last year.

Numbers like 1,275,985 would be reflected as shown.

## Numbers at Beginning of Sentences

Sentences that begin with numbers indicate the numbers as words, although when a sequence of numbers follows, figures may be used throughout to ensure a smooth reading of the record. Other exceptions to this rule include:

- Times expressed in hours and minutes—12:15 p.m.
- Dates stated numerically—8/8/00
- Weight references—160 poounds
- Decimals—1.4 million
- Ratios—11 to 8 is the ratio of children dressed as Indians in the school play versus children dressed as pilgrims
- Scores—8 to 2 was the score before the commercials
- Numbers accompanied by a dollar sign—$900

## The Word *Number*

The word *number* is usually spelled out in a transcript, for example, *The number 280 appears on the invoice circled;* however, it may be abbreviated in certain contexts, such as:

- *We've previously marked this as Plaintiff's Exhibit No. 3.*
- *In paragraph No. 9, subsection (b) of the declaration, it is clearly stated.*
- *I am going to read from interrogatory No. 11.*
- *Building No. 2 was 119 Main Street.*
- *Elevator No. 1 was out of order.*

## Fractions

Fractions are generally expressed in words, especially when a fraction is a non-modifier, for example, *Only a quarter of the battalion survived,* or precedes the words *of, of a,* or *of an,* such as *Six-eighths of us agreed.* However, if there is a sequence of measurements, figures may be preferred. For example:

A The measurements were in inches as follows: 9/16, 9/16, 2/5, 9/16.

## Dates

Months are written out, not abbreviated, in transcripts. If a date is stated numerically, use slashes; for example, *6/9/62* or *6/9/1962,* rather than dashes.

When a speaker says, for example, *March 3rd*, without stating the year, the *rd* after the *3* may remain in the transcript. The same would apply to the *st* following the *1* in *June 1st*. However, if the year follows the date, the ordinal number is removed; for example, *March 3, 1996, June 1, 1945.*

If a month falls on a separate transcript line than the day and/or year, move it to the following line. It should not appear as:

Q The accident happened on the 4th of January,
but I felt leg pain on January
6, 1998.

Rather, the correct form is:

Q The accident happened on the 4th of January,
but I felt leg pain on January 6, 1998.

## Time

***A.m./P.m.*** Numbers preceding a.m. or p.m. are written as figures except when beginning a sentence.

A.m. and p.m. are always written with periods in the context of time. Note that the *A* in *A.m.* in the prior sentence is uppercase, since it begins a sentence, and that *p.m.* is completely lowercase, since it does not. If not the first word of a sentence, a.m. and p.m. will be lowercase.

***O'clock*** Numbers lower than 10 that are followed by the word *o'clock* are traditionally written out as words, for example, *four o'clock,* yet some agencies may prefer their reporters to use figures for 10 o'clock and up. If a transcript contains multiple references to time, it is recommended to use figures for all times mentioned.

***When Not Followed by A.m., P.m., or O'clock*** If a time mentioned is not followed by the words *a.m., p.m.,* or *o'clock,* the number may be spelled out, for example, *He goes to bed at ten.* However, if the time is conveyed by hours and minutes or if the transcript mentions other times expressed in hours and minutes, numerals would be utilized, for example, *We arrived at 6:11.*

Ciphers, or the colon symbol, are used to express times that reflect minutes, for example, *4:42 a.m.* Times that are not inclusive of minutes, for example, *5 p.m.,* may be written with or without ciphers followed by 00, for example, *5:00 p.m.* When two or more times reflecting minutes are mixed with times reflecting only hours, the ciphers would be used, for example, *I generally only eat around 12:00 p.m. and 6:30 p.m.* Ciphers would also be used when tabulating, or listing, a series of times. For example:

A According to the log, the following people worked the following shifts:
"9:00 to 12:15, Anna Rosilio
"12:15 to 3:30, Richard Brent
"3:30 to 7:00, Esther Goldzweig."

## HYPHENS

Hyphens are used, in the context of numbers, after numbers as unit modifiers. This applies to numbers written as both numerals and words, for example, *They were a 13-child family, We polished off three-quarters of an 18-pound turkey for Thanksgiving.* When two numbers (or words) modify the same noun or unit, a hyphen is used for each number (or word). An example where this would occur might be:

Q Was it a one- or a two-family house?
A I don't know if it was a legal two-family house, but two-thirds of it was occupied by tenants and the landlord lived on the top floor.

Height is expressed in words rather than numerals. Oftentimes you will hear someone state his or her height as five-eight, and that is exactly how it would appear in the transcript, with the numbers spelled out, separated by a hyphen.

## QUOTATION MARKS

Reporters do not use a parenthetical such as *(Reading.)* to indicate that material was read into the record; they use quotation marks. When a quotation is read into the record, writing *KW-T* prior to the quote and *KW-T/KW-T* immediately after the quote (or whatever your theory teaches) will clarify for the record where the quotation began and ended. Sometimes an attorney will preface quoted material with an indication that he or she is reading something, such as, "You state in paragraph 2 of the complaint the following, quote:," which clues the reporter in to the fact that a quotation will follow. Other times, it may not be as clear. In addition, it is not always apparent where the quotation ends, especially if you forget to place an end quote in your steno notes. If the quoted material is not too lengthy or voluminous, it may be wise to request to view it on a break and make a notation to yourself about where the quote begins and ends, rewrite the quote into your steno notes as a note to yourself, or request a copy for scoping purposes.

Do not overquote—use quotes for distinguishing what is said from what is being read into the record, for emphasis, or for referral to previously mentioned words/sentences. When attorneys or witnesses say *quote/unquote,* it is usually written as such in the record, preceded and followed by commas, and obviates the need to place quotation marks around the quote. If you have occasion to review the actual document quoted from or you know exactly where the quotation begins and ends, you may remove the *quote/unquote* and use quotation marks if the text quoted is quoted verbatim.

## OBJECTIONS

If an attorney feels that a question asked by the examining attorney or an answer given by the witness is impermissible, the attorney may state an objection on the record to it. Objections are written in colloquy. The most common grounds for objections are:

- *Incompetent*—this objection challenges the competency of the person who said what is being objected to
- *Irrelevant*—this claims that what was said is not related to the case or discoverable material
- *Immaterial*— this claims that what was said is not germane or important to the case

Attorneys may also object, using the words:

- *Leading and suggestive*—claiming the attorney is encouraging the witness to answer in a certain way or suggesting an answer to the witness
- *Hearsay*—claiming the witness is simply relating what others have told the witness or what he or she heard others say
- *Argumentative/badgering the witness*—claiming that the question posed by the attorney is provoking an argument with the witness, evidenced by questions that begin with *why* and answers that begin with *because,* or demeaning the witness
- *Compound and complex*—claiming that the question, as posed, is asking multiple questions that require multiple answers within one question and/or is confusing
- *Vague and ambiguous*—claiming that the question asked requires clarification or may be taken two ways and should be rephrased
- *Without proper foundation*—claiming that the examining attorney is assuming facts not in evidence and must first lay the groundwork for the question before asking it
- *Privileged*—claiming that the question would lead to an answer that should not be on the record and is protected by legal privileges, such as the attorney work-product privilege and the attorney-client privilege, or privileges protecting certain professionals and their patients
- *Asked and answered*—claiming that the question was already asked of the witness and answered
- *Nonresponsive to the question*—claiming that the witness's response is beyond the scope of the information sought by the question

- *Not the best evidence*—claiming that an exhibit's marking is not the best tool to support the attorney's questioning/case or that a question posed would be better asked of a witness more knowledgeable of the facts
- *The evidence speaks for itself*—claiming the witness does not have to answer the question posed as the answer is found within the evidence already presented in the case
- *Beyond the scope*—claiming that the question asked exceeds the boundaries of the proceeding as set forth by Court order or Rules of Discovery
- *Self-serving*—claiming that the question asked by another attorney or the answer given by a witness was chosen for purposes of advancing one's case or making oneself look better
- *Self-incriminating*—claiming that the witness is protected by the Fifth Amendment and should not answer the question as the answer may lead to facts irrelevant to the case, the disclosure of which may lead to further legal action against the witness
- *Calls for a narrative*—claiming that the question calls for a lengthy, rambling, storylike response rather than a brief, specific answer
- *Calls for opinion evidence*—claiming that the question posed by the examining attorney calls for opinions of the witness rather than facts
- *Calls for a conclusion*— claiming that the question posed by the examining attorney requires the witness to conclude something rather than state facts
- *Calls for expert witness testimony*—claiming that the witness is a layperson and is not qualified or appearing in a capacity that would enable him or her to respond to the question posed

An attorney may object to an exhibit being offered for identification if the attorney does not feel it is properly characterized on the record or properly represents what it ought to. An attorney may also object if testimony offered by his or her client differs from the information provided by the client in preparation for the proceeding. Colloquy by the examining attorney and/or other attorneys present may ensue in response to the objection, the reporter may be asked to mark the prior question or answer for a ruling, or the examining attorney may choose to rephrase the question or move on to another.

## OTHER TIPS

Some do's and don'ts of preparing court reporting transcripts are:

- Don't begin a carryover line with dashes—bring the word preceding the dashes to the following line
- Don't divide a person's title onto two lines—move the *Mr., Mrs., Dr.,* and so on to the following line
- When addressing a doctor by the word *doctor,* it is written initial capped as *Doctor.* If the word *doctor* precedes the doctor's name, it is written *Dr.,* for example, *Dr. Dreyfuss.* If the attorneys are just referring to the doctor without saying the doctor's name, it is written in lowercase, for example, *The doctor has brought his CV with him.* The same rules apply for the word *judge*

- Don't divide addresses/state names by two lines—move the first word or street number to the following line
- Don't divide exhibit information onto two lines with just the exhibit number or letter beginning the following line—move the whole thing to the next line
- Don't prepare a transcript with numerous notations *(Indicating), (Nodding),* and *Uh-huh* in it; say something while on the job to get verbal answers for the record
- Don't use parentheticals unmercilessly—beginning a new paragraph may reflect an obvious action following previous testimony
- Don't begin parentheticals with the wording *Whereupon* or *At this time* (or both) unless that is agency preference
- Don't overcomma—if it reads okay without the comma, leave it out
- Don't overhyphenate—if unsure whether hyphens belong between words, consult *One Word, Two Word, Hyphen?,* the agency, or a scopist
- Don't add English to make the transcript read better—if you dropped something, dash it off and leave it out; the witness/attorney has an opportunity when reading the transcript to correct an obvious drop or erroneous word used. If a witness spoke poorly, that is just his or her recognized speech pattern. It is not your responsibility to clean up the grammar
- Don't delete anything from the transcript unless so directed by attorneys or the agency
- Don't include in a transcript repetition by the examining attorney of the witness's previous answer unless it is germane to the subsequent question
- Don't call a witness for assistance following a proceeding
- Do obtain permission from an agency to telephone an attorney if you require further information from the attorney, or ask the agency for assistance
- Do use paragraphing to break up lengthy text, but try to do so only in appropriate spots
- Do proofread for context as well as spelling/punctuation errors
- Do pay attention to singular and plural possessives, for example, student's versus students' or Plaintiff's versus Plaintiffs', and make sure they correspond properly to the subject matter/number of parties
- Do make sure your transcript is prepared in the agency's edit style and utilizes the agency's parenthetical preferences

## SHORT-ANSWER QUESTIONS

1. A ____ ____ may take place in the examination of a child witness to determine whether the child knows the difference between right and wrong, lying and telling the truth.
2. When spelling a word in the record, the reporter will stroke the ____ bank of the steno machine in conjunction with an ________ key.

3. Reporters use quotation marks at the beginning and end of a _____ to indicate that someone was reading from something.
4. Incompetent, irrelevant, and immaterial are examples of ____________ that are made during a proceeding.
5. If a speaker says or spells a word/date incorrectly, [___] should follow the word/date in the transcript.
6. The numbers __ through __ are generally spelled out in transcripts.
7. I, II, and III are examples of _____ numerals.
8. 1, 2, and 3 are examples of ______ numerals.
9. 1st/first, 2nd/second, and 3rd/third are examples of _______ numbers.
10. A ______, or colon, is used when time is expressed in both hours and minutes.
11. ________ preceding the words *of, of a,* or *of an* are generally written as words.
12. In the phrase *a quarter of the team,* the fraction *a quarter* is a non________.
13. ______ are used in conjunction with numbers as unit modifiers.
14. Beginning a new paragraph may eliminate the need for a ____________.
15. Reporters must make sure that the appropriate ________ __________, such as *Plaintiff's Exhibit,* and ______ ___________ such as *Plaintiffs' Exhibit,* are utilized within the transcript.

## TRUE/FALSE QUESTIONS

1. Objections made by attorneys appear in colloquy in a transcript.
2. The numbers 11 and above are usually reflected as numerals in transcripts.
3. Page, section, and paragraph numbers are always spelled out in transcripts.
4. In cases of ambiguities or when words and numerals are mixed together, all numbers should be converted to numerals for consistency.
5. It is recommended to use Arabic numerals rather than Roman numerals, as certain Roman numerals may conflict with letters or abbreviations.
6. Decimal points should be used when writing all dollar figures.
7. Dollar figures in the thousands and above should contain commas.
8. *A hundred* always appears in transcripts as a number, *100,* rather than the words *a hundred.*
9. Round figures in the millions or billions combine a number with the word *million* or *billion,* for example, *$3 million.*
10. Times expressed in hours and minutes at the beginning of a sentence should be written as numerals with ciphers.
11. Months are always abbreviated in transcripts.
12. Slashes rather than dashes are used to reflect dates stated numerically.
13. When a date includes an ordinal number and a year, the ordinal number should be changed to a cardinal number, for example, *January 3, 1990* as opposed to *January 3rd, 1990.*
14. Months and days in dates should be on the same line in a transcript.
15. Numbers preceding a.m. or p.m. are always written as numerals.
16. Numbers 1 through 9 followed by the word *o'clock* are usually written as words and 10 and above as numerals.
17. Ciphers are always used when a time is written.
18. Hyphens are placed after each number modifying the same noun or unit.
19. Height is expressed in numerals.
20. Unless referring to a date, the ordinal numbers 1 through 10 are written as words.

21. When ordinal numbers below 10 appear in a series with ordinal numbers above 10, all numbers should be converted to words.
22. Street names with ordinal numbers are commonly spelled out as words.
23. Ordinal numbers remain ordinal numbers in dates where the ordinal number precedes the month and/or year, for example, *the 4th of May.*
24. The word *number* is always spelled out in a transcript.
25. A person's title—Mr., Ms., Dr., and so on—should not be on a separate transcript line than the person's name.

## DISCUSSION QUESTIONS

1. Why is a voir dire of a child important before obtaining legal testimony from the child? A person on medication?
2. Why is it wise to verify spellings of words/names previously spelled on the record?
3. If you do not obtain a spelling of an unusual name mentioned on the record and cannot verify its spelling elsewhere, how should it be reflected in the transcript?
4. Why do reporters request speakers to use decimal points or state *dollars* and *cents* on the record when discussing numbers?
5. Why is the use of Arabic numerals often preferred over Roman numerals in transcripts?
6. What are some methods of obtaining for review a quotation read into the record?
7. When an attorney states an objection on the record, what should the reporter do?
8. Why can't reporters add English to a transcript?

# CHAPTER 11

# Freelancer Protocol

## ON THE RECORD VERSUS OFF THE RECORD

When I was a new reporter, the attorney that ordered me for a deposition got into an on-the-record argument with the other attorneys present. After words were exchanged, the attorney stood up and declared, "That's it. I'm outta here." As he began walking out of the room, one of the attorneys present in the room with me said, "On the record. We just want to note that Mr. -* has walked out of the deposition and we were still willing to proceed." At this point, the attorney who had left the room returned and began yelling at me for continuing to write on his record in his absence. I had no idea what my responsibility was and to whom in this scenario.

A similar situation was presented to NCRA's Committee on Professional Ethics, and the statement of facts, discussion, and conclusion, as published in Public Advisory Opinions, were as follows:

**PUBLIC ADVISORY OPINION**
**NO. 6 (1987)**

### Statement of Facts

A reporter is engaged by the attorney representing plaintiff to report a deposition. Attorney for the defendant and the witness appear at the designated time. After completing his examination, the hiring attorney states that the deposition is concluded. The defense attorney, wishing to examine the witness, does not agree to its conclusion. The hiring attorney then directs the reporter to go off the record since he is paying for it. The reporter declines to do so and continues to report the examination of the opposing counsel.

### Discussion

The question presented here is: Should the reporter have complied with the hiring attorney's request not to continue reporting his opponent's examination?

The answer is an emphatic no. It makes no difference who makes the request. Unless all counsel in an examination agree to go off the record, the reporter is duty-bound to continue reporting the proceedings even when the hiring attorney makes the request of the reporter. The reporter must act impartially and professionally in all proceedings that are reported.

### Conclusion

It is the Committee's opinion that the reporter was acting within the provisions of the Code of Professional Ethics, particularly Provisions 1 and 9, which state that the member shall:

**No. 1.** Be fair and impartial toward each participant in all aspects of reported proceedings.
**No. 9.** Maintain the integrity of the reporting profession.

If **counsel** other than the examining attorney should ask you to go off the record, a simple, "Counsel?" directed at the examining attorney should elicit a nod or a response that will imply consent or disagreement.

Extraneous comments by counsel or jokes are generally not meant for the record, but counsel often neglect to say "Off the record" to the reporter. Seasoned reporters develop an instinct for when to stop writing, but newer reporters should just write it and delete it upon preparation of the transcript. Do not be surprised if the attorneys glare at you while you are writing down an off-the-record-type joke as if you should have known better. You can simply respond by saying, "I'm just making a note to myself in the record," and then render that the truth as you make a note to yourself to delete the previous colloquy.

Occasionally witnesses will ask the reporter to go off the record. The appropriate response should be, "I can only go off the record at counsel's request," which will prompt counsel to direct you as to what to do. If the examining attorney nods his or her head in acquiescence, that is as good as a verbal okay.

There are other times reporters may intervene regarding on- or off-the-record material, such as if a lengthy heated dispute takes place on the record or if the attorneys are discussing a continuation date for the job and they forget to go off the record. You may suggest that they work things out off the record in an effort to save them paying for pages upon pages of colloquy and to save yourself reporting the whole thing only to be told at the end, "That was all off the record."

## MISSING SOMETHING THAT SHOULD BE ON THE RECORD

**Counsel:** A synonym for attorney; also a venerable title by which to address lawyers.

**Housekeeping:** A (generally) off-the-record discussion amongst the representatives of parties to a legal action regarding details about the case.

In the context of hearings, we have discussed **housekeeping,** a discussion by the attorneys about certain matters regarding the case. This can occur on depositions as well. While generally it is not on the record, occasionally attorneys may want it on the record and may not formally tell you to go on the record.

If attorneys begin to speak and it seems like it is substantial subject matter, interject immediately and ask, "Is this on the record, Counsel?" Otherwise, they may assume it was and go on for a number of minutes while you are missing an extensive amount of information. If you realize afterward that something was meant to be on the record but was not recorded, it is your duty to notify all present so that they can repeat what was said.

Once the job begins, if you drop something that was said, your obligation is to make an accurate record and get what it was that you missed. There are a number of methods of doing this. The preferred method is to stop the proceedings and politely ask for a repeat. However, you do not want to do this too often because it will become obvious to all present that you are unable to fulfill your job responsibilities, and it will instill doubt in the attorneys that the record will be accurate.

A common problem with asking the witness to repeat an answer is that frequently the witness will try to explain or elaborate on the answer and will ramble on without specifically stating what it was that was originally said. To prevent that from happening, you might say something like, "I'm sorry, but after 'Then we deposited the check into . . .,' what was it that you said?"

If someone is speaking too rapidly for you, it is important to communicate that. Saying something like, "Could I just ask you to speak a little slower for the record" should get your point across, but be forewarned that fast speakers tend to slow down for a minute or two and then return to their normal speaking pattern. There are cases where missing something may not be your fault at all. It is very rare that you have a 100 percent perfect environment for hearing. Sometimes you could be doing a deposition in a courthouse where 10 other cases are going on and people are speaking loudly. Sometimes construction is going on nearby. Or sometimes people at the proceeding speak over one another. It is always up to you, the reporter, to temporarily halt the proceedings if you are having difficulty hearing.

When people speak over one another, traditionally it was advised to take your hands off the machine and hold them up in the air, alerting those in the room that you are no longer writing. Personally, I do not find this to be a practical method because by the time that you raise your hands from the machine, you can lose pertinent information, as people keep speaking, and sometimes they will look at you angrily and say, "We're still on the record." How I handle this situation is to keep writing, but when it gets to be too much, I just say, at a pause in the proceeding or when I am at my breaking point, "I'm sorry, but I can only take down one person at a time."

Other disturbances involve people moving chairs, shuffling papers, or coughing over a question or answer; in these situations, it is perfectly acceptable to say, "Could you please repeat that?" You may request witnesses to speak louder or to remove their hand from covering their mouth. Do not be concerned about what the attorneys think of you. Just concern yourself with making a verbatim record and doing your job properly.

## GUIDELINES FOR PROFESSIONAL PRACTICE

The NCRA publishes a *Code of Professional Ethics,* which outlines how reporter members of NCRA should conduct themselves professionally. Section 1 of its *Guidelines for Professional Practice* states that:

> "Common sense and professional courtesy should guide the Member in applying the following guidelines.
>
> In making the official record, a Member should:

A. Accept only those assignments when the Member's level of competence will result in the preparation of an accurate transcript. The Member should remove himself from an assignment when the Member believes the Member's abilities are inadequate, recommending or assigning another reporter only if such reporter has the competence required for such assignment.
B. Prepare the record in accordance with the transcript-preparation guidelines established by statute or court order, by local custom and usage, or when not so established in accordance with the NCRA's recommended transcript format guidelines.
C. Notify, whenever possible, the parties engaging the Member if a substitute reporter, equally qualified, will be assigned to report the proceedings.
D. Preserve the shorthand notes in accordance with statute or court order, or for a period of no less than five (5) years through storage of the original paper notes or an electronic copy of either the shorthand notes or the English transcript of the notes on computer disks, cassettes, backup tape systems, or optical or laser disk systems.
E. Meet promised delivery dates whenever possible, make timely delivery of transcripts when no date is specified, and provide immediate notification of delays.
F. Strive to become and remain proficient in the Member's professional skills.
G. Keep abreast of current literature, technological advances and developments, and participate in continuing-education programs.
H. Assist in improving the reporting profession by participating in national, state, and local association activities that advance the quality and standards of the reporting profession.
I. Cooperate with the bench and bar for the improvement of the administration of justice.
J. Cooperate with qualified legal assistance organizations providing free legal services to the indigent, as part of the shorthand reporting profession's commitment to the principle that reporting services should be available to all. Such participation should be in accordance with the basic tenets of the profession: impartiality, competence, and integrity.

## SPOT CALLS

**Spot calls** are calls from attorneys who need reporters to be sent either immediately or within a few hours' notice. Freelance agencies are often hard-pressed to find available reporters to cover these calls. If you happen to be off on a business day and going to your office for any reason, be prepared for the possibility of a spot call. Dress casually but conservatively, and bring your equipment, if possible. The agency may have a spare machine in the office to loan you, but reporters are most comfortable with their own equipment and supplies. Helping an agency out of a jam helps you score some major points and earns you the reputation of a team player.

**Spot call:** When a freelance court reporting agency receives a request for a reporter to appear immediately at a proceeding and to record it stenographically.

I remember going to the office one summer's day in shorts, a T-shirt, sneakers, and sweat socks, only to find myself moments later taking down testimony.

If you are in casual clothing, do not worry. The attorneys are usually notified by the agency in advance that the reporter will be appearing in nonprofessional attire, and the attorneys are generally just grateful to know that someone will be there shortly.

If agency error led to the absence of a reporter on a job, the agency will attempt to make it appear as though the reporter scheduled for the job got ill or give some similar excuse, and will assure the attorneys that another reporter will be there shortly.

In either case, do not engage in conversation with the attorneys about how you were not prepared to work that day. Just get the necessary information, set up as soon as you can, and delve into the proceeding.

Many times agencies will send a reporter whose a.m. job has busted or ended early to cover a spot call. Agencies, therefore, request that all reporters call in before leaving a job location in case something else needs coverage.

## WHEN YOU ARE ASSIGNED AN A.M. AND A P.M. JOB

If you are assigned an A.M. and a P.M. job, when you arrive to the first job, you may inquire of the examining attorney if he or she thinks it will last all day. The attorney will generally give you an expected time frame with the caveat that "It depends on how much the witness knows." If it seems that the A.M. job is going to end too close to the time that you need to be at the P.M. job, request a break, let the attorneys know that you are scheduled to cover another job, stating the time you have to leave by, and ask if you should advise your office to cover the second job with another reporter.

## DO NOT SOLICIT WORK

If you are working for an agency, you must not solicit work for a different agency or private work, nor should you divulge that you are "just picking up" a job with the agency. **Picking up** connotes that you do not generally work for this agency but are just covering a job for them. It is best to simply state that you are working for the subject company and leave it at that. If an attorney recognizes you from a previous case on which you worked for a different agency and queries you about it, you can respond that you are a freelancer and work with both agencies; but unless you are asked, do not offer any information. Likewise, you should not give a business card out at a job for any agency other than the one that has hired you for the job.

## THINGS NOT TO SAY ON A JOB

Do not say anything negative about an agency to a client. Do not state your intention to leave an agency to an attorney who is a client of that agency.

Your role as a freelance court reporter includes confidentiality regarding any information that you obtain on the job. This applies to names of parties, attorneys, witnesses, and subject matter. You should not discuss details of a case or even make reference to a case you have worked on with an attorney within

**Picking up:** When an agency that a reporter is on staff with does not have an assignment for the reporter and the reporter then accepts an assignment from another agency.

earshot of anyone besides the attorney. Saying something like, "Didn't we work on the Jones job together?" or "I've deposed this witness before in three other cases like this" violates the Code of Ethics that reporters are governed by.

Do not make comments like:

- I'm picking up work with this company; I usually work for XYZ Company
- I'm new
- This is my first deposition
- I've never done a medical before
- I used to work for XYZ Company, but they fired me
- I'm just out of detox for alcohol/drugs

Similarly, do not assume everyone wants to know details about your personal life, for example, a recent breakup. Do not pull out pictures of your children unless specifically asked.

Witness information also should not be divulged. Saying to a witness, "Hi, Doctor. Didn't I take your testimony in the Smith case?" may lead to a dismissal of the doctor's testimony if the opposing side, for instance, can establish that this particular doctor only testifies on behalf of plaintiffs and never for defendants.

## NEUTRALITY

You should not get too chummy with the witness or opposing counsel, as your client might find this behavior offensive. Remember, you are supposed to be a neutral presence in the proceeding, so be equally friendly to all or reserved toward all. Many reporters choose to dine alone at lunchtime because it avoids the favoritism element that sides often push for. However, it is acceptable to dine with other neutral parties, such as interpreters and videographers. If the client who has retained you invites you to join him or her, or invites himself or herself to join you, that is acceptable. Otherwise, the attorney may prefer to discuss the case privately with a colleague or his or her witness or prepare for the afternoon session. Try not to spend too much time with the witness on a break. Witnesses like to tell you their side of the story and elicit empathy, which may make you subject to disapproval by the examining attorney.

Some attorneys may use your impression of a case against you to make a point with opposing counsel. If asked your opinion of a case, it is always best to find a way to remain neutral. One day, when I was a new reporter, I was reporting a deposition in a courthouse. Every time the examining attorney asked the witness a question, the witness's attorney would pull the witness out of the room to confer with him. This literally happened after each question. We had been there about three hours. On yet another one of these occurrences, the examining attorney asked me, "How many pages do you think you have there?" I looked at my paper and judged that I had about 30 pages. He then said, "Not a lot for three hours, huh?" I responded, "Not really."

We went back on the record when the witness and his attorney returned. Before answering the next question, the witness's attorney wanted to pull the witness out for another conference. An argument erupted between the two attorneys, and the examining attorney said, on the record, "Enough already with these breaks. Even the reporter said that she's been here all day and all she's written is 30 pages!" As I wrote the words, I could feel my face turn bright red, and then I had to experience the same feelings again when I scoped, proofread, and corrected the transcript. After that, I never offered my opinion on *anything*!

## WHEN ATTORNEYS TAKE YOUR ORDER

Occasionally attorneys will ask reporters if they would like anything to eat/drink for lunch/dinner or as a snack. Generally the attorney will be treating the reporter, but the reporter should not assume this is so and should offer to pay upon the attorney's return. Since the attorney is most likely treating, you should not order anything extravagant or anything that will cost more money than you have on your person. A sandwich *or* salad *or* soup, chips *or* cookies, and a drink are the norm for lunch or dinner. Be sure to thank the attorney if he or she treats you to anything.

If a spread is put out for opposing counsel and the witness, the reporter is usually entitled to partake but should politely ask, "May I?" and motion toward the food, rather than assuming that it is all right to join in. It is also proper protocol to let the witness and attorneys partake of the spread first.

Take care not to spill anything or leave a trail of crumbs in the conference room. Place cups, cans, wrappers, and so on in the garbage after eating.

Acknowledge the attorney's generosity at the end of the day with a "Thank you again for lunch/dinner." It may encourage the attorney to continue this practice with future reporters.

## KEEPING YOUR IMPRESSIONS TO YOURSELF

You may be asked by an attorney about your impression of a witness or the case. Again, the neutrality responsibility comes into play. This can be a dilemma because you want to appear friendly to the attorney who is asking you for your input. Try to think of a generic response that would remind the attorney of your role in the proceeding without seeming evasive. I like to say, "I just process what I hear; I don't pay attention to the details of a case until I proofread it."

## ATTORNEY CRITIQUES

You may encounter novice and/or insecure attorneys asking what you thought of their questioning technique. Do not offer advice or criticism. Try to find something positive to say or just say, "You did a great job." Do not make a negative comment about the opposing side or the witness in an attempt to compliment the attorney.

A new attorney may turn to you and whisper, "This is my first deposition." Do not respond with, "Yeah, I could tell" or "I thought so." Say something like, "You're doing better than some experienced attorneys I've worked for" or "Really? It didn't come off that way." Bolstering the confidence of a new attorney may result in the attorney's requesting you in the future.

## STOIC EXPRESSION AND CALM COMPOSURE

Court reporting protocol dictates that you keep a stoic facial expression during the proceedings. You do not want to express any sense of judgment regarding witness testimony, possible accents, the attorney's ability to form coherent questions, and so on. If a joke is made and all parties laugh, you may join in; but in general, offer no responses or opinions either verbally or nonverbally.

One time when I was sitting in on a trial at a nearby courthouse as part of my internship program, a fellow student and I were both brought into the same trial, as there was nothing else to sit in on at that time. We each sat beside the official reporter. Apparently, one party to the suit produced an unexpected medical witness, and this created quite a stir in the courtroom. Within seconds, everyone in the room was yelling. My colleague and I, barely having obtained a speed of 200 at this point, did not know whose comments should be taken down. Our heads were like Ping-Pong balls, trying to follow the proceedings. I was so overwhelmed that I stopped writing, took one look at my friend, and with a history of a nervous giggle, started to laugh uncontrollably. I just could not believe our luck. We were simply trying to have a rewarding sitting-in experience to confirm that we were almost ready to start working.

I then glanced at the official reporter, who was calmly continuing to write, and observed him maintaining his composure. I studied the injured child witness and his mother with tears in their eyes. Then I realized the gravity of the situation and the inappropriateness of my reaction. I managed to focus my gaze on my machine and continue writing.

Years of waiting for a trial date can mean millions of dollars expended, reputations, careers, and livelihoods at stake. This is not to be taken lightly by any person involved in the case on whatever level, especially the court reporter. Since that time I have developed a method of composure when things get out of control. I focus on the fact that this will be over with soon and stare at my machine for a few minutes, rather than at the faces of the participants. This talent, unfortunately, has earned me a reputation for being able to handle crazy situations and gives people the impression that nothing phases me. As a result, I often get called back on harrowing cases. However, that, in itself, makes me invaluable to the agencies that I work for.

You should anticipate that something will happen in your career where you will feel like laughing aloud. Find a spot on your machine to focus on or a serious thought that will keep you from showing emotions. Actors utilize this method to emote; reporters utilize it for just the opposite.

It is very embarrassing for many witnesses to testify about sexual issues, for example, dysfunctions, capabilities, and frequency due to an accident or incident, or subject matters such as rape. It is bad enough for them to have to be examined by a room full of lawyers, but having a court reporter, especially one of the opposite sex, staring at them adds to their discomfort. During this type of testimony, reporters may wish to look away from the witness, giving the impression that they are just recording testimony and doing their job. I cannot tell you how many times male witnesses have been uncomfortable by certain subject matters and have apologized to me personally for testimony given in this vein.

## TAPE-RECORDING PROCEEDINGS

There is a lot of controversy about tape-recording proceedings without the consent of both the agency and all those present at the proceeding. According to the *Code of Professional Ethics,* unless otherwise directed by a judge, reporters are under no obligation to provide a backup tape that they have made for their personal use in preparing a transcript, nor do they even have to disclose the fact that they are taping the proceeding. However, the discovery by those present at a proceeding that the reporter is tape-recording it can have some repercussions.

If a hidden tape recorder is discovered, all attorneys at the proceeding may demand copies. The agency's client may refuse to work with the agency again. Upon receipt of the transcript, the participants to the proceeding may look it over with a fine-tooth comb to make sure that on-the-record versus off-the-record discussions and other matters were handled appropriately by the reporter.

Even openly requesting to make a backup tape of a proceeding may lead to resistance. It may give attorneys the impression that you are incapable of producing a verbatim transcript. In addition, many attorneys view audiotape tape-recording as disruptive to the proceeding, since the reporter must request a pause in the proceeding to change cassettes.

Currently there is court reporting equipment on the market with built-in microphones or notebook computer attachments that provide an audio recording of the proceeding onto a diskette to facilitate editing for the reporter. If attorneys or witnesses claim that they did not say something on the record that they, in fact, did say, the recording serves as a backup verification method, despite the fact that the reporter's steno notes should accurately reflect what was said. However, the reporter had to have activated the taping device during that segment of the proceeding. There is also equipment on the market where a tape recorder is built into the reporter's writer case. These are nondisruptive methods of recording, since they do not require the reporter to request a pause in the proceeding to physically change a cassette tape. Therefore, many agencies welcome this advancement in technology.

A few methods of requesting permission to tape-record a proceeding are:

- Have the agency request it prior to the proceeding.
- Say, "I've been having some trouble with my equipment lately and would like to tape-record as a backup."
- Say in a multispeaker proceeding, "May I tape-record the proceeding as a backup, since there may be overlap of speakers?"
- Say, "I give my work to a scopist and if she has any questions, she'll be able to consult the tape for clarification."
- Ask the videographer for a courtesy copy of the proceeding if the proceeding is videotaped.

A major problem with tape-recording proceedings is that the reporter may begin to rely on the tape and not utilize the practices that he or she uses in a nontaped proceeding to ensure the accuracy of the record. I once encountered a job where an attorney via telephone from Florida was examining a medical expert. Present in the hotel room were myself and two attorneys. Since I was a relatively new reporter and had not done all that many medicals at that point, I was told by my agency that it would be all right to tape-record the proceedings. I notified the attorneys before the proceeding began that I would be running a backup tape and placed my cassette recorder on the table in front of me.

During the course of the doctor's testimony, the examining attorney (via telephone) started making insinuations about the doctor's integrity and credentials and a fight ensued, resulting in what seemed like a nervous breakdown on the part of the questioning attorney. The attorneys present in the room with me were astonished by what transpired next. The doctor began throwing the medical records all over the place, and the attorney on the telephone was screaming at what seemed at the time 500 words a minute.

I was shocked by the audacity of the attorney to make such insinuations, as were all parties present. I attempted to communicate that there was too much overlapping, that everyone was overlapping and speaking too rapidly for me to make a verbatim record, but I was told to keep writing. Sure enough, after the doctor walked out of the proceeding, the attorneys present asked for an expedited excerpt of the transcript where the attorney's fight-provoking questions and comments began. I thanked my lucky stars that I had tape-recorded the job. As I began to pack up my things, however, I realized that the doctor, in his fury, when he was throwing the medical records in the air, had accidentally knocked the tape recorder over, causing the charger to disengage and stop recording. At that time, recording devices built into the reporter's laptop were not yet available.

Sometimes you are requested to tape the proceedings in situations like public hearings and other difficult proceedings where people often talk over one another. With permission from the agency and the attorneys/administrators of the proceeding, this is acceptable. However, get there early and test-run the equipment, and do not rely on it to aid in your preparation of the transcript. Chances are if there was overlap or you could not make something out while it was said right before you, you will not be able to make it out from a tape. Ask for clarifications or repeats while you are at the proceeding. Modern technology enables court reporting software to decipher what is said on an audiotaped segment of a proceeding and synchronize it with the reporter's notes.

## CONFLICTS OF INTEREST

There may be times when you are presented with conflicts of interest. Say you show up to a deposition and a lawyer who is a family member of yours is representing one of the parties. As the reporter certifies in the certificate page at the end of the transcript that he or she is not related by blood or marriage to any party in the lawsuit or interested in the outcome of the matter, this is considered a conflict of interest. You must divulge this information to all present and let them decide how they want to proceed. If you are related to or know personally a *neutral* party at the proceeding, such as an interpreter or videographer, it is not considered a conflict of interest.

Another situation that could happen is you might personally know the witness or a party to the litigation. Whether or not that person is present at the proceeding, you have a duty to notify the attorneys that you know that person. They will determine if that creates any problems.

Bear in mind that if you show up to a med mal case where the doctor being sued is one of your personal physicians, the testimony may elicit a change in your attitude toward using the services of that doctor in the future. The same is true of any other service provider. The witness may not feel comfortable having you overhear details about the case and may request a different reporter. Do not take it personally.

## AGENCY PREFERENCES

When working for more than one agency, you will find that each agency may request specific things in a transcript from you, as well as specific procedural behavior. Unless it is something that you find ethically incorrect, follow the instructions given by the agency. It may be a painstaking detail that needs to be added manually throughout a transcript. Do not say to the agency, "But other agencies don't request this of me" or refuse the request, or you will lose your team-player status. Put up with it, or simply avoid working for that agency. As long as there is no conflict with NCRA's *Code of Professional Ethics,* there is no right and wrong way to do things, only recommended guidelines. Agency preference dictates.

## SHORT-ANSWER QUESTIONS

1. ____________ is a discussion by attorneys about certain matters regarding the case.
2. Professional conduct for court reporters is outlined in NCRA's ____ __ ____________ ______.
3. Reporters should avoid ____ while reporting.
4. ___ _____ are unexpected jobs that agencies are expected to cover with a reporter immediately.
5. Reporters should not _______ work for an agency while covering a job for a different agency.
6. _______ __ connotes that you do not generally work for an agency.
7. Reporters have a role of _______________ regarding any information obtained on a job.
8. Reporters are expected to maintain a _______ presence at and have no interest in a proceeding.
9. Reporters should have a _____ facial expression during a proceeding.
10. According to NCRA's *Code of Professional Ethics,* reporters are under no obligation to disclose to those present at a proceeding that they are ____-______ the proceedings.
11. If you show up at a job and find a relative of yours involved in the proceeding, there may be a ________ __ ________.
12. Reporters certify in the ___________ page of a transcript that they are not in any way interested in the outcome of the matter being reported.

## TRUE/FALSE QUESTIONS

1. Barring nonethical requests, directives of examining attorneys should be followed by reporters.
2. If you are retained by an attorney and he or she leaves the deposition and other attorneys wish to add something onto the record, you should notify them that you require the other attorney's presence and acquiescence and will not go back on the record without it.
3. If attorneys make extraneous comments or jokes on the record and do not tell you to go off the record, you should keep it as part of the transcript.
4. If you are told to go off the record and it sounds like the attorneys went back on without notifying you, you should wait until someone says, "Back on the record."
5. If you are not specific in your request to a witness for a repeat, the witness may try to explain or elaborate on the answer and may ramble on without specifically stating what it was that was originally said.
6. Reading back the portion of the witness's testimony previous to what you dropped may help a witness focus on what he or she originally said.
7. Taking your hands off your machine and holding them up in the air is the recommended way to halt a proceeding.
8. Reporters cannot interrupt deposition proceedings to ask for a repeat of something.
9. According the NCRA's *Guidelines for Professional Practice,* if an assignment is beyond a reporter's skills, he or she should not accept the assignment.
10. Reporters are required to provide their services to the indigent at least once a year.
11. Reporters should offer their opinions related to a case to attorneys or the witness if they are requested to do so.
12. The possibility of a spot call exists on a day when you are off, so you should bring your equipment with you if you are going to the agency.
13. When your job busts, you should pack up and go home immediately.
14. Reporters may be assigned an A.M. job and a P.M. job in two separate locations.
15. Attorneys always know how long their examination should last.
16. If your A.M. job is running late and you are scheduled to cover a P.M. job, you should ask for a break, state your predicament to the examining attorney, find out how much longer the attorneys expect the job to go, and advise your agency to try to cover the job with another reporter.
17. You should notify attorneys that you are covering a job for the agency that retained you but that you are on staff with another agency.
18. A reporter should not give a business card to an attorney that indicates an agency other than the one through which the attorney has contracted the reporter.
19. Making reference to previous cases or discussing the current case within earshot of other parties to the case or the witness violates the Code of Ethics by which reporters are governed.
20. Attorneys appreciate your honesty and want to know if you are a new reporter.
21. If you are assigned your first medical job, you should not tell the attorneys you have never taken one before.
22. Personal matters, such as drug/alcohol problems, should not be discussed on a job.
23. When asked for an opinion of the case or of the witness being deposed, reporters should find a way to evade giving an answer that may put them in a precarious situation.
24. If a witness says something during a deposition that seems funny to you, it is all right to laugh.
25. Tape-recording the proceeding may give attorneys the impression that the reporter is incapable of reporting the proceeding.
26. Audio recording devices may be contained within a reporter's writer case or software program.

27. It is important to arrive early at a proceeding that you will be tape-recording as well as reporting on your stenographic writer so that you can test-run the audiotaping equipment.
28. Tape recording is a 100 percent reliable method to obtain anything missed while stenographically recording a proceeding.
29. If you show up to a proceeding and note the name of someone you know personally in the caption, even if that person is not the witness being examined, you should mention this to the attorneys, as they may feel that there is a conflict of interest.
30. If your brother is the attorney at a proceeding where you are the court reporter, no conflict of interest exists.

## DISCUSSION QUESTIONS

1. If told to go off the record by an attorney other than the examining attorney, what should you do?
2. If told to go off the record by a witness, what should you do?
3. What should you do if you miss something that is said during a deposition?
4. What is a drawback of putting your hands up in the air when a proceeding gets out of control?
5. What methods would you employ if a proceeding got out of control?
6. What are some merits of tape-recording proceedings?
7. What are some drawbacks to tape-recording proceedings?
8. What impressions might an attorney have of a reporter who requests utilization of a tape recorder as a backup?
9. What are some ways to request permission to tape-record a proceeding?
10. What types of conflicts of interest might arise on a job?

# CHAPTER 12

# Beyond the Deposition

## DICTATING

Prior to the advent of electronic stenographic writers, reporters would take down a job on their writer and **dictate** the entire job, plus punctuation, into a Dictaphone, or hand their notes over to a notereader. Dictating is very time-consuming, not to mention the effects on the reporter's throat after hours of speaking into the Dictaphone. Electronic stenographic writers are quickly replacing the older writers, and dictating is rapidly becoming a thing of the past.

## NOTEREADERS

There are people skilled in reading steno notes who then prepare a transcript directly from those notes. These people are called **notereaders.** If a reporter does not possess an electronic stenographic writer, a notereader may come in handy. Likewise, if a reporter who writes a job on an electronic stenographic writer finds out that the disk the job was written on is defective or is lost and does not have time to rewrite his or her job, a notereader may be used.

**Dictate:** To read one's steno notes replete with punctuation into a Dictaphone for a scopist/typist to prepare a transcript from.

**Notereader:** A professional who prepares a transcript for a reporter from rough steno notes.

## SCOPING THE JOB

When you finish taking a job, you have the option to either scope it yourself or have it prepared by a scopist. Some of the advantages of using a scopist are:

- It frees the reporter to accept more jobs a week than the reporter might be able to handle if he or she had the additional responsibility of scoping jobs
- It enables the reporter to have free time to devote to other activities/family

- The reporter might not be able to scope the transcript within the turn-around time required
- The reporter may not have a software program to scope his or her work on
- The scopist serves as a second set of eyes and may catch errors that the reporter may not see
- Some agencies offer in-house scoping free of charge or require some/all jobs to be scoped in-house

Several reasons that reporters prefer to scope their own work are:

- The reporter may feel that no one can understand his or her notes as well as he or she can, especially after an off day of writing
- The reporter may not want to expend the additional cost of paying a scopist from his or her page rate
- Dissatisfaction with the skills of the scopist(s) previously utilized
- Inability to find a scopist with software compatible to the reporter's writer
- Inability to find a scopist who can handle the workload that the reporter wishes him or her to handle
- Slow turnaround by scopists previously utilized
- The reporter does not know how to find a scopist

## Finding a Scopist

Finding a scopist is not as difficult as it appears. Many advertise on court reporting school bulletin boards, in trade magazines, and on the Internet through NCRA and other court reporting–related Web sites. In-house scopists at freelance agencies often do scoping on the side. Ask fellow reporters who does their scoping. Since most transactions are done electronically or via regular mail, the scopist's location is not a major issue.

## Scopist-Reporter Compatibility

There is a certain element of compatibility that must be present between the reporter and the scopist. Preferred scopists are ones that follow reporter instructions well, are meticulous in spell checking/proofreading the transcript before sending it to the reporter to proofread, flag questions they have rather than making judgment calls unbeknownst to the reporter, and meet transcript deadlines. Similarly, scopists prefer to work with reporters who:

- Write clearly and legibly
- Prepare a sufficient glossary
- Provide clear instructions
- Estimate the amount of transcript pages fairly accurately
- State a specific date that the transcript should be returned by

Scopists are professionals in their own right, and all it takes is one memorable job to create a reporter-scopist bond that may last a lifetime. Treat them with the utmost respect, because they are truly invaluable.

## Scopist Rates

Prior to working with a particular scopist, the reporter should ask the scopist for his or her page rate. A reporter may attempt to negotiate with a scopist if the reporter pays other scopists *x* cents per page and the scopist's rate seems unusually high. Either the scopist will reduce the page rate, the reporter will pay the higher page rate, or the reporter will choose to use another scopist. After the scopist states the page rate, if a job is given to the scopist, it is assumed that the reporter accepts the page rate and agrees to pay it.

## How to Work with a Scopist

When the reporter finishes a job, if he or she has a software program, the job should be dumped, or entered into, his or her software program. Then the reporter should name or date the file. Many agencies prefer that the reporter use his or her initials followed by the date of the job, for example, *DC080100.* Then the reporter's **unedited notes** should be tranned against his or her main (personal) dictionary. If the scopist does not have a copy of the reporter's dictionary, or an updated one, the reporter should translate the job notes before copying them and sending them via disk or e-mail to the scopist.

**Unedited notes:** Rough notes prior to updating by a reporter or scopist.

## Include Files

The reporter may then want to insert some include files into the job. Include files are files that are programmed into a reporter's software system that indicate an agency's format for:

- Title page, appearance page, index page, stipulation page (if applicable), sworn/affirmed paragraph, and first two questions (name and address)
- Interpreter sworn/affirmed paragraph
- Parenthetical wording
- Time noted, jurat/acknowledgment page (if applicable), certification page

Include files also may be created for continuing cases or multiple witnesses on the same case. This way, when scoping, you already have the title page and appearance page of the case at your disposal, which you will modify to reflect new information.

## Sample Transcripts

When you start working for an agency, you can ask them for a sample:

- Title page
- Appearance page
- Index
- Stipulation page (if applicable)
- List of parentheticals
- Jurat/acknowledgment page
- Certification page

Agencies will usually help you set things up in your computer if you choose to do your own scoping. Some have a skeleton disk that they can give you containing formatting information and include files.

By studying a sample transcript of your agency, you can learn how they like their parentheticals to read, such as:

(Discussion held off the record.)
versus
(Discussion off the record.)

Each agency has its preferences, so it is important to communicate with the agency when you have scoping questions, punctuation questions, or when judgment calls need to be made.

## What to Send to the Scopist

You can either create include files in your software program and add them into the job file before sending it to a scopist or send the scopist a sample transcript and let the scopist add everything. If the reporter does not have an edit style sheet for that particular agency, either the scopist or the reporter can call the agency and speak to the key computer person to find out the edit style parameters, margins, tabs, and so on. The reporter may:

- Send the original disk to the scopist if the scopist's software program is compatible to the reporter's writer
- Transfer the job onto a disk that is compatible
- E-mail/modem the job directly to the scopist's software electronically

The reporter should then photocopy his or her work sheet and any additional material that he or she is sending to the scopist. If the reporter is faxing the material to the scopist, this is not necessary, although the reporter will still need a photocopy of the work sheet when he or she sends the original work sheet to his or her agency with the finalized transcript.

The additional material sent to the scopist should include a glossary, a photocopy of any material quoted from, and/or any exhibits that were referred to which may contain spellings of words or names that the reporter did not include in the glossary.

## Glossaries

When using a notereader or scopist, you should include an alphabetized glossary of names for the case, as well as short forms (briefs), for example, *LAERGS* for *laceration,* or outlines that you used on the job, such as *BEN/BEN* for *benefactor.* Arbitraries are short forms for lengthy or difficult-to-write words or phrases.

When preparing a glossary, list people's names under the last name first, separated by a comma, for example, *Jones, Bob,* under *J.* (See Figure 12–1 for a sample glossary.) If you are not sure whether the scopist or notereader will be able to decipher the last name from your steno notes, you may choose to cross-reference the name by also listing it under the letter for the first name, for example, *Bob Jones* under *B,* as well.

This glossary should be submitted to the agency with the finished transcript so that if another reporter is sent at a later time to work on the same case, that reporter will have access to your glossary as an assistive device.

**FIGURE 12–1**
Sample Glossary

| CASE: | DATE: | REPORTER: |
|---|---|---|
| A | H&I | P&Q |
| B | J | R |
| C | K | S |
| D | L | T-U-V |
| E | M | W-X-Y-Z |
| F | N | OUTLINES |
| G | O | |

### When the Scopist Finishes the Transcript

After the scopist performs the necessary scoping functions, the scopist will return the **edited notes** to the reporter by mail, delivery service, or electronically; or, if the scopist lives or works near the reporter's home/job location, the reporter may pick it up or the scopist may drop it off.

## PROOFREADING TRANSCRIPTS

**Edited notes:** Steno notes that have been "tranned" on CAT software and scoped.

The reporter is then responsible for proofreading the transcript. The reporter looks not only for spelling and punctuation errors, but also for hearing and spacing errors. As it is only human to make errors, it is important that you check *every* section of the transcript for accuracy. Do not assume a scopist caught everything, no matter how fastidious he or she may be.

When you finish proofreading the job, usually you will make corrections to the transcript. Some scopists will do corrections for the reporter, but they may charge an additional amount of cents per page for it. If you are working on a daily or an expedited transcript and time is of the essence, you can ask office personnel for assistance in doing corrections. On dailies, you are counseled not to proofread as critically as you might on a regular job, for example, minor punctuation corrections, but rather, just to focus on substantial corrections. You can always send a more conscientiously proofread trancript at a later date.

After proofreading, it is also essential that you do a spell-check of each job. This will aid you in the detection of errors that were missed by you and/or your scopist. Bear in mind, however, that if the error is that the word *their* appears in the transcript as *there,* since *there* is spelled correctly, the spell-check would not detect it as an error. That is something the reporter or scopist should have spotted. When doing corrections, you might make subsequent typos. Running the spell-check function on your software system once or even twice should pick them up.

### Using Proofreaders

Another professional you may encounter in the court reporting industry is the proofreader. Some reporters scope their work and pay a proofreader to read it in lieu of reading it themselves. Some reporters use professional proofreaders as a second (or third) set of eyes, whether the reporter scopes the job or not. The fee for the proofreader comes out of the reporter's pocket unless the agency supplies in-house proofreading services gratis. As with a scopist, the reporter should ask the proofreader his or her rate up front. Giving the proofreader a job means that you agree to pay the specified rate.

Proofreaders either provide the reporter an errata sheet or write directly on a draft of the transcript. The errata sheet is a form that would include:

- The agency's name, address, and telephone number
- A summarized title of the case
- The date of the proceeding
- The witness's full name
- Page and line numbers of each error
- Lines where the errors are filled in
- Lines for the corrections that are to be made

See Figure 12–2 for a sample errata sheet offered by a proofreader. The reporter would then make the corrections listed by the proofreader.

## PAYING SCOPISTS/NOTEREADERS/PROOFREADERS

If you use the services of a scopist, notereader, or proofreader, they will submit a bill with the return of the transcript/errata sheet. Generally, they do not expect to be paid until you are paid for the job, which can be weeks later. Some, however, request immediate payment. This should be discussed with the scopist/notereader/proofreader at the time he or she accepts the job. It aids scopists/notereaders/proofreaders in maintaining their records if you enclose a copy of their bill with your check. In the memo section of your check, you should write:

**FIGURE 12–2**
Sample Proofreader's Errata Sheet

CORRECTION/ADDITION SHEET

DEPOSITION OF: ____________________

TAKEN ON THE ____ DAY OF ____________, 20_____

IN THE MATTER OF: ____________________

| PAGE NUMBER | LINE NUMBER | SHOULD READ: |
| --- | --- | --- |

Sworn to before me this

____ day of ____________, 20_____

____________________

Notary Public

wp\forms\deposit.cor

- The agency the job was for
- The date of the job
- A summarized caption name
- The witness's or witnesses' name(s)
- Number of pages scoped/proofread

## IRS Form 1099

If an individual scopist/notereader/proofreader earns more than $600 from you in one year, you need to prepare or have your accountant prepare a 1099 form for that person by January 31st of the following year, filed with the IRS by

February 28th of the following year. Even if the amount this individual has earned is less than $600, if you wish to declare this as a business expense, you would do the same.

## BACKUP DISKS

A backup disk of each job should be maintained by the reporter as well as by the agency. Each backup disk should have a label on it that identifies:

- The agency the job was for
- Interoffice agency job number, if applicable
- The date of the job
- Summarized caption name
- Witness's or witnesses' name(s)

You can use one backup disk to archive several job files. These disks should then be stored in a fireproof box. *Always* double-check to make sure that the information you are copying onto the disk is indeed on the disk!

I once worked for an agency whose building burned completely to the ground in the middle of the night. All disks, finished transcripts, work sheets, and equipment in the office were gone, as well as the agency's archived transcripts and bookkeeping records. At that point in my court reporting career, all of my work was scoped in-house. Finished transcripts that had been sent to the office that were not yet forwarded to the lawyers were destroyed. Jobs either had to be noteread from the reporters' steno notes or scoped from the original job disks or job files previously **dumped** (downloaded) into the reporters' personal computers.

Lessons to Be Learned:

- When you get home from a job, if you are physically sending the original job disk to a private or office scopist, dump the job file into the computer. This way, you have a copy of your job if anything should happen to the disk that you mail. Reporters who do this are able to reprint a copy of the transcript without the need to have a job noteread
- Photocopy any paperwork, the original of which is being mailed somewhere
- Purchase fireproof/waterproof boxes for archiving disks of past jobs, bookkeeping records, and so on

The principal of the agency at that time learned the importance of fireproof boxes for archiving disks of past jobs as well as bookkeeping records.

## SENDING FINISHED TRANSCRIPTS TO AGENCIES

The transcript is now ready to be sent to the agency. Depending on your agency's software and preference, you will send:

- A printed transcript
- A printed transcript and an ASCII disk
- Just a disk with the transcript on it if the agency's software is compatible with yours
- An e-mailed transcript

**Dump:** To download steno notes from a job into CAT software.

The transcript of each witness in a multiple-witness deposition should be on a separate disk or sent in a separate e-mail attachment, each indicating:

- The date of the job
- A summarized caption name of the job
- The witness's name
- Witness #1, #2, #3 or Witness A, B, C, and so on to indicate that other disks/e-mails that contain the testimony of other witnesses will be forthcoming
- The agency the job was for
- Any agency interoffice job number
- The reporter's name

Additional services requested by the client or the agency will be discussed in Chapter 13. When sending a job to an agency, it is recommended to also add the job to your bill to that agency.

## BILLING AGENCIES

As mentioned earlier, each agency has a billing cycle and will tell you when your bill must be in the office by in order to get paid on a specified date. Agencies supply reporters with billing forms that usually ask for:

- The reporter's name and address
- The reporter's Social Security number
- The month and date of the billing cycle that the bill represents
- The date of the job
- A summarized caption
- The number of copies that were ordered
- The page rate utilized by the reporter in calculating the bill
- How many appearances the reporter should receive (A.M., P.M., A.M. and P.M., evening), if appearances are applicable in your area
- The number of pages billed for
- The total amount due the reporter
- Charges for litigation support, if applicable

See Figure 12–3 for a sample bill to be filled out by a freelance reporter.

In the event that no transcript is ordered from a freelance assignment, the reporter trans his or her notes on the computer, notes the estimated number of pages, and bills the agency for half of the total estimated transcript pages. The reporter also makes a notation on the bill that it is an estimate as no transcript was ordered. If and when the transcript is ordered, the reporter would bill the agency for the balance of transcript pages eventually transcribed,

Photocopy the bill in case it should get lost in the mail, or fax it, but beware that many eyes may view incoming fax transmissions. Many offices mail the reporter a check without a copy of the reporter's billing form. A photocopy enables the reporter to see which jobs were paid by a specific check from the agency. The reporter should enter the date and amount of the check by agency name and check off the individual jobs the check applied to in his or her ledger.

Telephone: (212) 684-7298
Fax: (212) 684-4360

PLEASE COMPLETE THIS SHEET CLEARLY

REPORTER: ______________________________

ADDRESS: ______________________________

______________________________

______________________________

SOCIAL SECURITY NO. ______________________

TO: REINIG REPORTING, INC.

(PLEASE CIRCLE)
BILLING PERIOD – 15th / 30th 1999
MONTH: ______

| DOJ | CAPTION | COPIES | PAGE RATE | A.M. P.M. | # OF PAGES | SUB TOTAL |
|---|---|---|---|---|---|---|
| | | | | | | |
| | | | | | | |
| | | | | | | |
| | | | | | | |
| | | | | | | |
| | | | | | | |
| | | | | | | |
| | | | | | | |
| | | | | | | |
| | | | | | | |
| | | | | | | |
| | | | | | | |
| | | | | | | |
| | | | | | | |
| | | | | | | |

**FIGURE 12–3**
Sample of Freelance Reporter's Bill

## DELETING JOB FILES

After a job is scoped, proofread, corrected, copied onto a backup disk, and sent to the agency, you may delete the job file from your software. The best practice for new reporters is to do this about once a month. This way if anything unusual occurs, such as an agency misplacing the disk subsequently created from your e-mail and then deleting your e-mail, the job will be readily accessible.

## LEDGERS

Each reporter should keep a ledger-type book tracking his or her job information for each year. At the top of each page should be the year to which the ledger sheet applies. The first page or section of the ledger should include columns specifying:

- The date of the job
- The agency that assigned the job
- A summary of the caption
- The witness's or witnesses' last name(s)
- An interoffice job number, if applicable
- The location of the proceeding—some agencies pay different rates depending upon the job location and distance traveled
- Page rate
- Whether the delivery of the transcript was regular, expedited, daily, or immediate/realtime
- The number of appearance fees received, if applicable
- The total number of transcript pages
- The amount billed for
- The date of your bill to the agency

If the reporter works for several agencies, instead of writing out each agency's name, the reporter may ascribe codes, for example, the first letter of the agency's name if the agencies all begin with different letters, to indicate which agency assigned the job.

When the reporter gets paid for a job, a check mark should be placed in the ledger next to the job to indicate that the reporter has been paid. This way, if you inadvertently forgot to bill for a job, the absence of a check mark upon review will remind you to bill for it at a later time. Double-check that the amount received for individual jobs and the total bill match the amounts billed for. Final payment may be off by a page or two upon final printing of a transcript, but substantial discrepancies should be looked into.

The next page or section of the ledger should list each agency for which the reporter has worked and the amount and date of each check received from that agency. The date of the check is important to note to avoid confusion in case two checks in the same amount are received by the reporter.

At the end of the year, total the amount paid by each agency, and double-check that your totals match the 1099 forms that the agencies send you by February of the subsequent year. Your figures may differ from those of the agencies for a number of reasons, such as:

- You might have neglected to record a check in your ledger
- You may have recorded a check twice into your ledger
- You may not be including checks dated by the agency before January 1$^{st}$ that were received after January 1$^{st}$ in your total
- An agency might have made an error

Do not assume an agency's figure is accurate. Do a little research and clear up the discrepancy with the agency's bookkeeper.

Another page of the ledger should be dedicated to recording tax-deductible expenses. Designate separate columns for:

- The lease/purchase of business-related equipment
- Repair and maintenance costs for business-related equipment

- Office supplies, steno paper, business cards, notepads, exhibit stickers, notary/signature stamps, and so on
- The vehicle(s) used to get to and from job destinations. Freelance reporters should record the mileage on vehicles utilized for work purposes at the beginning and end of each year, the purchase or lease payments made during a particular year, the cost of repairs to said vehicles, auto maintenance and part expenditures, the amount of car insurance paid throughout the particular year, and the amount paid for gasoline throughout the year
- Other transportation expenses, such as receipts or documentation for tolls, buses, trains, taxis, and so on
- Parking expenses
- Dues paid to associations
- Donations made to associations/schools/charities
- Seminar fees and related travel expenses
- Travel or entertainment expenses relating to job employment
- Telephone expenses
- Internet fees, if you send work to scopists, agencies, or directly to clients via e-mail
- Postage expenses
- Day care expenses
- Scopist/proofreader expenses

See Figure 12–4 for a sample ledger sheet.

Some reporters record what they earn on a month-by-month basis on a graph so that they can track when business is slower or busier and decide when to take time off/vacations.

## CONTINUING TO BUILD YOUR DICTIONARY

Either weekly or every couple of weeks, a review of your globals is recommended. New words appear on each job that should be added to your main (personal) dictionary. Additionally, combinations of words globalled together may help to resolve conflicts to some degree. Make a copy of your dictionary periodically so that you have an updated version of it. Then, if anything should happen to your dictionary file in your software system, you will have a fairly recent backup.

JOBS — YEAR 2000

| | Co. | Date | Caption | LOC. | Witness | Job # | Delivery | # Pgs. | Pg. Rate | App. | Amount Billed | Date of Bill | Check Rec'd |
|---|---|---|---|---|---|---|---|---|---|---|---|---|---|
| 1 | R | 1/3 | Church v. Larson | NYC | Larson | 3 | regular | 120 | | 2 | | 1/15 | 1 ✓ |
| 2 | B | 1/4 | Kramer hearing | White Plains | | 20 | expedited | 240 | | 2 | | 1/15 | 2 ✓ |
| 3 | R | 1/5 | EUO of Patterson | Long Island | Patterson | 1 | regular | 53 | | 1 | | 1/15 | 3 ✓ |
| 4 | A | 1/6 | Jones v. Smith | NYC | B. Smith<br>R. Smith | 3 | regular | 97 | | 1 | | 1/15 | 4 ✓ |
| 5 | B | 1/7 | Thomas v. ABC Hosp. | Bklyn | Okuko | 52 | daily | 136 | | 2 | | 1/15 | 5 ✓ |
| 6 | P | 1/10 | Kaplan v. XYZ Pizza | Bronx | Kaplan | 7 | regular | 205 | | 3 | | 1/30 | 6 ✓ |
| 7 | A | 1/11 | Finnegan v. Parambuli | Queens | Stokes | 2 | | 0 | | Bust | | 1/15 | 7 ✓ |
| 8 | R | 1/12 | Halpern v. Halpern | NYC | R. Halpern | 7 | expedited | 172 | | 2 | | 1/30 | 8 ✓ |
| 9 | R | 1/13 | Gordon v. Wilson | NJ | Cartright<br>Gordon<br>Wilson | 8 | regular | 273 | | 2 | | 1/30 | 9 ✓ |

**FIGURE 12–4** Sample Ledger Sheet

## SHORT-ANSWER QUESTIONS

1. Before electronic stenographic writers, reporters had to ______________ their jobs or have them noteread.
2. A __________ reads steno notes and then types a transcript up from them.
3. Using a _______ frees up a reporter's time so that he or she can spend more time reporting.
4. _______, or entering a job file into your software program, should be done the day of the job.
5. _______ ____ are files that are programmed into your software system that indicate an agency's transcript/parenthetical preferences or that may be utilized for continuing cases or multiple witnesses on the same cases.
6. You can learn about an agency's transcript style and preferences by requesting a ______________ _________.
7. A ________ is an alphabetized listing of names and words specific to a case.
8. __________ are short forms for a lengthy or difficult-to-write word or phrase.
9. A person's name is generally listed in a glossary under the initial letter of the person's ____ name.
10. ___________-_______________ is used on a glossary if the reporter foresees a problem that the scopist/notereader will have deciphering the name in steno.
11. _________ is done by reporters to correct spelling, punctuation, hearing, and spacing errors.
12. Court reporting software comes with a _____ _____ function that helps to detect errors in a transcript.
13. If a scopist/notereader/proofreader earns more than $600 a year from a reporter, the reporter, if claiming his or her services as a tax deduction, is required to send that person a ____ by January 31st of the following year.
14. If a scopist does not have a copy of your dictionary, you should ____ the job before sending it.
15. ______ disks should be maintained by reporters for every job.
16. Reporters should keep a ______ of their job information, income, and job-related expenses.
17. It is advised to store backup disks in _________ boxes.

## TRUE/FALSE QUESTIONS

1. Most reporters today dictate their jobs.
2. If a reporter's job disk is defective, the reporter might utilize the services of a notereader rather than rewriting the job.
3. Some reporters use scopists as a second set of eyes to catch errors the reporter may not catch.
4. All agencies have in-house scopists.
5. Reporters pay independent scopists a per-page amount.
6. A scopist may be used if a reporter cannot meet a job's turnaround time by scoping, proofreading, and correcting the transcript himself or herself.
7. No one can read a reporter's notes on an off-writing day, so the reporter should scope the job himself or herself.
8. Scopists/notereaders/proofreaders may advertise their services online.
9. Being scopist-friendly means you write clearly and ledgibly, prepare a sufficient glossary, provide clear instructions, estimate the amount of transcript pages fairly accurately, and state a specific date that the transcript should be returned by.
10. Scopists always return jobs to reporters within three days.
11. Scopist page rates are determined after they scope the job.
12. Include files of caption and appearance pages on continuing jobs are helpful to reporters.
13. The name Steven Albert would be listed under *S* on a glossary.
14. If a scopist is utilized, a reporter need not proofread the job.
15. Corrections are always done by scopists.
16. Reporters are counseled to focus on substantive corrections and not minor punctuation corrections when proofreading a daily.
17. Typos may occur while a reporter is making corrections to a transcript.
18. Spell-checks detect any error in a transcript.
19. Proofreaders generally make corrections for reporters.
20. Even if scopists/notereaders/proofreaders earn less than $600 from you during a given year, if you wish to claim their services as a tax deduction, you should issue them a 1099.
21. A backup disk should be prepared for each job.
22. All agencies require the reporter to send a printout of a finished transcript.
23. An agency's 1099 figure is always accurate.
24. Monthly automobile leasing payments may be a tax deduction for a freelance reporter.
25. Freelance reporters may not claim seminar fees as a tax deduction.
26. Tolls and parking expenses incurred on workdays are tax deductions for freelance reporters.
27. Once you graduate from court reporting school, your dictionary is complete.
28. Combinations of words globalled together may help to resolve conflicts.
29. Reporters should back up their dictionaries periodically onto disks.

## DISCUSSION QUESTIONS

1. If you were looking for a scopist/notereader/proofreader, how would you go about finding one?
2. What are some advantages of using a scopist?

3. Why might a reporter choose to scope his or her own work rather than use a scopist?
4. What are the benefits of obtaining sample transcripts from agencies?
5. Why might glossaries sent to agencies with finished transcripts be helpful to other reporters?
6. What information is contained on a proofreader's errata sheet?
7. When paying a scopist/notereader/proofreader, what information should be included on your check?
8. What information should be included on a billing sheet sent to an agency?
9. What information should be contained within a reporter's ledger?
10. What can a reporter do to make sure he or she has billed and/or been paid for a specific job?
11. What expenses may be claimed by freelance reporters each year?
12. Why do some reporters record what they earn on a monthly basis on a graph?

# CHAPTER 13

# The Transcript

## ELEMENTS OF A DEPOSITION TRANSCRIPT

A deposition transcript consists of:

- A title page
- An appearance page
- An index page, if warranted
- A stipulation page, if applicable
- The sworn/affirmed parenthetical, if applicable
- Testimony
- Colloquy
- A jurat or acknowledgment page, if applicable
- A certification page

See Figure 13–1 for a sample transcript employing usual stipulations (in New York), and see Figure 13–2 for a sample transcript employing federal stipulations.

### Title Page

The title page is the first page of the transcript. It contains the venue of the case, or the jurisdiction where the case is filed. The title page also includes the caption, which is the title or name of the case, and the case number, the wording of which varies depending on the jurisdiction. Title pages generally state:

- The location of the proceeding—usually just street address, city, and state
- The date of the proceeding
- The starting time of the proceeding
- The nature of the proceeding, for example, deposition or statement
- The classification of the witness(es)—plaintiff, defendent, claimant, respondent, nonparty witness, expert witness—if applicable
- The name of the witness(es)
- Whether the proceeding is pursuant to notice, order, subpoena, stipulation, or agreement
- The name and credentials of the reporter

**FIGURE 13–1**
Sample Transcript Employing Usual Stipulations

SUPREME COURT OF THE STATE OF NEW YORK
COUNTY OF NASSAU
\- - - - - - - - - - - - - - - - - - - - - - - - - -
HENRIETTA SILVER,

Index No.
Plaintiff, 75757/95

–against–

CARL KLUG, ALICIA TRIPPE AND MARIO TRIPPE,

Defendants.

\- - - - - - - - - - - - - - - - - - - - - - - - - -

EXAMINATION BEFORE TRIAL

of the Plaintiff,

HENRIETTA SILVER, pursuant to Court Order of the Hon. Justice Bertram L. Smith, held at the law offices of FEINSTEIN, FEINSTEIN & BERTOLI, LLP, 123 Buckeye Road, Merrick, New York 12345, on April 5, 1999, commencing at 10:15 A.M., before Dana Chipkin, a Registered Professional Reporter and Notary Public within and for the State of New York.

REINIG REPORTING, INC.
192 Lexington Avenue
New York, New York 10016
(212) 684-7298

**EXHIBIT 1**
A sample title page

(may be DEPOSITION in your state)

**EXHIBIT 2**
A sample of agency information on title page

If a caption is very lengthy, the title page may be divided into more than one page, or the spacing may be changed in order to include all the information on one page. If the title of the case contains multiple captions, an agency may instruct you to place the first two captions on the title page and place the balance of the captions on the following page(s). Each agency has a preference for how it likes the title page to appear, so request a format booklet or sample transcript from the agency.

See Exhibit 1 in Figure 13–1 for a sample title page. Note that:

- The classification of the proceeding may be in uppercase *(DEPOSITION)* or initial capped only *(Deposition)*
- The word *of* is lowercase
- The witness's name is uppercase

**FIGURE 13–1**
(continued)

APPEARANCES:

EXHIBIT 3
A sample appearance page

PANICO & PANICO, ESQ.
Attorney for Plaintiff
75 Parker Street
Croton on Hudson, New York 98765
BY: SHEILA PANICO, ESQ.

FEINSTEIN, FEINSTEIN & BERTOLI, LLP
Attorneys for Defendant
123 Buckeye Road
Merrick, New York 12345

BY: L. OLIVER BAINES, ESQ.

ALSO PRESENT:
BERNARD SILVER

REINIG REPORTING, INC. (212) 684-7298

EXHIBIT 4
A sample footer

- The classification of the witness is initial capped *(the Defendant herein)*
- The classification of attorney examining the witness is initial capped *(taken by the Plaintiff)*
- What authority the proceeding is pursuant to is initial capped, as well as the name of the judge *(pursuant to Court Order of the Hon. Justice Peter E. Gibbs)*
- The reporter's name and credentials are initial capped, with the words *before, a, and, of the,* and *of* lowercase *(before Dana Chipkin, a Registered Professional Reporter and Notary Public of the State of New York.)*

While standard deposition transcript pages contain 25 lines, some agencies' transcripts contain 28 lines. Each line is numbered chronologically (from

**FIGURE 13–1**
(continued)

IT IS HEREBY STIPULATED AND AGREED by and between counsel for the respective parties hereto that all rights provided by the C.P.L.R., including the right to object to any question, except as to the form, or to move to strike any testimony at this examination, are reserved; and, in addition, the failure to object to any question or to move to strike testimony at this examination shall not be a bar or waiver to make such a motion at, and is reserved for, the trial of this action.

IT IS FURTHER STIPULATED AND AGREED that this examination may be signed and sworn to by the witness being examined, before a Notary Public other than the Notary Public before whom this examination was begun, but the failure to do so, or to return the original of this examination to counsel, shall not be deemed a waiver of rights provided by Rules 3116 and 3117 of the C.P.L.R. and shall be controlled thereby.

IT IS FURTHER STIPULATED AND AGREED that the filing of the original of this examination is hereby waived.

REINIG REPORTING, INC. (212) 684-7298

**EXHIBIT 5**
A sample stipulation page

1 through 25 or 1 through 28), and the line numbers appear on the printed transcript. Transcript pages are numbered chronologically starting with page 1 (unless the proceeding was a continuation), and page numbers appear in the top right corner.

Some agencies like a box that surrounds all elements of a transcript page except page number and footer to appear on each transcript page. To accommodate this request, the reporter (or scopist) programs a specific number when setting the parameters of the agency's edit style sheet. Although the box does not appear on your computer screen, it will appear when the transcript is printed.

***Agency Information*** Below all the other information, the title page, and the title page only, may have the agency's name, address, and telephone number on

**FIGURE 13–1**
(continued)

HENRIETTA SILVER, having been duly sworn by a Notary Public within and for the State of New York, and having stated her address as 1818 Lockwood Court, West Hurley, New York 12491, was examined and testified under oath as follows:

EXAMINATION BY MR. BAINES:

Q Please state your name for the record.

A Henrietta Silver.

Q Please state your address for the record.

A 1818 Lockwood Court, West Hurley, New York 12491.

Q Ms. Silver, are you taking any medication that may affect your testimony this morning?

A Not that would affect my testimony, no.

Q What medications are you presently taking?

A Theo-Dur for my asthma and Tylenol with codeine for pain.

REINIG REPORTING, INC. (212) 684-7298

separate lines, centered. If there is no room for this information, the agency may divide the title page into two pages or choose to eliminate it. See Exhibit 2 in Figure 13–1 for agency information on the title page.

***Footers*** The footer is a single or double line that appears below the last line of each transcript page. It usually contains the agency's name and telephone number(s). If there is room, it may contain the agency's address and fax number as well. The footer is set in the edit style of the transcript and does not appear on the screen during the editing process. When the job is printed, however, the footer appears on every transcript page. Since the title page already contains agency information, the footer would be redundant, so agencies may ask you to delete the footer on the title page only. This is done by printing transcript pages 2 on (or if a continuation, the number of the second page of the transcript on)

**FIGURE 13–1**
(continued)

Silver

EXHIBIT 6
A sample header

Q What is your Social Security number?

MS. PANICO: Don't answer that.

MR. BAINES: On what grounds?

MS. PANICO: You know, I really don't have to - - let's go off the record for a minute.

(Discussion held off the record.)

MS. PANICO: You can answer the question.

A I don't have it memorized. Let me see if I have my card in my bag.

I can't find it.

MS. PANICO: Leave a space in the record and we'll fill it in upon execution of the transcript.

MR. BAINES: Okay.

*INSERT: - - - - - - - - - - - - - - -

Q Were you involved in an automobile accident on November 20, 1994?

A Yes.

Q Were you the driver or a passenger at the time of the accident?

A Well, my friend Estelle had

REINIG REPORTING, INC. (212) 684-7298

with a footer, then deleting the footer command on your CAT system, and then printing out the first page of the transcript. See Exhibit 4 in Figure 13–1 for a sample footer.

## Appearance Page

The appearance page is the next page in the sequence. The word *APPEARANCES,* uppercase, centered or left margin, followed by a colon, is on line 2. See Exhibit 3 in Figure 13–1 for a sample appearance page.

***Noting Attorney Appearances*** When listing the attorneys, who they represent determines their order on the appearance page. Look at the caption. Go party by party, listing their counsel in the same order.

**FIGURE 13–1**
(continued)

Silver
invited me - -
MS PANICO: Just answer the
question "yes" or "no," if you can.
THE WITNESS: You told me that
already. I'm sorry.
MS. PANICO: That's okay. You're
doing fine.
A What was the question again, I'm
sorry.
MR. BAINES: Let's have the
reporter read it back.
(The question is read back by the
reporter.)
A I was the driver.
Q What was the make and model of
the vehicle that you were involved in the
accident with?
A A Chrysler LeBaron.
Q Do you know what year?
A 1993.
Q Was the license plate of the
vehicle JHE157?
A You know, I really don't
remember.
REINIG REPORTING, INC. (212) 684-7298

As on your work sheet, you will list the name of the attorney's law firm, who the attorney represents, the street address of the law firm, city, state, and zip code, and the appearance of the attorney present at the proceeding. An example:

PETERSON & GORDON, ESQS.
Attorneys for the Plaintiff
123 Magnolia Street
Pittsburgh, Pennsylvania 15123
BY: LINDA PETERSON, ESQ.

The order of the information may vary, but the nature of the information will be the same. Note that uppercase is utilized for the name of the law firm, the word *BY,* and the name of the attorney present, while other words are initial capped and lowercase.

**FIGURE 13–1**
(continued)

Silver

MS. PANICO: Off the record.

(Discussion held off the record.)

Q Did you purchase the vehicle new or used?

A New.

Q How many miles did the vehicle have on November 20, 1994?

A Oh, I wouldn't remember that.

Q Did the vehicle have standard or automatic transmission?

A Automatic.

Q Power steering?

A Yes.

Q Did it have air bags?

A When the accident happened, I didn't - -

MS. PANICO: "Yes" or "no."

A Yes.

Q Was the radio on at the time of the accident?

A Yes, I always listen to those a.m. talk shows when I travel.

Q Are you familiar with the intersection of Julian Avenue and Kenny Court?

REINIG REPORTING, INC. (212) 684-7298

If the firm uses an ampersand *(&)* in its name rather than the word *and*, make sure you use an ampersand, or vice versa. If the firm is a multiple-name law firm, everything should correspond in the plural, for example, *ESQS.* rather than *ESQ.*, and *Attorneys for. . .* rather than *Attorney for. . . .* Even though only one attorney appeared on behalf of the firm, it is the firm name to which *ESQS.* and *Attorneys* must correspond.

If there are multiple plaintiffs or defendants named in the caption and an attorney represents one or more parties, in addition to listing the attorney as *Attorney for Defendant,* for example, note also the name of the defendant that the attorney represents, for example, *Attorney for Defendant 123 CORPORATION.* The name of the party may be written in uppercase letters or initial capped only. Some agencies like the reporter to place a hyphen between the party classification and the party name. For example:

**FIGURE 13–1**
(continued)

Silver

A Yes.
Q Had you driven by that intersection prior to November 20, 1994?
A Many times.
Q When had you driven there last prior to November 20, 1994?
A The day before.
Q Immediately prior to the accident on November 20, 1994, where were you?
A In my car.
THE WITNESS: What does he mean?
MS. PANICO: If you don't understand the question, tell him.
MR. BAINES: I'll rephrase the question.
Q Where had you gotten into your car just prior to the accident occurring?
A At my house.
Q That was at 1818 Lockwood Court in West Hurley on November 20, 1994?
A Yes.
Q If the accident had not occurred, where were you intending to go?
A Well, we were - - I wanted to - -

REINIG REPORTING, INC. (212) 684-7298

ANDREA DOCAMPO, ESQ.
Attorney for Defendant - 123 CORPORATION
54 Maiden Lane
New York, New York 10038

Others may prefer starting a new line with the party's name. For example:

ANDREA DOCAMPO, ESQ.
Attorney for Defendant
123 CORPORATION
54 Maiden Lane
New York, New York 10038

Check on your agency's preference.

**FIGURE 13–1**
(continued)

Silver

grocery shopping at Waldbaums with my friend Estelle. She doesn't drive and asked me to take her.

MR. BAINES: Move to strike the nonresponsive part of the answer.

Q You had been to the intersection of Julian Avenue and Kenny Court before?

MS. PANICO: Asked and answered.

MR. BAINES: Sorry.

Q What route did you take to go from your home at 1818 Lockwood Court to the intersection of Julian Avenue and Kenny Court on November 20, 1994?

A The way I always go.

Q We don't know the way you always go. You have to tell us.

A You mean north, south, east, west?

I don't know compass directions all that well.

Q No. I mean - -

A I don't study maps, you know.

Q - - when you left your home, what streets did you take, did you make a left or

REINIG REPORTING, INC. (212) 684-7298

***Listing Nonattorneys Who Might Question Witnesses*** Sometimes the person questioning the witness will state that he or she is not yet admitted to the bar. This person may be permitted to question a witness under the supervision of the attorneys of record or may be questioning a witness in a nondeposition setting. If affiliated with a law firm, the person's appearance will be listed on the appearance page in the same manner as an attorney with that firm; however, *ESQ.* will not follow the person's name. Anyone else affiliated with a law firm, such as a summer intern or clerk, would not be questioning the witness and would be listed under *ALSO PRESENT* on the appearance page. In a nondeposition setting, the person questioning would be listed on the appearance page with the company that person represents and its address, if applicable.

***Attorneys Representing Multiple Parties*** If an attorney represents more than one party named in the caption and the parties are named in different locations of the caption, the order of the attorney's appearance is determined by

Silver

right; that's what I'm looking for.

A Oh.

MS. PANICO: Just let him finish the entire question before you start to answer.

THE WITNESS: Okay.

A Sorry. I've never done this before.

Q First time for everything.

A I took Lockwood to Central Boulevard, made a left on Central, took it to Main Street, made a left on Main Street and continued on Main until it turned into Julian Avenue, and that's when the accident happened.

Q Were you wearing your glasses at the time of the accident?

MS. PANICO: Objection. Lack of foundation.

MR. BAINES: Strike that.

*RL Q Did your driver's license have any restrictions on it, such as your having to wear glasses while driving?

MS. PANICO: Objection.

MR. BAINES: On what grounds?

REINIG REPORTING, INC. (212) 684-7298

**FIGURE 13–1**
(continued)

the first-named party he or she represents. All the parties the attorney represents follow *Attorney for . . .* in the order in which they appear in the caption.

***Listing Of-Counsel Attorneys*** When an attorney says that he or she is appearing *of Counsel,* this means that the attorney is covering the proceeding for the official attorney(s) of record but is not officially a member of the law firm. You would reflect this on the appearance page by listing the information of the official attorneys of record and, where it says *BY:,* inserting the of-counsel attorney's name, followed by *ESQ., of Counsel.* For example:

SMITH & JONES, ESQS.
Attorneys for Third-Party Defendant
456 Logan Street
Darlington, New Jersey 07446
BY: RICHARD LEWIS, ESQ., of Counsel

**FIGURE 13–1**
(continued)

Silver

MS. PANICO: I don't have to tell you the grounds.

MR. BAINES: If we're operating under the usual stipulations, you do.

MS. PANICO: No, I don't.

MR. BAINES: Are you directing the witness not to answer?

MS. PANICO: Yes.

MR. BAINES: Mark it for a ruling.

Q Did you fill out an MV-104?

A A what?

MS. PANICO: An accident report.

A Yes.

Q Do you have the accident report here with you today?

A I thought I had brought it, but I can't seem to find it.

*REQ MR. BAINES: I call for production of the MV-104.

MS. PANICO: We will make a search for it and provide it.

I did find this in my file (indicating). Do you want to mark it?

REINIG REPORTING, INC. (212) 684-7298

Whether the *ESQ., of Counsel* is placed on the same line as the attorney's name or on the next line is a matter of agency preference. For example:

SMITH & JONES, ESQS.
Attorneys for Third-Party Defendant
456 Logan Street
Darlington, New Jersey 07446
BY: MIRIAM GREEN, ESQ.,
of Counsel

***Listing Of-Counsel Law Firms*** Sometimes the of-counsel attorney will be on behalf of a law firm that is of-counsel to the official attorneys of record. In

**FIGURE 13–1**
(continued)

Silver

MR. BAINES: Yes.

Mark this as Defendants' A for identification.

(Handwritten document entitled "Accident information - 11/20/94," dated November 24, 1994, is marked Defendants' Exhibit A for identification, as of this date.)

Q Do you recognize what we've had marked as Defendants' Exhibit A for identification?

A Yes.

Q What is it?

A This is my notes that I made following the accident.

Q This is your handwriting, Mrs. Silverstein [sic]?

A Silver.

Q Silver, sorry.

A Yes, it is.

Q Does this document list as a witness to the accident a Mr. Chadpuri (phonetic)?

A Looks like it. I can't read that

REINIG REPORTING, INC. (212) 684-7298

that case, note the firm's full name (but not its address) and the name of the of-counsel attorney. For example:

SMITH & JONES, ESQS.
Attorneys for Third-Party Defendant
456 Logan Street
Darlington, New Jersey 07446
BY: GREEN & GREEN, ESQS., of Counsel
BY: MIRIAM GREEN, ESQ., of Counsel

The address of the of-counsel firm/attorney is not necessary, as the transcript, if ordered, will go to the official attorneys of record, unless you are otherwise

**FIGURE 13–1**
(continued)

Silver

name too well.

Q It looks like C-h-a-d-p-u-r-i.

THE WITNESS: Is that the man who - -

MS. PANICO: Let him ask you questions and just answer what's asked of you.

THE WITNESS: Got it.

A That sounds familiar.

Q Were there any other witnesses to this accident, that you know of?

A No.

Q Do you have any other notes or documents which have this witness' name on it?

A Yes, his business card. I have it at home. It has his phone number on it as well.

*REQ MR. BAINES: I call for production of the business card.

MS. PANICO: May I?

MR. BAINES: Sure.

MS. PANICO: Didn't you mention a second witness to me?

THE WITNESS: Oh, I forgot about

REINIG REPORTING, INC. (212) 684-7298

directed. It is a good idea to double-check where the transcript should be sent and that you have the correct name and address of both law firms.

***Inclusion of File Numbers*** Agencies differ as to whether or not to include a file number on the appearance page below the attorney's information. Consult the agency for its preference.

***Personal Attorneys*** If a witness on behalf of a party company or entity has a personal attorney present in addition to the party company's/entity's official attorney of record on the case, the personal attorney is also listed as an attorney on the appearance page. However, he or she is listed after all attorneys of record are listed. In addition, since he or she is representing an individual and not a company, the listing will state *Attorney for* and the witness's name rather than the witness's classification (plaintiff, defendant, and so on). For example, say Millie Jones is the personal attorney for the plaintiff, ABC Corporation, and

**FIGURE 13–1**
(continued)

Silver

him.

MS. PANICO: Tell him.

A There was another gentleman.

Could we go off the record for a second?

Q Sure.

(Discussion held off the record.)

MS. PANICO: The witness has notified us that she is not feeling well enough to continue and would like to adjourn for the day. We will arrange for a continuation of the plaintiff's examination at a mutually convenient time and place.

MR. BAINES: With that, we are adjourned.

(Time noted: 11:24 a.m.)

______________

HENRIETTA SILVER

**EXHIBIT 7**
A sample jurat

Subscribed and sworn to before me

this _____ day of ____________, 1999.

________________________________

NOTARY PUBLIC

REINIG REPORTING, INC. (212) 684-7298

A. J. Wells is the witness appearing on behalf of ABC Corporation. The appearance page will be as follows:

SCHWARTZ, GOLDBERG & FEIT, P.C.
Attorneys for Plaintiff
99 Park Avenue
New York, New York 10016
BY: JILL SCHWARTZ, ESQ.

BONILLO & BONILLO, ESQS.
Attorneys for Defendant
103 Cuttermill Road
Briantown, OH 97034
BY: JOHN BONILLO, ESQ.

**FIGURE 13–1**
(continued)

ACKNOWLEDGMENT

**EXHIBIT 8**
A sample acknowledgment page

STATE OF NEW YORK )

: ss.

COUNTY OF )

I, HENRIETTA SILVER, hereby certify that I have read the transcript of my testimony taken under oath in my depostion of April 5, 1999; that the transcript is a true, complete and correct record of my testimony, and that the answers on the record as given by me are true and correct.

------------------

HENRIETTA SILVER

Signed and Subscribed to

before me, this _____ day

of __________, 1999.

--------------------

Notary Public, State of New York

REINIG REPORTING, INC. (212) 684-7298

MILLIE JONES, ESQ.
Personal Attorney/Counsel for A. J. Wells
12 Clinton Avenue
Garden City, New York 11530

At the beginning of the proceeding, when obtaining your work sheet information, ask for the personal attorney's card or firm name and address.

***Co-counsel*** When a party witness has representation by more than one law firm for an action, subsequently retained attorneys are delineated in the record as *co-counsel.* Co-counsel are listed on the appearance page right after the original attorneys of record. When you are given information from which to copy the caption, search for attorney information and note which law firm is listed first. If you do not find this information, you can deduce that the attorney who

**FIGURE 13–1**
(continued)

INDEX

**EXHIBIT 9**
A sample index page

| WITNESS | PAGE |
|---|---|
| HENRIETTA SILVER | |
| Examination by: | |
| MR. BAINES | 4 |

EXHIBITS

| DEFENDANTS' | DESCRIPTION | PAGE |
|---|---|---|
| A | Handwritten document entitled "Accident information - 11/20/94," dated November 24, 1994 | 12 |

DOCUMENTS AND/OR INFORMATION REQUESTED

| DESCRIPTION | PAGE |
|---|---|
| 1) Social Security number | 5 |
| 2) MV-104 | 11 |
| 3) Business card | 13 |

QUESTIONS MARKED FOR A RULING

| PAGE | LINE |
|---|---|
| 10 | 21 |

REINIG REPORTING, INC. (212) 684-7298

is sitting closest to the witness and who is more verbal during the proceeding should be listed first. The appearance page would appear as follows:

SMITH & DARGE, ESQS.
Attorneys for Plaintiff
77 Havana Boulevard
Barrington, Rhode Island 02806
BY: SKYLAR SMITH, ESQ.

-and-

JONES & JONES, ESQS.
Co-Counsel for Plaintiff
32 Floral Lane
Yucca Valley, California 92284
BY: KATHY JONES, ESQ.

**FIGURE 13–1**
(continued)

STATE OF NEW YORK )
ss
COUNTY OF NASSAU )

I, DANA CHIPKIN, a Registered Professional Reporter and Notary Public within and for the State of New York, do hereby certify:

THAT HENRIETTA SILVER, the witness whose examination is hereinbefore set forth, was duly sworn by me and that this transcript of such examination is a true record of the testimony given by such witness.

I further certify that I am not related to any of the parties to this action by blood or marriage and that I am in no way interested in the outcome of this matter.

IN WITNESS WHEREOF, I have hereunto set my hand this 12th day of April, 1999.

---------------

DANA CHIPKIN

REINIG REPORTING, INC. (212) 684-7298

If two attorneys within a single law firm are both examining a witness, they may also be referred to as co-counsel. The first attorney to question should be listed first on the appearance page. For example:

SMITH & DARGE, ESQS.
Attorneys for Plaintiff
77 Havana Boulevard
Barrington, Rhode Island 02806
BY: JOHN L. SMITH, ESQ.
-and-
PRISCILLA V. MANN, ESQ.

Format as to how to reflect this varies, so consult the agency you are working for regarding this.

UNITED STATES DISTRICT COURT
EASTERN DISTRICT OF NEW YORK
-----------------------------
PETER LEE,

Plaintiff, Civil Action No.: 98 Civ. 48935

–against–

OAK LAKE DENTISTRY and OAK LAKE MEDICAL CENTER,

Defendant.

-----------------------------

92 Third Street
Garden City, New York

December 12, 2000
2:45 p.m.

DEPOSITION of OAK LAKE DENTISTRY by TRAVIS JEAN, a Defendant herein, pursuant to Notice dated November 29, 1999, before Dana Chipkin, a Registered Professional Reporter and Notary Public within and for the State of New York.

ARISTA COURT REPORTING CO.
192 Lexington Avenue
Suite 802
New York, New York 10016
(212) 684-6100

**FIGURE 13–2**
Sample Transcript Employing Federal Stipulations

***Pro Se Witnesses*** When a pro se witness—one who is appearing on his or her own behalf without legal representation—is a named party in the caption, the witness should be listed on the appearance page in the order of the parties in the caption. Therefore, if the pro se witness is a plaintiff, his or her appearance will be noted first; if a defendant, his or her appearance will be noted after the appearance of the attorney for the plaintiff. The pro se witness's appearance will be as follows:

Casey Brian, Pro Se Witness
45 Center Road
Rutledge, Tennessee 37861

Placing the witness's name in uppercase is a matter of agency preference.

**FIGURE 13–2**
(continued)

APPEARANCES:

ROBINSON, TURNER & PODHA, ESQS.
Attorneys for Plaintiff
  92 Third Street
  Garden City, New York 11530

BY: REGINALD L. ROBINSON, ESQ.

WILLIE, MILES & DOTTIE, P.C.
Attorneys for Defendant -
OAK LAKE DENTISTRY
  125 Tilden Lane
  Lancaster, Pennsylvania 17600

BY: LILY LANCE, ESQ., of Counsel

HADDEN, PHOEBES AND DRUCKER, L.L.C.
Attorneys for Defendant -
OAK LAKE MEDICAL CENTER
  8 Atinborough Lake
  Barton, Ohio 43905

BY: ALLYN PHOEBES, JR., ESQ.

ALSO PRESENT: KENDRA CHAPPAQUA, Videographer
REMY JULIENNE, French
Interpreter

ARISTA COURT REPORTING CO. (212) 684-6100

***Listing Nonpresent Law Firms*** If you obtain the name and address of a nonpresent law firm that represents a party to the action and you are not told by the examining attorney to do otherwise, with agency approval, you may list the nonpresent law firm on the appearance page. The nonpresent law firm would be listed in the order of parties named in the caption. The *not present* notation may appear before or after the appearance. Examples are:

JULIAN, ALEXANDER, LANE & OLIVER, ESQS.
Attorneys for Defendant - 123 CORPORATION
  919 Sullivan Street
  Addison, Illinois 60101
  (Not Present)

or

STIPULATIONS

IT IS HEREBY STIPULATED AND AGREED by and between the attorneys for the respective parties hereto that filing, sealing and certification be and the same are hereby waived.

IT IS FURTHER STIPULATED AND AGREED that all objections, except as to the form of the question, be reserved to the time of the trial.

IT IS FURTHER STIPULATED AND AGREED that the within examination may be signed and sworn to before any Notary Public with the same force and effect as though signed and sworn to before this Court.

ARISTA COURT REPORTING CO. (212) 684-6100

**FIGURE 13–2**
(continued)

NOT PRESENT
JULIAN, ALEXANDER, LANE & OLIVER, ESQS.
Attorneys for Defendant - 123 CORPORATION
919 Sullivan Street
Addison, Illinois 60101

Again, consult the agency for its recommendation, as some agencies advise against listing firms that, unbeknownst to the reporter, may have been officially let out of the case.

If a law firm does not send someone to attend the proceeding but you are notified that the firm would like a copy of the transcript, you definitely list the firm, who it represents, and its address. You should then request that the court reporting agency confirm the transcript delivery information with the law firm.

**FIGURE 13–2**
(continued)

REMY JULIENNE, called as the
interpreter in this matter, was first
duly sworn to faithfully and accurately
translate questions propounded to the
witness from English to French, and the
answers given by the witness from French
to English.

TRAVIS JEAN, having been duly
sworn by a Notary Public within and for
the State of New York, and having stated
his address as 8090 Barclay Plaza, Shady
Valley, Tennessee 37688, was examined
and testified under oath as follows:

EXAMINATION BY MR. ROBINSON:

Q Please state your name for the
record.

A Travis Jean.

Q What is your present home
address?

A 8090 Barclay Plaza, Shady Valley,
Tennessee 37688.

ARISTA COURT REPORTING CO. (212) 684-6100

***Also Present*** As discussed in Chapter 5, you will list under *ALSO PRESENT* people present at the proceeding who are not attorneys of record or witnesses being examined in that particular transcript. Whether or not their names are listed as uppercase or initial capped is at the discretion of the agency you are working for.

## Index Page

Depending on the state that you report in, the index page may follow the appearance page of the transcript or may appear toward the end of the transcript. The word *INDEX* is indicated on line 2 of the page in uppercase letters, centered, often with spaces between each letter. Agencies differ in their index styles, so obtain a sample from the agency.

Index pages specify the page on which each witness's testimony began. In the case of multiple attorneys examining, it provides the page number on which each attorney's examination commenced or continued following examination by another attorney.

Indexes may include:

- **Requests**—a brief description of each request made and the corresponding page and (sometimes) line numbers where it was made. The inclusion of line numbers is a matter of agency preference. Some agencies have reporters list only page and line numbers on transcripts where numerous requests are made; others may require descriptions
- **Inserts**—the page and line numbers where blank lines were left for information to be inserted and a brief description of the information called for. Some agencies omit the description and list only page and line numbers. The inclusion of line numbers varies from agency to agency
- **Rulings**—the page and line numbers where items were marked for rulings
- **Exhibits**—whether exhibits were marked for identification or in evidence, deemed marked for identification or in evidence, a brief description of the exhibit, how the exhibits were marked—Plaintiff's, Plaintiffs', Defendant's, Defendants', Third-Party Plaintiff's, Third-Party Defendants', the name of the witness, and so on—the number or letter of the exhibit, and the page number corresponding to where in the transcript the exhibit was physically marked by the reporter

Depending upon the agency, an index page may also include page numbers of directions to a witness not to answer a question and **motions** made by the attorneys.

If there was only one witness who was examined by one attorney and there were no requests for information, inserts, rulings marked, or exhibits marked, then it is not necessary to have an index page in the transcript. See Exhibit 9 in Figure 13–1 for a sample index page.

## Stipulation Page

In states where it is the practice to insert stipulation pages in deposition transcripts, a transcript may have a stipulation page if the case is pursuant to state/usual or federal stipulations and not a continuation. Some states, however, do not insert stipulation pages at all. If you are reporting in a state that does not utilize stipulations, you may disregard the stipulation information presented in this book. Note also that stipulation pages are not used for transcripts of hearings, arbitrations, or nonlegal proceedings.

In states where the index page is toward the end of the transcript, the stipulation page may appear after the appearance page in the beginning of the transcript. Some agencies begin the stipulations on the same page as the appearance page rather than starting a new page in the transcript. In states where the index page follows the appearance page, the stipulation page will be placed after the appearance page.

Each agency has a format preference regarding state/usual and federal stipulations and whether a separate page should contain stipulations or be placed at the end of the appearance page, so consult the agency's sample transcript

**Motion:** An application to the Court for specific relief. This maybe in written or verbal form, but is usually in writing in accordance with specific Court rules.

booklet. Some agencies center *STIPULATIONS* at the top of the pages; others do not.

See Exhibit 5 in Figure 13–1 for a sample stipulation page.

## Sworn/Affirmed Paragraph

The paragraph for the swearing/affirming of the witness appears on line 2 of the subsequent page in deposition transcripts. It is preceded only by a paragraph for the swearing/affirming of an interpreter, if applicable. The interpreter paragraph will read something like:

> J O S E     P E R E Z, called as the official interpreter in this matter, was duly sworn by a Notary Public to accurately and faithfully translate the questions propounded to the witness from English into [translated language] and the answers given by the witness from [translated language] into English.

Whether or not colloquy appears in the record before the witness is sworn or the witness's examination begins, the sworn/affirmed paragraph will be placed first in a deposition transcript.

The sworn/affirmed paragraph conveys to the transcript reader that the witness (and interpreter, if applicable) swore/affirmed to tell the truth in the testimony that follows that paragraph. Although agency preference determines the wording of this paragraph, the paragraph begins with the witness's name in uppercase letters with a space between each letter, five spaces between each name, followed by a comma. For example:

> P E R R Y     I R A     C U L K I N, a Witness herein, residing at 78 Patterson Street, Magdalena, New Mexico 87825, after having been first duly sworn by a Notary Public of the State of New Mexico, testified as follows:

If the witness's name is lengthy, leave less than five spaces between the names. Try to keep the full name on one line.

Some agencies like to include the witness's address in the sworn/affirmed paragraph even if the first two questions of the transcript repeat this information; others prefer not to do so. Note that the word *Witness,* the street address, the words *Notary Public,* and the city and state are initial capped. Consult the agency's sample transcript or format booklet for the agency's preference.

If the job is a continuation, then the sworn/affirmed paragraph may include wording such as *recalled as a witness, resworn,* or *reminded,* to indicate which has occurred. Wording may also be changed to reflect that the witness has been sworn prior to this proceeding. For example:

> P E R R Y     I R A     C U L K I N, recalled as a Witness herein, after having been previously sworn by a Notary Public of the State of New Mexico, testified as follows:

There would be no need to restate the witness's address or include the witness's name and address as the first two questions in the transcript, since that information has already been included in the transcript of the first session of the witness's testimony. (See Figure 13–3).

It is important to note that hearings and arbitrations may involve numerous witnesses, and the sworn/affirmed paragraph in those transcripts will appear immediately prior to each witness's testimony, not at the beginning of the transcript.

## Examination By

The sworn/affirmed paragraph will be followed by a new line—or two lines, depending on agency preference—that will read *EXAMINATION BY* and the examining attorney's name in uppercase letters followed by a colon. Examples are:

EXAMINATION BY
MR. HARRIS:

or

EXAMINATION BY MR. HARRIS:

Some localities specify direct versus cross-examination in deposition transcripts; others do not.

If on-the-record colloquy immediately follows the swearing/affirming of the witness, then place the *EXAMINATION BY* information after the colloquy.

*EXAMINATION BY* is also placed within the transcript to reflect a change of examining attorney. When scoping, an asterisk *(*)* is usually placed before *EXAMINATION BY* so that the reporter can locate the page number where examination by each attorney appears in order to list it on the index page. The asterisk is removed after proofreading when corrections are done.

When an attorney is questioning a witness, his or her examination is interrupted by extensive colloquy, and it is unclear who the examining attorney is, *BY MR./MS. [ATTORNEY'S NAME]:* may be placed in the transcript before Q&A continues. This is common practice. However, certain agencies utilize *EXAMINATION BY MR./MS. -** or *BY MR./MS. -** after every colloquy. Check with the agency.

*EXAMINATION BY* is always followed by *MR.* or *MS.* and the attorney's last name in uppercase letters, never *MRS.* for female attorneys. If *JR.* or *SR.* or *III,* for example, follows the attorney's name and there are no other attorneys present with the same last name, it will follow the attorney's name in his or her appearance on the appearance page, but it is not necessary to include it after *EXAMINATION BY* or for colloquy. If another attorney at the proceeding has the same last name, then the *JR., SR.,* and so on will be included.

## Headers

The title page, appearance page, index page, stipulation page, page where the witness is sworn/affirmed, and certification page do not contain headers of witnesses' names. A header appears above the first line of a transcript page or on line 1. It may be centered or may appear in the left or right corner; most frequently it is centered. See Exhibit 6 in Figure 13–1 for a sample header.

For depositions, headers may include just the witness's last name, the initial of the witness's first name and his or her full last name, or the witness's full name. If the witness's name was Alice Jones, for instance, the header may appear *Jones, A. Jones, or Alice Jones,* depending on the agency's preference. Whether the header is initial capped or completely uppercase is a matter of agency preference. The header does not appear on the page where the witness is sworn. Reporters place the header command below the sworn parenthetical and *EXAMINATION BY* line with the attorney's name. This brings the header up on all the following pages.

**FIGURE 13–3**
Continuation Transcript

SUPREME COURT OF THE STATE OF NEW YORK
COUNTY OF KINGS
-----------------------------
MILDRED CHARLES, an infant over the
age of 14 years, by her mother and
natural guardian, FLORENCE CHARLES,

Plaintiffs, Action No. 1
Index No.
–against– 9889/98

BARTLETT SCHOOL DISTRICT and BARTLETT
INTERMEDIATE SCHOOL,

Defendants.

-----------------------------
BARTLETT SCHOOL DISTRICT and BARTLETT
INTERMEDIATE SCHOOL,

Third-Party Plaintiffs,
Action No. 2
–against– Index No.
81922/96
DORIS IRVING WINDOWS and HELEN SOPHIE
CONTRACTING,

Third-Party Defendants.

-----------------------------

CONTINUED EBT of HELEN SOPHIE
July 3, 1998

REINIG REPORTING, INC.
192 Lexington Avenue
New York, New York 10016
(212) 684-7298

In cases where the testimony of two witnesses sharing the same last name is booked together, such as Ed Smith and Alice Smith, use the first initial and the last name, initial capped, of the witness in the header, for example, *E. Smith* and *A. Smith,* or each person's full name.

If you have an Ed Smith, Sr. and an Ed Smith, Jr., for example, the header should include the *Sr.* or *Jr.* in order to distinguish between the witnesses, for example, *E. Smith, Sr.* and *E. Smith, Jr.* If Ed A. Smith and Ed R. Smith are being deposed, the headers may be, respectively, *E.A. Smith* and *E.R. Smith* or *ED A. SMITH* and *ED R. SMITH.*

Other headers are used for hearings and arbitrations, such as *PROCEEDINGS, DIRECT EXAMINATION - Jones, CROSS-EXAMINATION - Connor, SUSAN BREEZY - REDIRECT EXAMINATION,* and so on.

**FIGURE 13–3** (continued)

CONTINUED EXAMINATION BEFORE TRIAL of the Third-Party Defendant HELEN SOPHIE CONTRACTING by HELEN SOPHIE, taken by all parties, pursuant to Subpoena dated May 3, 1997, held at the law offices of Whitney, Brock & Blazer, Esqs., 44 College Point Boulevard, College Point, New York, on July 3, 1998, commencing at 12:12 P.M., before Dana Chipkin, a Registered Professional Reporter and Notary Public within and for the State of New York.

REINIG REPORTING, INC. (212) 684-7298

## Q&A and Colloquy

Q&A and colloquy are the meat and potatoes of the transcript.

***Q&A*** On the line following *EXAMINATION BY* and the attorney's name with a colon, the witness's examination by the attorney is recorded in a Q&A, or a question and answer, format. Some agencies place a period after the *Q* and *A;* others do not.

Margins and tabs vary from agency to agency, so get the agency's format parameters and create an edit style sheet before translating your job file on the computer. This way, transcripts may be translated into the agency's format without having to reprogram the format each time a job is taken for that agency.

**FIGURE 13–3**
(continued)

APPEARANCES:

WHITNEY, BROCK & BLAZER, ESQS.
Attorneys for Plaintiffs
44 College Point Boulevard
College Point, New York 11356

BY: BERNARD M. BROCK, ESQ.

STERN & ASSOCIATES, P.C.
Attorneys for Defendants
21 Suzanna Street
Glen Cove, New York 11542

BY: KENNEDY A. ROTH, ESQ.

O'REILLY, SULLIVAN & O'CONNOR, L.L.P.
Attorneys for Third-Party Defendant -
DORIS IRVING WINDOWS
64 East 47th Street - Suite 250
New York, New York 10017

BY: ROBERT R. BRODKIN, ESQ.

SCIORRA, VITELLI & DUDIE, ESQS.
Attorneys for Third-Party Defendant -
HELEN SOPHIE CONTRACTING
707 Rockaway Boulevard
Howard Beach, New York 11414

BY: VINCENT A. VITELLI, JR., ESQ.

REINIG REPORTING, INC. (212) 684-7298

Generally, the *Q* or the *A* in the transcript is set at the first tab, and the actual question or answer begins at the second tab. If it carries over to the next line, it will go back to the left margin. However, I have worked for agencies that place the *Q* and *A* at the left margin, followed by block-style text beginning at the first tab.

Software programs are set up so that questions automatically have a question mark and answers automatically have a period. If you do not punctuate while writing, this is how it will appear when the job is translated. Therefore, if a question is more of a statement or polite request, use a period. If the witness asks a question, use a question mark. Use commas to reflect pauses and a listing of separate items. The wrong punctuation can completely change the context of testimony. For example:

HELEN SOPHIE, recalled as a
witness, having been previously sworn,
continued to testify as follows:

EXAMINATION BY MR. BROCK:

Q When we left off at our last session, we were speaking about the windows that your company installed at the Barlett Intermediate School on February 9, 1995.

A Yes.

REINIG REPORTING, INC. (212) 684-7298

**FIGURE 13–3**
(continued)

Q. You stole supplies from the company?
A. I stole supplies from the company?
Smith stole supplies from the company.

versus

Q. You stole supplies from the company?
A. I stole supplies from the company, Smith stole supplies from the company.

Do not rely on your memory to assist you with punctuation after the job. It is nearly impossible to remember how something was said when listening to hours upon hours of testimony each week and reading numerous transcripts.

It is also important, when writing, to use dashes to reflect a change in thought or correction of a false start. A false start occurs when the examining attorney wishes to change the course of what is said but forgets to say something like "Strike that," "Physically strike that," "Withdrawn," or "Let me rephrase." A false start may be deleted in a deposition if it is less than five words long and if its deletion is not integral to what follows; however, some agencies advise you to leave everything in the transcript.

*Strike that,* when said by an attorney to a reporter, should be noted on the record. If it was to correct a false start or a sentence with less than five words, it may later be deleted. If the following thought is meaningless without the stricken portion, keep it in the transcript. If there is subsequent dialog that makes sense only with its presence, keep it. Whether *strike that* is preceded by dashes and kept within the Q&A format or is written as colloquy depends upon agency preference. If *strike that* is said by a witness, it should remain in Q&A in the transcript, preceded by dashes, unless *all* attorneys present direct you to delete it.

*Physically strike that,* when requested by an attorney in a deposition setting, may be deleted if what was said was inconsequential or was agreed to by *all* attorneys present Again, if what follows the stricken portion is meaningless without it or if it follows five or more words, keep it in the record. Whether *physically strike that* is preceded by dashes and kept within the Q&A format or is written as colloquy is a matter of agency preference. A request from a witness to physically strike something from the record should be ignored unless consented to by *all* attorneys present.

*Withdrawn* should be left on the record. It merely reflects recognition of an error that may be subsequently corrected or a desire to have what has just been said on the record disregarded. If the speaker intends only for the word preceding *withdrawn* to be changed and subsequently chooses another word to replace it and continues on with his or her thought, add dashes before and after the word *withdrawn* and continue the thought within the Q&A format. For example:

Q How are the people - withdrawn - workers compensated?

If the speaker intends to change the entire course of what he or she is saying, begin a new paragraph after *withdrawn.* In this scenario, whether *withdrawn* is preceded by dashes and kept within the Q&A format or is written as colloquy is a matter of agency preference. Examples with Mr. Wilkins as the examining attorney are:

Q How can you say that - withdrawn.
On what do you base that statement?

or

Q How can you say that?
MR. WILKINS: Withdrawn.
Q On what do you base that statement?

When an attorney is responding to another attorney's objection or saying *withdrawn* after colloquy, an off-the-record conversation, or a break, *withdrawn* will appear as colloquy.

*Let me rephrase* should be kept on the record as well. It is just an indication to those present that the attorney will reword the question/statement. Generally a new paragraph is begun after *let me rephrase* or a variation thereof is uttered. Since it is sometimes difficult to determine whom the attorney is directing it at, *let me rephrase,* in the course of examining a witness, is generally kept within the Q&A format. If it follows a line of colloquy, then it will appear as colloquy.

***Colloquy*** Colloquy is the format utilized to reflect words spoken on the record outside of the Q&A format. Colloquy occurs when:

- A witness says something in a nonexamination context to someone other than the examining attorney on the record
- The examining attorney speaks to anyone at the proceeding on the record other than the witness
- Directions are given to the reporter
- Objections/motions/directions to a witness not to answer/requests are stated
- A few questions are asked of the witness by an attorney other than the examining attorney
- Anyone else present at the proceeding speaks on the record (attorneys, videographers, people listed as *ALSO PRESENT*)
- An interpreter speaks on the record outside of the translation function
- Rulings are recorded

Punctuate colloquy while writing, as something may read both as a question or a statement and you may not be able to remember which when preparing the transcript. As with Q&A, the wrong punctuation may completely change the context of what is said.

Colloquy is reflected by the speaker's name followed by a colon, for example, *MR. POWELL:,* two spaces, and then the spoken material. Colloquy margins vary from agency to agency. Generally, the reporter tabs twice before placing the speaker's name in the transcript. By placing a computer command before colloquy begins, when colloquy continues onto the next line, it falls right below the *Q* or *A* symbol at the first tab. Contact school personnel, the agency's computer personnel, court reporting software personnel, or a scopist to learn how to program commands. If the speaker addresses a different person within his or her colloquy, a new paragraph is made to so indicate.

When colloquy reverts back to Q&A, another command is programmed into the computer manually to properly set up the Q&A format while scoping. If examination by a different attorney follows the colloquy, *EXAMINATION BY (ATTORNEY'S NAME):* will precede the Q&A.

If the colloquy is not lengthy and examination by the same attorney who questioned prior to the colloquy continued, no notation is necessary. If the colloquy is extensive and it seems unclear as to who had been questioning, *EXAMINATION BY (ATTORNEY'S NAME):* or *BY (ATTORNEY'S NAME):* may be inserted prior to the Q&A while scoping.

## Change of Examining Attorney

As mentioned in Chapter 9, if there is a change of attorney examining, your steno notes should so indicate. When the transcript is prepared, you will add a new line—or two, depending on agency preference—*EXAMINATION BY* and the attorney's name in uppercase letters, followed by a colon. When the attorney's examination ends and another attorney's begins, the same is done.

When an attorney who has previously examined the witness asks some follow-up questions after examination by other attorneys, preceding his or her questioning may be *CONTINUED EXAMINATION BY, FURTHER EXAMINATION BY,* the attorney's name, and a colon, or *EXAMINATION (Cont'd.) BY,* the attorney's name, and a colon, depending upon agency preference.

### Time Noted

At the end of all of the testimony and colloquy, the ending time of the proceeding is noted. It appears on a separate line in colloquy margins or centered. For example:

(Time noted: 4:56 p.m.)

The agency also may wish to specify whether the witness's examination was concluded or adjourned. For example:

(At 3:45 p.m., the examination of this witness was concluded.)

or

(At 5:25 p.m., the hearing was adjourned.)

Agency preference will dictate on this matter.

### The Jurat

On the same page, some agencies place a jurat, unless the jurat cannot completely fit on the last page of testimony, in which case you add a blurb like:

(Continued on following page to include jurat.)

The page where the jurat is placed should have a line or two of text on it. If no text falls on the jurat page, move a line or two of text from the previous page onto the jurat page.

The jurat consists of a space for the witness's signature above his or her name in uppercase letters and provides spaces for a notary to fill in the date subscribed and sworn to before him or her, as well as the notary's signature. If the witness had been affirmed rather than sworn, the word *affirmed* appears in the jurat instead of *sworn.*

When a witness's signature must be notarized, a jurat is used instead of an acknowledgment page and appears prior to the certification page. See Exhibit 7 in Figure 13–1 for a sample jurat.

### Acknowledgment Page

Instead of a jurat, in some states, a new page known as an acknowledgment page is used. The acknowledgment is basically a witness's certification that the transcript is a true, complete, and accurate record of the testimony given (that the answers on the record are true and correct). The witness will sign the acknowledgment on the line above his or her name, which appears in uppercase letters, and have it notarized. The county of the notary's license should be left blank for the notary to fill in when the transcript is signed by the witness. The acknowledgment page may contain a header with the witness's name.

See Exhibit 8 in Figure 13–1 for a sample acknowledgment page. Either a jurat or an acknowledgment page is generally used. Both a jurat and an acknowledgment are included in Figure 13–1 solely as examples.

### Certification Page

Lastly, you have the certification page. This is the court reporter's certification that the witness was sworn/affirmed by him or her, that the transcript of the examination is a true and accurate record of the testimony given by that witness, and that the reporter is not related to any of the parties to the action by blood or marriage and is in no way interested in the outcome of the matter. Generally, either *CERTIFICATION* or *CERTIFICATE* appears on line 2 of the page, centered, and states the state and county where the court reporter's notary public license is registered, as well as the date that the reporter certified to what appears above. It has a line above the reporter's name, which is in uppercase letters, for the reporter's signature.

Reporters must sign the certification page in pen on the original transcript or provide signature stamps to agencies to stamp onto the certification page in lieu of the reporter's signature. A signature stamp can be made up at your local print shop.

## ERRATA SHEETS

Freelance agencies in certain localities utilize errata sheets for a witness (or attorney) to note any errors and return to the agency for corrections. The errata sheet is placed toward the end of the transcript. There is no header on an errata sheet.

Errata sheets usually contain:

- The agency's name, address, and telephone number
- A summarized title of the case
- The date of the proceeding
- The witness's full name
- Page and line numbers of each error
- Lines where the errors are filled in
- Lines for the corrections that are to be made
- A signature line for the witness above his or her printed name in uppercase letters
- A place for the notary to date and sign the execution of the errata sheet

See Figure 13–4 for a sample transcript errata sheet.

The order of the acknowledgment, index, errata, and certification pages may vary according to agency preference. Ask your agency what order it prefers.

## COMPATIBLE DISKS/ASCII DISKS

Depending on the agency, the reporter may be required to furnish the agency with:

- A printed transcript and disk of the job if the reporter's software is compatible to the agency's
- Just a disk of the job if the reporter's software is compatible to the agency's
- A printed transcript and an ASCII disk of the job
- A transcript sent electronically only

**FIGURE 13–4**
Sample Errata Sheet

* * * ERRATA SHEET * * *
ABC REPORTING CO.
85 123RD STREET
NEW YORK, NEW YORK 10022
(212) 123-1234

NAME OF CASE: SMITH -v- JONES
DATE OF DEPOSITION: JUNE 18, 1999
NAME OF WITNESS: JIM NASIUM

| PAGE | LINE | FROM | TO |
|---|---|---|---|
| ---- | ---- | ----------------- | ---- |
| ---- | ---- | ----------------- | ---- |
| ---- | ---- | ----------------- | ---- |
| ---- | ---- | ----------------- | ---- |
| ---- | ---- | ----------------- | ---- |
| ---- | ---- | ----------------- | ---- |
| ---- | ---- | ----------------- | ---- |
| ---- | ---- | ----------------- | ---- |
| ---- | ---- | ----------------- | ---- |
| ---- | ---- | ----------------- | ---- |
| ---- | ---- | ----------------- | ---- |
| ---- | ---- | ----------------- | ---- |

______________________
JIM NASIUM

Subscribed and sworn before me
this ____ day of ____________, 1999.

-------------- ---------------
(Notary Public) My Commission Expires:

ASCII disks are disks that are compatible to most computer systems. Some agencies use them to make minor edits to the transcript or to create a concordance/keyword index and/or condensed transcript.

## CONCORDANCES/KEYWORD INDEXES

**Concordance:** A listing at the end of a transcript (or separately bound) that indexes every work and name mentioned in a transcript by page and line number.

**Concordances,** also known as keyword indexes, may be placed at the very end of a transcript. A concordance is an alphabetical listing of each word in the transcript that provides page and line numbers where the word is found. All current software programs on the market have the capability to produce concordances.

Although some agencies automatically attach a concordance to the end of a transcript, others do so only at the request of an attorney. The concordance enables the attorney to locate text by a *key* word.

The pages of the concordance are unnumbered and are affixed to the transcript after the certification page. If the reporter is unable to provide a concordance, the agency can create one in-house upon receipt of a DOS disk, an ASCII disk, or a disk that is compatible with the agency's software program.

See Figure 13–5 for a sample concordance/keyword index.

## CONDENSED TRANSCRIPTS

Sometimes attorneys will request a **condensed transcript** in lieu of or in addition to the regular-sized transcript. Condensed transcripts shrink the print of a transcript page so that multiple transcript pages may be placed onto a single page. The transcript pages within the condensed transcript retain the same page numbers as in the regular transcript. It is not as if the first four pages of the original transcript, when merged into one page on the condensed transcript, become collectively page 1. The words **Min-U-Script** or *Xmax* are sometimes used to connote a condensed transcript, since they are software programs that are known in the industry in conjunction with creating condensed transcripts. Other synonyms are *mini* and *4-up.*

Attorneys often request condensed transcripts if a transcript is particularly voluminous. Once condensed, it is obviously much lighter for the attorney to carry around. Also, during a deposition, sometimes attorneys like to refer to testimony or quotes from other depositions in the case, and condensed transcripts enable the attorney to carry multiple transcripts to a proceeding.

Some agencies request reporters or reporters' scopists to produce condensed copies, while others will condense the transcript in-house upon receipt of a DOS disk, ASCII disk, or e-mailed transcript. Some agencies may offer a condensed copy of a transcript to an attorney free of charge, while others may charge extra for it.

See Figure 13–6 for a sample condensed transcript.

## EXCERPTS

If attorneys request an **excerpt** from the transcript, they are looking for a portion of the transcript to be sent under separate cover from the rest of the transcript prior to the delivery of the entire transcript. For expedition of the excerpt, if not lengthy, the excerpt may be faxed or e-mailed rather than mailed/messengered to the attorney. Depending on the relationship that the agency has with its client, the attorney may or may not be billed for a brief excerpt. The reporter, however, can bill the agency for the excerpt pages in addition to the amount of total transcript pages. Since the excerpt is usually requested expedited or daily, the reporter will bill for the amount of excerpted pages at the expedite or daily page rate.

When an excerpt is requested, you would prepare a title and appearance page, followed by the excerpted material. The title page should be unnumbered, unless the computer automatically places it onto the page. The appearance page should be page 2. The excerpted page numbers will begin after the appearance page(s) and continue sequentially.

**Condensed transcript:** A transcript format that places multiple transcript pages onto a singular page. Popular brands are Min-U-Script and Visual Xmax. Condensed transcripts are often referred to as Min-U-Scripts, Minis, or 4-ups.

**Min-U-Script:** A popular brand name of a condensed transcript.

**Excerpt:** A portion of a transcript requested prior to the delivery of the entire transcript.

**FIGURE 13–5**
Sample Concordance Keyword Index

BSA — **Henrietta Silver** — Look-See(6)

**Look-See**
**Concordance Report**

- - -

UNIQUE WORDS: **384**
TOTAL OCCURRENCES: **795**
NOISE WORDS: **384**
TOTAL WORDS IN FILE: **1,879**

- - -

SINGLE FILE CONCORDANCE

- - -

CASE SENSITIVE

- - -

INCLUDES ALL TEXT OCCURRENCES

- - -

DATES **ON**

- - -

INCLUDES PURE NUMBERS

- - -

POSSESSIVE FORMS **ON**

**– DATES –**

**11/20/94** [2] *12:6; 16:9*
**April, 1999** [1] *17:17*
**April 5, 1999** [2] *1:15; 15:11*
**November 20, 1994** [7] *5:21; 7:8; 8:4, 7, 10, 21; 9:14*

**– 1 –**

**1** [1] *16:12*
**10** [1] *16:17*
**10016** [1] *1:22*
**10:15** [1] *1:15*
**11** [1] *16:13*
**11/20/94** [2] *12:6; 16:9*
**11:24** [1] *14:17*
**12** [1] *16:9*
**123** [2] *1:14; 2:9*
**12345** [2] *1:15; 2:9*
**12491** [2] *4:7, 16*
**12th** [1] *17:17*
**13** [1] *16:14*
**1818** [4] *4:5, 15; 8:20, 9:12*
**192** [1] *1:21*
**1993** [1] *6:21*
**1994** [7] *5:21; 7:8; 8:4, 7, 10, 21; 9:14*
**1999** [4] *1:15; 15:11, 22; 17:17*

**– 2 –**

**2** [1] *16:13*
**20** [7] *5:21; 7:8; 8:4, 7, 10, 21; 9:14*
**21** [1] *16:17*
**212** [1] *1:22*

**– 3 –**

**3** [1] *16:14*
**3116** [1] *3:19*
**3117** [1] *3:19*

**– 4 –**

**4** [1] *16:5*

**– 5 –**

**5** [3] *1:15; 15:11; 16:12*

**– 6 –**

**684-7298** [1] *1:22*

**– 7 –**

**75** [1] *2:5*
**75757/95** [1] *1:4*

**– 8 –**

**802** [1] *1:21*

**– 9 –**

**98765** [1] *2:5*

**– A –**

**A.M.** [1] *1:16*
**a.m.** [2] *7:23; 14:17*
**Accident [2]** *12:6; 16:9*
**accident** [15] *5:21, 24; 6:18; 7:16, 21; 8:9, 18, 23; 10:15, 17; 11:14, 16; 12:15, 22; 13:11*
**action** [2] *3:11; 17:13*
**addition** [1] *3:8*
**address** [2] *4:5, 13*
**adjourn** [1] *14:11*
**adjourned** [1] *14:16*
**affect** [2] *4:18, 20*
**against-CARL** [1] *1:5*
**AGREED** [3] *3:2, 12, 21*
**air** [1] *7:15*
**ALICIA** [1] *1:6*
**answer** [7] *5:4, 10; 6:3; 9:6; 10:6; 11:8; 13:6*
**answered** [1] *9:9*
**answers** [1] *15:14*
**April** [3] *1:15; 15:11; 17:17*
**arrange** [1] *14:12*
**asthma** [1] *4:24*
**Attorneys** [2] *2:4, 8*
**Automatic** [1] *7:12*
**automatic** [1] *7:11*
**automobile** [1] *5:21*
**Avenue** [5] *1:21; 7:25; 9:8, 13; 10:15*

**– B –**

**bag** [1] *5:13*
**bags** [1] *7:15*
**BAINES** [19] *2:10; 4:9; 5:5, 18; 6:11; 8:15; 9:5, 10; 10:20, 25; 11:4, 7, 10, 20; 12:2; 13:18, 21; 14:15; 16:5*
**bar** [1] *3:10*
**begun** [1] *3:16*
**BERNARD** [1] *2:13*
**BERTOLI** [2] *1:13; 2:8*
**Bertram** [1] *1:12*
**blood** [1] *17:13*
**Boulevard** [1] *10:12*
**Buckeye** [2] *1:14; 2:9*
**Business** [1] *16:14*
**business** [2] *13:15, 19*

**– C –**

**C-H-A-D-P-U-R-I** [1] *13:2*
**C.P.L.R.** [2] *3:4, 19*
**call** [2] *11:20; 13:18*
**car** [2] *8:11, 18*
**card** [4] *5:13; 13:15, 19; 16:14*
**Central** [2] *10:11, 12*
**certify** [3] *15:9; 17:7, 12*
**Chadpuri** [1] *12:22*
**CHIPKIN** [2] *17:5, 20*
**Chipkin** [1] *1:16*
**Chrysler** [1] *6:19*
**codeine** [1] *4:25*
**commencing** [1] *1:15*
**compass** [1] *9:20*
**complete** [1] *15:12*
**continuation** [1] *14:12*
**continue** [1] *14:10*
**continued** [1] *10:14*
**controlled** [1] *3:20*
**convenient** [1] *14:14*
**counsel** [2] *3:3, 18*
**COUNTY** [3] *1:2; 15:6; 17:3*
**COURT** [1] *1:2*
**Court** [8] *1:11; 4:6, 15; 7:25; 8:20; 9:8, 12, 13*
**Croton** [1] *2:5*

**– D –**

**DANA** [2] *17:5, 20*
**Dana** [1] *1:16*
**date** [1] *12:8*
**day** [4] *8:8; 14:11; 15:21; 17:17*
**deemed** [1] *3:18*
**DEFENDANTS** [1] *16:7*
**Defendants** [5] *1:8; 2:8; 12:3, 7, 10*
**deposition** [1] *15:11*
**DESCRIPTION** [2] *16:7, 11*
**directing** [1] *11:7*
**directions** [1] *9:20*
**Discussion** [3] *5:9; 7:3; 14:7*
**document** [3] *12:5, 21; 16:8*
**DOCUMENTS** [1] *16:10*
**documents** [1] *13:14*
**doesn't** [1] *9:3*
**drive** [1] *9:3*
**driven** [2] *8:3, 6*
**driver** [2] *5:23; 6:15*
**driver's** [1] *10:21*
**driving** [1] *10:23*
**duly** [2] *4:3; 17:9*

**– E –**

**east** [1] *9:18*
**entitled** [2] *12:5; 16:8*
**ESQ** [3] *2:4, 6, 10*
**Estelle** [2] *5:25; 9:3*
**EXAMINATION** [2] *1:10; 4:9*
**Examination** [1] *16:4*
**examination** [9] *3:7, 9, 13, 16, 17, 22; 14:13; 17:9, 10*
**examined** [2] *3:14; 4:7*
**except** [1] *3:6*
**execution** [1] *5:17*
**Exhibit** [3] *12:3, 7, 10*

**– F –**

**failure** [2] *3:8, 16*
**familiar** [2] *7:24; 13:9*
**feeling** [1] *14:9*
**FEINSTEIN** [4] *1:13; 2:8*
**file** [1] *11:24*
**filing** [1]

From **11/20/94** to **filing**

An attorney may make special requests regarding an excerpt, such as taking two separate portions of the transcript and placing them together in the excerpt prepared. You should follow instructions to the letter.

Agencies may have certain preferences regarding excerpted material and should be consulted before the excerpt is finalized.

## CONFIDENTIAL MATERIAL

Attorneys may request that an entire transcript or portion(s) of the transcript be designated confidential. The reporter may even be asked by the attorneys to sign a confidentiality agreement, depending upon the subject matter contained within the transcript. If the entire transcript is to be labeled confidential, the

**FIGURE 13–5**
(continued)

BSA | **Henrietta Silver** | Look-See(7)

*3:22*
**fill** [2]
*5:16; 11:12*
**find** [3]
*5:14; 11:19, 24*
**fine** [1]
*6:8*
**finish** [1]
*10:4*
**First** [1]
*10:10*
**following** [1]
*12:15*
**follows** [1]
*4:8*
**forgot** [1]
*13:24*
**form** [1]
*3:6*
**forth** [1]
*17:9*
**foundation** [1]
*10:19*
**friend** [2]
*5:25; 9:2*

**– G –**

**gentleman** [1]
*14:3*
**given** [2]
*15:14; 17:11*
**glasses** [2]
*10:16, 23*
**gotten** [1]
*8:17*
**grocery** [1]
*9:2*
**grounds** [3]
*5:5; 10:25; 11:3*

**– H –**

**hand** [1]
*17:17*
**handwriting** [1]
*12:16*
**Handwritten** [2]
*12:5; 16:8*
**held** [4]
*1:12; 5:9; 7:3; 14:7*
**HENRIETTA** [6]
*1:3, 11; 15:8, 18; 16:3; 17:8*
**Henrietta** [1]
*4:12*
**HEREBY** [1]
*3:2*
**hereby** [3]
*3:23; 15:8; 17:7*
**hereinbefore** [1]
*17:9*
**hereto** [1]
*3:3*
**hereunto** [1]
*17:16*
**home** [3]
*9:12, 24; 13:16*
**Hon** [1]
*1:12*
**house** [1]
*8:19*
**Hudson** [1]
*2:5*
**Hurley** [3]
*4:6, 16; 8:21*

**– I –**

**I've** [1]
*10:8*
**identification** [3]
*12:4, 8, 11*
**Immediately** [1]
*8:9*
**INC** [1]
*1:20*
**Index** [1]
*1:4*
**INFORMATION** [1]
*16:10*
**information** [2]
*12:6; 16:9*
**INSERT** [1]
*5:19*
**intending** [1]
*8:24*
**interested** [1]
*17:14*
**intersection** [4]
*7:25; 8:4; 9:7, 13*
**invited** [1]
*6:2*
**involved** [2]
*5:20; 6:17*

**– J –**

**JHE157** [1]
*6:23*
**Julian** [4]
*7:25; 9:8, 13; 10:14*
**Justice** [1]
*1:12*

**– K –**

**Kenny** [3]
*7:25; 9:8, 13*
**KLUG** [1]
*1:6*

**– L –**

**Lack** [1]
*10:18*
**last** [1]
*8:6*
**law** [1]
*1:13*
**Leave** [1]
*5:15*
**LeBaron** [1]
*6:19*
**Let's** [1]
*6:11*
**let's** [1]
*5:7*
**Lexington** [1]
*1:21*
**license** [2]
*6:22; 10:21*
**LINE** [1]
*16:17*
**list** [1]
*12:21*
**listen** [1]
*7:22*
**LLP** [2]
*1:14; 2:8*
**Lockwood** [5]
*4:6, 15; 8:20; 9:12; 10:11*
**Looks** [1]
*12:24*
**looks** [1]
*13:2*

**– M –**

**Main** [3]
*10:13, 14*
**man** [1]
*13:3*
**maps** [1]
*9:23*
**MARIO** [1]
*1:6*
**Mark** [2]
*11:10; 12:3*
**mark** [1]
*11:25*
**MARKED** [1]
*16:16*
**marked** [2]
*12:7, 10*
**marriage** [1]
*17:14*
**matter** [1]
*17:15*
**mean** [3]
*8:12; 9:18, 22*
**medication** [1]
*4:18*
**medications** [1]
*4:22*
**memorized** [1]
*5:12*
**mention** [1]
*13:22*
**Merrick** [2]
*1:14; 2:9*
**miles** [1]
*7:7*
**minute** [1]
*5:8*
**model** [1]
*6:16*
**morning** [1]
*4:19*
**motion** [1]
*3:10*
**Move** [1]
*9:5*
**move** [2]
*3:6, 9*
**MR** [18]
*4:9; 5:5, 18; 6:11; 8:15; 9:5, 10; 10:20, 25; 11:4, 7, 10, 20; 12:2; 13:18, 21; 14:15; 16:5*
**Mr** [1]
*12:22*
**Mrs** [1]
*12:17*
**MS** [23]
*5:4, 6, 10, 15; 6:3, 7; 7:2, 18; 8:13; 9:9; 10:4, 18, 24; 11:2, 6, 9, 14, 22; 13:5, 20, 22; 14:2, 8*
**Ms** [1]
*4:17*
**mutually** [1]
*14:13*
**MV-104** [3]
*11:12, 21; 16:13*

**– N –**

**name** [3]
*4:10; 12:25; 13:14*
**NASSAU** [2]
*1:2; 17:3*
**nonresponsive** [1]
*9:6*
**north** [1]
*9:18*
**Notary** [6]
*1:17; 3:14, 15; 4:3; 15:24; 17:6*
**noted** [1]
*14:17*
**notes** [2]
*12:14; 13:13*
**notified** [1]
*14:9*
**November** [7]
*5:21; 7:8; 8:4, 7, 10, 21; 9:14*
**number** [3]
*5:3; 13:16; 16:12*

**– O –**

**oath** [2]
*4:8; 15:10*
**object** [2]
*3:5, 8*
**Objection** [2]
*10:18, 24*
**occurred** [1]
*8:23*
**occurring** [1]
*8:18*
**offices** [1]
*1:13*
**Oh** [3]
*7:9; 10:3; 13:24*
**Okay** [2]
*5:18; 10:7*
**okay** [1]
*6:7*
**OLIVER** [1]
*2:10*
**operating** [1]
*11:4*
**Order** [1]
*1:11*
**original** [2]
*3:17, 22*
**outcome** [1]
*17:15*

**– P –**

**PAGE** [4]
*16:3, 7, 11, 17*
**pain** [1]
*4:25*
**PANICO** [26]
*2:4, 6; 5:4, 6, 10, 15; 6:3, 7; 7:2, 18; 8:13; 9:9; 10:4, 18, 24; 11:2, 6, 9, 14, 22; 13:5, 20, 22; 14:2, 8*
**Parker** [1]
*2:5*
**part** [1]
*9:6*
**parties** [2]
*3:3; 17:13*
**passenger** [1]
*5:24*
**phone** [1]
*13:16*
**phonetic** [1]
*12:23*
**place** [1]
*14:14*
**Plaintiff** [3]
*1:4, 10; 2:4*
**plaintiff's** [1]
*14:13*
**plate** [1]
*6:22*
**Please** [2]
*4:10, 13*
**Power** [1]
*7:13*
**PRESENT** [1]
*2:12*
**presently** [1]
*4:23*
**prior** [4]
*8:4, 7, 9, 18*
**production** [2]
*11:21; 13:19*
**Professional** [2]
*1:17; 17:6*
**provide** [1]
*11:23*
**provided** [2]
*3:4, 19*
**Public** [6]
*1:17; 3:15; 4:3; 15:24; 17:6*
**purchase** [1]
*7:4*
**pursuant** [1]
*1:11*

**– Q –**

**question** [9]
*3:5, 8; 5:11; 6:4, 9, 13; 8:14, 16; 10:5*
**QUESTIONS** [1]
*16:16*
**questions** [1]
*13:6*

**– R –**

**radio** [1]
*7:20*
**read** [4]
*6:12, 13; 12:24; 15:9*
**recognize** [1]
*12:9*
**record** [12]

From **fill** to **record**

title page must so indicate. Agencies may utilize a stamp that reads *Confidential* or *Confidential—For Attorneys' Eyes Only.* If a portion of the transcript is to be designated confidential, it may be done within the transcript itself, or it may be bound under separate cover. Ask for the attorneys' preference.

If the confidential section occurs at the beginning of a transcript or is an excerpted confidential portion of a transcript, the title page should be amended to read *Confidential portion of the Deposition of . . .* followed by the witness's name. There should be a notation about the confidentiality throughout the confidential section of a transcript in the page header next to the witness's name, such as *Smith—Confidential.* Check how confidential transcripts are handled in your agency.

A transcript that contains a confidential section may have something like *Confidential—Pages 45–97* stamped onto the title page. The transcript would be

**FIGURE 13–5**
(continued)

BSA **Henrietta Silver** Look-See(8)

*4:11, 14; 5:8, 9, 16; 7:2, 3; 14:4, 7; 15:13, 14; 17:11*
**Registered** [2]
*1:16; 17:5*
**REINIG** [1]
*1:20*
**related** [1]
*17:12*
**remember** [2]
*6:25; 7:9*
**rephrase** [1]
*8:15*
**report** [2]
*11:14, 16*
**Reporter** [2]
*1:17; 17:6*
**reporter** [2]
*6:12, 14*
**REPORTING** [1]
*1:20*
**REQUESTED** [1]
*16:10*
**reserved** [2]
*3:7, 11*
**respective** [1]
*3:3*
**restrictions** [1]
*10:22*
**return** [1]
*3:17*
**right** [2]
*3:5; 10:2*
**rights** [2]
*3:4, 18*
**RL** [1]
*10:21*
**Road** [2]
*1:14; 2:9*
**route** [1]
*9:11*
**Rules** [1]
*3:19*
**RULING** [1]
*16:16*
**ruling** [1]
*11:11*

**– S –**

**search** [1]
*11:23*
**second** [2]
*13:23; 14:5*
**Security** [2]
*5:2; 16:12*
**SHEILA** [1]
*2:6*
**shopping** [1]
*9:2*
**shows** [1]
*7:23*
**Signed** [1]
*15:20*
**signed** [1]
*3:13*
**SILVER** [7]
*1:3, 11; 2:13; 15:8, 18; 16:3; 17:8*
**Silver** [4]
*4:12, 17; 12:18, 19*
**Silverstein** [1]
*12:17*
**Smith** [1]
*1:12*
**Social** [2]
*5:2; 16:12*
**Sorry** [2]
*9:10; 10:8*
**sorry** [3]
*6:6, 10; 12:19*
**sounds** [1]
*13:9*
**south** [1]
*9:18*
**space** [1]
*5:15*
**ss** [2]
*15:5; 17:3*
**standard** [1]
*7:10*
**start** [1]
*10:5*
**STATE** [3]
*1:2; 15:4; 17:2*
**State** [4]
*1:18; 4:4; 15:24; 17:7*
**state** [2]
*4:10, 13*
**stated** [1]
*4:5*
**steering** [1]
*7:13*
**STIPULATED** [3]
*3:2, 12, 21*
**stipulations** [1]
*11:5*
**Street** [3]
*2:5; 10:13*
**streets** [1]
*9:25*
**Strike** [1]
*10:20*
**strike** [3]
*3:6, 9; 9:5*
**study** [1]
*9:23*
**Subscribed** [1]
*15:20*
**Suite** [1]
*1:21*
**SUPREME** [1]
*1:2*
**sworn** [3]
*3:13; 4:3; 17:9*

**– T –**

**talk** [1]
*7:23*
**testified** [1]
*4:7*
**testimony** [7]
*3:7, 9; 4:18, 21; 15:10, 13; 17:11*
**Theo-Dur** [1]
*4:24*
**thereby** [1]
*3:20*
**times** [1]
*8:5*
**transcript** [4]
*5:17; 15:9, 12; 17:10*
**transmission** [1]
*7:11*
**travel** [1]
*7:23*
**TRIAL** [1]
*1:10*
**trial** [1]
*3:11*
**TRIPPE** [2]
*1:6, 7*
**true** [3]
*15:12, 15; 17:11*
**Tylenol** [1]
*4:25*

**– U –**

**understand** [1]
*8:14*
**usual** [1]
*11:5*

**– V –**

**vehicle** [5]
*6:17, 23; 7:4, 7, 10*

**– W –**

**waived** [1]
*3:23*
**waiver** [2]
*3:10, 18*
**Waldbaums** [1]
*9:2*
**wanted** [1]
*8:25*
**we'll** [1]
*5:16*
**we're** [1]
*11:4*
**we've** [1]
*12:9*
**wear** [1]
*10:23*
**wearing** [1]
*10:16*
**West** [3]
*4:6, 15; 8:21*
**west** [1]
*9:19*
**what's** [1]
*13:6*
**WHEREOF** [1]
*17:16*
**WITNESS** [8]
*6:5; 8:12; 10:7; 13:3, 8, 24; 16:3; 17:16*
**witness** [8]
*3:14; 11:8; 12:22; 13:14, 23; 14:8; 17:8, 11*
**witnesses** [1]
*13:10*
**wouldn't** [1]
*7:9*

**– Y –**

**year** [1]
*6:20*
**YORK** [3]
*1:2; 15:4; 17:2*
**York** [11]
*1:14, 18, 22; 2:5, 9, 4:4, 6, 16; 15:24; 17:7*

From **Registered** to **York**

prepared as it usually is. The page before the confidential segment, for example, page 44, should contain a blurb to the effect that the following pages are designated confidential, such as:

(The following portion, pages 45 through 97, has been deemed confidential.)

Pages 45 through 97 would have the *Confidential* notation in the header. No information contained within the confidential portion should be alluded to elsewhere within the transcript. Therefore, a separate index page may be included within the confidential section. At the conclusion of the confidential section, there should be a blurb to so indicate, such as:

(End of confidential portion of transcript.)

or

(Continued in nonconfidential portion of transcript.)

**FIGURE 13–6**
Sample Condensed Transcript

**Examination of Henrietta Silver**

**SILVER -v- KLUG, et al.**

**Page 1 to Page 17**

APRIL 5, 1999

PREPARED BY:

**REINIG REPORTING, INC.**
**192 Lexington Avenue**
**Suite 802**
**New York, NY 10016**
**Phone: (212) 684-7298**
**FAX: (212) 684-4360**

The nonconfidential portion of the transcript would continue starting on page 98. The header on page 98 would revert back to just the witness's name, that is, *Smith*.

If the confidential section is to be placed under separate cover, the nonconfidential transcript is prepared as per a regular transcript; however, preceding the confidential excerpted portion should be a blurb, such as:

> (Pages 45 through 97 are designated confidential and are bound under separate cover.)

The excerpted portion would have an unnumbered title page that would be stamped *Confidential.* A separate index may be included in the confidential transcript relating to material within the confidential pages. This index page would be unnumbered. The appearance page would likewise be unnumbered.

**FIGURE 13–6**
(continued)

BSA **Henrietta Silver** XMAX(1/1)

Page 1

SUPREME COURT OF THE STATE OF NEW YORK
COUNTY OF NASSAU
---------------------
HENRIETTA SILVER,
Index No.
Plaintiff, 75757/95
-against-
CARL KLUG, ALICIA TRIPPE and MARIO TRIPPE,
Defendants.
---------------------

EXAMINATION BEFORE TRIAL of the Plaintiff, HENRIETTA SILVER, pursuant to Court Order of the Hon. Justice Bertram L. Smith, held at the law offices of FEINSTEIN, FEINSTEIN & BERTOLI, LLP, 123 Buckeye Road, Merrick, New York 12345, on April 5, 1999, commencing at 10:15 A.M., before Dana Chipkin, a Registered Professional Reporter and Notary Public within and for the State of New York.

REINIG REPORTING, INC.
192 Lexington Avenue
Suite 802
New York, New York 10016
(212) 684-7298

Page 2

APPEARANCES:
PANICO & PANICO, ESQ.
Attorneys for Plaintiff
75 Parker Street
Croton on Hudson, New York 98765
BY: SHEILA PANICO, ESQ.
FEINSTEIN, FEINSTEIN & BERTOLI, LLP
Attorneys for Defendants
123 Buckeye Road
Merrick, New York 12345
BY: L. OLIVER BAINES, ESQ.
ALSO PRESENT:
BERNARD SILVER

Page 3

IT IS HEREBY STIPULATED AND AGREED by and between counsel for the respective parties hereto that all rights provided by the C.P.L.R., including the right to object to any question, except as to the form, or to move to strike any testimony at this examination, are reserved; and, in addition, the failure to object to any question or to move to strike testimony at this examination shall not be a bar or waiver to make such a motion at, and is reserved for, the trial of this action.

IT IS FURTHER STIPULATED AND AGREED that this examination may be signed and sworn to by the witness being examined, before a Notary Public other than the Notary Public before whom this examination was begun, but the failure to do so, or to return the original of this examination to counsel, shall not be deemed a waiver of rights provided by Rules 3116 and 3117 of the C.P.L.R. and shall be controlled thereby.

IT IS FURTHER STIPULATED AND AGREED that the filing of the original of this examination is hereby waived.

Page 4

HENRIETTA SILVER, having been duly sworn by a Notary Public within and for the State of New York, and having stated her address as 1818 Lockwood Court, West Hurley, New York 12491, was examined and testified under oath as follows:

EXAMINATION BY MR. BAINES:

Q Please state your name for the record.
**A Henrietta Silver.**
Q Please state your address for the record.
**A 1818 Lockwood Court, West Hurley, New York 12491.**
Q Ms. Silver, are you taking any medication that may affect your testimony this morning?
**A Not that would affect my testimony, no.**
Q What medications are you presently taking?
**A Theo-Dur for my asthma and Tylenol with codeine for pain.**

**REINIG REPORTING, INC.** (212) 684-7298 **Page 1** to **Page 4**

The subsequent material would begin with the page number it appeared on in the original transcript and continue sequentially, that is, pages 45 through 97. At the conclusion of the confidential excerpted material, there would not be a jurat or acknowledgment page, unless the witness's testimony was concluded within the confidential excerpted section, in which case another jurat/acknowledgment page would be placed in the original transcript for the witness's signature and execution as well. The certificate page requiring the reporter's signature is generally added to the original transcript only, and not to the confidential portion bound separately.

**FIGURE 13–6**
(continued)

BSA | **Henrietta Silver** | XMAX(2/2)

Page 5

Q What is your Social Security number?
MS. PANICO: Don't answer that.
MR. BAINES: On what grounds?
MS. PANICO: You know, I really don't have to – let's go off the record for a minute.
*(Discussion held off the record.)*
MS. PANICO: You can answer the question.
**A I don't have it memorized. Let me see if I have my card in my bag. I can't find it.**
MS. PANICO: Leave a space in the record and we'll fill it in upon execution of the transcript.
MR. BAINES: Okay.
INSERT: ------------------
Q Were you involved in an automobile accident on November 20, 1994?
**A Yes.**
Q Were you the driver or a passenger at the time of the accident?
**A Well, my friend Estelle had**

Page 6

**invited me –**
MS. PANICO: Just answer the question "yes" or "no," if you can.
THE WITNESS: You told me that already. I'm sorry.
MS. PANICO: That's okay. You're doing fine.
**A What was the question again, I'm sorry?**
MR. BAINES: Let's have the reporter read it back.
*(The question was read back by the reporter.)*
**A I was the driver.**
Q What was the make and model of the vehicle that you were involved in the accident with?
**A A Chrysler LeBaron.**
Q Do you know what year?
**A 1993.**
Q Was the license plate of the vehicle JHE157?
**A You know, I really don't remember.**

Page 7

MS. PANICO: Off the record.
*(Discussion held off the record.)*
Q Did you purchase the vehicle new or used?
**A New.**
Q How many miles did the vehicle have on November 20, 1994?
**A Oh, I wouldn't remember that.**
Q Did the vehicle have standard or automatic transmission?
**A Automatic.**
Q Power steering?
**A Yes.**
Q Did it have air bags?
**A When the accident happened, I didn't –**
MS. PANICO: "Yes" or "no."
**A Yes.**
Q Was the radio on at the time of the accident?
**A Yes. I always listen to those a.m. talk shows when I travel.**
Q Are you familiar with the intersection of Julian Avenue and Kenny Court?

Page 8

**A Yes.**
Q Had you driven by that intersection prior to November 20, 1994?
**A Many times.**
Q When had you driven there last prior to November 20, 1994?
**A The day before.**
Q Immediately prior to the accident on November 20, 1994, where were you?
**A In my car.**
THE WITNESS: What does he mean?
MS. PANICO: If you don't understand the question, tell him.
MR. BAINES: I'll rephrase the question.
Q Where had you gotten into your car just prior to the accident occurring?
**A At my house.**
Q That was at 1818 Lockwood Court in West Hurley on November 20, 1994?
**A Yes.**
Q If the accident had not occurred, where were you intending to go?
**A Well, we were – I wanted to –**

**REINIG REPORTING, INC.** (212) 684-7298 **Page 5** to **Page 8**

## WHEN TWO REPORTERS WRITE SIMULTANEOUSLY

In cases where there are two reporters writing simultaneously, since the official reporter will deliver the original transcript and copies to his or her agency's client (and others) and the nonofficial reporter will deliver a transcript to his or her client only, the title page will only contain the name of the reporter preparing that particular transcript. On the appearance page, under *ALSO PRESENT,* you will list the appearance of the other reporter and whether that reporter was the official reporter of record for that proceeding. Certain agencies may have you include the reporter's agency; others may not. Examples are:

**FIGURE 13–6**
(continued)

BSA **Henrietta Silver** XMAX(3/3)

Page 9

**grocery shopping at Waldbaums with my friend Estelle. She doesn't drive and asked me to take her.**
MR. BAINES: Move to strike the nonresponsive part of the answer.
Q You had been to the intersection of Julian Avenue and Kenny Court before?
MS. PANICO: Asked and answered.
MR. BAINES: Sorry.
Q What route did you take to go from your home at 1818 Lockwood Court to the intersection of Julian Avenue and Kenny Court on November 20, 1994?
**A The way I always go.**
Q We don't know the way you always go. You have to tell us.
**A You mean north, south, east, west? I don't know compass directions all that well.**
Q No. I mean –
**A I don't study maps, you know.**
Q – when you left your home, what streets did you take; did you make a left or

Page 10

right? That's what I'm looking for.
**A Oh.**
MS. PANICO: Just let him finish the entire question before you start to answer.
THE WITNESS: Okay.
**A Sorry. I've never done this before.**
Q First time for everything.
**A I took Lockwood to Central Boulevard, made a left on Central, took it to Main Street, made a left on Main Street and continued on Main until it turned into Julian Avenue, and that's when the accident happened.**
Q Were you wearing your glasses at the time of the accident?
MS. PANICO: Objection. Lack of foundation.
MR. BAINES: Strike that.
RL Q DID your driver's license have any restrictions on it, such as your having to wear glasses while driving?
MS. PANICO: Objection.
MR. BAINES: On what grounds?

Page 11

MS. PANICO: I don't have to tell you the grounds.
MR. BAINES: If we're operating under the usual stipulations, you do.
MS. PANICO: No, I don't.
MR. BAINES: Are you directing the witness not to answer?
MS. PANICO: Yes.
MR. BAINES: Mark it for a ruling.
Q Did you fill out an MV-104?
**A A what?**
MS. PANICO: An accident report.
**A Yes.**
Q Do you have the accident report here with you today?
**A I thought I had brought it, but I can't seem to find it.**
MR. BAINES: I call for production of the MV-104.
MS. PANICO: We will make a search for it and provide it. I did find this in my file. Do you want to mark it?

Page 12

MR. BAINES: Yes. Mark this as Defendants' Exhibit A for identification.
*(Handwritten document entitled "Accident information – 11/20/94," is marked Defendants' Exhibit A for identification, as of this date.)*
Q Do you recognize what we've had marked as Defendants' Exhibit A for identification?
**A Yes.**
Q What is it?
**A This is my notes that I made following the accident.**
Q This is your handwriting, Mrs. Silverstein?
**A Silver.**
Q Silver, sorry.
**A Yes, it is.**
Q Does this document list as a witness to the accident a Mr. Chadpuri *(phonetic)*?
**A Looks like it. I can't read that name too well.**

**REINIG REPORTING, INC.** (212) 684-7298 **Page 9** to **Page 12**

ALSO PRESENT: Betty Tilden, ABC Reporting, Official Reporter

or

ALSO PRESENT: Betty Tilden, Official Reporter

or

ALSO PRESENT: Betty Tilden, Reporter

If you were not the official reporter of record, since the other reporter swore/affirmed the witness, the sworn/affirmed paragraph must reflect this in the transcript. For example:

B O B M I L L E R, called as a witness, having been duly sworn by the Notary Public [other reporter's name] was examined and testified as follows:

**FIGURE 13–6**
(continued)

BSA | **Henrietta Silver** | XMAX(4/4)

Page 13

Q It looks like C-H-A-D-P-U-R-I.
THE WITNESS: Is that the man
who –
MS. PANICO: Let him ask you
questions and you just answer what's
asked of you.
THE WITNESS: Got it.
**A That sounds familiar.**
Q Were there any other witnesses to
this accident, that you know of?
**A No.**
Q Do you have any other notes or
documents which have this witness' name on it?
**A Yes, his business card. I have**
**it at home. It has his phone number on it as**
**well.**
MR. BAINES: I call for
production of the business card.
MS. PANICO: May I?
MR. BAINES: Sure.
MS. PANICO: Didn't you mention a
second witness to me?
THE WITNESS: Oh, I forgot about
him.

Page 14

MS. PANICO: Tell him.
**A There was another gentleman.**
**Could we go off the record for a**
**second?**
Q Sure.
*(Discussion held off the record.)*
MS. PANICO: The witness has
notified us that she is not feeling
well enough to continue and would like
to adjourn for the day. We will
arrange for a continuation of the
plaintiff's examination at a mutually
convenient time and place.
MR. BAINES: With that, we are
adjourned.
*(Time noted: 11:24 a.m.)*

Page 15

ACKNOWLEDGMENT
STATE OF NEW YORK )
: ss
COUNTY OF )
I, HENRIETTA SILVER, hereby
certify that I have read the transcript
of my testimony taken under oath in my
deposition of April 5, 1999; that the
transcript is a true, complete and
correct record of my testimony, and
that the answers on the record as given
by me are true and correct.
----------------------
HENRIETTA SILVER
Signed and Subscribed to
before me, this -------- day
of ---------------, 1999.
------------------------------
Notary Public, State of New York

Page 16

INDEX

WITNESS PAGE

HENRIETTA SILVER
Examination by:
MR. BAINES 4
EXHIBITS

DEFENDANTS' DESCRIPTION PAGE

**A Handwritten document entitled**
**"Accident information – 11/20/94" 12**
**DOCUMENTS AND/OR INFORMATION REQUESTED**

**DESCRIPTION PAGE**

**1) Social Security number 5**
**2) MV-104 11**
**3) Business card 13**
**QUESTIONS MARKED FOR A RULING**

**PAGE LINE**

**10 21**

**REINIG REPORTING, INC.** | (212) 684-7298 | **Page 13** to **Page 16**

Check with the agency for its preference on wording.

You would include a copy of your agency's stipulations, if applicable, into the transcript.

If a readback was done by the other (official) reporter, certain agencies place a readback blurb into the transcript to so indicate, such as:

(Record read by official reporter.)

The nonofficial reporter would just use a regular readback blurb; for example, *(Record read.)*. Other agencies may choose to implement the regular readback blurb for both the official and nonofficial reporter, figuring that it is obvious from the transcripts who did the readbacks.

If a ruling took place, both the official reporter and the nonofficial reporter would report it and transcribe it. The nonofficial reporter's placement of the

**FIGURE 13–6**
(continued)

BSA | **Henrietta Silver** | XMAX(5/5)

Page 17

**STATE OF NEW YORK )**
**ss**
**COUNTY OF NASSAU )**
**I, DANA CHIPKIN, a Registered**
**Professional Reporter and Notary Public within and for**
**the State of New York, do hereby certify:**
**THAT HENRIETTA SILVER, the witness whose**
**examination is hereinbefore set forth, was duly sworn**
**by me and that this transcript of such examination is**
**a true record of the testimony given by such witness.**
**I further certify that I am not related**
**to any of the parties to this action by blood or**
**marriage and that I am in no way interested in the**
**outcome of this matter.**
**IN WITNESS WHEREOF, I have hereunto set**
**my hand this 12th day of April, 1999.**
**--------------------**
**DANA CHIPKIN**

**REINIG REPORTING, INC.** | (212) 684-7298 | **Page 17** to **Page 17**

official reporter under *ALSO PRESENT* on the appearance page implies that exhibits are marked by the official reporter. The nonofficial reporter's transcript should include the time that the proceeding began and ended and a jurat/acknowledgment page for the witness even though the witness will sign and have notarized the original transcript. If you are the nonofficial reporter, eliminate that portion of the certification page that indicates that the witness was sworn/affirmed by you or reword it to indicate that the witness was sworn/affirmed by the official reporter.

If you are the official reporter of record, the only variation from a single-reporter proceeding is the inclusion of the nonofficial reporter's name under *ALSO PRESENT* on your transcript's appearance page.

## WHEN THERE IS A RELIEF REPORTER

A relief reporter is brought in to continue the recording of testimony begun by another reporter. One transcript is prepared that merges the testimony reported by both the initial reporter and the relief reporter. The title page should include the names and credentials of both reporters reporting the proceeding.

The appearance page will be the same as in a single-reporter proceeding. You do not list the relief reporter under *ALSO PRESENT,* as it is assumed from the title page that you left the proceeding when the relief reporter began writing. Likewise, the relief reporter does not list the other reporter under *ALSO PRESENT.* The two reporters' index pages will be merged into one index page. It will be obvious by the page numbers of each item which reporter's record the item fell within. A single stipulation page will appear in the transcript.

The agency usually prepares the final transcript once the two reporters have turned in their transcripts. At the conclusion of the first reporter's transcript, a notation is placed that indicates the time that the first reporter left the proceeding and the relief reporter took over. Consult the agency for the proper wording. There is no jurat or acknowledgment page added when the initial reporter's portion of the transcript ends. The pages written by the relief reporter follow the initial reporter's pages sequentially (numerically). The relief reporter fills in the time that the proceeding ends, and the agency places two certification pages at the end of the (merged) transcript, which each reporter then signs.

## BOOKING TESTIMONY TOGETHER

In cases where testimony is booked together, such as that of a husband/wife or parent/child, if your agency uses jurats, a jurat will appear following the first witness's testimony, and the second witness's testimony will begin on the subsequent page. The header is changed to reflect the new witness's name. You have your sworn/affirmed paragraph, *EXAMINATION BY* and the attorney's name, followed by a colon, and then the Q&A on the next line. A separate jurat will appear at the conclusion of the second witness's testimony. If your agency uses acknowledgment pages, a single acknowledgment page will include both witnesses' names and have a signature line for each witness. The only variation in the index page is that it should list each witness, by whom he or she was examined, and the page number that each examination began/continued on.

## SHORT-ANSWER QUESTIONS

1. The first page of a transcript is called the _____ page.
2. A ______ appears above the first line of a transcript page after testimony begins.
3. A ______ is a single or double line that appears below the last line of each transcript page reflecting agency information.

4. The __________ page follows the title page and lists those present at the proceeding.
5. A multiple-name law firm representing either the plaintiff or defendant will be delineated as _________ *for the Plaintiff(s)* or _________ *for the Defendant(s)* on the appearance page.
6. When an attorney appears __ _______, it means that attorney is covering the deposition for the attorney(s) of record but is not officially a member of the law firm.
7. Since a _______ _______ represents an individual and not a party company/entity, he or she is listed as *Attorney(s) for,* followed by the individual's name.
8. When a party witness has representation by more than one law firm for an action, the subsequently retained attorneys are delineated in the record as ____ - ____________.
9. If a law firm does not send someone to a deposition and you are told that the firm wants a copy of the transcript, you should list the firm on the appearance page with a ____ ________ notation.
10. ___________ __ is placed into the record to reflect the commencement or continuation of an attorney's questioning of a witness.
11. Examination of a witness by an attorney is recorded in a _____ format.
12. Qs and As in a transcript are set at the _____ tab, and the actual question or answer begins at the ______ tab.
13. Speaker designations in colloquy generally begin at the ______ tab.
14. ______ are used to reflect a change in thought or a false start.
15. ____ _____ is written by the reporter at the end of a proceeding to indicate when the proceeding concluded.
16. A _____ may be used instead of an acknowledgment in localities where the witness's signature must be notarized.
17. An ______________ page is a witness's certification that the transcript is a true, complete, and accurate record of the testimony given.
18. The ___________ page is the reporter's attestation that the transcript is a true and accurate record of a witness's testimony, that he or she is not related to any of the parties to the action, and that he or she has no interest in the outcome of the matter.
19. ______ _____ are used by witnesses/attorneys in certain localities to make corrections to a transcript.
20. A ___________, or keyword index, is an alphabetical listing of each word in a transcript and the page and line numbers where it appears.
21. A _________ __________ may be referred to as a Min-U-Script, mini, or 4-up.
22. An _______ is a portion of a transcript sent prior to delivery of the entire transcript under separate cover.
23. When a transcript or portion of a transcript is marked ____________, public viewing of the transcript is prohibited.
24. When two reporters write simultaneously, the ________ reporter provides the original transcript and does readbacks and marking of exhibits.
25. A ______ reporter continues recording testimony begun by another reporter.

## TRUE/FALSE QUESTIONS

1. A header is placed on every page in the transcript.
2. The header command is placed below the *EXAMINATION BY* line with the attorney's name immediately prior to the beginning of a witness's testimony.

3. If a law firm represents one defendant in a multiple-defendant action, it is sufficient to list the law firm as *Attorneys for the Defendant* on the appearance page without specifying which defendants.
4. If an attorney represents multiple defendants in the caption, the order of the attorney's appearance is determined by the first-named party he or she represents.
5. File numbers are never included on the appearance page.
6. A personal attorney is listed under the attorney(s) of record on the appearance page.
7. A pro se witness who is a named party in the action should be listed on the appearance page among the attorneys in the order of parties named in the caption.
8. Index pages list the page number each attorney's questioning began on and/or continued on when more than one attorney examines the witness.
9. *EXAMINATION BY*—or just *BY*—and the attorney's name may be placed into the transcript when an attorney continues his or her examination after a brief colloquy.
10. The nature of an exhibit, how it was designated, its numerical or alphabetical designation, and a brief description of the exhibit are listed on the index page by page number.
11. Every transcript contains an index page.
12. The order in which a stipulation page, if applicable, appears within a transcript varies from locality to locality.
13. All states insert stipulation pages in deposition transcripts.
14. Stipulation pages are not used for hearings/arbitrations.
15. The interpreter sworn/affirmed paragraph follows the paragraph for the swearing/affirming of a witness.
16. The sworn/affirmed paragraph is the same for the first session of a witness's testimony as a continuation.
17. Reporters must always note the time the proceeding concludes.
18. Jurat wording must be changed if a witness is affirmed rather than sworn.
19. The title page of an excerpt is considered page 1, the appearance page is page 2, and the subsequent pages are numbered sequentially.
20. Confidential material is always bound separately from the nonconfidential portion of the transcript.
21. A blurb must be added to a transcript to indicate where confidential material begins and ends.
22. When two reporters write simultaneously, the nonofficial reporter delivers a copy of the transcript to his or her client only.
23. When two reporters write simultaneously, the title page lists the names of both reporters.
24. When two reporters write simultaneously, each lists the other reporter on their transcript appearance page.
25. When two reporters write simultaneously, the sworn/affirmed paragraph and the sworn/affirmed portion of the certification page should reflect which reporter swore/affirmed the witness.
26. When there is a relief reporter, the agency merges the testimony recorded by the two reporters into one transcript that contains both reporters' names on the title page.
27. When there is a relief reporter, separate certifications are placed at the end of the transcript and signed by the two reporters.
28. When testimony is booked together, a jurat is placed at the end of the first witness's testimony, and the second witness's testimony begins on the subsequent page.
29. When testimony is booked together, a single acknowledgment page with a signature line for both witnesses may be placed in the transcript.
30. When testimony is booked together, indexes must list the witnesses' names, who they were examined by, and the page number that each examination began/continued on.

## DISCUSSION QUESTIONS

1. What are the elements of a transcript?
2. What should you do if there is a lengthy caption?
3. What agency information appears on the title page of a transcript?
4. If testimony was booked together for two witnesses who share the same last name, how can you differentiate the witnesses in the header?
5. What types of headers are used for hearings or arbitrations?
6. How is the order of attorneys on the appearance page determined?
7. If the person questioning the witness is not yet admitted to the bar, how it that person's appearance reflected on the appearance page?
8. How is the appearance of an of-counsel attorney indicated on an appearance page?
9. What information is contained within an index?
10. How may the continuing testimony of a witness be reflected in the sworn/affirmed paragraph?
11. How might lack of punctuation or incorrect punctuation affect a transcript?
12. In what forms may reporters present a finished transcript to an agency?
13. What are some reasons why a reporter should not call an attorney or witness for assistance in the preparation of a transcript?
14. How might you search your steno notes to locate a requested excerpted protion of the testimony?
15. List some scenarios where two reporters may end up writing simultaneously.

# CHAPTER 14

# Being an Independent Contractor

## WHAT IS AN INDEPENDENT CONTRACTOR?

Freelancers are generally considered independent contractors rather than employees by taxing authorities. Freelance reporters fall into the independent contractor category because:

- Most of the reporter's training to do his or her job takes place in school. The agency does not offer a paid training period, despite the fact that the agency offers transcript assistance and guidance
- The reporter is usually not reimbursed for expenses related to performance of his or her job by an agency
- The reporter's equipment is not paid for by an agency
- The reporter does not receive weekly paychecks with state and federal taxes taken out
- The reporter's principal place of work is not the agency's office
- The reporter is not automatically entitled to benefits provided by an office, such as health or disability insurance, pension plans, paid vacation, and sick days
- The reporter, after having his or her taxes prepared, may recognize a profit or a loss for a particular year
- The reporter does not usually have a written contract with the agency that ensures employment for a specified period of time

## IRS FORM 1099

At the end of the year, you will receive a Form 1099 from everyone that you have worked for, provided the amount is above $600. Some agencies will issue you a 1099 even if you have earned less than $600 with them. It is then your responsibility to report this income in your yearly tax return, as the Internal Revenue Service performs comparisons of 1099-MISC forms submitted by companies, which list the names of reporters who have earned income with that agency, against the reporters' income tax returns.

## ESTIMATED TAXES

Freelance reporters pay estimated taxes throughout the year. If you are a new reporter, you would base your yearly income on a projection of how much you have earned thus far divided by the number of months that amount was earned over multiplied by 12. For instance, say that you have been reporting for three months and have earned $12,000. You would divide $12,000 by the number of months (3), which averages out to $4,000 a month. Multiplying $4,000 by 12 equals $48,000, which would be your projected income for the year. Your accountant will assist you in figuring out the amount of the quarterly payments that should be made to the proper tax authorities.

If you are a freelance reporter who has been working for more than a year, your estimated taxes would be based upon the prior year's earnings.

## MONEY MANAGEMENT

Many freelance reporters have experienced problems in money management as a result of not setting aside a portion of their earnings for taxes. A good rule of thumb is to put a third of each paycheck into a separate account reserved for paying taxes. Some reporters simply deposit every third check received into this type of account.

## TAX DEDUCTIONS

Freelance reporters should be aware of the types of tax deductions they are entitled to and the importance of retaining receipts and documentation concerning:

- The lease/purchase of business-related equipment
- Repair and maintenance costs for business-related equipment
- Office supplies—steno paper, notepads, exhibit stickers, notary/signature stamps, and so on
- Business cards
- The vehicle(s) used to get to and from job destinations. Freelance reporters should record the mileage on vehicles utilized for work purposes at the beginning and end of each year in their work ledgers, the purchase or lease payments made during a particular year, the cost of repairs to said vehicles, maintenance and part expenditures, the amount of car insurance paid throughout the particular year, and the amount paid for gasoline throughout the year
- Other transportation expenses, such as receipts or documentation for tolls, buses, trains, taxis, and so on
- Parking expenses
- Dues paid to associations
- Donations made to associations/schools/charities
- Seminar fees and related travel expenses

- Travel or entertainment expenses relating to job employment
- Telephone expenses
- Internet fees
- Postage expenses
- Printing expenses
- Day care expenses—to claim as a deduction, you must submit either a federal tax ID number for the day care institution or an individual's Social Security number. You can claim up to $2,400 per child yearly as of the date of publication of this book
- Scopist/notereader/proofreader expenses
- A portion of your home as an office

Reporters must designate a percentage of their mileage and expenses for telephone, Internet, and postage, as these categories are frequently used for personal use as well as business use.

## THE IN-HOME OFFICE

Although Section 280A of the Internal Revenue Code has made it very difficult for freelance reporters to claim a portion of their home as an in-home office, the Taxpayer Relief Act of 1997, by utilizing words such as "principal place of business," has enabled some reporters to do so. These reporters' in-home offices must, however:

- Be used exclusively for the reporter's business, which means that if the office contains a couch and a home entertainment system, for example,

**FIGURE 14–1**
A Typical Court Reporter's Home Office

the deduction will not be allowed. One can claim a portion of a room containing these items, but that portion of the room must contain solely work-related items

- Be used regularly for the reporter's business, which means that the freelance reporter performs work-related functions at this location rather than half at the agency and half at home
- Be the reporter's principal place of business, which means that it is the sole location where the reporter conducts a substantial portion of his or her business activities. It is this third requirement that is the most controversial, as freelance reporters have four basic elements to their job—reporting, scoping, proofreading, and correcting the transcript—and may argue that, therefore, a greater percentage of their job requirements are performed in the home office, if they scope and do their corrections themselves. It might be argued that the reporter can utilize the agency's office, but for some, that is just not feasible, especially when logistics and late-night hours are taken into account

It may not even be worth it to claim a home office. Check with your accountant as to the benefit of claiming it weighed against the possibility of placing a red flag onto your return, which may lead to an audit. (See Figure 14–1 for an example of a typical court reporter's home office.)

## NO BENEFITS

Employee benefits may be offered to reporters working for agencies that do contract work or that focus on stenocaptioning; however, most freelance court reporters are independent contractors and do not receive such benefits. Being an independent contractor means that you are on your own as far as health and disability insurance goes. Although some agencies today are forming group insurance plans for their reporters, it is not all that common.

If you are married and your spouse has insurance benefits, then you may obtain insurance at a rate lower than if you had to take out a plan independently. However, not everyone fits into this category. As a member of NCRA, you may be eligible to participate in a group plan. Contact the NCRA for details.

Another option may be to find out whether an organization you belong to offers health benefits to its members. Some associations have very reasonable membership fees, such as NAFE, the National Association for Female Executives, which provides discounts on special packages. You can contact NAFE by writing to 135 West 50th Street, 16th Floor, New York, NY 10020; by calling (800) 634-NAFE; by faxing a letter on a company letterhead requesting membership to (212) 445-6228; or by e-mailing them at nafe@nafe.com. Check out their Web site, www.nafe.com.

Disability insurance is a must, and especially important is having a policy with a rider to protect your most precious of work tools, your hands. You are no different than a concert pianist or an athlete when it comes down to it, so think ahead and provide for your future.

As an independent contractor, maternity/paternity leave, vacation time, and sick days are all benefits that you do not receive, so try to make provisions for these occurrences ahead of time by alloting a portion of your income to a slush fund.

## TAX-FREE/TAX-DEFERRED PLANS

As I am a freelancer myself and not a financial advisor, my best advice to you would be to retain a financial consultant to familiarize you with the various plans that permit you to place a certain amount of money into them each year that would be either tax-free or tax-deferred. Terms to ask about are:

- A traditional IRA
- The new Roth IRA
- A SEP—Simplified Employee Pension—plan
- A Keogh plan
- A 401K plan—these are utilized by corporations only, and you would not need to concern yourself with this type of plan unless you were planning on starting your own agency

## SHORT-ANSWER QUESTIONS

1. Freelance court reporters are generally considered __________ __________ as opposed to employees.
2. Freelance reporters receive ____ from the agencies where their earnings have totaled $600 or more yearly.
3. Freelance reporters are required to pay ________ taxes throughout the year to avoid penalties by the taxing authorities.
4. It is a good rule of thumb to place ___-_____ of your paycheck or every third paycheck into an account reserved for the payment of taxes.
5. Freelance reporters should maintain receipts and documentation of certain expenses that may be claimed as ___ _________.
6. Section ____ of the Internal Revenue Code has made it very difficult for freelance reporters to claim a portion of their home as an in-home office.
7. Being an independent contractor means that _______ such as health and disability insurance are not provided by the agencies that the freelance reporter works for.
8. An __ - ____ ______ is the portion of a reporter's home where he or she performs the majority of his or her court reporting functions.
9. Being a member of ____ may enable you to participate in group insurance plans.
10. A special rider to one's __________ insurance is recommended regarding injury to one's hands.
11. ___ - ____ and ___ - ________ plans allow reporters a tax exemption on certain accounts.
12. If you are starting your own freelance agency, a ____ plan should be a consideration.

## TRUE/FALSE QUESTIONS

1. Reporters who are trained stenocaptioners and who work for one company and receive weekly paychecks with federal and state taxes taken out are considered employees.
2. Most freelance court reporting agencies pay for their reporters' equipment.
3. A reporter's principal place of work is considered the job setting by taxing authorities.
4. Most freelance court reporting agencies offer health/disability insurance benefits to their reporters.
5. If you earn $550 with an agency for a given year, you have no obligation to report it to the tax authorities.
6. The Internal Revenue Service compares agency 1099-MISC forms against the tax returns of individual reporters listed on the 1099-MISC forms.
7. In projection of their first year's earnings, new reporters base their estimated taxes on a $50,000 income.
8. Working freelance reporters base their estimated taxes upon their prior year's earnings.
9. Freelance reporters can claim 100 percent of their home telephone expenses as a tax deduction.
10. Dues paid to NCRA are a valid tax deduction for court reporters.
11. To claim a portion of one's home as a tax deduction, the reporter cannot utilize the in-home office as a family room also.
12. Nonreporting-related associations may offer group insurance plans that freelance court reporters may participate in if a member.
13. Freelance reporters receive three months' paid maternity leave.
14. Having a slush fund cushions a reporter's lack of income from unpaid sick and vacation days off.

## DISCUSSION QUESTIONS

1. Why are freelance court reporters viewed as independent contractors rather than employees by the taxing authorities?
2. How would a reporter or his or her accountant arrive at an estimated tax figure if the reporter just began freelancing? If the freelance reporter is already working?
3. What is the rule of thumb utilized by freelance reporters regarding setting money aside for taxes?
4. What expenses can freelance court reporters claim as tax deductions?
5. Should the in-home office be considered a tax deduction? Why or why not?
6. With what organizations might a freelance reporter associate that would enable the reporter to participate in a group health/disability/dental plan?

# CHAPTER 15

# Every Court Reporter's Nightmare

A subject that I would like to talk about is what to do in case of court reporting catastrophes or situations that every reporter fears. Although I cannot cover every situation that could occur in the course of your reporting career, I will endeavor to discuss a few scenarios and share with you some valuable lessons learned and practical solutions.

## IN CASE OF FIRE

From the incident previously mentioned where my agency's office was destroyed by fire, I learned about the importance of dumping jobs into my personal computer upon the conclusion of each job, photocopying work sheets and related materials, and maintaining disks and financial records in fireproof boxes.

## THE UNITED PARCEL SERVICE STRIKE

After a very technical job where documents were quoted from extensively and the terminology was mind-boggling, I managed to procure the original exhibits from the examining attorney. I promised to return them to his office by the following Monday. I wanted my agency's in-house scopist to check a few quotes against my notes, so I mailed the exhibits, together with my work sheet, to the agency. The job was scoped and sent back to me with the exhibits via United Parcel Service (UPS). That night, UPS workers went on strike, and it took approximately three weeks to obtain the exhibits so that I could proofread the job and return it to the attorney. My agency called and explained the situation to the attorney, who turned out to be very understanding and supplied me with a copy of the documents to utilize in the preparation of the transcript in the interim.

This is a situation where agency intervention and explanation helped the reporter to maintain her reputation as reliable despite unfortunate circumstances and to obtain what she needed in order to provide an excellent transcript.

Lessons to Be Learned:

- Copies of documents should be made before mailing out original documents
- Keeping abreast of current events is always recommended—threats of the UPS strike had been mentioned in the news prior to the actual strike, and delivery could have been arranged with another service
- There is nothing wrong with agency intervention
- Attorneys usually have copies of documents marked as exhibits at proceedings

## THE IRS INVESTIGATION

When I had been reporting for only a year or so, I was sent to a hotel conference room to cover an investigation by the Internal Revenue Service (IRS). When I began taking appearances, I noted about 10 people present on behalf of the IRS and about 25 people present on behalf of the company being investigated. The representative for the IRS told me that all of the people present on behalf of the IRS would be questioning about three witnesses at a time. The table was so long, I could not even see the people at the end of it. Since I had arrived early, I excused myself after setting up and went into the ladies room to compose myself. I cannot tell you how tempted I was to just leave!

When I returned to the conference room, I located my contact from the IRS and said, "In order to make a clear record, I can't have everyone speaking at once, and I will need a second, since there will be so many people speaking, to identify each speaker, so here's what we're going to have to do: I'm going to get placards from the hotel desk downstairs with which I will identify each speaker, and before anyone begins questioning besides yourself, I want them to raise their hand and lift their placard in the air so that I can identify the person before he or she speaks. Since there will be three witnesses on the panel responding to questions, I would like each person questioning, if possible, to address the person that they would like to answer the question so that I will know in advance how to designate who will be answering."

My contact for the IRS and I set up the ground rules before the investigation began, and everything ran smoothly. He was so impressed with how I had handled the situation that, during our lunch break, he called my agency to thank them for sending such a conscientious and personable reporter.

What began as a dreaded situation turned into a challenging but rewarding job when I thought about what I, as the reporter, needed and then communicated that to the parties involved. Had I not said anything before we began, the proceeding would have been totally disorganized, and I would not have been able to predict who was going to speak when. My assertiveness made the parties aware of the difficulty of reporting such a proceeding and prompted them to work with me as a team to create a clear and accurate transcript.

Lessons to Be Learned:

- Arriving early to a job gives the reporter time to devise a set of ground rules in difficult situations
- Communicating your needs to the contact person/client may turn an unreportable proceeding into an organized one
- Placards, nametags, and other forms of identification may be necessary for multiple-speaker proceedings—some reporters carry oak tag in their bag for this reason
- People are often impressed by reporter insight regarding transcript ambiguitiy and clarity

## THE BURGLARY

One night when I was alone in my home and sleeping, a burglar entered. I heard someone in the house, but assumed it was my husband, who at that time worked nights. I noted the time as 3:00 A.M., then turned over and went back to sleep. The next morning, when I was getting ready to leave for work, I went to grab my work bag and could not find it.

Being a creature of habit, I had always left the work bag in the same place each night. I searched and searched the house, then searched my car, and still I could not find it. I asked my husband what time of the morning he had arrived home, and he said, "5:00 A.M." It was then that I realized that we had been burglarized.

Aside from the trauma that set in, what worried me most was that in the bag were my steno notes and paperwork from a job taken the previous day on a very technical computer case. During the job, I had used *short forms*—brief outlines for difficult-to-write or lengthy words or phrases—in lieu of extensive computer terms for speed-saving purposes. Without my notepad notes, I could not remember what word or group of words each short form represented. Left without a work sheet on the job, I could not prepare a title, appearance, stipulation, jurat/acknowledgment, or index page, nor could I identify speakers in colloquy.

Agency intervention was required. A caption was faxed to us from our client's office, and a few phone calls were made to obtain attorneys' names, addresses, file numbers, and so on. I asked the examining attorney if I could call him when short forms came up that were undecipherable, and he was able to help me figure them out and spell them accurately. As it is my practice to utilize a short form shortly after the word or phrase it represents comes up or is used repetitively, most of the outlines were identifiable.

Lessons to Be Learned:

- Always dump your computerized notes into your CAT system the day of the job
- Place job-related paperwork in close proximity to your CAT system (and hope the CAT system is not stolen!)
- Only utilize short forms if you have a good memory
- Only utilize short forms after you have written the word or phrase each form represents into the record clearly

- Only utilize short forms for difficult-to-write or lengthy words or phrases that are used repeatedly
- Always make a notation in the record as to what your outline represents, and spell it out if you can. Then, if necessary, you can recreate your globalling system
- There is nothing wrong with agency intervention.
- Captions can always be faxed to you
- Your client can usually provide enough information about those present at a proceeding for you to contact those who were present and obtain further information

## CALL IN THE EMS

I was once working in an air-conditioned office during a summer heat wave. Despite having eaten a healthy lunch, as we neared the end of the deposition, I began to feel dizzy and nauseous. I talked myself into continuing because it was almost five o'clock. The questioning attorney asked for a break to look over his notes, so I figured I was almost out of the woods.

During the break, I felt lightheaded, as if I were going to faint. One of the (female) attorneys present told me to lie down on a nearby cot and brought me a cool compress for my head. I was embarrassed, but what could I do but accept the situation at hand? I called the agency, but there were no relief reporters available at the time. I rested for a few minutes until the examining attorney returned to the room and said he had a few more questions he would like to ask. Diehard reporter that I am, I said, "Okay."

The attorney who had tended to me during the break explained to the examining attorney what had happened. They both agreed that they could finish the deposition of the witness in written interrogatories or over the telephone at a later time, as the witness was from out of town. At that point, despite my determination to continue, I suddenly felt like I was going to faint and an ambulance was called. As they were carrying me out of the conference room on a stretcher, I was repeatedly saying, "Let me just take down the last few questions. No, really, I'm all right." The attorneys told me not to worry about it, to just take care of myself.

I was concerned about my machine as well as my notes, which the emergency medical technicians were not allowing me to bring into the ambulance. The office we were at agreed to keep my things there until I could arrange to have them picked up. I was taken to the hospital where I was found to be severely dehydrated and required I.V. hydration. I called my husband, and we retrieved my belongings after I was discharged from the hospital.

Was I embarrassed? Yes. But I got over it. The reaction of the attorneys made me realize that my health was more important than reporting the last few questions. They even called my agency the next day to ask how I was feeling.

Lessons to Be Learned:

- The reporter should always communicate with her client and agency if he or she is ill
- A relief reporter may be available in the case of reporter illness

- If a reporter is ill, a deposition may be continued via written interrogatories, continued on another day, or continued over the telephone
- Serious health problems should not be overlooked

## COMMOTION AT THE COURTHOUSE

When I was a new reporter, I accepted a job from a plaintiff in a case who was having financial problems and could not afford to pay a freelance agency's rates for a court reporter. The plaintiff, who was acting pro se, was going to depose an attorney whom she had fired for legal malpractice after he failed to fulfill duties on her behalf, resulting in the inability to obtain financial damages after a horrific accident.

The plaintiff had asked me to tape-record the proceedings and said that at the end of the examination she would provide me with a list of the questions that she had asked. I did not know until the job began that the reason for this was because she would be yelling throughout the proceeding at a speed that I was not able to keep up with. About a half hour into the questioning, she was speaking so fast, the fighting was so frenetic, and there was so much overlapping of words that I was practically in tears. I asked for a break. I met a reporter friend in the courthouse hallway, who said, "Did you hear what's going on in Room 7? We can hardly hear our witness over all the commotion." I said, "Hear it? I'm reporting it."

I asked the plaintiff if I could speak with her outside of the deposition room. I told her that I was unable to continue because I was not getting everything and, frankly, was getting nervous from all the screaming. She tearfully begged me to continue anyway, as she was a disabled person and it was very hard for her to physically get to the courthouse, to get the attorney to finally appear, and so on. She asked me to stay and write and said that she would have a typist produce the transcript from the audiotapes so I would not have to certify to what I was not getting. Reluctantly, I agreed.

I wrote hundreds of pages from 9:00 in the morning till 4:30 in the afternoon, at which time I was ready to quit court reporting, feeling totally incompetent. After the job, I declined to accept payment. I felt I had not fulfilled my job responsibilities and just wanted to forget about the whole experience.

I received a call from the woman a few weeks later saying that typists were declining to certify to the accuracy of the audiotapes, since there was so much overlap and so many inaudible exchanges, and that she really needed me to audit nine hours of tapes against my steno notes to create a transcript. I did not know what to do. I asked colleagues and people whose opinions I respected for advice, and the concensus was that if I could not certify to something in good conscience, I should explain that to the woman and walk away from the job, which is what I did, after many apologies.

About two years later, I received a call from the plaintiff who explained that at the time of the deposition, she had been on heavy medication that made her belligerent. She said that it had been unfair to put me in the position I was put in and that she had worked out the problem and redeposed the attorney through written interrogatories. She wanted to pay me what she felt I had rightfully earned at the deposition two years before just by staying there and being a calming influence to her. I refused to accept payment, but a month later a check arrived with a lovely letter about how she felt I had earned my fee by remaining at the deposition even though I could not produce a transcript of the testimony and certify to it.

Lessons to Be Learned:

- Make sure your level of experience is appropriate for the prospective assignment prior to accepting the job
- Pro se witnesses and people representing their own cases who are non-attorneys may ramble incessantly or get out of control, as there is no one present on their behalf to offer guidance or calm them down
- Certain situations are unreportable, and you can only do your best given the circumstances
- If you are having difficulty, most reporters would experience the same difficulty; it does not mean you are a bad reporter
- Do not let one bad reporting experience influence you to quit the field.
- If communicating your needs does not change the reporting environment, the responsibility for a less-than-perfect transcript rests on the client
- If you cannot hear something at the proceeding, do not expect to be able to make it out from a tape recording of the proceeding
- If in a questionable situation, consult your court reporting school, state association, the NCRA, freelance agencies, colleagues, or people knowledgeable about the matter at hand for guidance
- Do not sacrifice peace of mind for a paycheck

## AN AWFUL TRANSCRIPT

One time I went to take down the testimony of a new witness for a case I had been on before. When I arrived, the attorney told me what every reporter dreads, that my transcript of the last deposition was the worst one he had ever received. I immediately got a knot in my stomach but inquired further, as I am a very thorough proofreader. He then went on to explain that there were strange letters in it and things that were undecipherable. I asked him to show me what he was talking about. When he showed me the transcript, it was obvious that somehow he had received an unedited transcript with steno throughout. Certain words that were unique to the subject matter of the case came up with improper spellings. I explained that this was not the edited copy and called my agency, which had the edited transcript messengered to the deposition while we were on the record. This reinstated my credibility with the attorney.

Lessons to Be Learned:

- If told there is a problem with a transcript, do not be defensive. First, make sure you were the reporter. Do not bad-mouth the agency, scopist, or another reporter if the error was theirs. Inquire about the nature of the problem, and seek to rectify it
- Have a corrected copy of the transcript sent to the parties as soon as possible
- Agencies sometimes have to fly through hoops to meet the needs of their clients and reinstate credibility when problems arise

## THE ALL-NIGHTER

After two months off due to a broken kneecap, I was preparing to go back to work the following Monday. On the Wednesday previous, the principal of my agency asked if I would do him a favor and take a job on Thursday in my neck of the woods, stating it would not be anything difficult. Always willing to do a favor for a principal when asked, I complied. Despite the fact that I had not touched my machine for two months, I figured a little brush-up practicing the night before should do the trick.

When I called for my assignment, I was told that it was going to be a two-day arbitration and that the transcript was a going to be a daily, which needed to be delivered to a medical expert witness the next morning by 9:00 A.M. for review before the witness testified at the arbitration later that morning. I immediately made baby-sitting arrangements for my children because I anticipated reading throughout the night and was not sure what time my husband would be arriving home.

The office was sending me a scopist to prepare the transcript while I was on the record. I was to give her disks at every break. The scopist was top-notch, and I knew she would do a great job, which she did.

Reporting on the arbitration entailed taking down the testimony of a panel of arbitrators and two attorneys for each side who flew through their opening statements. I pushed for speed, wrote sloppy at times, but rose to the challenge.

What the scopist and I did not anticipate was the length of the job, 327 pages, and the fact that at one point one of the attorneys would be reading Q&A directly from a deposition transcript into the record, which led to the transcript not even being close to finished upon the conclusion of the arbitration. We looked at one another and came to the conclusion that there was no way I could read all night and report the arbitration the following day. We arranged for another reporter to cover the next day's proceedings, which were, luckily, not requested daily.

I invited the scopist to my home to finish scoping the job while I attempted to print part of it out to begin proofreading. Imagine my reaction when I found out that my printer was not working! The cool, calm, and collected computer person at my office suggested we merge the finished files, make an ASCII disk of the transcript, and print it out on my husband's printer, which was connected to a computer that did not have court reporting software in it. We did so, and I was able to begin proofreading.

The scopist scoped until after midnight and I proofread the job until 7:00 A.M. the following morning, when my computer person had to have me e-mail the still-unfinished transcript to the office to bind a transcript to deliver to the doctor. The night before, the computer person had driven an hour to my home to drive the scopist home, went home for a short while, then left his home to return to the office at about 5:00 in the morning.

I worked until about 9:30 A.M., when I made my last correction. By this point, the doctor and the parties had all received transcripts that were about 20 pages shy of corrections, but at least the doctor was able to read the testimony he was to be examined on. By 11:00 A.M., all parties received fully scoped and corrected copies of the transcript.

Having a relief reporter for the following day enabled me to catch up on sleep and rest my hands, which were sore beyond belief at this point. The teamwork displayed by the agency personnel kept everything running smoothly even when the road took a few unexpected turns. Three of us went far beyond the call of duty to fulfill our responsibility to our client.

Lessons to Be Learned:

- Try to do favors asked of you by a principal
- Practice after taking a hiatus from reporting
- Have backup day care arrangements available to you
- Arrange for access to backup computer/printer equipment if roadblocks arise with yours
- Know your limits, and properly estimate required scoping/proofing/correcting time
- Make arrangements for a relief reporter, if necessary
- Have a computer-knowledgeable person to consult in times of trouble
- Do not focus on insubstantial corrections when under a time pressure
- Know how to e-mail, modem, and fax
- Court reporting is not a 9 to 5 job!

## "NONDROWSY" COLD MEDICINE

One time I woke up with a bad cold and did not want to cancel my morning job. I took some "nondrowsy" cold medicine and went on my way. I started falling asleep while driving to the job. Even coffee could not dispel the drowsiness that set in. I arrived at the deposition safely and did all I could to stay awake and alert, but my fingers had a mind of their own. Luckily, the job was a short one. Later, when my scopist saw my notes, she asked what happened. She could see an obvious change in my writing.

Lessons to Be Learned:

- Do not take nonpreviously tested "nondrowsy" medication on workdays
- Medications may affect your driving/comprehension/writing on the job
- You may choose to scope your own work on bad writing days

## FAST FINGERS

It once took me many hours to finish scoping a difficult medical job that involved a doctor with a foreign accent that was practically unreportable. On my yellow pad, I had pages upon pages of notations about what some words I transcribed in error should be, spellings of medications that I could not make out when the witness was uttering them, and so on. When I finally proofread and corrected the transcript, I felt that the result was commendable, and I was pleased that the job was done. While at the job, I had asked the examining attorney for a copy of a medical report that the witness read from during the deposition, and she had asked me to call her after the deposition so she could fax it to me. I had done so, but I never received the fax. I had left the scoped, proofread, and corrected job in my software program so that when I received the medical report, I could just check my transcript against it and make any necessary corrections.

Two weeks passed, and I had taken some time off to work on this book. I decided that since I had finished all the jobs taken prior to that time, I would clear all remaining job files from my CAT system. Remembering only that I had read and corrected the transcript of the medical job, I assumed that I had copied it onto a backup disk and sent it to my agency. I forgot about the long-awaited fax. I deleted the job along with my completed jobs, only to learn that I had neither copied it nor sent it to my agency. Since I had already reformatted and reused the disk the job was initially recorded on, the next three days were spent notereading the job from my steno notes; rewriting the job onto my stenographic writer; rescoping, reproofreading, and recorrecting it; and finally delivering it to the agency.

Lessons to Be Learned:

- Do not be too quick to reformat and reuse job disks—keep them around until the transcript is delivered to the agency
- Do not be too quick to delete jobs from your CAT system—maybe removing them once a month would be a reasonable time period
- Always check that you have backed up the job onto a disk before removing it from your CAT system
- Always check that the office has received the transcript prior to removing a job from your CAT system
- Do not rely on the "Call me and I'll fax it to you" promise; get a copy of it before leaving the proceeding

Once deleted from your CAT system, the job is unretrievable—so back up *everything!*

## A REAL REALTIME FIASCO

Around the time that I was pondering whether or not I was realtime-ready, a realtime assignment came up that my principal was confident I could cover. It was through a Spanish interpreter, so it was the perfect realtime job to cut one's teeth on. I accepted even though I had just purchased a laptop computer the week before and had not worked out the glitches yet to write realtime. The principal said I could use the agency's laptop and that he'd send me the office computer expert to get me up and running.

The first thing I did was to call a reporter who had worked on the case previously to get from her a job dictionary, directions to the job setting, and the lowdown on the terminology and lawyer personalities involved. After getting the necessary information and confirming that the job was indeed through an interpreter, I was actually looking forward to my first realtime experience.

The second thing I did was to speak to the office computer person on the phone and take instruction on copying my personal dictionary onto disks that we would enter on the agency's laptop when we met at the job setting the following morning. Since my dictionary was extensive (about 65,000 words), it took me a few hours to flag each item and then divide the entire dictionary into three separate disks.

The office had mentioned that I was to record the proceeding on audiotape at the request of one of the attorneys. The agency did not have a tape recorder accessible at the time and asked me to bring one of my own. After saying that I would, I could not find a working tape recorder. My husband suggested I use our camcorder with the lens cap over the lens to tape audio only. I took a brief lesson on its operation and packed it with my things.

The following day, I arrived almost two hours early to have my dictionary installed and the realtime situation set up by my office's computer expert. I handed over the disks supposedly containing my dictionary only to learn they were blank. Since I was going to utilize the office's laptop, I had not thought to bring my own, as I was still troubleshooting with it. I called my husband and asked him to get dressed, grab my laptop, dress the kids and take them to day care, and meet me at the job setting as soon as possible on his way to work. Fortunately, he agreed and was there within 45 minutes. It was also fortuitous that I was working fairly close to my home that day.

We now had to copy the dictionary from my laptop computer onto the office's, as my computer was not at the point of performing realtime functions yet. When it was time for the first of five depositions to begin, our client suggested we start the deposition without realtime and try to get it happening on one of the breaks. While I had been setting up my writer and the camcorder, assuring the attorneys I was not videoing the proceeding, realizing the disks were blank, calling my husband, and testing to see if the realtime functions were working (which they were not), I had totally forgotten to program the other reporter's job dictionary for use at the proceeding. I managed, however, to job global some outlines and my speaker designations—only to learn three hours later, when the realtime writing began, that my writer and the software were incompatible. I discovered that what I had job globalled, what was coming up transcribed on my writer's LCD screen in English, was not corresponding with what was appearing on the laptop screen. Even the speaker designations were coming up as untranslates. These distractions and the many breaks in between testimony led to my forgetting to turn the camcorder back on after a lengthy break and completely missing the audiotaped testimony of one of the five witnesses.

About the time I was finally getting over my fear of realtiming and actually enjoying working with it, the attorney who had requested it packed up his laptop and left the proceeding to go on vacation, leaving a colleague from his firm to take over the examination. The colleague had no laptop and no apparent interest in the realtime service. I turned my agency's laptop his way and let him use it. He was as inexperienced with a laptop as I was, so he was even more understanding about the technical problems.

As I was unfamiliar with the office's laptop, I was unable to edit on breaks and clean up the transcript. When the proceeding ended, I was under pressure to create the ASCII files, to make ASCII disks for two attorneys, and to pack up my writer, camcorder, personal laptop, office's laptop, and so on, while being told that the building was being closed for the night. I decided to give the attorneys a dirty daily because of the late hour. In my haste, I accidentally gave one attorney a regular note file rather than an ASCII file. He could not open the file on his computer over the weekend, so he was not able to review it before testimony began the following Monday. (Monday's reporter relayed that bit of information to me.)

I later offered to make copies of the audiocassettes rather than have my office do it. I used a machine that, unbeknownst to me, did not work properly and copied one side of the master tape onto both sides of the second-generation tape rather than copying both sides A and B onto it. After much confusion while trying to label the tapes, I finally decided to turn the master tapes over to the agency and have it copy them.

Lessons to Be Learned:

- Do not accept assignments that you are not ready for
- Practice realtiming with a laptop on jobs prior to actually being requested to do it
- Do not use unfamiliar equipment
- Test-run your equipment before using it on a job
- Double-check that information copied onto a disk is indeed on the disk
- Bring backup equipment/a backup dictionary, if possible, to a realtime job
- Try to get as much information as possible from a reporter who has worked on a realtime case prior to you
- Utilize the job dictionary of reporters who have worked on a case prior to you
- Make sure your writer and software are compatible so that job globals will be translated properly onto the laptop screen
- Remember to turn tape recorders off before breaks and back on after breaks, if applicable
- Attorneys are generally understanding about realtime glitches
- Edit realtime jobs on breaks rather than at the end of the proceeding
- Make sure that you give ASCII files to the attorneys requesting realtime jobs and that the files are indeed on the disks
- Stay on good terms with family members in case major favors need be asked of them!

## REPORTER FREEZE-UP

Lawyers at a deposition I was reporting were talking about a transcript they had never received from a reporter on a med mal in which they were both representing parties. One asked the other, "Whatever happened to that transcript?" The other explained that he had seen the reporter at a later time and asked her why he had not received the transcript. She told him that they were questioning the expert witness about the same medical condition from which her mother had died and that the trauma of the loss had caused her to freeze up on the job, losing important testimony. The doctor could have been redeposed, but the fees and time incurred to do so would have lost the reporter's agency a client. A situation like this is also damaging to the reputation of the reporter.

Lessons to Be Learned:

- If unable to report a proceeding, call your agency for guidance or communicate this to the attorneys at a break—do not pretend to be writing
- Call for a relief reporter in dire situations
- If there are problems with a transcript, have the agency communicate to the client what has happened

## HERE COMES THE JUDGE

Another situation that sometimes happens to reporters in the field is that they are called into court over disputed testimony and asked by the judge to read their notes. One reason for this scenario might be if attorneys are challenging the competency of an interpreter and the reporter has a response from the witness in English that differs from the interpreted answer. Although these situations are rare, and I cannot imagine anyone who would not be nervous in such a situation, there are ways to prepare for it:

- Do not add English to testimony. That way, your steno notes will correspond with your readback to the judge
- Find your steno notes for the job and, if you have the time, reconcile them with your transcript. Place a fold in your notes where each page begins and mark it with the page number so that if you are asked to read, for example, pages 55 through 58, you will be able to locate the material more easily

Reporters are human, and sometimes hearing errors occur and they make mistakes. You should remember, however, that the witness, in some states, has an opportunity to correct mistakes upon reading the transcript by filling out an errata sheet or change sheet. The attorneys are also free to do the same with any obvious corrections if all parties to the proceeding agree to the changes. Such changes in a transcript, however, should be handled only through your agency; do not take it upon yourself to make them.

## COMMUNICATION

The bottom line, when unusual or bizarre situations occur, is to always communicate with your agency and take instruction from them. It is also necessary to have the agency communicate with its client to apprise the client of the problem and request any assistance required.

Every career has its share of bad moments, but I do not want to give the impression that freelance court reporting is full of only negatives. For me, personally, it has provided many rewards. I can earn in a day what I used to make in a week in prior careers. I have been able to take my husband on a surprise romantic vacation to Spain on a whim. I am able to take off personal days when my children are sick or I just need or want a day off. I also feel that I am a member of an industry that has greatly enhanced my knowledge on many issues, boosted my self-esteem as a professional, and brought me many new friends.

## SHORT-ANSWER QUESTIONS

1. It is recommended that job backups and financial information be preserved in _________ boxes.
2. Placards, nametags, and other forms of identification are useful in _____ - _______ proceedings.
3. _____ ____ are brief outlines used for difficult-to-write or lengthy words or phrases.

4. A ______ ________ may be called to take over if a reporter becomes ill on the job.
5. A deposition may be done via written ______________.
6. ___ __ witnesses may ramble, since there is no one representing them at proceedings and cautioning them to just say *yes* or *no*.
7. If communicating your needs does not change an unreportable reporting environment, the responsibility for a less-than-perfect transcript rests on the _____.
8. Taking __________ may negatively affect a reporter's job performance.
9. A job should always be ______ up on a disk before it is deleted from a reporter's CAT system.
10. A reporter should practice ________ writing before accepting ________ assignments.
11. Using a ___ __________ of a reporter who has reported the same case may be beneficial to a realtime reporter.
12. Realtime reporters should double-check that the disk provided to the attorney(s) after the job contains an _____ file of the realtime job.

## TRUE/FALSE QUESTIONS

1. Reporters should dump their jobs as soon as they possibly can.
2. Short forms should never be used.
3. Reporters should communicate if they detect anything that may lead to confusion on the record.
4. If you become ill during a proceeding, there is nothing that can be done, so you should keep writing.
5. All situations are reportable.
6. If you cannot get everything while reporting a job, you should give up reporting.
7. If you cannot hear something at a proceeding, you can always figure it out from a tape recording of the proceeding.
8. If there is a problem with a transcript, you should blame it on the agency or the scopist.
9. If a client complains about a transcript error, a corrected copy should be sent to the client as soon as possible.
10. Reporters should practice writing steno after a hiatus from reporting.
11. Reporters should proofread the same way on a daily as they do on a transcript requested by regular delivery.
12. Editing realtime jobs should be done at the end of the proceeding.
13. There is no need to become familiar with realtime equipment prior to taking a realtime job.
14. No comprehension is required by reporters on the job, only writing skills.
15. Reporters should reformat and reuse job disks immediately after dumping jobs into their computers.
16. Backup disks should be checked to make sure that the information was in fact copied onto them.
17. Test-running equipment is unnecessary.

## DISCUSSION QUESTIONS

1. What can reporters do to safeguard job-related material from a fire at their agency? At their home?
2. How can keeping up with current events alter a reporting scenario?
3. What difficulties may be encountered by reporters/agencies/clients as a result of problems with mail/delivery services?
4. What benefits are there to arriving early to your assignment?
5. What can you do if your notes and related paperwork are stolen?
6. Who should you consult regarding a questionable or ethical reporting situation?
7. If you become ill during an assignment, what should you do?
8. Prior to accepting an assignment, if you think it may be over your head, what should you do?
9. While at a job, if you feel it is beyond your reporting capabilities, what are your options?
10. How might you respond to an attorney who tells you that there is a problem with a transcript?
11. Why might a reporter need day care backups?
12. If your equipment fails you, what can you do?
13. How can medication negatively affect you?
14. How might you prepare to do a readback of disputed testimony before a judge?

# CHAPTER 16

# Making Changes

## SWITCHING AGENCIES

Very few freelance reporters remain with the same agency throughout their entire reporting career. Therefore, you need to know why reporters switch agencies and how it is done successfully.

### The Reporter-Agency Relationship

The on-staff reporter-agency relationship is like a romantic relationship between two people. When it is good, it is good; but when it is not working, there are three options: work harder to fix its weaknesses, grin and bear it, or move on. Sometimes the problem lies in the nature of the work the agency has you doing. Sometimes it is about the people that you work with in the agency. Sometimes it is simply about receiving a better offer elsewhere regarding page rate, volume of workload, locations where you will be working, or for a variety of other reasons.

### Make a Plan B

In your spare time, you may wish to develop a Plan B in case the situation with your agency cannot be worked out. You should investigate your other options, interview with other agencies, and compare page rates and workload promises. Ask colleagues if their agencies are looking for reporters, check the classifieds in the association magazines, on court reporting school/courthouse bulletin boards, online, or cold-call. Let prospective agencies know that you have not said anything to the agency you are leaving yet and that you would like the interview to be kept confidential. Also tell them that you wish to give your current agency two weeks' notice as a courtesy if you should make the decision to leave. This shows the prospective agency an element of respect toward your current principal. Do not bad-mouth the agency or principal that you are planning to leave.

### Communicate with the Agency

Before making the decision to leave an agency if you are on staff, consider whether or not the problems you are experiencing can be worked out between you and the agency. Identify the specific problems and try to come up with practical solutions to those problems. Make an appointment to speak with the principal and communicate the difficulties you are having. Offer your suggestions, giving the principal an opportunity to keep you as a reporter but modify the relationship to better suit your needs. If the principal is unwilling or if the problems are such that no solution is apparent, then you have done the right thing by communicating your decision to leave.

### Do Not Burn Bridges

The important thing to learn, when making an agency switch, is not to burn bridges. It is best to try to maintain a relationship with the agency that you are leaving. If you are going on staff with another agency, tell the agency you are leaving you will give them second call if you are available for work. These instructions apply, obviously, in situations where you leave on a good note with the agency and it is your choice to leave rather than their choice to let you go.

### Grudge Holding

After leaving an agency, sometimes when you call them to pick up work, they will politely not offer you any until, after a period of time, you realize that they have hard feelings. Some will cut off their nose to spite their face, so to speak, and not call you even if they need you, just as a matter of principle, which in the freelance reporting field is not too wise a tactic. In any case, stop calling and find another agency to call when you need to pick up work.

### If the Agency Lets You Go

Agencies rapidly become disenchanted with reporters who:

- Whine about their chosen assignment
- Show up late to assignments
- Say inappropriate things to people at assignments or within the agency itself
- Do not follow reporter protocol
- Have weak reporting skills
- Produce transcripts with notable or multiple errors
- Do not meet turnaround times
- Withhold important information from the agency, such as continuation dates, a request to expedite a transcript, and so on
- Frequently overbill or underbill for jobs

If it was the agency's decision to let you go, unless you have done something really unethical or horrendous, most principals will either tell you they are letting you go or just not assign you work for a period of time. Barring major holidays, a week without work is a pretty good barometer that the agency is unhappy with your services. Sometimes it may be that the agency is slow and just has very little work, in which case you may want to consider working with an agency that has a busier calendar.

When you interview with prospective agencies, rather than offering negative information about what has happened, simply say that you have been freelancing among many agencies and now wish to go on staff with an agency. Do not offer the prior agency as a reference, because the court reporting community in certain areas is very small and people tend to know one another; the principal may call your prior principal and get the lowdown. You want to start with a clean slate.

Negative incidents happen. Let them go and do not look back. You may find yourself happier and doing a lot better with the next agency. Do not let any single incident sour you to court reporting. It is like any other job; it has its good days and its bad days.

## NETWORKING

As court reporting is a communications business, networking is an integral part of a reporter's success.

### What Is Networking?

Networking is developing relationships with others that may lead to possible job opportunities in one's field. The same methods apply to networking as to interviewing for a position in a freelance court reporting agency with the agency's principal, only the subject base is broadened to include people/entities related to the legal field and people acquainted with anyone related to the legal field.

### How Do Court Reporters Network?

In Chapter 6, the methods discussed for freelance court reporters to learn about job opportunities were:

- Speaking to the owner/staff of one's court reporting school
- Asking reporter acquaintances about walking you into their agency
- Browsing through trade magazines
- Checking bulletin boards in court reporting schools and courthouses
- Surfing the Internet
- Cold-calling

Networking involves going a few steps further.

### Personal Business Cards

A freelance reporter should have personal business cards printed that have the reporter's home telephone number on them, as one never knows when a situation may present itself. It may be as simple as someone at a party saying, "Oh, you're a court reporter? My husband's a lawyer. Let me introduce you." I know a reporter whose husband, by handing out her business cards to lawyers he meets while traveling on business, has helped establish a substantial client base for her.

Give your cards to your personal lawyers or to lawyers you meet *outside* of your assignments through agencies. You then have the option of taking on all the responsibilities for any assignments obtained or referring the client to one of the agencies that you freelance with.

### Maintain Contacts with Others in the Field

Do not be competitive with fellow reporters. Rather, help them out whenever possible, as you will find that having friendly and supportive reporter relationships will benefit you tremendously. Swap telephone numbers with friends in court reporting school and reporters you speak to on jobs. You never know when they may:

- Give your phone number to their principal when he or she is looking for a reporter
- Open/purchase an agency and contact you for work
- Be called for an assignment they cannot accept and recommend your services
- Be selling equipment you are interested in purchasing, and vice versa

Compete within yourself for excellence. A good reputation in the field will open doors for you; stepping on others to reach your goals will not.

Befriend reporters you meet on jobs, state and national court reporting association personnel, scopists, proofreaders, notereaders, agency personnel, and principals of agencies. New reporters who sat in with me and office staff I befriended or to whom I sent a condolence card or birth-of-a-child card are now agency owners and have called me to go on staff with them.

### The Internet

A reporter may network through the Internet. Some agencies have Web sites or links to other Web sites and invite prospective reporters to contact them. You can develop relationships with principals and even fax your resume via e-mail. You can contact state associations on the Internet, authors of reporting-related material, other reporters, and so on. This may be extremely helpful for reporters moving to another state.

Court reporting forums, such as NCRA's Online Forum through www.ncraonline.org, ReporterCentral.com, and DanaChipkin.com, encourage dialog between reporters. A reporter may also wish to create a personal Web site with links to court reporting–related sites to let the world online know of his or her existence.

### Attending Seminars/Conventions

As a member of state and national court reporting associations, you are notified of seminars/conventions in your area as well as in other locations that can be attended at a discounted membership fee. Attending them should not be viewed solely as a means of obtaining CEUs but, rather, as an educational, social, and professional networking experience. You never know when you will meet a colleague with whom you once worked, a fellow student from court reporting school, a principal you have heard good things about, people knowledgeable about the field and willing to offer guidance, and so on.

I once attended an NCRA convention in Washington, D.C., and was in a rather boisterous mood, participating in some of the question-and-answer sessions that were offered by the speakers. Finding what I said impressive, an agency owner from my area met me in the vendor display area and asked who I worked for and whether I was happy there. Even though I told him at that time that I had no plans of leaving the agency that I was on staff with, he gave me his card and told me if I ever changed my mind, to please give him a call.

A few weeks later, finding myself available for an assignment, I called him and received an assignment. I asked if it would be all right to pick up work with his agency on other such occasions, and he agreed. When the agency I was on staff with was slow, I would pick up jobs with his agency. A year or two later, I decided to go on staff with his agency, all as a result of networking at a seminar.

At that same convention was an agency owner to whom I had been referred by colleagues. I had covered jobs for him via telephone, but we had never met personally. I introduced myself to him, and further assignments followed.

### Liaison Companies

There are companies that function as liaisons between freelance agencies/entities seeking reporters and freelance reporters. Someone in need of a reporter for the following day will contact the company and be matched with a reporter who has contacted the company in search of work. After a reporter has accepted just one job with the freelance reporting agency, if the agency is satisfied with the reporter's services, a seed has been planted for a future relationship (staff or freelance) with that agency.

These companies may access reporters by their membership in state or national associations or trade listings, such as the NCRA *Sourcebook* and *Campbell's List.*

### The NCRA *Sourcebook*

The NCRA publishes a sourcebook annually that contains member contact information. (See Figure 16–1.) A reporter who has read an article in the *Journal of Court Reporting* pertaining to an aspect of reporting that he or she wishes to know more about can access the author's information through the sourcebook. Reporters can find principals of freelance agencies in the sourcebook. A reporter also may randomly choose from the sourcebook the name of a reporter in a certain state to contact about the reporting environment in that state.

### *Campbell's List*

*Campbell's List* is a listing of professionals within the legal environment. (See Figure 16–2.) It is published annually and distributed every March to 12,000 law offices, corporate legal departments, foreign consulates, process servers, and other legal professionals, both in book form and on the Internet. Through your listing in *Campbell's List*, you may be contacted by lawyers or freelance agencies looking for a reporter within a specific area to cover a job, or you may be contacted for a staff position. A nominal fee is required, and discounts are offered for advance payments. In the standard listing, reporters may list:

- Name
- Firm name
- Home/business address
- Home telephone number
- Cell phone number
- Beeper number

**FIGURE 16–1**
The NCRA *Sourcebook*

- Fax number
- E-mail address
- Web site address

In the deluxe listing, reporters may choose to include up to 250 words of detailed information about services offered, along with one graphic, such as an agency logo. Links to e-mail and Web site addresses are provided to subscribers at no extra charge. Reporters who subscribe will receive a copy of the publication in early April of each year.

You may contact *Campbell's List* via e-mail at info@campbellslist.com. Their mailing address is 100 E. Ventris Avenue, P.O. Box 428, Maitland, FL 32751. Telephone numbers are (800) 249-6934 or (407) 644-8298. The fax number is (407) 740-6494. You may visit their Web site at www.campbellslist.com.

**FIGURE 16–2**
*Campbell's List*

## SHORT-ANSWER QUESTIONS

1. If a reporter is leaving a staff position with a freelance agency, he or she should offer ___ weeks' notice as a courtesy.
2. If switching agencies, a freelance reporter should offer to give the agency he or she is leaving ______ call.
3. If as much as a ____ passes without an assignment from an agency, barring holidays, it may be an indication that the agency is unhappy with your services.
4. _______ is developing relationships with others that may lead to possible job opportunities in one's field.
5. Reporters should have ________ ________ ____ printed with their home telephone number for networking purposes.
6. NCRA publishes member contact information annually in its ____ __________.
7. Creating a personal ________ is one method of networking online.
8. Reporters may meet principals by attending _______.
9. _______ companies help find reporters for agencies/entities requiring reporting services.
10. _________ _______ is an annual publication of professionals in the legal environment.

## TRUE/FALSE QUESTIONS

1. Freelance reporters only switch agencies for financial reasons.
2. Showing common courtesy toward a freelance agency a reporter is leaving reflects positively on the reporter with prospective agencies.
3. If an agency fires a reporter, the reporter should continue to call the agency for assignments.
4. If an agency is dissatisfied with a reporter's work or behavior, they may tell the reporter, or they may just withhold work from the reporter until the situation improves.
5. Repeatedly showing up late to assignments is grounds for agency dissatisfaction with a reporter.
6. Freelance reporters should tell prospective agencies about all the problems they experienced with the agency/agencies they are leaving.
7. Cold-calling principals is the only way freelance court reporters network.
8. It is acceptable to hand personal business cards to attorneys you meet on an assignment from a freelance court reporting agency.
9. All freelance court reporting agencies have Web sites.
10. Reporters attend seminars just to obtain CEUs.

## DISCUSSION QUESTIONS

1. What are some ways to investigate the reporting environment when you are unhappy with your present situation?
2. How can you differentiate between whether the reporting environment is slow or the agency is choosing not to give you work?
3. Why might an agency be dissatisfied with a reporter?
4. Can you think of other ways to network your reporting skills?
5. What benefits are there to obtaining contact information of other people in the reporting profession?
6. How is the Internet beneficial to reporter networking?
7. How can listing one's contact information in NCRA's sourcebook and/or *Campbell's List* benefit reporters?

CHAPTER

17

# Other Forums for Your Skills

Freelance court reporting is by no means the end of the line. Although a large majority of reporters enjoy freelancing, some venture into other areas of reporting, which include:

- Information reporting
- Realtime/CIC reporting
- Realtiming to assist in education
- Reporting religious services
- Providing CART services
- Closed captioning
- Per-diem reporting in the court system
- Official reporting in the court system
- Legislative reporting
- Pro bono work
- Workers'/Workmen's Compensation
- Speech/voice recognition
- Political activities
- Public speaking
- Writing about the profession
- Outside projects
- Appearing on television/in films

## INFORMATION REPORTING

Many businesses today are employing court reporters both part-time and full-time to report information. A speed of 225 words per minute may be helpful but is not a necessity for this type of reporting. Therefore, court reporting students may engage in this type of work while attending court reporting school. If the reporter has knowledge of a specific type of terminology—medical, legal, insurance, chemical, and so on—he or she should focus on marketing his or her services within that field. The reporter may contact public agencies related to his or her field of expertise or simply contact the human resources departments of large companies. A resume highlighting education and work experience should be prepared. The reporter should expect to perform a demonstration of his or her skills during the in-person interview.

Medical dictation is one form of information reporting. Some court reporting schools offer courses in medical dictation for reporters who wish to specialize in this area.

Dictations taken by reporters may be in person, via telephone, via Dictaphone, and so on. Generally reporters are paid at a rate per transcribed line, so the faster you are at transcribing, the more money you will earn.

Information reporting is generally done through DOS software, such as WordPerfect, with the reporter performing realtime. Therefore, a stenographic writer and computer notebook containing both DOS and court reporting software are required.

## REALTIME/CIC REPORTING

Realtiming is the process whereby reporters provide instantaneous translation of the proceedings on a computer screen. Computer-integrated courtroom (CIC) reporting involves realtiming in a courtroom where there are multiple hookups for participants of the proceeding to observe. In the realtime proceeding, the reporter may scope the proceeding on breaks and then provide an ASCII disk of the **updated** (edited) **transcript** of the proceeding, or the attorneys are given what is called a **dirty daily,** which is an on-the-spot, unedited disk of the reporter's rough notes. **Rough notes** are notes that are unedited but may be partially translated into English to the extent that the words are contained within the reporter's main (personal) or job dictionary.

Arrive very early to these types of proceedings so that you have an optimum setup time and opportunity to test-run everything. Many reporters bring scopists with them to edit as they are writing. Speak to reporters who have worked on the case previously and obtain a job dictionary. Have a good breakfast and some coffee or tea for maximum concentration the morning of the job. Get as much information as you can before going on the record. Ask the attorneys in advance for a word list of common words or terms that may be used and spellings of names that will be mentioned. You can then global them into your job dictionary, and the correct spellings will appear when they are mentioned on the record.

In the NCRA's *Code of Professional Ethics, Guidelines for Professional Practice,* Section II, entitled Realtime Reporter as Assistive Technology in Legal Proceeding, describes the role of the realtime reporter member of NCRA. It states:

> A realtime reporter in this setting is a court reporter using realtime skills and equipment to provide on-screen translation for use in a legal proceeding by a deaf defendant, plaintiff, juror, or perhaps for a particular witness. The realtime reporter is not there to make the official verbatim record, and a clear explanation and understanding of the realtime reporter's role is necessary among all parties to the proceeding.

**Updated transcript:** An edited transcript or ASCII disk.

**Dirty daily:** An unedited ASCII disk or printout of a proceeding given to attorneys at the conclusion of a proceeding, which will be superseded by an edited version of the transcript subsequently delivered.

**Rough notes:** Unedited steno notes prior to being tranned.

Common sense and professional courtesy should guide the Member in applying the following Guidelines. In legal proceedings, a Member acting as a realtime reporter with assistive technology should:

A. Establish before beginning realtime reporting a clear understanding of who has hired the reporter, what is to be reported, and whether the realtime is to be used as assistive technology or if a verbatim record is required in addition to the assistance being provided.
B. Establish before beginning realtime reporting a clear understanding with all parties as to who owns the residual computer note file and who, if anyone, has access to sell and/or distribute the same and to whom, if anyone. Each situation will be unique.
C. Keep all assignment-related information strictly confidential.
D. If realtime is used as assistive technology and a verbatim record is not required, render as near a verbatim translation as possible, always conveying the content and spirit of the speaker, using substitute language which is computer-translatable when necessary to be understood by the person being served. Use parentheticals to describe sounds, laughter, anything that detracts attention from the proceedings to explain to the nonhearing participant what is going on.
E. Not counsel, advise, or interject personal opinions.
F. Accept assignments using discretion with regard to skill, setting, and the consumers involved, and shall accurately represent their qualifications for realtime reporting.
G. Know the software and hardware system used and be able to do simple trouble-shooting.
H. Strive to further their knowledge and skill through participation in workshops, professional meetings, interaction with professional colleagues and reading of current literature in the field, and to achieve realtime certification on a state or national level.
I. Save hard copy or disk of actual translation as it was seen on screen before editing the file in any way. Job defines can be added as the day goes on so long as they don't alter what was seen on screen earlier. The actual record as seen by the deaf party or juror should be saved.

Some realtime reporters choose to report in nonlegal settings, such as educational or religious settings.

## REALTIMING TO ASSIST IN EDUCATION

Realtiming to assist in education involves a reporter aiding deaf/hard-of-hearing students in following and participating in classes/seminars via the reporter's laptop computer. If you are interested in realtime to assist in education, you should market your skills to schools and agencies related to the deaf and hard-of-hearing community. You may want to contact:

- Disabled students' services on campuses
- Interpreter coordinators

- Interpreter-referral services
- Centers for disability-related services
- Community service centers for the deaf and hard of hearing
- Deaf/hard-of-hearing individuals directly—hand out business cards or brochures explaining the services that you provide
- Services for public accommodation of large companies

It is the responsibility of the reporter to enlighten people about the ways in which his or her services may be utilized. A demonstration of one's skills is standard, as is having backup equipment and a backup reporter lined up in case of emergencies. Knowledge of sign language is recommended but not mandatory.

In a school setting, generally students read directly from your laptop computer, so a large-screen display projector is not necessary. Oftentimes, the logistics are not ideal. Reporters are expected to accompany the consumer from classroom to classroom, often with little time in between classes. The reporter must be able to break down and set up equipment very quickly. This puts a lot of wear and tear on equipment, and reporters providing these services may need to purchase equipment and equipment accessories more frequently than other types of reporters. Business and/or homeowners insurance is a must to protect against such problems as theft of equipment.

Many colleges and universities are now offering full-time positions to reporters who realtime to assist in education. Reporters seeking to perform educational-related services should not expect these positions to be among the highest-paying positions in the reporting field but should focus on the positive differences that these positions offer, such as:

- The reporter not having to work with lawyers
- No transcript preparation if the student takes notes directly from the reporter's notebook
- Flexible hours
- Summers off, if one chooses
- Benefits, such as medical/surgical insurance
- Feedback from an appreciative audience
- Knowing that one's skills are being utilized to make a difference in someone's life

Colleges and universities pay for the reporter's services. If the reporter is full-time, an annual salary is arrived at, and benefits are usually part of the employment package. If the reporter is part-time, benefits are not usually offered. Part-time reporters are expected to provide invoices delineating the days and hours worked and are paid per class hour. Their hourly rate should include preparation time and travel time as well as the actual time realtiming. Part-timers also receive minimums for busts.

Twenty-four-hour cancellation notice is expected of a reporter who assists in education. There will also be a predetermined grace period for the reporter to wait for a student to show up.

Section III of NCRA's *Code of Professional Ethics, Guidelines for Professional Practice,* states:

> The Realtime Educational Reporter will be assigned to one or more students for a particular class or classes for the term of each class. This reporter will accompany the student(s) to each class. Through the use of

realtime translation, the reporter will write the teacher's spoken words; the text of this lecture will display on a computer monitor or other display device in English for the deaf or hard-of-hearing student(s) to read. At the conclusion of each class, the reporter will provide the student(s) with a copy of the lecture text from the realtime translation either in the format of an unedited ASCII file on a diskette or a printed copy of the edited text.

The Realtime Educational Reporter should:

A. Work with the instructor for each assigned class to assure that all the technical terminology for that particular class will be provided in advance so that it can be entered into the reporter's computer dictionary. This will help the reporter maintain a high translation rate, which is advantageous for both the reporter and the student(s).
B. Keep all assignments strictly confidential.
C. Not participate in class discussion or provide any advice to the student whom the reporter is assisting. The reporter is there only to facilitate communication between the student, the instructor, and the student's classmates. The reporter will realtime lectures and classroom activities including orally presented assignments.
D. Arrange equipment so that the student being assisted is able to watch the reporter's computer screen and the speaker at the same time. The translation and text display are usually one to four seconds behind the speaker, and for this reason it may take the student a few seconds longer to respond. If at all possible, the instructor must limit the class discussion to one person speaking at a time.
E. Follow the intent of the speaker at all times. The reporter shall render as near a verbatim translation as possible, always conveying the content and spirit of the speaker. If a new term is introduced that will not translate properly, the reporter may use substitute language that is computer-translatable when necessary to be understood by the student.
F. Reflect in the text on the reporter's screen everything going on in the environment including environmental sounds and speaker token (identifiers). Examples include:

    INSTRUCTOR:
    MALE STUDENT:
    FEMALE STUDENT:
    (LAUGHTER)
    (APPLAUSE)
    (BELL RINGING)

G. Inform the student(s) being assisted that the student is responsible for recording all nonspoken information, such as material presented on the chalkboard.
H. Accept assignments using discretion with regard to skill, setting, and the consumers involved, and accurately represent his or her credentials for realtime reporting.
I. Work with instructors and all students in each class to secure cooperation.
J. Have a backup reporter to take over the class in case of illness.

## REPORTING RELIGIOUS SERVICES

Some reporters market their services to religious entities that have deaf/hard-of-hearing members or wish to have special events or services captioned. The basic procedures are the same as those for captioning seminars/videoconferencing. The reporter will need to approach the entity and possibly audition for the entity. Demonstration tapes are also handy marketing tools. When accepting the assignment, the reporter should cover details about the necessity of a large-screen projection display, the fees for the reporter's service, and payment terms. At this time, in advance of the proceeding, the reporter will also attempt to obtain an agenda and names of participating speakers.

Early arrival is recommended in order to find the best location to set up and to run an equipment test. Bring backup equipment, as well as business cards to hand out after the service upon request.

## PROVIDING CART SERVICES

CART is an acronym for Communication Access Realtime Translation (formerly known as Computer-Aided Realtime Translation). It is a realtime service that translates the spoken word into English text. CART is utilized mainly by people with hearing/learning disabilities or whose native language is not English. The person performing CART services is known as a CART provider, not to be confused with a court reporter, as the CART provider's functions extend beyond those of a court reporter. In the legal setting, a CART provider may assist a deaf/hard-of-hearing juror in the courtroom and jury room or may be allowed to participate in confidential caucuses amongst lawyers. And while CART providers must maintain a backup of the realtime text as reporters would for a freelance/official assignment, jury deliberation or confidential attorney-client text is subsequently deleted.

CART providers should possess the RPR certification, as well as any mandatory state certification. CART candidates should not attempt to interview for CART assignments before training to be a CART provider. One's realtime skills must be excellent. Writing must be conflict-free and inclusive of punctuation. One must have nonconflicting user-defined prefixes and suffixes. Speed must be there in order to job-global outlines for words unique to the assignment, for example, NAOUM/NAOUM for pneumothorax, and to fingerspell untranslated words, for example, pneumothorax as P-N-E-U-M-O-T-H-O-R-A-X. CART providers must know how to use the phonetics table when writing so that steno untranslates are not visible on the screen. Stamina must be good to enable the verbatim recording of straight matter without breaks. Although CART providers attempt to write verbatim, there are times when substitutions are acceptable; this is another area in which CART differs from standard reporting protocol.

One may amass information about CART through continuing education seminars, books/articles on CART, exchange of information with CART providers, and sitting in with CART providers. Learning sign language and joining organizations related to the deaf and hard of hearing may serve to bridge gaps in communication that may occur, even though there may be a sign language interpreter present. The ability to follow a sign interpreter's rules and regulations is an integral part of performing CART services. CART providers should be knowledgeable of etiquette regarding politically correct versus incorrect terminology and exhibit sensitivity to the CART consumer's needs. The CART provider should also familiarize himself or herself with telephone relay systems to facilitate dealing directly with a person who is deaf/hard of hearing, since, prior to the assignment, a preliminary discussion or meeting should be had with the CART consumer to go over display options.

The ADA (Americans with Disabilities Act) made it mandatory for companies to provide services for the deaf and hard of hearing so that they could conduct their lives similar to those without hearing disabilities. The company, not the CART consumer, absorbs these services. This applies to everything from assistance in a school setting to appointments for professional services, work-related seminars, meetings with supervisors/bosses, job interviews, police interrogations, immigration and naturalization matters, and so on. The ADA mandates local captioning of:

- Government-sponsored programming
- Political debates
- City/county/town/village council meetings
- School board hearings/meetings
- Local cable network programming of emergency news, such as weather forecasts and updates, and school closings

Local captioning must also be provided for other events where it will assist in ensuring the deaf and hard-of-hearing community equal rights to those without hearing impairments.

CART providers may work through a company or freelance. In order to be successful as a freelance CART provider, the reporter must market his or her services to organizations, companies, and deaf/hard-of-hearing individuals in order to become known as a CART provider. There may be some degree of advertising expense. Numerous phone calls may be required to make oneself known. Business cards or advertisements may be placed on bulletin boards with the permission of the entity. Mailing lists of group members may be purchased or furnished. The Internet may prove helpful in marketing your services. Demostration tapes and cold-calls auditioning the CART provider's services are standard.

Freelance CART providers should be familiar with their equipment and know how to troubleshoot when problems arise. They should be able to adjust font size and color as well as line spacing to accommodate consumer preferences, operate and troubleshoot basic display equipment, and have access to a large-screen projection display when required. Knowledge and maintenance of one's equipment is key to succeeding at CART. The recommended CART-performance equipment to date, according to an article in the April 1999 *Journal of Court Reporting* entitled "An Introduction to CART," written by Nancy L. Catuogno, is shown in Figure 17–1.

Once contacted for a CART assignment, the reporter should attempt to obtain a word list from the client requesting the service. If you are going to assist in a deaf person's consultation with a doctor, for example, you may ask the doctor about terminology that may come up in advance of the meeting. You may be asked to sign a confirmation of identification as a CART provider, since privileged medical information may be discussed. After signing the confirmation,

**FIGURE 17–1**
Recommended CART-Performance Equipment

**VII. Equipment**

It is important to keep current with rapidly advancing technologies in order to meet consumer preferences. The following is a listing of the displays known at this time for CART.

The CART provider should furnish and know how to operate all equipment necessary for basic display. Asterisked items are recommended but not required. A backup steno machine, computer and software key should be readily available.

**A. Basic Display**
1. Stenotype machine with realtime cable
2. Notebook computer
3. CAT/realtime software
4. Text-enlarging software
5. Diskettes
6. Extension cords of different lengths
7. Surge protector with indicator light
8. Three-prong to two-prong ground cord adapter
9. Duct tape or gaffer's tape for taping down cables
10. Additional realtime cable
11. Twenty-five-foot realtime cable*
12. Notebook computer tray/tripod*
13. Equipment case with wheels*
14. Chair (make arrangements)*
15. Infrared/FM listening device*

The additional equipment necessary for the following displays can be furnished either by the CART provider or the hiring party. In all cases, before accepting an assignment to display with external monitors or equipment, the CART provider must establish and test hardware and software compatibility.

**B. Computer Monitor Display**
1. Splitter box for additional monitors
2. Twenty-five-foot monitor cables
3. Multiline block or digital sharing device (for interactive realtime)*

**C. Television Display**
1. Digital signal converter (computer to television)
2. Coaxial cable to daisy chain multiple TV monitors

**D. Projection Screen Display**
1. LCD plate and projector or combination unit
2. Projection screen
3. Extra projector light bulbs (must know how to replace)

**E. L.E.D. Display**
1. L.E.D. message boards in various sizes and colors for indoor use
2. L.E.D. message board for outdoor use

**F. Encoded Display**
(Closed-circuit sites such as conventions or classrooms)
1. Captioning software (requires training)
2. Encoder or character generator
3. Camera
4. BNC cables
5. Null modem cable and/or modem

**G. Remote CART**
1. Telephone line(s)
2. Voice/data modem (for use with single phone line)
3. Special microphone (for speaker)
4. CAT software which supports Remote CART
5. Communication software (computer to computer)

you may be able to obtain a copy of the patient's medical records in advance of the meeting in order to global words into your main or job dictionary. In the case of a seminar, ask the client for names of speakers/people referred to, a copy of the agenda or speech, if possible, and any handouts.

Dress is dictated by the CART assignment. While you would dress professionally for a seminar or job interview, more casual attire will suffice for providing CART in a school setting. An early arrival, once again, allows for a less stressful setup time. It allows the reporter to locate:

- Outlets (a surge protector, three-to-two ground cord adapter, and multiple varying-length extension cords are a staple of the CART provider)
- The best lighting
- The best view of blackboards, slides, overheads, and so on
- The sign interpreter/teacher/audiovisual personnel

An uncaptioned film or videotape may be shown that you will need to translate in realtime. Therefore, you should have pregloballed designations of speakers, such as:

- NARRATOR:
- VOICE:
- MAN:
- WOMAN:
- CHILD:

As opposed to freelance court reporting, where reporters are encouraged to keep parentheticals to a bare minimum, when providing CART services, the provider is expected to write parentheticals of sounds or distractions into the realtime text. CART providers are expected to adhere to the NCRA *Code of Professional Ethics* and maintain impartiality and confidentiality at all times. Authorization may be required for distribution of the realtime text. A rough edit should be done before turning over a disk or hard copy of the realtime text.

The fee for CART services and terms of payment should be determined at the time the assignment is accepted, as should fees for rough-edited diskettes or hard copies of the realtime text, if required.

If you are interested in becoming a CART provider, contact the NCRA at (800)272-6272 for information. There currently exists a CART Task Force that serves to promote CART as a career, among its many other functions. It may be contacted on the Internet by visiting www.machineshorthand.com, clicking on *Associations,* and then clicking on *CARTWheel.* Recommended reading about CART may be found in *Alternative Realtime Careers* by Gary D. Robson (NCRA press, ISBN No. 1-881859-51-7).

## CLOSED CAPTIONING

**Closed captioning** superimposes realtime captions onto visual media. Anyone possessing a decoder for a television has access to it. It is not to be confused with open captioning, such as captioning on a large-screen display projector at a covention, where anyone can see the caption whether or not he or she possesss a decoder.

Closed captioning may be done anywhere provided the necessary equipment is present, that equipment being:

- A computer
- Captioning software
- An electronic stenographic writer
- Three telephone lines for **remote captioning,** which is captioning done by a reporter at a location other than the broadcast site (phone line 1 to listen to the program on television, satellite dish, or audio on the telephone; phone line 2 to send the caption via modem to the TV station; phone line 3 as an emergency/trouble line for contact during a broadcast or as a fax line to receive information during the broadcast)
- A headset for the telephone
- An uninterruptable backup power system

A majority of reporters work for captioning agencies that furnish them with captioning assignments and the requisite (not to mention costly) captioning software. Full-time employees of captioning companies are on a salary and receive benefits. They generally work out of the company's office. Full-timers

**Closed captioning:** Superimposing a caption onto a visual media via realtime.

**Remote captioning:** The performance of captioning from a location other than the broadcast site.

work a 40-hour workweek; part of their time is spent captioning, while part of their time is spent preparing to caption. Captioning agencies use captioners to caption live events, such as sporting events, presidential speeches, and events seen on channels such as CNN, TNN, and The Weather Channel. Captioning for sitcoms, soap operas, news, and other shows, is not live and uses postproduction TelePrompTer captions rather than captioning by reporters.

Reporters should not contact captioning agencies before obtaining a state reporting certification, if applicable. Having the RPR certification from NCRA will be a plus. A resume should then be prepared that lists court reporting schooling, work experience to date, notable accomplishments, and prior realtime/captioning experience. A separate list of references of people/entities that the reporter has realtimed/captioned for should accompany the resume. Check, recheck, and have someone else check both the resume and reference list for errors, as errors detected at this stage may prevent your advancement to the in-person interview stage. Demostration tapes of your realtime skills are standard in the captioning industry. Research the company you will be interviewing with and update your dictionary with the agency name, names of key people in the interviewing process, as well as its clientele, if known. You will then be expected to audition, so to speak, for the captioning agency so that the agency can assess your realtime skills on the spot. Therefore, your dictionary should contain the information found in a January 1998 *Journal of Court Reporting* article entitled "How to Get Captioning," subheaded "Developing Your Stenocaptioning Skills" (see Figure 17–2). Some captioning companies will test your English and grammar skills in addition to your reporting skills.

Captioning agencies prefer to work with on-staff captioners and commonly require captioners to sign anticompetition agreements, stating that they will not work for competitors of the agency or work privately for the agency's clientele. Captioners usually receive their assignments well in advance of the job date. This gives them ample time to do some much needed preparation work. For instance, if you are captioning a baseball game, it is your responsibility to obtain information such as the names of teams and players.

Closed captioning reporters train to transcribe live broadcasts into English while the program is airing. This type of reporter is referred to as a stenocaptioner. The stenocaptioner records every word spoken, and the words appear on viewer television screens within seconds. The stenocaptioner needs a stenographic writer and a CAT system. The television stations usually possess caption-encoding equipment that takes the reporter's translation and makes it broadcast ready.

Although many closed captioning assignments may be done from the reporter's home, other captioning assignments, such as those at seminars and video-conferencing, for example, are done at the event site. Captioners may market their skills privately for like assignments. Therefore, freelance captioners need to be real go-getters.

When captioning independently, arriving at least an hour early to set up and test the equipment is recommended. A big screen projector is often required, and many freelance captioners will rent rather than purchase one for such assignments. Backup equipment is a necessity when captioning. There is rarely, if ever, a transcript required of the captioned assignment, so reporters can say goodbye to the transcript-preparation function encompassed within freelance reporting.

**FIGURE 17–2**
Information to Include in Court Reporter's Dictionary

- Presidents (past, present and potential)
- First Ladies
- Cabinet members
- Senate
- House of Representatives
- National figures (government, religious, entertainment, criminal, etc.)
- All the countries in the world and their capitals
- All the states and their capitals
- All major U.S. cities and some of the smaller ones
- Geographical information such as mountain ranges, mountain peaks, oceans, rivers, lakes, local creeks
- Meteorological terms, weather terms
- World leaders, including United Nations leaders
- World history terminology, as in *Tet Offensive, Bolsheviks, Chairman Mao,* etc.
- Major wars, domestic and international
- Terms related to world organizations like NATO, OPEC, etc.
- Nationalists and languages for foreign nations
- Supreme Court Justices and important Supreme Court decisions
- Military leaders; Joint Chiefs of Staff; military bases; weapons of war, like *A-10 tank killers, F-15s, Tomahawk missiles, Scuds,* etc.
- National parks
- Colleges, universities and their team names
- Local stuff for the area you plan to caption in: landmarks, hospitals, junior colleges; prominent people, etc.
- All the professional sports teams, their nicknames, players and coaches
- Sports terminology, awards and organizations, both amateur and professional
- Makes and models of automobiles
- Major businesses, brand names, trading organizations, stock terms
- Currencies and major banks around the world
- All the colors, and their shades and hues
- Dog and car breeds
- Foods and their measurements and the spices that go with them
- Holidays: Christian, Jewish and all other faiths
- Special events, like *Kwanzaa, Cinco de Mayo,* etc.
- Religious structures, like mosques, temples, etc.
- Books of the Bible and of religions around the world
- Basic chemicals
- Drug names and manufacturers, both legal and illegal
- Common first and last names
- World literature, philosophy and religious terms, like *Aesop, orthodox, Buddhism, Eucharist, the brothers Grimm,* etc.
- Political terms, like *glosnost, apartheid, anarchy, propaganda, caucus, expatriate, Kremlin, Parliament,* etc.
- Computer terms
- Commonly used foreign words and phrases, such as *adieu, aloha, de rigeur, fait accompli, modus operandi,* etc.

Billing for captioning assignments is based on minimums and broadcast hour rates. Captioning agencies have standard hourly rates that are discussed in the interview process with a potential captioner. Freelance captioners may command whatever rate the client agrees to, but should price themselves competitively to the local market for captioning services. Freelance captioners will also include in their hourly rate fair compensation for hours of prep time for the assignment, which are generally twice the amount of broadcast time. Therefore, captioning tends to be more lucrative than realtiming depositions, but again, income will depend on frequency of captioning jobs and must take into account the hefty investment in captioning equipment (a minimum of about $20,000 to $25,000) that is required if the reporter is planning to be an independent captioner.

Some companies conduct training seminars via satellite and may use the services of a captioner. Colleges and universities may likewise hold classes via satellite. Government agencies and religious institutions may broadcast via satellite, requiring captioners as well.

For more information on captioning, check out *Inside Captioning* by Gary D. Robson, (Cyber Dawg Publishing, ISBN No. 0-9659609-0-0) and *Alternative Realtime Careers* by Gary D. Robson (NCRA Press, ISBN No. 1-881859-51-7).

## PER-DIEM REPORTING IN THE COURT SYSTEM

Another option for freelance court reporters is per-diem reporting. Oftentimes, courts are short-staffed as far as their official reporters and welcome freelancer coverage. Freelance agencies may contract with the court to provide reporters, or reporters may offer their services to courthouses independently.

To enlist yourself independently, you can give your name, home telephone number, cell phone number, beeper number, and resume to the chief court reporter at the courthouse, who may call you in on a per-diem, or day-by-day, basis. You may want to request to sit in on a proceeding to learn the ropes before actually working.

Higher courts often require the reporter to have achieved specific certifications, such as being an RPR or having passed at least the lower court test, as well as having a few years of freelance experience. This is, again, an important reason to take as many tests as you can while your skills are at their peak, right after finishing court reporting school.

When you are called to do per-diem work, you will go early to the court reporters' office. Usually there will be a contact person who will walk you through your responsibilities, such as telling you:

- What to expect
- Where to sit
- Information about the judge and the cases
- When to take lunch/return from lunch
- When to leave for the day

In court, generally the clerk of the court or the judge will administer oaths. Occasionally you are asked to do so. Your notes, known as minutes, are not transcribed except when specifically requested, so your per-diem service is remunerated in a flat fee for the morning session, afternoon session, or both. You will fill out a slip with some basic information on it, and you will subsequently receive a check in the mail for your services.

Doing per-diem work is an excellent pathway toward making contacts and building a resume in preparation for a career in the court system.

## OFFICIAL REPORTING IN THE COURT SYSTEM

Although each state differs in its requirements for reporters to attain positions as officials in its court system, the minimum requirement is a court reporting school diploma and a state certification, if applicable in your state. The lower courts (traffic court, family court, and so on), when short-staffed, may utilize per-diem reporters with no additional certification or work experience, but the higher courts (state and federal courts, bankruptcy courts, and so on), require reporters to have passed the RPR exam and the lower court test and to have a certain level of reporting experience.

If interested in court work, you may contact the court directly and ask the clerk of the court or the chief court reporter to mail you an application, or you may physically go to the court to apply. Inquire first about the qualifications that you must meet in order to apply and about per-diem/full-time official reporter remuneration. Prepare a resume. Ask if you can sit in on a trial/hearing to gain knowledge of your responsibilities before you begin working there. Read as much material as you can about the court system, and contact official reporters for guidance.

## LEGISLATIVE REPORTING

Some reporters choose to specialize in **legislative reporting,** which is reporting in the United States Senate and House of Representatives. Legislative reporters primarily work in the Capitol on Capitol Hill, Washington, D.C. They are required to obtain security clearance before being awarded a permanent position.

### Reporting in the House of Representatives

Reporters who work in the House of Representatives are referred to as official reporters. The official reporters in the House are designated to report either Committee meetings or House Chamber proceedings incorporating parliamentary procedure. These reporters record individual speeches of representatives, as well as the consideration of bills, the subsequent voting process to have them passed, and resolutions. They also report any other business taking place in the House Chamber. If the House and Senate both pass similar legislation, it then goes to conference, and if both the House and Senate agree on a conference report, the legislation is sent to the president of the United States for his ratification or veto.

Committee meetings entail the reporter sitting at a table located by the witnesses in a hearing room and reporting for a predetermined amount of time—one hour, two hours, the full session—known the day before the meeting. Although the hearings generally take place from 9:00 to 5:00, they may be shorter or longer. Reporters may obtain from Committee staff copies of statements and witness lists to assist in their preparation of the record. Experienced reporters supervise reporters new to Committee meetings for a period of time until they learn the drill.

Reporting in the House Chamber is known as reporting on the Floor of the House. Reporters take 15-minute turns reporting and then spend the time between reporting preparing the record for the members to review. There are about seven official reporters in the pool, so reporters have about one and one-half hours between reporting shifts. When reporting, the reporters are seated at a table in the front of the House Chamber. There are two electronic steno writers on either side of the table for the smooth transition of shift changes. Reporters use earpieces to hear all of the speakers, but sessions are audio/videotaped, so if a reporter did not hear something, the tape could be listened to. New reporters undergo a period of training with the chief floor reporter in parliamentary procedure before working on the Floor.

In addition to these two functions, official reporters of the House may report:

- A State of the Union address
- A meeting with a head of State
- A special ceremony
- Party caucuses
- Press conferences

**Legislative reporting:** Reporting for either the United States Senate or House of Representatives.

**FIGURE 17–3**
*Congressional Record*

Official reporters of the House are expected to:

- Add parliamentary procedure into the record
- Convert the record into proper language
- Place headlines into the record
- Set phrases through include files
- Identify all 435 members of the House, which changes every two years; however; House staff assist reporters by giving them a seriatim, which identifies speakers, and copies of statements made
- Read and adhere to the Parliamentary Procedure Manual, which is given to each new House official
- Not take any breaks whatsoever during their reporting shifts
- Report whenever called
- Remain on hand until the record is closed no matter how late it is

The procedure for preparation of the transcript is: the reporter reports a 15-minute turn and translates that text, inserting proper parliamentary procedure; the record is then handed to transcribers for review and returned to the House Chamber, to clerks and members. If a member needs to add or delete anything, the member can make the correction. The record is returned to the chief reporter, who checks it for conformance to parliamentary procedure and style. The chief court reporter sends the record electronically to the Government Printing Office, which places the record into a book that also contains the Senate record. The office of official reporters receives it the following day. If any minor corrections need to be made at this point, such as grammar or spelling corrections, they may be made to the permanent record. Considering how many sets of eyes have checked the record before it is sent to the Government Printing Office, corrections at this stage are rare.

Reporters interested in a position with the House of Representatives should get an application from the Clerk of the House or from the court reporters' office of the House. Upon receipt of the reporter's resume and a number of interviews, the reporter will then be asked to sit in with an official about two to three times. The official reporter will check the applicant's notes, and the applicant's record will be looked at by the House transcribers and others.

Applicants should have about ten years' experience (this may be waived in lieu of outstanding reporting accomplishments). Experience doing committee work tends to prepare reporters better for a legislative reporting career than simply doing court work. The reporter must be knowledgeable about parliamentary procedure, history, and current events. The reporter's dictionary should include hot topics and names of prominent people in the news. The reporter should possess excellent English (grammar and spelling) skills and endeavor to constantly increase his or her vocabulary. He or she should watch C-SPAN and practice against televised proceedings. Closed captioning experience is a plus.

The beginning salary in the House is $75,000 as of the date of publication of this book. There are then pay scale-with-longevity raises. Official reporters in the House receive full government benefits. There is a six-month probationary period for new reporters, and permanent positions are offered only to those who obtain a security clearance.

When the Floor is not in session, reporters work on Committee hearings. They generally take vacations around major holidays and during August. They are allowed a certain number of days off each year in addition to vacation days, but their schedules are dependent upon the House calendar.

In terms of upward mobility, an official reporter in the House may aspire to become chief court reporter.

### Reporting in the Senate

Reporters who work in the Senate are called **official reporters of debates.** They write according to the Senate schedule, so when the senators are off, the Senate reporters are off. They generally enjoy a three-week vacation in August, but when the Senate is in session, the official reporters of debates must be available. They are on call on a 24-hour basis. They are at the beck and call of the Senate calendar. While the Senate is not in session, they are expected to come into the office for one day to perform routine clerical assignments.

A typical day for an official reporter of debates consists of reporting for 10 minutes of every hour the Senate is in session. There is a staff of about seven reporters who share in the preparation of the record by taking turns reporting 10-minute segments of the entire record. They carry their writers on shoulder harnesses that contain platforms for their machines, and they report the record while standing. It is the responsibility of the official reporters of debates to anticipate who will be speaking next and to position themselves by the senators, who stand at their respective desks.

At the conclusion of an official reporter of debates' 10 minutes, the reporter returns to the official court reporters' room and spends the remainder of the hour preparing the record of that 10-minute segment. The reporter will hand the record over to professional transcribers who:

- Check it against the Government Printing Office Style Manual for spelling, grammar, style, and so on—the transcript has a wall-to-wall style, meaning the transcript margins begin at the left margin and go all the way to the right margin
- Ensure that the transcript follows the preferences of the chief court reporter

**Official reporters of debates:** The title held by court reporters who work in the United States Senate.

- Research information contained or referred to in the record
- Make changes in the record to anything that was incorrectly stated by a speaker
- Assist the reporter in parliamentary procedure
- Print the transcript
- Return the transcript to the reporter to proofread

The official reporter of debates then proofreads the transcript and turns it over to the chief court reporter for an additional proofreading. Senate staff may assist in the preparation of the record electronically or by physically going to the court reporters' room. About one-third of the transcripts require Senate staff collaboration.

At the conclusion of this 50-minute period, the record is sent electronically to the Government Printing Office along with a hard copy of the record. The following day, the Government Printing Office produces the *Congressional Record* (see Figure 17–3), which contains both the Senate and House transcripts of the previous day. It is rare, but if a senator detects an error at this stage, a call would be placed to the Government Printing Office and the correction would be made.

Other functions of Senate reporters would be to record:

- Caucuses of the Senate and House each week
- State of the Union messages, which are done in the House and may be done by either Senate or House reporters—preference may be given to those reporters with prior captioning experience
- Inaugural speeches—one reporter is selected on the basis of seniority, and these speeches take place in front of the Capitol
- Special events required by the readership of the Senate

What qualifications do Senate reporters need? Certainly, a writing speed of about 240 words per minute in word density (literary/straight writing) is a requirement. National certifications are recommended, with a minimum of at least an RPR certification. There is no state certification in Washington, D.C., as of this book's publication date. Educational/academic backgrounds count significantly, as legislative reporters must be well-versed in English, history, and politics. Interviewers generally will not consider reporters with less than 20 years of reporting experience, although exceptions are made for reporters with outstanding reporting-related accomplishments. Reporting experience in the House of Representatives is the best training ground for Senate reporting. Otherwise, state or federal government experience, such as hearings for state public service commissions, and/or medical conference and convention reporting experience, is noteworthy. The reporter should be a team player, as the official reporters of debates work together as a team to create the Senate portion of the record.

Official reporters of debates are responsible for proper production of calendar work, which involves the passage of bills by unanimous consent, so they must be familiar with and knowledgeable about parliamentary procedure and the legislative process. A knowledge of current events is a must, as is having already defined the names of world leaders and names in the news in the reporter's main dictionary. Contrary to the traditional method of verbatim reporting, legislative reporters are expected to edit grammar either while writing or in the transcript-preparation process. In addition to years of freelance/official reporting experience, committee/conference reporting would best prepare a reporter for legislative reporting. Excellent writing skills and stamina are necessities. Availability around the clock is a key element, as Senate reporters often know the evening before what the following day's start time is but are not permitted to leave until the record is concluded.

If interested in applying for a position with the Senate, an application may be obtained from the Senate directly. A resume highlighting reporting experience and accomplishments should be prepared and sent along with the application. Favorable recommendations also should be included in the application packet. Although no test is given by the Senate, reporters can expect about two to three interviews to take place. There is no training process that the reporter undergoes; he or she is thrown into the pool of reporters in turn.

The starting salary for an official reporter of debates is negotiable depending upon one's qualifications. Benefits are included, as official reporters of debates are considered employees of the United States Government. The Senate pays for the reporter's equipment. An official reporter of debates may utilize spare equipment provided by the government or borrow another reporter's equipment if technical difficulties arise.

Additional tips for preparing for a career in legislative reporting include:

- Reading Robert's Rules of Order for an introduction to parliamentary procedure
- Keeping abreast of current events—read the *New York Times, Wall Street Journal,* and so on
- Reading everything you can, especially books that expand your knowledge of history
- Doing crossword puzzles
- Studying words

In terms of upward mobility, an official reporter of debates may aspire to become chief reporter of the official reporters of debates. The chief reporter has the option to continue to report the record in this capacity in conjunction with his or her duties or to focus solely on his or her other duties, which include:

- Interviewing prospective official reporters of debates
- Overseeing the official reporters of debates—maintaining a smooth flow of 10-minute shifts
- Assisting in the preparation of the record, making sure it conforms to government standards
- Locating proper parties to aid in research
- Providing senators with a copy of the record for review
- Ensuring that both a hard copy and an electronic copy of the record are sent to the Government Printing Office

## PRO BONO WORK

The NCRA, as well as state associations, welcome pro bono, or free-of-charge, services from reporters. They are in touch with a myriad of people and entities that cannot afford to pay the reporter or are not-for-profit organizations. There is no better feeling in the world than donating your services to a worthy cause. Sometimes you are touched by a story and feel that you cannot accept a fee for your service.

One day I was on a job at a law firm, and a partner in the firm, an elderly gentleman, approached me and asked me if I ever did any projects on the side. I said, "Sure," and asked what he had in mind. He asked if I could transcribe a videotape and asked how much it would cost. Never having done it before, I told him I would let him know when I saw how much time would be involved. It turned out to be a videotape of his dead son's eulogy.

While transcribing the eulogy, I was so moved by the extraordinary things said by family and friends, some of which were celebrities and bigwigs in the music industry, that I could not take any payment from this man who spoke to me of his only son with such love and sadness in his eyes. I attached to the transcript a cover letter stating that we should all be so lucky to be remembered by our loved ones in such a beautiful light and that he and his wife should be proud that they had raised such a wonderful human being who was spoken about in such an unusual way. The lawyer and his wife were deeply touched by my words. They offered to buy me a gift or take me to lunch, but I declined. My reward was the way I felt following the project.

## WORKERS'/WORKMEN'S COMPENSATION

Workers' Compensation and Workmen's Compensation are non–civil service entities that reporters may choose to work for rather than freelancing. Employment at these entities is on a full-time basis rather than a per-diem basis. The appeal of Workers'/Workmen's Compensation is the provision of benefits to reporters and a steady income. Reporters at Workers'/Workmen's Compensation do calendar calls for ALJs (Administrative Law Judges), as well as reporting hearings that determine:

- Whether or not the claimant should receive compensation for accidents or incidents that occurred on or at their job sites
- If the claimant can receive a lump-sum payment in lieu of periodic payments
- If an ALJ's decision should be appealed

Participants in the hearings may be medical witnesses, employment witnesses, lay witnesses, and attorneys representing insurance carriers. Most of the content of the hearings is medical testimony.

Calendar call entails parties coming before the ALJ to set a date for their hearing, to adjourn a hearing, to settle a case, and the like. Reporters are often rotated to different parts within Workers'/Workmen's Compensation, as well as being rotated on A.M. and P.M. sessions.

## SPEECH/VOICE RECOGNITION

Speech, or voice, recognition reporting is an alternative to manual reporting. Like realtiming, it is an instantaneous translation method by which the spoken word is converted to printed text. However, it requires the voice writer to feed verbal commands to a computer and repeat what is said at a proceeding verbatim into a device called a silencer. Unlike the replacement of the reporter as with audiotaping of legal proceedings, speech/voice recognition still requires the human element to record proceedings, as voice-recognition software can only recognize the user's voice. Speech/voice recognition offers people with limited or no use of their hands an opportunity in the court reporting field, as well as those who just prefer verbal court reporting to manual court reporting. Speech/voice recognition is popular in some localities and not yet used at all in others.

The National Verbatim Reporters Association (NVRA) offers voice writers membership benefits similar to those provided by NCRA. Three certifications are granted by the NVRA: the Certified Verbatim Reporter (CVR), the Certificate of Merit (CM), and the Realtime Verbatim Reporter (RVR); all require membership in NVRA to qualify to take the examination.

To obtain the Certified Verbatim Reporter (CVR) certification, a basic knowledge written examination; a set of three five-minute dictation tests at 200 wpm (literary), 225 wpm (jury charge), and 250 wpm (Q&A); and a silence test must be passed. The silence test judges whether the voice silence device used by a voice writer candidate will disturb participants in a courtroom setting. If audible, the candidate is immediately disqualified from taking the examination at that time. The Certified Verbatim Reporter candidate must attend one basic workshop prior to taking the CVR examination, must score 75 or above on the written examination, and must score 95 on each dictation. CVR candidates are credited for passing single legs of the dictation segment of the examination.

To obtain the Certificate of Merit (CM) certification, a voice writer candidate must have passed the Certified Verbatim Reporter examination, scored 90 or above on a basic knowledge written examination, and scored 97 on three five-minute dictations at 225 wpm (literary), 250 wpm (jury charge), and 300 wpm (Q&A). Candidates are credited for passing single legs of the dictation segment of the examination.

To obtain the Realtime Verbatim Reporter (RVR) certification, the voice writer candidate must have the Certified Verbatim Reporter certification and subsequently pass a realtime competency examination consisting of a five-minute Q&A dictation ranging in speeds from 180 to 200 wpm, whereby the RVR candidate must repeat the dictation into a speech silencer and convert this material to an ASCII disk with 96 percent accuracy. The RVR candidate is not permitted to make any corrections to the text.

Each certification examination is offered, generally, at the NVRA's annual convention and a couple of other times throughout the year. Examination results are received in the mail within four to six weeks after the examination is given. Upon passing, the certification recipient's name and passing grade are listed in *The Verbatim Record,* a publication of NVRA. In order to maintain the certifications, 30 continuing education credits must be achieved within every consecutive three-year cycle from the NVRA.

For more information about speech/voice recognition, contact the National Verbatim Reporters Association. Their address is 2729 Drake Street, No. 130, Fayetteville, Arkansas 72703; their telephone number is (501) 582-2200; their fax number is (501) 521-7459; and their Web address is www.nrva.org.

## POLITICAL ACTIVITIES

There are many issues affecting the court reporting profession today, such as the threat of live reporters being replaced by audio/videocassette in the courts, that the national and state court reporting associations attempt to combat through political measures. The presence of reporters as a group rather than as a couple of individuals obviously can make a difference. Attending continuing education seminars, reading trade magazines, and conversing with fellow reporters will keep you abreast of pressing issues. Contact your state or national court reporting association to see how you can help.

## PUBLIC SPEAKING

If you are the least bit outgoing and knowledgeable on any given subject(s), offer to speak at court reporting schools. Simply call the school and ask to be a guest speaker. Even if you have just been working for a short while, students are starved for contact with working reporters. Do not focus on the negatives of the industry, as the students need positive feedback in order to stay motivated. Follow your talk with a question-and-answer session so you can address the students' concerns on a one-on-one basis, offer your services as a mentor, or make contacts with future reporters. Try to transcend the two most commonly asked questions of working reporters: (1) How many days a week do you work? and (2) What's the money like?

You might also contact your state association or local high schools about speaking at career nights to offer information about court reporting as a profession. Career expos may be another venue for public speaking about the court reporting field.

## WRITING ABOUT THE PROFESSION

If you feel like you have something to say or share with fellow reporters or students, both the national and state court reporting associations welcome articles for their magazines. Take some time off and write a book on a related topic. Both the NCRA and Stenograph Corporation have catalogs for court reporting–related books that they market to reporters if the content is deemed appropriate. There have been books on court reporting–related stories/humor, cookbooks for reporters with limited time to cook, realtiming, captioning, and so on. This is a communication business, so communicate with your colleagues!

## OUTSIDE PROJECTS

Through word of mouth or personal interrelationships that you have, you may be requested to do outside projects. I was once asked to produce a transcript from a cassette tape wherein a detective hired by a man involved in a divorce action befriended the former wife by helping her out when her car would not start. He had been staking out her premises for information. She was suing the former husband for damages, claiming she now had no income, had to rent a place to live, and so on. During their tape-recorded conversation, she asked the detective what he did for a living and he told her he served summonses. Grateful for the assistance, she then offered her services as a legal secretary, told him where she worked, mentioned she was living with a boyfriend, and so on. The transcript, which proved that she had been lying to the Court, was a key factor in dismissing her case.

## APPEARING ON TELEVISION AND IN FILMS

Reporters have landed roles on television and in films as reporters. They can actively seek roles by getting a portfolio together and contacting an agent, or sometimes a camera crew appears to film in a courthouse and just happens to need an extra to act as a court reporter, as was the case with the reporter in the film *Philadelphia*.

Whatever venue you choose to pursue, I wish you much success.

## SHORT-ANSWER QUESTIONS

1. Medical dictation is a form of __________ _______.
2. ___ _______ allows participants at a proceeding whose computers are integrated with the reporter's to view the record within seconds of the reporter's recording it.
3. An _____ disk containing unedited, or rough, notes is given to attorneys after a realtime proceeding.
4. _______ is another word for editing one's job at a realtime proceeding.
5. ____ stands for computer-integrated courtroom and involves multiple-computer hookups within a courtroom setting.
6. Realtiming __ ______ __ ________ involves a reporter aiding deaf/hard-of-hearing students in following and participating in classes/seminars via the reporter's laptop computer.
7. If you are realtiming to assist in education and know in advance that you cannot make a scheduled class, __ - hour notice should be given or a backup reporter summoned.
8. ____ is an acronym for Communication Access Realtime Translation.
9. A ____ _______ may assist a deaf/hard-of-hearing juror in a jury room during jury deliberations.
10. The _________ ____ __________ Act made it mandatory for companies to provide services for the deaf and hard of hearing so that they could conduct their lives similar to those without hearing impairments.
11. ______ _______ superimposes realtime captions onto visual media for those with decoders to view.
12. ____ _______ is visible to all participants at a convention.
13. ______ _______ is captioning done by a reporter at a location other than the broadcast site.
14. ______ and ____ tapes are standard submissions when interviewing for a captioning position.
15. Captioning agencies may require reporters to sign _____________ agreements stating they will not work for competitors of the agency or privately for the agency's clientele.
16. A reporter who transcribes a live broadcast into English while the program is airing is referred to as a ____________.
17. Billing for captioning assignments is based on _______ and ________ ____ rates.
18. _______ or _______ Compensation are non–civil sevice entities that employ reporters.
19. If a courthouse is short-staffed, it may accept reporters on a ___ - ___ basis.

20. __________ reporting is reporting done in the United State Senate or House of Representatives.
21. Reporters in the House of Representatives are called ________ reporters.
22. Reporters in the Senate are called ________ __________ __ ________.
23. __________ scope for the legislative reporters.
24. The __________ ________ ______ receives the record electronically and prints a book containing both the House and Senate record for each day.
25. House applicants should have about __ years' reporting experience.
26. Senate applicants should have about __ years' reporting experience.
27. Reporters in the ______ report caucuses of the House and Senate, as well as inaugural speeches.
28. Reading _______ _____ __ _____ is recommended to become familiar with parliamentary procedure.
29. When reporters do ___ ____ work, they offer their services for free.
30. Court reporting schools welcome _____ _______ who educate and motivate court reporting students.

## TRUE/FALSE QUESTIONS

1. A speed of 225 words per minute is required for information reporting.
2. Information reporters are paid a flat fee for their services.
3. Realtime or audio recording equipment should be test-run prior to the proceeding.
4. Reporters who realtime to assist in education must own large-screen projector displays.
5. Reporters who realtime to assist in education may put a lot of wear and tear on their equipment due to frequent and hurried equipment setups and breakdowns.
6. Deaf/hard-of-hearing students pay reporters for educational-related services.
7. Reporters who realtime to assist in education may leave immediately if the student(s) utilizing their services do not show up within five minutes of the class's start time.
8. Reporters must be fluent in sign language to provide CART services.
9. CART providers should always wear business suits to assignments.
10. When performing CART services, one should be sparing with regard to using parentheticals.
11. If a film or videotape without captioning is shown, the CART provider is expected to translate it into realtime.
12. Captioning agencies require reporters to purchase their own captioning equipment.
13. Captioning agencies give interviewing preference to reporters with a state certification and an RPR certification over candidates who do not have them.
14. It is not necessary to prepare a resume when interviewing with a captioning agency.
15. Closed captioning reporters usually receive their job assignments the day prior to the assignment.
16. Full-time captioners of captioning agencies are on salary and receive benefits.
17. Most full-time captioners of captioning agencies are remote captioners who work from the captioning agency's office or their home.
18. If a demo tape is submitted during the interviewing stage of applying for a realtime/CART/captioning assignment or position, an audition of one's skills is waived.
19. Captioners should set up at least an hour prior to a captioning assignment.
20. Backup equipment is a necessity when captioning or providing CART services.
21. Reporters gain excellent experience with medical terminology while working at Workers'/Workmen's Compensation.

22. Higher courts tend to have more stringent requirements than lower courts when it comes to per-diem reporters.
23. Security clearance is a must for permanent legislative reporters.
24. Official reporters of debates stand while reporting.
25. Senate reporters report for 50 minutes and spend the remainder of the hour preparing the record.
26. Only Senate reporters report State of Union addresses.
27. Legislative reporters provide verbatim transcripts.
28. Legislative reporters are not permitted to take breaks during a reporting shift.
29. A minimum speed of 240 wpm is required for reporting in the Senate.
30. Speaking at high-school career nights or career expos helps to raise awareness of freelance court reporting as a profession.

## DISCUSSION QUESTIONS

1. What are some incentives for reporters who choose to realtime to assist in education?
2. What steps would one take to train to be a CART provider?
3. How might one become involved in reporting religious services?
4. How does legislative reporting differ from verbatim reporting?
5. Are you cut out for public speaking?
6. Where else might public speaking about the court reporting profession be warranted?

# Answer Key

# Answer Key

## CHAPTER 1

### Short-Answer

1. freelance
2. legal
3. homonyms/soundalikes
4. Frank Sarli Memorial Scholarship
5. official
6. freelance, official
7. 225, 200, 180
8. good hearing, dexterity, good physical condition, stamina
9. provisional
10. professionalism

### True/False

1. F
2. F
3. T
4. F
5. F
6. F
7. T
8. F
9. T
10. T
11. F
12. T
13. T
14. F
15. T
16. T

## CHAPTER 2

### Short-Answer

1. 225, 200, 180
2. Anatomy/Medical Terminology
3. Court Procedures
4. internship
5. 40
6. Machine Shorthand
7. STPH, SKWR, FPLT, RBGS
8. Jury charges
9. scopist
10. main/personal
11. job
12. official reporter
13. notary public

### True/False

1. F
2. T
3. T
4. F
5. T
6. T
7. T
8. T
9. T
10. T
11. T
12. T
13. F
14. F
15. F
16. T

## CHAPTER 3

### Short-Answer

1. Rhode Island
2. CSR/CCR
3. RPR
4. Hawaii
5. RMRs, 3.0
6, Home Study
7. RMR
8. RDR
9. CRR
10. Realtiming
11. CLVS
12. Workers'/Workmen's Compensation

### True/False

1. F
2. T
3. T
4. T
5. F
6. F
7. F
8. T
9. F
10. T
11. T

## CHAPTER 4

### Short-Answer

1. realtime, realtime
2. CAT
3. edit
4. AICR
5. Leasing
6. used
7. key
8. dictionary conversion
9. Maintenance
10. cold
11. heat
12. overhaul
13. refurbishment
14. work sheet
15. bust
16. Maintenance
17. service
18. Laptop
19. e-mail, fax
20. PDR

### True/False

| | |
|---|---|
| 1. T | 11. T |
| 2. F | 12. T |
| 3. T | 13. F |
| 4. T | 14. F |
| 5. F | 15. T |
| 6. T | 16. T |
| 7. F | 17. F |
| 8. T | 18. T |
| 9. F | 19. F |
| 10. F | 20. T |

## CHAPTER 5

### Short-Answer

1. caption
2. venue
3. civil action, criminal action
4. index
5. d/b/a
6. a/k/a
7. a/s/o
8. n/k/a
9. f/k/a
10. s/h/a
11. PC
12. LLC
13. LLP
14. Esqs./Esquires
15. ESQ., of Counsel
16. federal
17. *The American Bench*
18. nonparty
19. expert
20. *ALSO PRESENT*
21. husband-wife, parent-child

### True/False

| | |
|---|---|
| 1. T | 6. T |
| 2. F | 7. F |
| 3. F | 8. F |
| 4. T | 9. F |
| 5. T | 10. F |

## CHAPTER 6

### Short-Answer

1. Workers' Compensation
2. freelance
3. On-staff
4. Turnaround
5. daily
6. resume
7. Realtime, CART, closed captioning
8. Call-in
9. job diaries
10. backlogged
11. holiday, holiday
12. scoped
13. scopist
14. evening
15. Immediate
16. Daily
17. Expedited
18. appearance
19. bust
20. subsidiary

### True/False

1. T
2. T
3. F
4. F
5. T
6. F
7. T
8. T
9. F
10. F
11. F
12. F
13. T
14. F
15. T
16. T
17. F
18. F
19. T
20. T
21. T
22. F
23. T
24. F
25. T
26. F

## CHAPTER 7

### Short-Answer

1. 50-h
2. Examination Under Oath, EUO
3. claimant, respondent
4. plaintiff, defendant
5. counterclaim
6. cross claim
7. third-party impleader
8. depositions
9. first
10. med mals
11. interrogatories
12. default statement
13. Answers to Interrogatories
14. Legal mals
15. Maritime
16. Bankruptcy
17. debtor, petitioner, creditor
18. petitioner, respondent
19. statement
20. statement
21. stipulations
22. hearing, arbitration
23. opening statements
24. direct examination
25. cross-examination

### True/False

1. F
2. T
3. F
4. F
5. F
6. T
7. F
8. T
9. F
10. T
11. F
12. F
13. T
14. T
15. T
16. F
17. T
18. T
19. T
20. T
21. T
22. T
23. F
24. T
25. T
26. F
27. T
28. F
29. F
30. T

## CHAPTER 8

### Short-Answer

1. practice
2. Dating
3. Bill of Particulars
4. Globalling
5. Job/J globalling
6. prepping
7. *Not Present*
8. speaker designations
9. *SNAO*
10. *SKWRAO*

### True-False

1. F
2. T
3. T
4. T
5. F
6. T
7. T
8. T
9. F
10. T

## CHAPTER 9

### Short-Answer

1. continuation
2. swearing, affirming
3. interpreter

4. first two questions
5. *TITLE/TITLE*
6. begins, ends
7. stipulations, stipulations
8. exhibits
9. Plaintiffs', defendants'
10. for identification
11. for identification, in evidence
12. Parentheticals
13. *OFF/OFF*
14. *READ/READ*
15. *KWERD*
16. *Question, Answer*
17. ruling
18. **RL*
19. **RQ, *REQ*
20. Inserts
21. five
22. *Time Noted:*
23. O+1
24. 1cc
25. pro se
26. requests
27. steno notes
28. numbered
29. rubber band
30. five

### True/False

1. T
2. F
3. T
4. T
5. T
6. F
7. F
8. T
9. T
10. F
11. F
12. F
13. T
14. F
15. F
16. T
17. T
18. T
19. F
20. F
21. T
22. T
23. F
24. F
25. T
26. T
27. F
28. T
29. F
30. T

## CHAPTER 10

### Short-Answer

1. voir dire
2. left, asterisk
3. quotation
4. objections
5. sic
6. 1, 10
7. Roman
8. Arabic
9. ordinal
10. cipher
11. Fractions
12. modifier
13. Hyphens
14. parenthetical
15. singular possessives, plural possessives

### True/False

1. T
2. T
3. F
4. T
5. T
6. F
7. T
8. F
9. T
10. T
11. F
12. T
13. T
14. T
15. F
16. T
17. F
18. T
19. F
20. T
21. F
22. T
23. T
24. F
25. T

## CHAPTER 11

### Short-Answer

1. Housekeeping
2. *Code of Professional Ethics*
3. emoting
4. Spot calls
5. solicit
6. Picking up
7. confidentiality
8. neutral
9. stoic

10. tape-recording
11. conflict of interest
12. certification

### True/False

| | | | |
|---|---|---|---|
| 1. | T | 16. | T |
| 2. | T | 17. | F |
| 3. | F | 18. | T |
| 4. | F | 19. | T |
| 5. | T | 20. | F |
| 6. | T | 21. | T |
| 7. | F | 22. | T |
| 8. | F | 23. | T |
| 9. | T | 24. | F |
| 10. | F | 25. | T |
| 11. | F | 26. | T |
| 12. | T | 27. | T |
| 13. | F | 28. | F |
| 14. | T | 29. | T |
| 15. | F | 30. | F |

## CHAPTER 12

### Short-Answer

1. dictate
2. notereader
3. scopist
4. Dumping
5. Include files
6. sample transcript
7. glossary
8. Arbitraries
9. last
10. cross referencing
11. Proofreading
12. spell check
13. 1099
14. tran
15. Backup
16. ledger
17. fireproof

### True/False

| | | | |
|---|---|---|---|
| 1. | F | 16. | T |
| 2. | T | 17. | T |
| 3. | T | 18. | F |
| 4. | F | 19. | F |
| 5. | T | 20. | T |
| 6. | T | 21. | T |
| 7. | F | 22. | F |
| 8. | T | 23. | F |
| 9. | T | 24. | T |
| 10. | F | 25. | F |
| 11. | F | 26. | T |
| 12. | T | 27. | F |
| 13. | F | 28. | T |
| 14. | F | 29. | T |
| 15. | F | | |

## CHAPTER 13

### Short-Answer

1. title
2. header
3. footer
4. appearance
5. Attorneys, Attorneys
6. of counsel
7. personal attorney
8. cocounsel
9. *NOT PRESENT*
10. *EXAMINATION BY*
11. Q&A
12. first, second
13. second
14. Dashes
15. Time Noted:
16. jurat
17. acknowledgment
18. certification/certificate
19. Errata sheets
20. concordance
21. condensed transcript
22. excerpt
23. *Confidential*
24. official
25. relief

### True/False

1. F
2. T
3. F
4. T
5. F
6. T
7. T
8. T
9. T
10. T
11. F
12. T
13. F
14. T
15. F
16. F
17. T
18. T
19. T
20. F
21. T
22. T
23. F
24. T
25. T
26. T
27. T
28. T
29. T
30. T

## CHAPTER 14

### Short-Answer

1. independent contractors
2. 1099s
3. estimated
4. one-third
5. tax deductions/business expenses
6. 280A
7. benefits
8. in-home office
9. NCRA
10. disability
11. Tax-free, tax-deferred
12. 401K

### True/False

1. T
2. F
3. T
4. F
5. F
6. T
7. F
8. T
9. F
10. T
11. T
12. T
13. F
14. T

## CHAPTER 15

### Short-Answer

1. fireproof
2. multiple-speaker
3. Short forms
4. relief reporter
5. interrogatories
6. Pro se
7. client
8. medication
9. backed
10. realtime, realtime
11. job dictionary
12. ASCII

### True/False

1. T
2. F
3. T
4. F
5. F
6. F
7. F
8. F
9. T
10. T
11. F
12. F
13. F
14. F
15. F
16. T
17. F

## CHAPTER 16

### Short-Answer

1. two
2. second
3. week
4. Networking
5. personal business cards
6. sourcebook
7. Web site
8. seminars/conventions
9. Liaison
10. Campbell's List

### True/False

1. F
2. T
3. F
4. T
5. T
6. F
7. F
8. F
9. F
10. F

## CHAPTER 17

### Short-Answer

1. information reporting
2. CIC reporting
3. ASCII
4. Updating
5. CIC
6. to assist in education
7. 24
8. CART
9. CART provider
10. Americans with Disabilities
11. Closed captioning
12. Open captioning
13. Remote captioning
14. Resumes, demonstration
15. anticompetition
16. stenocaptioner
17. minimums, broadcast hour
18. Workmen's, Workers'
19. per-diem
20. Legislative
21. official
22. official reporters of debates
23. Transcribers
24. Government Printing Office
25. 10
26. 25
27. Senate
28. Robert's Rules of Order
29. pro bono
30. guest speakers

### True/False

1. F
2. F
3. T
4. F
5. T
6. F
7. F
8. F
9. F
10. F
11. T
12. F
13. T
14. F
15. F
16. T
17. T
18. F
19. T
20. T
21. T
22. T
23. T
24. T
25. F
26. F
27. F
28. T
29. T
30. T

# Court Reporting Terminology

# Court Reporting Terminology

## A

**Affirm** To have a witness who prefers not to be sworn attest that he or she is telling the truth under pains and penalties of perjury without mention of the word *God.*

**AICR** (Artificial Intelligence-Conflict Resolution) A method by which CAT software attempts to resolve conflicts for reporters.

**Appearance** A fee paid a reporter in some localities in addition to his or her page rate that is determined by the reporter's presence at a proceeding within specified time periods. *Appearance* may also be used synonymously with *bust fee, minimum,* or *per diem* to reflect a fee paid reporters by freelance agencies to compensate them for their time when the proceeding they are assigned to report does not take place.

**Arbitrary** A singular stroke that represents multiple words; synonymous with *brief* or *short form.*

**ASCII** (American Standard Code for Information Interchange) A standard type of file that is compatible to most computers and software.

## B

**Backup** May refer to having a copy of a file/job in case anything happens to the original or may refer to having extra equipment in case one's equipment fails to operate properly.

**Blurb** A parenthetical conveying information to the reader of a transcript.

**Brief** A singular stroke that represents a commonly used word or phrase.

**Bust** Cancellation of a proceeding for which a reporter receives a minimum fee; may only apply in certain localities/agencies.

## C

**Calendar** The book in which freelance agencies record jobs that are subsequently assigned to reporters.

**Call-in time** A specific time of the day that a freelance court reporting agency has reporters call for job assignments.

**Caption** The title or name of a legal action filed with a court that lists the court and county the action is filed in, the parties in the suit and their classifications, and the case number assigned the action by the court. When speaking about closed captioning, a caption would refer to words superimposed onto a visual media, such as a television program.

**CART** (Communication Access Realtime Translation) A realtime service that is provided for people with hearing/learning disabilities or whose native language is not English.

**Case number** The number given to an action upon its being filed in a particular jurisdiction.

**CAT system** (Computer-Aided Transcription system) Court reporting software that enables reporters to create transcripts from electronic steno writers.

**CCR** (Certified Court Reporter) A state certification in certain states.

**CIC reporting** Realtiming in a courtroom when there are multiple hook-ups for participants of the proceeding to observe.

**Civil (Civ.) action number** The docket or identification number assigned to a civil action by a federal court. It is the equivalent of an index number, or case number, in state/lower courts.

**Civil service** An adjective pertaining to working for an administrative service of the state or United States Government—*i.e.,* official reporting and legislative reporting.

**Closed captioning** Superimposing a caption onto a visual media via realtime.

**CLVS** (Certified Legal Video Specialist) A voluntary certification offered by the NCRA for legal videographers.

**CM** (Certificate of Merit) A national reporting certification now replaced by the RMR certification.

**Colloquy** A method of recording text on the record outside of Q&A that reflects: the witness speaking to someone other than the examining attorney, the examining attorney speaking to someone other than the witness, or speaking by anyone else present at the proceeding.

**Concordance** A listing at the end of a transcript (or separately bound) that indexes every word and name mentioned in a transcript by page and line number.

**Condensed transcript** A transcript format that places multiple transcript pages onto a singular page. Popular brands are Min-U-Script and Visual Xmax. Condensed transcripts are often referred to as Min-U-Scripts, Minis, or 4-ups.

**Conflict** Two words/phrases written exactly the same way that requires the computer, reporter, or scopist to figure out which of the two should be selected.

**Conflict-free writing** Following a shorthand theory or principles that provide the reporter a method of writing words and phrases so as to avoid conflicts.

**Continuation/continuance** When a proceeding is adjourned and resumes on a subsequent day.

**Counsel** A synonym for attorney; also a venerable title by which to address lawyers.

**Court reporter** A generic phrase referring to stenographers, whether freelance, official, or otherwise.

**Criminal action no.** The docket or identification number assigned to a criminal action by a federal court. It is the equivalent of an index number, or case number, in state/lower courts.

**Cross-examination** Examination of a witness by opposing counsel.

**CRR** (Certified Realtime Reporter) A voluntary certification offered by the NCRA for reporters who perform realtime.

**CSR** (Certified Shorthand Reporter) A state certification in certain states.

**Cycle-charging** A method of charging one's electronic steno writer's battery to increase its longevity.

## D

**Daily delivery** A term used to indicate delivery of the final edited transcript the (business) day following the proceeding.

**Deem marked** To identify an exhibit on the record without physically marking it. It has the same effect as if the exhibit had been physically marked and is listed on the index page of the transcript.

**Deposition/depo** A process within the discovery phase of litigation whereby examinations are taken under oath and recorded by a stenographer who subsequently provides a transcript of the proceeding.

**Dictate** To read one's steno notes replete with punctuation into a Dictaphone for a scopist/typist to prepare a transcript from.

**Dictionary** A file that reporters program to define words. Main, or personal, dictionaries are all-inclusive; job dictionaries are used for globals pertaining to a specific case.

**Dictionary conversion** When the vendor of a software different from that which the reporter's dictionary is programmed on takes the reporter's dictionary and makes it compatible to its CAT software.

**Direct examination** Examination of a witness by the attorney who has called that witness on behalf of the party he or she represents.

**Dirty daily** An unedited ASCII disk or printout of a proceeding given to attorneys at the conclusion of a proceeding, which will be superseded by an edited version of the transcript subsequently delivered.

**Disclosure** The exchange of relevant material prior to trial, as well as the exchange of material that may lead to the discovery of relevant material.

**Discovery** A pretrial phase of litigation wherein pertinent information is procured or exchanged by the parties in preparation for trial; referred to as *disclosure* in New York civil practice.

**Drop** To fail to record spoken text that should be on the record.

**Dump** To download steno notes from a job into CAT software.

## E

**Edited notes** Steno notes that have been "tranned" on CAT software and scoped.

**Edit style** Transcript-formatting parameters applicable to a particular freelance court reporting agency that take a reporter's rough steno notes and place them into a chosen format.

**Examination** The questioning of a witness under oath by parties seeking to elicit information pertaining to a legal action; also includes questioning of a witness at a trial, arbitration, and so on.

**Excerpt** A portion of a transcript requested prior to the delivery of the entire transcript.

**Exhibit** Material marked for identification at legal proceedings that may be used as evidence at the time of trial. Not all material so marked is admissible in evidence.

**Expedited delivery** A term used to indicate that delivery of a transcript must be made before the regular delivery date, usually within three to five days of the proceeding or by a specific date requested by an attorney.

**Expert witness** A witness who, by virtue of education, work experience, and/or publications in a specific field, is asked to give testimony on a particular subject matter. This term has specific definitions in state and local practice that normally imply that such a witness is testifying regarding subject matter that is beyond the ken of normal or ordinary understanding.

## F

**Federal stipulations** Stipulations applicable to actions venued in federal courts.

**First call** A reporter's giving first priority to a freelance court reporting agency over other agencies for assignments at designated call-in times.

**Format** A process done on an electronic steno writer or CAT software that clears a floppy disk and prepares it for use in an electronic steno writer; also may refer to the manner or style of transcripts produced by freelance agencies.

**Freelance court reporter** May refer in general to a court reporter not employed full-time by an agency or court; may also refer to a freelance reporter who freelances among many agencies as opposed to being on staff with just one agency.

## G

**G Global** To define a steno outline permanently in one's main (personal) dictionary.

**Global** To define steno outlines in English.

**Glossary** A sheet on which a reporter lists words and names alphabetically to assist a scopist in preparing a transcript.

## H

**Housekeeping** A (generally) off-the-record discussion amongst the representatives of parties to a legal action regarding details about the case.

## I

**Immediate delivery** Delivery of a transcript (usually via ASCII disk) at the conclusion of a proceeding.

**Index** A page in a transcript that indicates the page numbers that each witness's testimony began on, page numbers that each attorney's examination of each witness began/continued on, and information regarding requests, inserts, rulings, and exhibits marked or deemed marked during a proceeding. Indexes sometimes include directions not to answer and motions, depending upon the agency.

**Index number** Identification number assigned by the court clerk to an action in state or lower court. It is the equivalent of a case number (Civil Action No./Criminal Action No.) in federal court.

**Initial capped** When only the first letter of a word is capitalized (uppercase), such as in English.

**Interrogatory/interrogatories** A question or number of questions set forth in a written document that are required to be answered under oath. Depending on the circumstances, the services of a court reporter may be used in lieu of an attorney's presence to read the questions to the witness and record the answers.

## J

**J (job) global** To define outlines from steno to English for definitions utilized for a specific job that will not be programmed into the reporter's main (personal) dictionary.

**Job file** A file on one's steno writer or CAT software containing steno and English notes of a proceeding.

**Jury charge** A judge's instruction to a jury during a trial before the jury deliberates on the case. Examinations in court reporting schools, as well as state and national examinations, include dictations whereby straight matter is dictated simulating a judge's charge to a jury to assess reporters' skills at specific speed levels.

## K

**Key** A device that attaches to computer hardware and prevents pirating, or copying, of CAT software systems.

**Keyword index** An alphabetical listing of each word in a transcript that provides page and line numbers where the word is found; synonymous with *concordance.*

## L

**Laptop computer** Portable hardware programmed with CAT software that enables reporters to perform realtime or transcription functions anywhere; synonymous with *notebook computer.*

**LCD screen** A small liquid crystal display screen found on electronic steno writers that enables reporters to view a portion of what they are writing in English or steno, program J globals, set the writer's date and time, adjust steno note spacing, and so forth.

**Leg** One of the three elements comprising the skills portion of a court reporting examination; that is, Q&A, jury charge, or literary.

**Legal mal** Examination of a witness who is an attorney.

**Legislative reporting** Reporting for either the United States Senate or House of Representatives.

**Literary** Straight matter containing content of a literary or current events nature. *Literaries* are dictated to court reporters at various speed levels to assess their skills during court reporting school examinations and state and national examinations.

**Litigation** The legal process whereby parties seek the court's assistance in resolving disputes and awarding damages (financial rewards) for their grievances.

**Litigation support** Tools that assist attorneys in litigation, such as ASCII disks, that enable attorneys to search information on their laptop computers that was given at previous depositions for use during an examination without having to physically carry multiple transcripts to the examination.

**Lowercase** Small or noncapital letters of the alphabet.

## M

**Maritime** An examination where the subject matter involves navigation, commerce, or other happenings on the sea.

**Machine shorthand theory** A method of writing on a stenographic machine that enables the reporter to attain higher levels of speed than if the reporter were writing by pen or typing.

**Med mal** Examination of a medical-related party to an action or an expert medical witness.

**Minimum** A fee that a reporter receives for his or her appearance when he or she arrives at an assignment and the proceeding does not take place (sometimes paid to reporters before their arrival to the job location); synonymous with *bust fee.* Reporters also receive the minimum fee when billing for a job that amounts to less than the minimum amount.

**Min-U-Script** A popular brand name of a condensed transcript.

**Motion** An application to the Court for specific relief. This may be in written or verbal form, but is usually in writing in accordance with specific Court rules.

## N

**Named party** A person listed individually or appearing on behalf of an entity listed in a caption.

**NCRA** National Court Reporters Association.

**Non–civil service** An adjective pertaining to non-government or state agencies.

**Nonparty witness** A witness who is not individually named or appearing on behalf of an entity listed in a caption.

**Notebook computer** A portable, or laptop, computer that is programmed with CAT software which enables reporters to perform realtime or transcription functions anywhere.

**NoteMarker** A buttonlike device found on a steno writer utilized by reporters to mark or flag spots within their steno notes.

**Notereader** A professional who prepares a transcript for a reporter from rough steno notes.

## O

**Of counsel** This is placed after the appearance of an attorney appearing on behalf of a law firm he or she is not regularly employed by.

**Official court reporter** A court reporter employed full-time by the court system or the United States House of Representatives. *Official reporter* may also refer to the reporter who provides the original transcript at a proceeding where two freelance reporters are present and who performs the requisite functions of the proceeding.

**Official reporters of debates** The title held by court reporters who work in the United States Senate.

**On staff** When a freelance court reporter has a first-call agreement with one agency.

**O+1 (original and one)** The original transcript and one copy. (O+2 indicates the original plus two copies, and so on.)

**Opposing counsel** Any attorney representing an adversary (opponent) in an action.

**Outline** The steno that represents an English word or phrase.

**Overhaul** A process that is recommended to be performed on a steno writer as part of equipment maintenance once every two years or as needed.

**Overruled** A ruling by a judge, hearing officer, or arbitrator rendering an objection inappropriate and permitting the question objected to to be answered.

## P

**Page rate** The amount that a freelance court reporting agency will pay a reporter per transcript page.

**Parenthetical** A description of a nonverbal activity in a transcript, set in parentheses, that assists readers of the transcript in understanding what transpired during the proceeding.

**Party** A person or entity named in a caption.

**Per-diem reporter** A reporter who works for an entity on random days as needed and is paid a flat fee for the day.

**Picking up** When an agency that a reporter is on staff with does not have an assignment for the reporter and the reporter then accepts an assignment from another agency.

**Pirating** The illegal copying of CAT software.

**Principal** An owner of a freelance court reporting agency.

**Proofreader** A professional who reads a reporter's scoped transcript for detection of errors and lists the errors on an errata sheet or on a copy of the transcript itself.

**Provisional reporter** A reporter who works regularly in a courthouse who has not yet received an official reporter position.

**Push** To attempt to report at a writing speed that the reporter is not comfortable at or that is beyond the reporter's capabilities.

## Q

**Q&A (question and answer)** The format by which the examination of a witness is recorded stenographically. Reporters are tested at different levels of Q&A to obtain a court reporting school diploma and various certifications.

## R

**RDR** (Registered Diplomate Reporter) A meritorious certification offered by the NCRA.

**Readback** Reiteration of the record at a proceeding by a reporter as requested by a judge, a jury, an attorney, or a witness.

**Realtiming** The process whereby reporters provide instantaneous translation of the proceedings on a computer screen.

**Refurbishment** The process whereby a steno writer is overhauled and old parts are replaced with new or updated parts.

**Remote captioning** The performance of captioning from a location other than the broadcast site.

**RMR** (Registered Merit Reporter) A meritorious certification offered by the NCRA.

**Rough notes** Unedited steno notes prior to being tranned.

**RPR** (Registered Professional Reporter) A certification offered by the NCRA.

## S

**Scope** The process of editing rough steno notes, adding in parentheticals and include files, and setting commands to distinguish colloquy from Q&A.

**Scoped page rate** The amount a freelance court reporting agency pays a reporter per page for a transcript that the reporter scopes himself or herself or pays an independent scopist to prepare.

**Scopist** A professional knowledgeable in steno theory who assists reporters in the preparation of a transcript.

**Short form** A brief, abbreviated method of writing an otherwise multiple-stroke outline, such as *SDOEFR* instead of *DIS/KOF/RAOE*.

**Sitting in** When a court reporting student attends a proceeding as a learning experience and sits next to the reporter assigned to report the proceeding, prepares a work sheet, reports the proceeding unofficially, and transcribes a few pages of the transcript for review by a court reporting school or a freelance court reporting agency.

**Solo practitioner** An attorney in private practice who is not a member of a multiple-name law firm.

**Speaker designation** An outline ascribed to each speaker in a proceeding for identification during a proceeding.

**Spot call** When a freelance court reporting agency receives a request for a reporter to appear immediately at a proceeding to record it stenographically.

**StenoMark** A buttonlike device found on a steno writer utilized by reporters to mark or flag spots within their steno notes.

**Stroke** The pressing of one key or a combination of keys on a steno machine to write a number, letter, word, or phrase.

**Subsidiary** A company that a freelance court reporting agency contracts work for and provides court reporters on behalf of, that has a separate clientele than that of the agency.

**Sustained** A ruling by a judge, hearing officer, or arbitrator that validates an objection and precludes a witness from answering the question objected to.

**Swear** To have a witness raise his or her right hand and vow to tell the truth during the examination. This procedure involves mention of the word *God* as opposed to affirming, which does not.

## T

**Technical support** Service provided by a court reporting equipment vendor to answer questions or troubleshoot problems regarding equipment.

**Tran** To run electronic steno notes through a personal dictionary, a job dictionary, if applicable, and an agency's edit style sheet.

**Transcribe** To translate steno notes into English.

**Transcript** A document prepared by a court reporter (and/or scopist), which is certified by the court reporter, consisting of a verbatim recording of a proceeding and parentheticals describing nonverbal occurrences.

**Turnaround time** The time between the reporter's recording of a proceeding and the court reporting agency's receipt of the transcript to prepare it for delivery to a client.

## U

**Unedited notes** Rough notes prior to updating by a reporter or scopist.

**Unscoped page rate** The page rate that a reporter receives from a freelance court reporting agency for pages scoped by an in-house scopist.

**Untranslate** Undefined steno words after steno notes have been tranned against a reporter's personal (main) dictionary and/or job dictionary.

**Updated transcript** An edited transcript or ASCII disk.

**Uppercase** Capital letters.

**Usual (state) stipulations** Stipulations agreed to by and amongst counsel regarding how they will conduct an examination before trial of a witness for a case venued in a state or local civil court.

## V

**Venue** The court and county in which a legal action is filed.

**Voice recognition software** Software trained to recognize and respond to verbal directives as opposed to a court reporter manually creating the record with physical strokes. Stenomask is a popular form of voice-recognition technology currently utilized in the legal setting.

**Voir dire** Questioning of a witness by an attorney to find out whether or not the witness is competent to testify. Most commonly done with child witnesses, aged or ailing witnesses, or those whose testimony may be affected by medication. A second meaning is a brief examination by an opposing party to determine whether or not the witness is the proper witness to bring in evidence versus another witness or to determine if a witness is qualified to provide testimony on a specific subject, or if a sufficient foundation has been laid in order to offer a document or testimony into evidence at a trial.

## W

**Work sheet** A sheet provided by a freelance court reporting agency to reporters for the recording of pertinent data necessary for preparation of the transcript of a proceeding.

# Index

# Index

## D

## E



## F



## G



## H



## I

## Q



## R



## S



## T

## U



## V



## W

**$15.00**

TO RECEIVE A CURRENT NCRA STORE CATALOG, CALL TOLL-FREE (800) 272-6272 OR VISIT THE NCRA STORE ONLINE AT WWW.VERBATIMREPORTERS.COM

The National Court Reporters Association
8224 Old Courthouse Rd.
Vienna, VA 22182
(800) 272-6272
Email: msic@ncrahq.org

# NCRA STORE CATALOG GIFT CERTIFICATE

This certificate is good toward the purchase of any item(s) in the NCRA Store Catalog. It may not be redeemed for cash, and must be used in its entirety at point of purchase.

Coupon Code: DCOO Dept. Code: Membership & Marketing

Name: ______________________________
Address: ____________________________
City: _______________________________
State, Zip: __________________________
Phone: ______________________________
Email: ______________________________
Name of your school: __________________

NCRA
Guardians of the Record